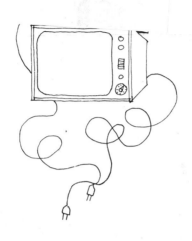

ISSUES IN BROADCASTING

RADIO,
TELEVISION,
AND CABLE

Edited by
Smythe

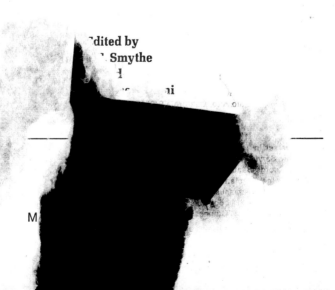

M

Library of Congress Catalog Card Number: 74-33884
International Standard Book Number: 0-87484-330-8

Manufactured in the United States of America

Mayfield Publishing Company
285 Hamilton Avenue, Pa   A

This book was set in T
by Typographic Servi
bound by the George
was Alden C. Paine, Ca
and Marilyn Palmer was ma
supervised production, the boo
by Nancy Sears, and Jim M'Guinness

CONTENTS

iii

Contents

vi

PREFACE

From its beginning in 1920, the American broadcasting industry has been involved in controversy, and from then on scholars, practitioners, and critics have been ready to evaluate elements of the changing controversies, offering their many points of view for discussion, debate, and action. It is a pattern that has continued, but it is also one that tends to be dated. Looking at the few collections of articles available on broadcasting, we saw that they would be of limited use to us in teaching in the seventies mainly because of their lack of timeliness. We were seeking to provide material in a rapidly changing field that would supplement some of the existing textbooks by supplying more current information, primarily by focusing on the most recent controversial issues.

Even as we surveyed the field to determine which issues seemed to be of more than seasonal interest, we found limitations of our own with respect to the size of the book we were planning and the way we expected it to be used. Another consideration was the kinds of articles we felt would be desirable in a book that was to be a supplementary reader. That is, we wished to include both scholarly journal articles (from sources such as the *Journal of Communications* and the *Journal of Broadcasting*) and those from the trade (*Broadcasting* and *Television/Radio Age*) and the popular press. Wherever possible, we wanted to include complete articles, keeping excerpts to a minimum, in an effort to let the authors have their full say.

The result of our planning was our decision to reduce the total number of selections in order to offer as many complete articles as possible within a book of manageable size. Consequently, issues covered as well as the number of viewpoints offered are not as numerous as we might have wished. Since we also sought to present articles that were topical, we generally avoided historical articles (except for those that provided needed background) or articles that reflected earlier issues. We have, therefore, concentrated on what we consider to be the key issues of the seventies, insofar as our powers of prophecy have enabled us to foresee the next few years. We have sought to present views on a variety of issues that deal with social criticism, professional problems, government regulation, minority interests, and technological effects.

In attempting to present those key issues, we have included authors who express strong, one-sided viewpoints. We feel these authors crystallize the issues, even though we ourselves may disagree with their views (as we sometimes have). Other writers have been included because they place an issue in perspective and provide a general understanding of the ramifications of proposed solutions. It is, perhaps, needless to add that in selecting these articles over others some important issues and viewpoints undoubtedly have been omitted, for which we ask the reader's indulgence. Without pretext to comprehensive coverage, this book of readings is intended as a sampling and a supplement or as a text in an issues-oriented seminar.

We thank those writers and publishers who have permitted us to reprint these articles and chapters. We have left the articles in their original form in most cases; a few articles have been edited for space considerations by eliminating footnotes and statistical references. It is our hope, as editors, that the readers of this book will be stimulated to seek further information about these issues so that they can make informed personal decisions regarding them.

We also wish to thank all those who helped in the preparation of this book through their advice and their willing assistance and expertise: Alden Paine, Carole Norton, Marilyn Palmer, Freda Nichols, and Cheryl McElvain. We also appreciate the contributions of April Orcutt, who carefully worked on many of the small details in the final preparation of the materials. Especially, we want to thank our wives, Barbara Smythe and Nancy Mastroianni, who observed the project from beginning to end with patience and good humor.

Fullerton, California

Ted C. Smythe
George A. Mastroianni

INTRODUCTION

The social and political turmoil of the sixties profoundly affected
American social institutions, and many segments of society exerted
pressure for changes in education, religion, political parties, private
industry and the mass media. All of these institutions responded in some
way to the pressure and criticism, and many of them made major
adjustments in their methods and goals. The highly visible and powerful
institutions of the mass media (print media and broadcasting) were
vigorously attacked by groups that sought to use them to influence social
change. The broadcast media, which are the most pervasive and perhaps
the most persuasive media, received special attention from minority and
activist groups. Their attention was well placed, because the Federal
Communications Commission (FCC) provided the legal tools for those
groups that wanted to use broadcasting. (The electronic media in this
country are still the only mass media regulated by the government.) The
development of cable television and its spread to urban areas also
stimulated many groups to seek immediate access to these primarily
local media.

Social groups were not the only critics of broadcasting practices.
Indeed, many of the "professionals" in broadcasting have had severe

disagreements with industry-wide practices such as rating systems, news policies, and technological improvements, in addition to minority group proposals, FCC restrictions, and court rulings. There are also issues concerning ethical considerations in programming and broadcasting. An ongoing conflict between broadcasters and cablecasters over copyright and pay television is still to be resolved.

The role played by public broadcasting (noncommercial education and community stations) has from its earliest days been one of promise and unfulfilled promise. Within the predominately commercial system of broadcasting that we have in the United States, public broadcasting is a supplementary system, and it has had to perform a different role from that assigned to it in countries where it is the dominant system. In the United States public broadcasting's role primarily is to provide a wide range of programming designed to meet minority tastes. Perhaps the most pressing and continuing issues in the public broadcasting area are those of long-term financing and independence from government control—two issues that are separate yet interdependent.

Broadcasting and cablecasting, commercial and public, have performed a useful social role in American society by entertaining the public, informing it, directing its attention to issues of importance, and, in general, giving the public a shared experience. There is much to praise in American broadcasting, whether it concerns quality drama (such as the recent production of *Hamlet* or the award winning *The Autobiography of Miss Jane Pittman*), or public affairs (such as the moon probes, the Kennedy assassinations, or the Watergate hearings). However, there also is much to condemn among those individuals in broadcasting who all too frequently have sought the easy way to fame and fortune by appealing to the lower instincts of the public through violence and sex in entertainment, vaudevillian tactics in the news and exclusion of certain groups from the media.

These, then, are some of the broad issues we will consider here. Again, in a book of this size, we cannot present all sides of all issues nor even include all of the issues. Indeed, we have focused attention on those key issues that we believe will have meaning not only for today but through the decade of the seventies.

Each chapter deals with a different aspect of broadcasting—types of programming, government policy, cable television, public broadcasting, international broadcasting, and technology. Our commentaries introduce the chapters and seek to structure the issues presented in the articles so that the reader will be able to pick out the general relationships among discordant views. Where needed, we have provided background information on an issue to help the reader develop a perspective for interpreting the opinions in the readings.

Each chapter introduction closes with a selective bibliographical essay evaluating some of the books and magazine articles that deal with the issues in that particular chapter. By using the bibliography, the reader also will be able to find related articles and books that fill in those content areas not covered in our selections. The study questions, which follow the bibliographical essays, can serve as guides both before and after reading the articles: (1) the reader can gauge his familiarity with current broadcasting issues by trying the questions before reading the articles and (2) the questions can be used as a self-check after reading the articles.

BIBLIOGRAPHICAL ESSAY

The bibliographical essays will enable students to find additional related books, articles, reports, and government studies that appear relevant to the topics in the chapters. They are designed to be convenient research tools, but do not strive for comprehensiveness; instead, they seek to highlight the more important and more accessible sources of information.

During the life of this book, many additional articles and books will be published that could not have been included here. Therefore, this essay deals with standard publications in the field which will permit the reader to keep up-to-date on the issues that confront broadcasting—today and tomorrow. We will first describe periodicals in broadcasting or periodicals which frequently carry articles dealing with broadcasting. Second, we will note several standard books in the field that are requisite background for many of the issues we discuss. The student who reads carefully two or three of these books will have an excellent background for discussing the issues; he or she will then need to read regularly in two or three of the periodicals suggested.

Periodicals

Periodicals dealing with the broadcast field fall mainly into five categories: professional, scholarly, governmental, popular, and criticism. In the professional category, the best single publication is *Broadcasting,* a weekly news magazine that covers the entire field of broadcasting, including cable television. This publication is especially valuable for its coverage of federal legislation and hearings related to broadcasting, its up-to-the minute coverage of the FCC and its infrequent but highly useful special articles. *Variety,* also a weekly, is devoted to far more "media" than broadcasting, including film, stage, music, and records. It tends to give good economic background on broadcasting, particularly the entertainment side of the field. It has annual international editions that are especially useful for their coverage of foreign broadcast systems. *Television/Radio Age* meets management as well as technical objectives. Many of the issues that are peculiarly related to interindustry practices find good expression here. For instance, the problem of advertising clutter (a problem advertising and broadcasting share) has received excellent coverage. There also is thorough coverage of FCC actions and proposals. *Broadcast Management/Engineering* (*BM/E*) is described by its title. Students interested in the applications of new technology, whether in news or production, will find good treatment in this publication.

Scholarly journals are numerous, but tend to concentrate articles on certain aspects of broadcasting or more general mass media concerns. The most general and most useful broadcasting quarterly is the *Journal of Broadcasting*. It is a broad-scan publication, giving historical, legal, and statistical treatment to broadcasting. It frequently includes special bibliographies on subtopics of broadcasting. In the educational broadcasting field, the best of several journals is *Public Telecommunication Review;* formerly entitled *Educational Broadcasting Review,* this new-format monthly is now more aptly described by its title, since much of the content of the magazine deals not only with the educational side of broadcasting but also with those public broadcast stations that are incidentally oriented to education or linked to a school system. The renovated *Television Quarterly* concentrates on the commercial television industry and on research studies and viewpoints that might not find expression elsewhere.

Three scholarly publications that are more general in nature frequently contain articles dealing with broadcasting: *Journalism Quarterly, Public Opinion Quarterly,* and the *Journal of Communications.* All three are highly regarded publications. *Journalism Quarterly* (*JQ*) is especially useful for its good coverage of books (brief annotations of many books that will not be reviewed in full are included) and for its excellent compilation of articles which are taken from a rich variety of publications. Although the citations are always dated by at least three months, they are conveniently categorized for research needs, and there are excellent cross-citations. *Public Opinion Quarterly* (*POQ)* emphasizes the subject of its title. Therefore, articles on the influence of television news, advertising, or perhaps entertainment, particularly as it relates to the political process, frequently appear in this journal. The *Journal of Communications* has been editorially and visually revamped and now offers many articles that are related more to the impact of the mass media, especially television, than was true before. The journal covers the domestic and international fields. Somewhat related to this class of journal is the *EBU Review* (European Broadcasting Union). This publication deals primarily with the European broadcasting scene. There are two issues: one covers general and legal issues, the other covers technical problems and solutions. This is an excellent source of information on European systems of broadcasting and sometimes contains articles on non-European countries as well.

Federal publications are few in number but they are highly useful sources of information because of the relationship between broadcasting and the FCC. The Federal Communication Commission issues *Annual Reports* that summarize the activities of the Commission during the year. In addition, there are FCC *Reports* on an ongoing basis that provide revealing insight into Commission response. The *Federal Communications Bar Journal* is a nongovernmentally supported publication that deals with a very specialized area of broadcast regulation, but it is well worth the serious reader's attention.

Popular publications dealing with broadcasting are numerous, but only a few are useful. One of the best is *TV Guide.* Many of the issues of concern to the television viewer receive topical coverage in this weekly publication. It frequently is difficult to locate back copies of the magazine, however, because few libraries keep it on file. Sometimes the television comment in metropolitan newspapers contains useful information about issues on the medium, but this is not true of all newspapers.

Criticism of broadcasting, particularly by consumer groups of one type or another, has been a fairly recent innovation. One critic is *ACT News* (Action for Children's Television), which is a news quarterly dealing with ACT efforts in regulation or local broadcasting across the country. Another is *Cable Report,* an outgrowth of the *Chicago Journalism Review* from which it is separated. Several of the journalism reviews that now dot the publishing landscape also include criticism of broadcast media, as well as of local newspaper and editorial practices; perhaps the most useful and easily obtainable are *Columbia Journalism Review,* which is the best of the group, *Chicago Journalism Review,* and (*More*). The last publication is issued from New York City and tends to concentrate on the media in the city.

Students interested in seeing what other publications are available in broadcasting should consult Kenneth Harwood, "A World Bibliography of Selected Periodicals on Broadcasting (Revised)," *Journal of Broadcasting* (Spring, 1972), 131–146.

Many other magazines and journals carry articles on broadcasting issues. The best way to keep abreast of the comment appearing in other periodicals, including legal publications, is to consult several indexes. *Topicator* is a monthly publication that covers the advertising-broadcasting trade press. Unfortunately, it seldom annotates the articles so the researcher must depend upon the title for useful information. The classified index of periodical articles that appears in the back of *Journalism Quarterly,* which already has been mentioned, is another excellent source. Indexes of more general nature include the reliable and wide-ranging *Reader's Guide to Periodical Literature, Business Periodicals Index,* the *Applied Science & Technology Index,* and the *Social Science* and *Humanities Index* (the latter two grew out of the former *International Index*). In addition, the *Index to Legal Periodicals* and *Index to Periodical Articles Related to Law* are useful sources for viewpoints on broadcasting.

Standard Books

Books on broadcasting are numerous, but the following titles offer extensive background information for the reader who wishes to quickly grasp the heritage and structure of the medium. The standard history is Erik Barnouw's *A History of Broadcasting in the United States,* Oxford University Press, New York, issued in three volumes in 1966, 1968, and 1970. These constitute the best history available. Two additional volumes that include useful historical treatments which emphasize the relationship of television and radio to society are by Sydney W. Head, *Broadcasting in America,* 2nd ed., Houghton-Mifflin, Boston, 1972; and Giraud Chester, et al., *Television and Radio,* 4th ed., Appleton-Century Crofts, New York, 1971. An excellent survey by Wilbur Schramm and Janet Alexander entitled "Broadcasting" appears as a chapter in the *Handbook of Communication,* edited by Ithiel de Sola Pool, Wilbur Schramm, et al., Rand McNally, Chicago, 1973. We reprint just a fraction of the chapter in this reader; students should consult the full chapter as well as the useful bibliography that accompanies it. Three additional sources should be mentioned. They are Warren C. Price, compiler, *The Literature of Journalism,* 1959, and Price and Calder M. Pickett, *An Annotated Journalism Bibliography, 1958-1968,* both published by the University of Minnesota Press, Minneapolis; and "Broadcasting and Mass Media: A Survey Bibliography," compiled annually in January by Christopher H. Sterling of Temple University. The first two books are baseline—any serious research in the field starts with them. Sterling's mimeograph edition has been published since 1970 and is a highly selective list of titles that generally are current in the field; it is categorized, which makes it useful, but it is not annotated, which detracts from its usefulness. For annotations, the student should consult Sterling's *Mass Media Booknotes*, a monthly listing of titles in the field of mass communications that is a highly useful source of information on current books and on their strengths.

STUDY QUESTIONS

1. What were the key inventions that led to the development of radio as we know it today? Of television?

2. What are the key elements in the structure of the U.S. broadcasting industry?

3. Describe the differences of operation between a network-affiliated station and an independent station in regard to their program functions.

4. What are some of the specific responsibilities of the Federal Communications Commission?

5. What are some of the policy issues of concern to broadcasters, government, and the people?

6. What reasons can you give for the changes in attitudes toward television between 1960 and 1970 as suggested by the results of the study by Dr. Robert T. Bower?

7. Are there observable differences in your own or your family's viewing of particular types of TV programming?

Survey of Broadcasting:
Structure, Control, Audience

WILBUR SCHRAMM and JANET ALEXANDER

Wilbur Schramm and Janet Alexander, "Broadcasting," in Ithiel de Sola Pool, Wilbur Schramm, et al., *Handbook of Communication*, © 1973 by Rand McNally College Publishing Company, Chicago, pp. 583-586, 588-589, 591-597, 599, 601-602. Wilbur Schramm, former director of the Institute for Communications Research, Stanford University, now heads the Communications Institute, East-West Center, Hawaii. He has published extensively in the broadcast field. Janet Alexander is a staff member in the Institute at Stanford University.

DEVELOPMENT OF BROADCASTING

Seeing, hearing, communicating over great distances have always been part of man's dream. During the Renaissance, when the study of magnetism led to the first primitive understanding of electronics, these dreams took a new form.

As early as 1558, Giovanni Battista della Porta described a "sympathetic telegraph" which could send messages through magnetism. . . . Joseph Glanvil predicted in London in 1661 that "the time will come, and that presently, when by making use of the magnetic waves that permeate the ether which surrounds the world, we shall communicate with the Antipodes." There were many such predictions in the seventeenth and eighteenth centuries, and in the nineteenth century they began to come true.

In 1844 Samuel F. B. Morse sent from Washington to Baltimore the first official message by wired telegraph, said to have been "What hath God wrought!" (What *un*official messages preceded that, we do not know, but anyone who has tried to get a new communication link to work will suspect that "What hath God wrought!" came fairly late in the process of trial.) Marconi demonstrated in 1897 that dots and dashes could be sent through space without wires, and in 1899 he sent Morse code across the English channel; in 1901, across the Atlantic.

Meanwhile work was under way in transmitting the human voice itself. Alexander Graham Bell demonstrated in 1876 that understandable speech could be sent over a wire. Edison was working on the phonograph by 1877. Just before the turn of the century experiments in sending the human voice by "wireless" were in progress. Stubblefield claimed to have sent and received a voice one mile without wires in 1899.

A key development at this time was the invention of the Alexanderson alternator, which produced a smooth continuous set of high frequency waves, suitable for voice modulation. Using this method, Fessenden, a former Westinghouse engineer who had gone to teach at the University of Pittsburgh, began to experiment with sending both music and voice through the air. Ham operators and ship radio officers began to report as early as 1905 that they occasionally received voice programs from Fessenden's laboratory.

DeForest's triode tube, patented in 1907, made voice broadcasting easier, and DeForest himself entered voice radio experimentation. He did a voice broadcast from the Tour Eiffel in 1909, and in 1910 put Caruso on the air, to be heard by ships at sea. In 1916 he broadcast election returns from New York City; like most other newsmen on that election day, he announced that Charles Evans Hughes was the next president of the United States.

One of the first official uses of voice radio was a broadcast made by President Wilson (who *had* won the 1916 election) from his ship returning from the Paris Peace Conference in 1919. Unfortunately, he seems to have been heard only by ships at sea.

Marconi and other European innovators had been very active with radio-broadcast experiments during the first two decades of the century, and experimental stations were springing up in both Europe and America. One of the first of these was KQW, San Jose, California, which was on the air in 1909. It was a short step from "ham" and experimental stations to stations designed to serve homes. The present KCBS in San Francisco is a lineal descendant of KQW.

In 1888, Edward Bellamy's book *Looking Backward* had contained a passage that drew more attention thirty years later than when it was first published. He described a scene in the year 2000, in which a hostess asked a guest whether he wanted to hear some music. She handed him a list of titles and let him make a selection, then "crossed the room and as far as I could see merely touched one or two screws and at once the room was filled with the music of a great organ anthem."

Probably Bellamy's imagination was stimulated by Edison's new phonograph, but thirty years later a telegrapher for the American Marconi Company (who later became president of the Radio Corporation of

America) believed that he saw a way to make the scene come true long before the year 2000. This was David Sarnoff, who wrote a memorandum to his superiors, as follows:

> I have in mind a plan of development which would make radio a household utility. . . . The idea is to bring music into the home by wireless. The receiver can be designed in the form of a simple "Radio Music Box" and arranged for several different wavelengths, which can be changeable with the throwing of a single switch or the pressing of a single button. . . . The same principle can be extended to numerous other fields, as for example receiving lectures at home, which could be perfectly audible; and events of national importance which can be simultaneously announced and received. Baseball scores can be transmitted in the air. . . . This proposition would be especially interesting to farmers and others living in outlying districts. . . .

The same vision came to others. Radio station 8MK, Detroit, became station WWJ. Out of the Westinghouse experimental station, in 1920, came station KDKA. There were 30 licensed stations on the air in the United States by the end of 1921, and 500 by the end of 1922. At that time approximately three million receivers were in use.

The Growing Pains of Radio

With the development of home radio in this country and elsewhere, problems swiftly developed: how to support it, how to regulate it, how to guide its use. It was thought at first that stations could be maintained by the sale of receivers and by the tangible or intangible returns from the prestige of broadcasting. Sarnoff himself did not conceive of radio as a vehicle for direct profit-making. He spoke of it as something that will "be regarded as a public institution of great value in the same sense that a library, for example, is regarded today." . . . In 1922, however, the American Society of Composers, Authors, and Publishers demanded payment for music that was played on the air. This pointed to even greater program expenses in the future, and forced the new stations to look for an additional source of substantial income. They found it in advertising.

The first recorded radio commercial was sold in 1922 by station **WEAF**, New York, to promote the sale of real estate lots on Long Island. Thereafter, advertising was to be the chief method of support for broadcasting in the United States.

There were vigorous protests against a commercial system. Secretary of

Commerce Hoover said in 1922, "It is inconceivable that we should allow so great a possibility for service, for news, for entertainment, for education, and for vital commercial purpose, to be drowned in advertising chatter.". . . He predicted that "the American people will never stand for" advertising on the radio. It was a celebrated miscalculation. By 1930, radio advertising had risen to $60 million a year, and there were 14,750,000 receivers in use. Presently, the bill for radio advertising is over a billion dollars a year, and for television more than two billion.

One of the chief reasons for the formation of networks (NBC in 1926, CBS in 1927) was the need to make it easier for advertisers and their agencies to deal quickly and efficiently with a group of stations. The first network show on American radio, at the inaugural of NBC on 15 November, 1926, illustrated the quality of talent that was on radio at that time, and also indicated what kind of display window radio was prepared to provide for the commercials on which it subsisted. The program originated at the Waldorf-Astoria in New York, and included the New York Symphony Orchestra under Walter Damrosch, the humorist Will Rogers, opera singers Mary Garden and Tito Ruffo, and the dance bands of Vincent Lopez and Ben Bernie, among others.

It is interesting to speculate what might have happened to radio in the United States if in 1922 it had chosen the way that most European countries took: government-owned radio supported wholly or in part by a tax on receiving sets. This was a fundamental decision for the United States communication system. It built commercial competition for audiences (and consequently for advertising dollars) into the system for as long as can be foreseen. It created property values for frequency assignments so that, in practice, they came to be treated as the broadcasters', rather than the public's, channels. It transferred the responsibility for programming to the broadcasters rather than to the government, and government regulatory agencies ever since have had the greatest difficulty doing anything about it. It tended to substitute audience size and resultant profit for other measures of public service. And, most obviously, it determined that American broadcasting thereafter would be a showcase for sales messages that were permitted to intrude into entertainment and informational programming.

Before radio could realize the financial and entertainment success it was destined to attain, however, it was necessary to regulate the assignment of frequencies to stations. American radio began with one frequency, then two, and finally the whole band of 550 to 1600 kilohertz (kHz). As more stations came on the air, and as power was increased, stations began to interfere with each other.

Secretary Hoover called a conference on standards and allocations as early as 1922, and most of the 1920s was taken up in sorting out frequency assignments and providing a way to make and enforce them. Finally the chaos on the air became so intolerable that the broadcasters themselves petitioned for regulation. The result was passage of the Federal Radio Act of 1927, which established the Federal Radio Commission. Seven years later the Federal Communications Act of 1934 replaced the 1927 law and established the Federal Communications Commission. We shall have more to say later about the FCC and the problems of broadcast regulation.

Once these basic decisions had been made and order established on the airwaves, radio became a thriving industry. Despite the depression, more than 50 million sets were in use and 700 stations operative by the end of the 1930s. Income from the sale of time was approaching $200 million. Radio won a historic victory over the newspapers in gaining the right to buy wire news services.

The new medium came to absorb somewhere near three hours of the average American's day. It contributed to everyday American life and experience familiar voices like those of Ed Murrow, William L. Shirer, H. V. Kaltenborn, and Lowell Thomas; the Philharmonic with Toscanini and the Saturday afternoon Metropolitan opera broadcast; quality drama such as CBS Playhouse; family serial drama, some of it as memorable as "One Man's Family"; satiric comedy like that of Fred Allen.

On Halloween, 1938, Orson Welles scared substantial numbers of listeners out of their lounge slippers with a program that demonstrated what radio had come to mean to Americans. It was outwardly innocuous—a dramatization of H. G. Well's novel, *War of the Worlds*, which tells the story of an imagined invasion from Mars. It was well labeled as fiction and radio drama—but it was in the form of news broadcasts. In less than twenty years radio had come to be so deeply trusted, so much depended on for news, that in several parts of the country uncritical listeners literally ran for the hills.

The Coming of Television

Even as early as 1938, a shadow was beginning to fall over the prosperity and popularity of radio. The shadow came from a new medium, still in an experimental stage, called television.

The development of television traces back at least as far as the invention of the daguerreotype, about 1839. Within a little over forty years, people found out how to make the picture move. Senator Leland Stanford of California bet that at one point in its stride a horse has all four feet off the ground. The photographer Eadweard Muybridge took a series of consecutive still pictures and mounted them on a rotating disc so that only one picture could be seen at a time through an aperture: the result was the illusion of a running horse. Stanford won his bet; there *was* one point at which all four of the horse's hooves were off the ground.

When Eastman's films became available in the late 1880's, Edison used them to develop the Kinetoscope, which was long used in penny arcades. In France, Auguste and Louis Lumière invented the Cinématographe which projected these consecutive exposures in a large room. Films began to be shown in nickelodeons, theaters where the admission was as low as five cents, and where a piano thumped out mood music for whatever action was being shown.

Barnouw . . . notes wryly that as early as 1907 the *Chicago Tribune* was charging that films were ministering to the "lowest passions of children." A judge wrote that "nickelodeons indirectly or directly caused more juvenile crimes coming into this court than all other causes combined.". . . Many of the same things were said in the 1950s and 1970s of television. But motion pictures gained more respectability with the coming of great stars such as Mary Pickford who by 1914 was being signed to annual contracts of more than $100,000 a year. And when a standard film width of 16 mm., and a fire-resistant film substance were agreed upon, teaching and training films began to come into use. The first sound films were shown in theaters in 1926, and sound took over most of the field from silent films during the early thirties.

Dizard . . . feels that the marriage of films and radio, resulting in television, is most appropriately dated at 2 November 1936 when the British Broadcasting Corporation inaugurated the first continuing public television broadcasting service in the world, from an experimental studio at Alexandra Palace on the north edge of London. But there were many developments before that. The scientific sources were international.

Jakob Berzelius, a Swedish chemist, discovered the element selenium that became the basic component of photoelectric cells. In 1875 Carey, an English scientist, designed a plan for "television" using selenium cells. Caselli, an Italian, claimed to have transmitted a picture by wire in 1862.

Paul Nipkow, a Russian living in Germany, developed a scanning disc in 1884 for transmitting pictures by wireless, an idea developed into working systems in the 1920s by Jenkins in the United States and Baird in England. Vladimir Zworykin, a Russian employed by Westinghouse in the United States, patented an electron-beam pickup that led to an all-electronic system and to the iconoscope or electronic camera tube, and the kinescope or electronic receiver system.

Development and testing went forward, on a variety of systems, throughout the late twenties and thirties. Television transmission over a wired circuit between New York and Washington was demonstrated by Bell Laboratories in 1927. On 11 May 1927, Station WGY, Schenectady, started experimental telecasts three afternoons a week. By 1932, twenty-five experimental television stations were operating in the United States; thirty-six were operating on 2 November 1936, which Dizard proclaimed the birthday of television. In 1938 David Sarnoff, echoing his famous memorandum about radio, wrote that he felt television was now feasible for use in the home.

The Federal Communications Commission approved a plan for commercial telecasting in 1940. Both CBS and NBC began television operations in July 1941, in New York, fifteen hours a week. Within a year, eight other commercial television stations came on the air, and six of them continued to broadcast throughout World War II.

The war, however, held up the development of television throughout the world. The United Kingdom, France, and the Soviet Union all stopped their television services in 1939. The British had 20,000 receivers when they ceased broadcasting at the start of the war. They resumed in 1946. France stopped in 1939 and resumed on a very limited scale after liberation in 1944. The Soviet Union had begun television in 1938, using equipment purchased from RCA. They also resumed on a limited scale in 1946. No other country except the United States had a regular television service before 1950.

In the United States only a small amount of television was available during the war, but the service and the industry grew rapidly when the war ended. In one year alone, 1948, the number of TV sets in this country increased from about 100,000 to about one million.

The Federal Communications Commission had to make two fundamental decisions before television in the United States could develop as it was destined to do. One of these concerned frequency allocation. It became apparent that there was not enough room in the frequency spectrum for all the stations that would be needed to bring three networks, as well as independent programming, to the whole country. For nearly four years (1948–1952), therefore, the commission maintained a freeze on new station authorizations until a satisfactory allocation plan could be developed for the country.

One result of this freeze and the new allocations was that American educators were able to secure 242 channel assignments, both very high frequency (VHF) and ultra high frequency (UHF)—12 percent of all those available at that time—for educational noncommercial use, making it possible for a second system to grow beside the commercial one. The first ETV station, KUHT at Houston, went on the air 8 June 1953. Thanks in no small degree to strong and continuing support from the Ford Foundation and later to the Educational Facilities Act of 1962 and the Public Broadcasting Act of 1967, there are now 191 of these noncommercial stations owned by citizens' groups or by educational institutions.

The second decision had to do with color television. The introduction of color was delayed for several years while the networks and their engineers battled over whether the approved color system should be "compatible" with black-and-white television—that is, whether color and black-and-white broadcasts should be receivable on the same set. The noncompatible system, built around a rotating color disc, was ready earlier. But the compatible system, based on the electronic system of Zworykin, ultimately won out; when color sets appeared in the stores they could receive either black-and-white or color programs.

Once these decisions were taken, television swept over the country. Less than twenty years had elapsed between the time television receivers were in 5 percent of American homes and the time they were in 90 percent. Radio had grown at nearly the same rate twenty-five years earlier. But when the Old Champion faced the New Challenger in the 1950s, it was a clear victory for the challenger. Television took from radio its position as the home entertainment center, its huge audiences, and its fat national advertising contracts. At the same time it kept a substantial part of movie audiences at home looking at the picture tube rather than at theaters watching the silver screen. . . .

Some Characteristics of the U.S. System

Before leaving the development of broadcasting, let us note several characteristics of the system that emerged in the United States.

For one thing, it emerged ad hoc. Regulation and direction came after technology. In the past decade, certain Asian and African nations have been able to plan and introduce their media systems in a way that integrates them smoothly into their existing sociopolitical systems and their goal patterns. In the United States, however, the technology was in use before there were appropriate governmental structures to regulate and control its development. Therefore, the broadcast system reflects many of the conflicts prevailing at the time of its growth.

Nevertheless, the ideology that shaped the system was based consistently on the First Amendment and the idea of free enterprise. For example:

The airwaves are recognized as belonging to the public. Private interests are merely franchised to use a portion of the spectrum, for a three-year period, "in the public interest, convenience, and necessity." The franchise granted by the FCC does not in any way constitute legal ownership, but rather public trusteeship whose renewal is dependent on the licensee's performance.

The profits belong to the licensee. Broadcasting requires the investment of risk capital by the private sector, with little or no regulation of rates, profits, or services.

Broadcast frequencies are allocated to local communities. The FCC assumes that the best frequency allocation is one that assures each local community a voice of its own. The licensee is charged with fulfilling this public service for the community. This is one reason why stations, rather than networks, are licensed, and why the licensee is required to return to the FCC every three years for the renewal of his license.

Consequently, the proper working of the system requires a balance between private and public interest. In return for the use of a public resource, the broadcaster is responsible for serving the public. What this "service" consists of is necessarily worked out in a balance of power and authority between the public and private sectors. The broadcasters are charged with providing a "free market place of ideas," and yet the government is loath to do anything about the programming of the stations. The private licensees operate franchises that acquire fabulous property values (for example, in a large city a television station may represent a capital investment of less than $5 million, but a property value of $50 million), and yet the broadcaster feels himself in jeopardy every three years when he faces the possibility (a very small possibility, it must be admitted) that the license may be taken from him.

STRUCTURE OF THE INDUSTRY

Perhaps the best way to approach the complex structure of the United States broadcasting industry is by means of a simple chart (Figure 1).

In essence, that is the way it works. With the aid of outside program sources, stations and cable services produce and transmit programs for audiences. Because it is a private enterprise system, it necessarily has a double goal—not only to please and serve audiences but also to attract the kind and size of audiences that in turn will attract advertisers to buy time on the system and, consequently, to make a profit for the owners. The system therefore serves two masters, and operates within limits set by government regulatory agencies that have rigorously maintained a policy of keeping hands off programs.

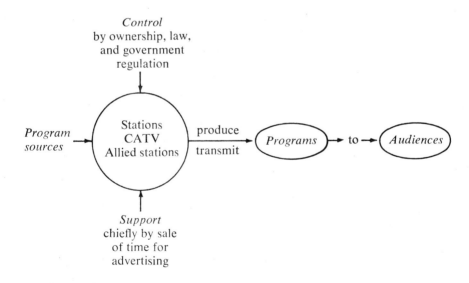

Figure 1
Structure of the U.S. broadcasting industry.

This is simple enough, but the picture is complicated when we start to fill in some of the details. For example, the mere matter of size—much larger than any other broadcasting system in the world—itself adds an element of complexity. Suppose we fill in some numbers for the circles in the previous chart (see Figure 2).

Schramm/Alexander

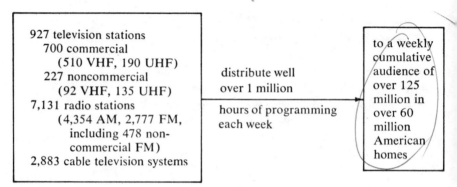

Figure 2
Size of the U.S. broadcasting industry.

927 television stations
   700 commercial
     (510 VHF, 190 UHF)
   227 noncommercial
     (92 VHF, 135 UHF)
7,131 radio stations
    (4,354 AM, 2,777 FM,
     including 478 non-
     commercial FM)
2,883 cable television systems

distribute well
over 1 million

hours of programming
each week

to a weekly cumulative audience of over 125 million in over 60 million American homes

The figures are for about the beginning of 1972: true totals will doubtless be larger by the time this is in print.

Because of the many different types of stations, their interrelationships in networks and chains of ownership, and their relationships to cable transmission of signals, most of which originate with stations; because of the great variety in programming; and because of the number of different audiences to be served—for these reasons it is impossible to describe American television and radio in any such simple way as one can describe, for example, the broadcasting system of a country that has a state-owned network or a single public corporation responsible for broadcasting. For the majority of American stations, their programming and their policies are their own; they are responsible to their owners rather than to a government agency or public corporation. They all come together under the umbrella of benevolent government regulation for, as indicated, the Federal Communications Commission since its founding in 1934 has been considerably more interested in allocating frequencies than in concerning itself over what a broadcaster does with his frequency.

The system is complex also because it includes a number of organizations and agencies that have become essential to the operation of broadcasting but are separate from the act of broadcasting. In Figure 3 we have inserted some numbers, where they are readily available, in order to provide some idea of the magnitude of these related services.

This is the kind of structure that broadcasting has evolved in the United States. . . .

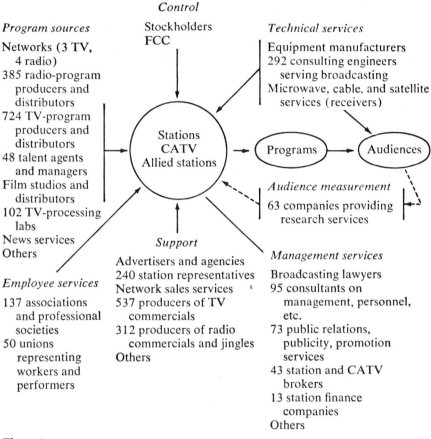

Control
Stockholders
FCC

Program sources

Networks (3 TV,
   4 radio)
385 radio-program
   producers and
   distributors
724 TV-program
   producers and
   distributors
48 talent agents
   and managers
Film studios and
   distributors
102 TV-processing
   labs
News services
Others

Technical services

Equipment manufacturers
292 consulting engineers
   serving broadcasting
Microwave, cable, and satellite
   services (receivers)

Stations
CATV
Allied stations

Programs

Audiences

Audience measurement

63 companies providing
   research services

Support

Advertisers and agencies
240 station representatives
Network sales services
537 producers of TV
   commercials
312 producers of radio
   commercials and jingles
Others

Employee services

137 associations
   and professional
   societies
50 unions
   representing
   workers and
   performers

Management services

Broadcasting lawyers
95 consultants on
   management, personnel,
   etc.
73 public relations,
   publicity, promotion
   services
43 station and CATV
   brokers
13 station finance
   companies
Others

Figure 3
Related agencies and services essential to U.S. broadcasting-industry.

The appetite of the American broadcasting system for programs is
gargantuan. Over one million hours per week must be programmed. This
is a quantum jump from the programming needs of a system like that of
France or Britain, where independent stations are almost nonexistent and
most programming comes from a few networks. That is why such a large
number of programming-production services are needed by the American
broadcasting structure.

Relatively little of a station's programming actually originates within the
station itself. A network station signs a contract that commits the network to

Schramm/Alexander

furnish a certain number of hours of programming in return for which the station promises to take a certain number of these programs and to permit the network to sell a certain amount of the station's time to national advertisers. The station thus receives programs of broad audience interest and also a substantial share of the time charges collected by the network.

The network makes some of the programs it distributes and contracts for the making of others. Behind the network, as behind the individual station, stand the program producers and distributors, the film studios and distributors, feature services, wire news services, and many other program sources. Where possible, the network covers live events of wide interest. For some of these (e.g., football games), the network must pay for the privilege of broadcasting; for others (e.g., a presidential press conference, a moon shot, or a public meeting or demonstration), it pays no fee but must meet the very considerable expense of coverage.

A network station receives by no means all of its programs from the network. The station provides some of its own programs and buys others, which means that it, too, deals with wire services, film distributors, program producers, and the like. Stations that are not affiliated with networks make even more use of these programming services, and often buy network shows that are available for reshowing after a season or two. Independent radio stations in particular build as much of their program as possible around low-cost programming, such as disc jockeys playing phonograph records or tapes, or talk shows relying upon telephone calls to the station.

Approximately one-tenth of broadcasting time can be filled by commercials. Some of these are read by station announcers from scripts written in the station or provided by advertisers. A national television commercial or a radio jingle, however, usually originates in an advertising agency or in the studio of a producer hired by the agency. In the case of television, particularly, loving care is usually lavished on the commercial, and the process of planning, studying, pretesting, making, and remaking usually costs considerably more per minute than does the program that the commercial accompanies. It comes to a station usually on film or magnetic tape, or embedded in a network program.

Noncommercial stations do not have quite the same relationship to their network, if they belong to one. The noncommercial network does not act as a national advertising salesman, and the station's promise of how much programming it will take is somewhat less strict, but the network does provide a certain number of programs. Like the programs of a commercial network (NBC, CBS, or ABC), the programs circulated by the Public Broadcasting System may be made by the affiliated national program center NET (as, for example, was "Sesame Street") or purchased from other sources (as were "The Forsyte Saga" and "Civilisation," which were purchased from BBC). Noncommercial stations also exchange a certain number of their own best programs.

Because of the need to transmit so many programs promptly, a nationwide microwave . . . and [coaxial cable has] . . . become necessary, and numerous proposals have been made to supplement these with domestic satellites. Because of the number of individual outlets that must be maintained and the great number of programs that must be paid for, a very large system of advertising sales has become necessary. We shall say something in the next section about the size of this support structure. Here we should merely note that it includes, in addition to the network sales departments, many hundreds of advertising agencies handling radio or television advertising, many hundreds of sales representatives who solicit and sell spot announcements for local stations and, of course, many thousands of local station sales departments which deal directly with local and regional advertisers. The stations and networks themselves employ over 100,000 persons.

The number of local units in the system and the intensely competitive nature of the industry place rather heavy responsibility on management for the economic survival of the station, and for dealings with unions and national professional organizations as well as with government regulatory agencies and local pressure and power groups. Whether the responsibilities are any less in a less-fragmented industry is debatable, but observers have continually noted the intensely competitive nature of American broadcasting in comparison, for example, with European broadcasting systems built around national networks.

Support of U.S. Broadcasting

The advertising support of commercial broadcasting in the United States amounts to more than $4.5 billion per year, of which almost two-thirds goes to television. It is interesting to observe how this support has grown.

. . . The swift rise of television, after the freeze ended in 1952, . . . [affected radio revenues, especially radio network advertisers income.]

The first year in which the total income of television exceeded that of radio was 1955, and 1956 was the first year since before World War II when radio's total sales fell below the level of the preceding year. After 1956, radio's national nonnetwork and local advertising began to rise again, but the rate of total growth in support was only about half that of television.

How does a station spend its money? . . . The radio station spends relatively more on sales because a greater part of its support has to come from selling local advertising. The television station has higher technical costs because it is technically more complex, and it spends more on programs because television material costs more than sound broadcast material.

How profitable is broadcasting? The question cannot be answered simply because there is a great variation among types of stations. VHF stations, carrying network service in metropolitan markets, may be immensely profitable whereas many UHF stations have been in severe financial difficulty. *Broadcasting Yearbook's* 1970 "typical TV station," which was supposedly a VHF station, reported a profit of 18.1 percent on gross before federal income taxes. The "typical radio station" for the same year made 8.7 percent before federal income taxes. These compare favorably with profits from other industries. For example, the steel industry has been making about 7 percent before federal income taxes, and printing and publishing has reported something over 9 percent.

Illustrating how unevenly the returns from broadcasting are divided, however, are the FCC financial reports for 1970, which show that almost 40 percent of the total income of television went to the three networks and their fifteen owned and operated stations.

Fifteen advertisers provided about one-third of television income in 1970. These were Procter and Gamble, General Foods, Colgate-Palmolive, Bristol-Myers, American Home Products, R. J. Reynolds, Lever Brothers, General Motors, Warner-Lambert, Sterling Drug, Phillip Morris, Gillette, General Mills, Ford Motor, and Miles Laboratories. All of these corporations deal in products with very wide appeal over economic, age, and social groups. That is, they sell goods like soaps, toothpastes, cigarettes, automobiles, and the contents of the home medicine cabinet. The top twenty advertisers—dealing almost wholly with the same kind of products —provided more than 40 percent of television income.

It might be predicted that this concentration of income in products of general, rather than specific, interest would encourage television programming of a kind that would also have the widest possible audience appeal; and this is precisely what we find. Programs of broad interest = large audiences = large product sales = large time sales and high advertising rates.

There is a corresponding concentration of this flow of advertising in a few large agencies. One advertising agency alone (J. Walter Thompson) was responsible for nearly 15 percent of all television time sales in 1969. The top ten agencies together were responsible for nearly two-thirds of total television time sales.

What does it cost to make a sales pitch to a large television audience? More than one-third of all the television homes in the United States are in the ten largest markets: New York, Los Angeles, Chicago, Philadelphia, Boston, San Francisco, Detroit, Cleveland, Washington, and Pittsburgh. To buy 1 percent of these television homes (one rating point) costs on the average $850 during prime time. This is for a brief spot announcement during prime time, 7:30 to 11:00 P.M. In the daytime it costs less, but the maximum audience is much less and does not include many adult males.

In the smaller markets of the country, an audience of the same size would cost more. The individual station time rates are lower, but the audiences are smaller, too. This is one reason why stations in large cities have a market value far above the investment that has been made in them: With the same program and corresponding facilities, they can reach a vast audience; consequently, they charge very high rates and still offer an attractive buy to national advertisers.

The heavy flow of advertising support and the need for programs of wide interest have had effects far beyond the broadcasting industry itself. For example, much of the entertainment of the country is dependent in no small part on television and radio. Exposure on the air is almost a requirement for successfully building an entertainer's career. Most professional sports would be much less popular and less prosperous without broadcasting. For example, the networks alone pay professional football about $50 million a year—$2.5 million of it for one game, the Super Bowl. Professional football schedules and times (e.g., whether the game is played on Saturday, Sunday, or Monday, and at what hour) will often depend more on the needs of television than the convenience of the local audience. And in order that commercials may get enough attention during a game, special time-outs for advertising are called a number of times during the game.

THE PATTERN OF CONTROL

No broadcasting system is completely free from control. There are countless degrees of political control between the extremes that Terrou and Solal (1951) describe as "subordination to political authorities" and "nonsubordination."

Toward one end of that spectrum would be a country like Spain, in which broadcasting is actually a part of the government and its content is carefully watched; or a country like the Soviet Union, in which broadcasting operates under the minister of culture and under the careful surveillance of the Party. Toward the other end would be a country like Sweden in which television operates as a private company under the direction of a board of eleven members, the chairman and five other members being appointed by the government; or the United States, where most stations are privately owned and subject to very light government regulation.

Between those extremes lie a variety of patterns. For example, the British Broadcasting Corporation operates under a nonprofit, corporate body set up by a royal charter with a board of governors appointed by the queen; BBC is given almost complete freedom in its programming policies and is expected to exercise responsibility. NHK in Japan is a public juridical person, free in large part from government control although regulated by a governmental agency much like the Federal Communications Commission in the United States. Both Britain and Japan have a parallel system of commercial stations, but neither BBC nor NHK takes advertising.

German broadcasting is conducted by chartered corporations in the several Länder (states); they are neither government agencies nor private companies, and are designed to be as free as possible of government control. Radiodiffusion-Télévision Française (RTF) in France is a public establishment under the joint supervision of the minister of information and the minister of finance and economic affairs, who have in the past exercised rather close control over the news policies of the organization.

There are thus many patterns of relationship to government, subtly different from each other . . . but even the systems that seem to be most free are not completely free. Any nation feels the obligation to allocate frequencies for its stations to prevent interference or chaos on the air. Any nation is almost certain to have a law protecting copyright owners from unauthorized broadcast, protecting audiences against obscenity or libel, and protecting the state against treason or sedition. Additional policies and legal controls vary in their strictness. But governmental control is not the only kind of control exerted upon broadcasting.

When a Western broadcaster says that Soviet broadcasting is not "free" he means that it is not *politically* free. When a Soviet broadcaster says that American broadcasting is not "free" he probably means that it is not *economically* free. That is, he would argue that it is owned by wealthy people and financial organizations, and is likely therefore to be in the control of owners who represent a class interest. The interests of ownership are likely to be reflected in the content. . . . There are differences of opinion as to how much control is exerted by ownership in different privately owned systems, but at least one can hardly contend that the need to make a profit from advertising does not affect the content of commercial broadcasting.

There is also the kind of social control that is expressed in the United States by the act of viewing or not viewing, listening or not listening, in letters and messages to stations and networks, in criticisms and rewards.

All broadcasting systems are to some degree subject to each of these kinds of control. It happens that the United States system is uncommonly free from control by government, and ownership is (except for noncommercial stations) private rather than public or governmental. The owner has a great amount of freedom to set policy for the same public service concerning which many governments are so concerned that they own and operate it themselves or control it tightly.

The agency by which the United States government chiefly exercises its regulatory control over broadcasting is the FCC—the Federal Communications Commission. This was actually the third pattern by which the United States tried to regulate broadcasting. The first such attempt to control general broadcasting was the Radio Act of 1912. It made the secretary of commerce and labor (these were then combined in one department) responsible for licensing radio stations and operators.

When stations multiplied rapidly in the 1920s, however, the courts decided that the secretary did not have the authority, under this act, to limit broadcast time and power, enforce frequency allocations, and cure the growing chaos on the air waves. President Coolidge asked Congress for new legislation, and the result was the Dill-White Radio Act of 1927, which established a five-member Federal Radio Commission with regulatory powers over licensing, allocating frequency bands to different services, assigning frequencies to stations, and controlling power. The Radio Commission went to work to straighten out the mess in frequency use, and its new rules forced about 150 of the more than 700 existing stations to surrender their licenses.

In 1933 President Roosevelt appointed an interdepartmental committee to restudy the needs of broadcast regulation in the context of national and international electronic communication as a whole. This committee recommended that "the communication service, as far as congressional action is involved, should be regulated by a single body. It recommended · that a new agency be created with responsibility for regulating all interstate and foreign communication by wire or by radio, including telephone, telegraph, broadcast, and other uses of the radio spectrum." . . .

This agency, the Federal Communications Commission, was created by the Communications Act of 1934 which, with its subsequent amendments, is the main body of U.S. communication law. The FCC was to carry out the law as written by Congress, and to promulgate new rules and regulations not contained in the law but necessary to carry out the law's intent. Thus, at the outset, the FCC became administrator, legislator, and judge.

The FCC is an independent regulatory commission. It consists of seven commissioners, appointed by the president with the advice and consent of Congress. Appointments are for seven years, and no more than four members may belong to a single political party. The commission has a staff numbering about fifteen hundred, a large number of whom are assigned to engineering work, such as monitoring the use of frequencies and power, and tracing interference.

The responsibilities of the FCC are far wider than broadcasting. They include the management, in the public interest, of the entire radio spectrum, the allocation of frequencies to different services, and the coordination of the United States' position regarding new spectrum allocations for the meetings of the International Radio Consultative Committee (CCIR— Comité Consultatif International des Radio-Communications), which is the international frequency-allocation board. The commission also regulates common carriers engaged in interstate and foreign communication by telephone and telegraph, and in so doing decides upon rates and charges. It examines and licenses radio operators of many kinds. These and others. But the best known of its activities, and the ones that chiefly concern us here, are those that relate to broadcasting, where it is responsible, among other things, for licensing every radio and television station.

In carrying out its responsibilites for broadcasting, the commission has made decisions of far-reaching importance. Among these are the frequency allocation plan for television that came into effect in 1952, opening up the UHF band, and providing much more complete coverage for the country. Another influential decision was the so-called chain regulations concerning monopoly of ownership: No individual or group may own more than one network, or more than seven AM, seven FM, or seven TV commercial stations anywhere in the United States, and no more than five of the seven TV stations may be in the VHF band.

Still another important decision had to do with adoption of a television system that would provide for "compatible" color—the reception of both black-and-white and color television on the same receiver. The FCC also reacted firmly to the "payola" and "quiz" scandals of the 1950s; as a result, the Communications Act was amended in 1960 to prohibit the plugging of phonograph discs or other commercial items without making clear when money had been received for doing so; and also to prohibit the broadcasting of quiz shows that were "fixed." . . .

A great deal of the argument generated around the commission, however, has arisen from the responsibility for licensing stations, and in particular from the possible relation of that responsibility to station programming.

Let us make clear that the commission has no direct authority over programs. It can neither put a program on or take it off the air. The Communications Act says:

> Nothing in this Act shall be understood or construed to give the commission the power of censorship over the radio communications or signals transmitted by any radio station, and no regulation or condition shall be promulgated or fixed by the commission which shall interfere with the right of free speech by means of radio communication.

The act stipulates certain requirements that must be met by applicants for a broadcast license. They must be legally, technically, and financially qualified to operate a station. They must be citizens of the United States. No officer or director of a corporation applying for a license may be an alien, nor may more than one-fifth of the capital stock of such a corporation be held by foreign owners. And an applicant must show that the proposed operation will be in the public interest.

Schramm/Alexander

That is where programming enters into the act of licensing. When a broadcaster endeavors to show that his operation will be in the public interest, he has to talk about what kind of programming he proposes to provide.

In this respect, the commission has not been dogmatic. . . . In practice the commission has paid relatively little attention to an applicant's programming except in two circumstances—when there is competition for the frequency, and (recently) when an applicant returns for a renewal of his license after three years (and there are complaints on file regarding his services). In the former circumstance, when the commission has before it more than one applicant for the same channel, all of whom are apparently adequately qualified legally, financially, and technically, then it has seemed necessary to examine the kind of programming they propose. And in the latter circumstance, when an applicant has received a license because he promised to provide certain kinds of programming, the commission has come to think that perhaps before it renews the license it should examine the program records he submits to see whether he has kept his promises.

The commission has been most loath to take any action based on programming. It does little more than pass on to a station any complaints that come to the commission concerning the station's programming. It has almost never revoked a license at the time of renewal, although it has sometimes renewed the license for less than three years.

In the last few years, however, the commission has taken a few actions of this kind. Certain commissioners have spoken very frankly about the level of broadcast programming (former chairman Newton Minow's "Vast Wasteland" speech still echoes through the stations and the networks), a "fairness doctrine" providing the right of reply to a political nonnews broadcast has been promulgated (see Kahn, 1972) and, in general, the matter of program quality and station responsibility for programs has been brought to public attention more vividly than in the past. This has frightened many broadcasters and raised the specter of the First Amendment and government control. We shall return to this and related problems of policy in the next section. Here it need merely be said that the degree of government control over broadcasting represented by the FCC is very mild indeed in comparison with many other systems in the world. . . .

THE BROADCASTING AUDIENCE

According to the Nielsen Television Index, during the measurement period ending in March of 1972 the average American home used its television receiver forty-two hours and fourteen minutes a week, or just over six hours a day. Over one-third of this was in the "prime time" hours—7:30 to 11 P.M. This pattern varies by day of the week, time of the year, and individual homes. For the kind of day we have described, however, it comes close to being the average for a supposedly representative sample of American homes.

There are no precisely comparable figures for radio because radio receivers are so widely distributed and, consequently, more difficult to survey. The common estimate of time devoted by a family to radio is about half the time for television. Yet radio in one day or one week reaches more people than does television, if we can depend upon an NBC audience study that was reported in *Broadcasting Yearbook* for 1972 beside the 1972 Nielsen figures. The cumulative audiences of people eighteen years of age and over reached by the two broadcast media are shown in Table [A].

Table [A]
Cumulative audiences of radio and television

	In one day	*In seven days*
Radio	92,100,000 (75.1%)	111,000,000 (90.5%)
Television	80,900,000 (65.9%)	106,500,000 (86.8%)

These figures are highly approximate, and may or may not be comparable. NBC says that it regards the radio estimates as "approximate" but "conservative" benchmarks, and that the comparison "does not imply that television and radio are equal in impact or effectiveness" but "does suggest that radio's broad reach makes the medium an ideal choice for backing up television advertising." . . .

One other note of interest is that radio reaches a higher proportion of teen-agers (twelve to seventeen) than of adults. The difference is only a few percentage points, but suggests the attractiveness of radio's popular music programs. . . .

Who is viewing, and how many? Latest answers to these questions come from Nielsen, for February 1971, and are presented in Table [B].

These figures indicate that television is largely a women's and children's medium through the working hours of the day, an all-family medium in the

Table [B]
Composition of the TV audience

	Homes using TV	Viewers per home	% of viewing audience made up of			
			Men	Women	Teens	Children
Monday-Friday						
10:00 A.M.-1:00 P.M.	25.3%	1.33	17	57	5	21
1:00-5:00 P.M.	32.8	1.42	16	56	8	20
All Nights						
7:30-11:00 P.M.	65.1	2.07	32	41	11	16

evening. About three out of five homes, on the average, will have the TV receiver turned on in prime time. In ten representative homes, we should expect in prime evening time to find about six sets in use, about thirteen people viewing, of whom four would be men, five women, one or two teen-agers, and perhaps two or three children. Of course, audience composition would vary greatly by program and by family.

The average network prime-time evening program will go into 15 to 20 percent of television homes. Daytime programs will get a much lower rating. Top network news programs will draw an audience nearly comparable to that of prime-time entertainment. Reruns of popular comedies like "I Love Lucy," in good time slots, will draw very well. Evening programs on public television, in competition with the top commercial entertainment, will draw at the most 5 to 10 percent of homes, and on the average 2 or 3 percent. The most popular of the independent stations will average higher ratings than the public stations: some of the independents, particularly those on UHF, will average less. . . .

Television gathers its largest audiences for coverage of great events. One of the largest audiences ever in front of television in this country was for the first moonwalk, covered by all three networks, and viewed in American homes by perhaps 125 million people. When President John F. Kennedy was killed, it is estimated that 166 million Americans viewed the ensuing events on television at some time during that weekend.

PROBLEMS OF POLICY AND PERFORMANCE

Any industry that serves as many people with information and entertainment, and commands as many of the waking hours of a nation as does American broadcasting is bound to raise problems of public policy.

In many countries these problems are internalized within the
government. In the United States, however, the private enterprise nature
of the system and the historic relations of mass media to government give
matters of this kind a high public visibility.

Most of these problems are twofold: Does some aspect of the industry or
its performance involve the public interest? What, if anything, should
the government do about it?

Needless to say, American tradition has been that the government should
do as little as possible, and the media should be as free as possible to
operate within a freely competitive situation. Therefore the public problems
of broadcasting, as they have grown more urgent, have raised over and
over again long-standing and still sensitive issues of private versus public
interest, licensing and censorship, freedom and control, and the degree
of public responsibility to be expected of a broadcaster. These are familiar
issues but the impact of electronic technology has modernized them. . . .

The Bower Report:
Attitudes Toward Broadcasting

BROADCASTING

Copyright 1973, Broadcasting Publications, Inc., publishers of *Broadcasting,*
newsweekly of broadcasting and allied arts, *Broadcasting Yearbook,* and *Broadcasting
Cable Sourcebook* (annual). Reprinted by permission from the June 11, 1973 issue of
Broadcasting. This *Broadcasting* magazine article is a condensation of Robert T.
Bower's book *Television and the Public.* Dr. Bower has been director of the Bureau
of Social Science Research in Washington, D.C. since 1950.

In the public mind American television has ceased to be primarily
an entertainment center and has become a major force in journalism as well.

This change occurred in a decade when, paradoxically, viewers were
losing some of their enthusiasm for television but nevertheless were
watching it more—and enjoying it more—than when the decade began.   **31**

Table 1
"Now, I would like to get your opinions about how radio, newspaper, television, and magazines compare. Generally speaking, which of these would you say . . . ?"
In percentages

Which of the media:	Television		Magazines		Newspapers		Radio		None/NA	
	1960	*1970*	*1960*	*1970*	*1960*	*1970*	*1960*	*1970*	*1960*	*1970*
Is the most entertaining?	68	72	9	5	13	9	9	14	1	0
Gives the most complete news coverage?	19	41	3	4	59	39	18	14	1	2
Presents things most intelligently?	27	38	27	18	33	28	8	9	5	8
Is the most educational?	32	46	31	20	31	26	3	4	3	5
Brings you the latest news most quickly?	36	54	0	0	5	6	57	39	2	1
Does the most for the public?	34	48	3	2	44	28	11	13	8	10
Seems to be getting worse all the time?	24	41	17	18	10	14	14	5	35	22
Presents the fairest, most unbiased news?	29	33	9	9	31	23	22	19	9	16
Is the least important to you?	15	13	49	53	7	9	15	20	7	5
Creates the most interest in new things going on?	56	61	18	16	18	14	4	5	4	5
Does the least for the public?	13	10	47	50	5	7	12	13	23	20
Seems to be getting better all the time?	49	38	11	8	11	11	10	15	19	28
Gives you the clearest understanding of the candidates and issues in national elections?	42	59	10	8	36	21	5	3	7	9

1960 base: 100 percent = 2427
1970 base: 100 percent = 1900

These are among many findings made public [in 1973] from 1970 research that duplicated—and thus permitted direct comparisons with—major elements of the 1960 surveys that formed the basis of the late Dr. Gary Steiner's landmark volume, "The People Look at Television" (*Broadcasting*, Feb. 18, 1963, et seq.).

Other major findings and conclusions from the 1970 study:

Viewers in 1970 found TV less "satisfying," "relaxing," "exciting," "important" and generally less "wonderful" than had those in 1960 (possibly, the report suggests, because some of the newness had worn off), but the change was not from "praise" to "condemnation"—more nearly is was from "summa to magna cum laude." (Table 2.)

Better-educated viewers in 1970, as in 1960, held TV in lower esteem than did other viewers, but they watched as much—and essentially the same things—as everybody else.

Table 2

"Here are some opposites. Please read each pair quickly and put a check some place between them, wherever you think it belongs, to describe television. Just your offhand impression."

Proportion of 1960–1970 samples choosing each of six positions

Television is generally:	(1) 1960	(1) 1970	(2) 1960	(2) 1970	(3) 1960	(3) 1970	(4) 1960	(4) 1970	(5) 1960	(5) 1970	(6) 1960	(6) 1970	
Relaxing	43	33	21	23	19	27	9	11	3	4	4	3	Upsetting
Interesting	42	31	21	23	19	24	9	13	4	5	4	3	Uninteresting
For me	41	27	16	20	19	24	10	15	6	8	8	6	Not for me
Important	39	30	17	19	21	24	10	15	7	7	6	6	Unimportant
Informative	39	35	25	27	20	23	8	9	5	3	3	3	Not informative
Lots of fun	32	22	20	20	25	31	12	16	5	6	6	5	Not much fun
Exciting	30	19	18	17	29	35	13	17	5	7	4	6	Dull
Wonderful	28	19	16	15	33	36	16	22	4	6	3	3	Terrible
Imaginative	26	19	21	20	28	33	14	15	6	7	5	6	No imagination
In good taste	24	18	21	19	31	33	19	19	6	7	4	4	In bad taste
Generally excellent	22	15	19	18	32	36	18	21	5	6	4	4	Generally bad
Lots of variety	35	28	16	20	19	21	12	14	10	9	8	8	All the same
On everyone's mind	33	21	22	18	24	29	15	20	4	7	3	5	Nobody cares much
Getting better	25	16	19	15	24	23	16	21	8	11	9	15	Getting worse
Keeps changing	23	22	17	18	22	24	18	20	10	9	9	8	Stays the same
Serious	8	7	8	8	31	35	29	33	12	10	12	7	Playful
Too "highbrow"	4	3	3	4	29	28	42	43	11	12	9	11	Too "simple minded"

1960 Base: 100 percent = 2427
1970 Base: 100 percent = 1900
(Excluding NA's which vary from item to item)

Table 3

Proportion of each group taking most extreme position on two scales.

	Superians Percent who check extreme positive positions				Vilifiers Percent who check extreme negative positions					
	"Wonderful"		"For me"		"Terrible"		"Not for me"		Base: 100% =	
	1960	1970	1960	1970	1960	1970	1960	1970	1960	1970
Sex:										
Male	27	17	40	24	3	4	7	7	1177	900
Female	28	20	41	31	3	2	9	6	1246	982
Education:										
Grade school	44	33	54	43	3	3	9	7	627	367
High school	26	19	42	28	3	3	7	6	1214	1030
College	12	7	20	15	3	2	11	8	516	490
Age:										
18-19	32	17	44	25	0	2	6	7	84	182
20-29	19	17	33	29	3	1	8	6	473	331
30-39	23	18	39	24	2	3	7	6	544	356
40-49	27	13	38	23	2	3	7	9	463	378
50-59	34	21	44	27	4	2	10	5	400	311
60+	36	24	50	33	4	5	10	6	440	419

In 1970 as in 1960 viewers showed a high degree of acceptance of commercials. At most, viewer attitude had become only slightly more negative. "The average viewer still overwhelmingly accepts the frequent and long interruptions by commercials as 'a fair price to pay.' " (Table 4.)

Most adults in both surveys felt children are better off with television than they would be without it, but the percentage has increased from 70% to 76%. College-educated parents now give TV the heaviest vote on this score (81%, up from 68% 10 years earlier), and grade-school-educated parents the lowest (68%, down from 75%).

Educational benefits remain the biggest advantage adults see in television for children, but by a much bigger percentage in 1970 than in 1960 (80% versus 65%), and entertainment has replaced the baby-sitting function as the second greatest advantage. (Table 6.)

"Seeing things they shouldn't" is still the top-rated disadvantage of TV for children in adults' minds, but there have been some changes since

Table 4

"Here are some statements about commercials. I'd like you to read each statement and mark whether you generally agree or disagree with each statement."

Percent who agree that:	1960 total	1970 total	1970 occupation of head of household	
			White collar	Blue collar
Commercials are a fair price to pay for the entertainment you get	75	70	69	71
Most commercials are too long	63	65	67	65
I find some commercials very helpful in keeping me informed	58	54	50	57
Some commercials are so good that they are more entertaining than the program	43	54	56	52
I would prefer TV without commercials	43	48	49	47
Commercials are generally in poor taste and very annoying	40	43	42	43
I frequently find myself welcoming a commercial break	36	35	31	38
I'd rather pay a small amount yearly to have TV without commercials	24	30	30	29
There are just too many commercials	(Not included in 1960)	70	71	70
Having special commercial breaks during a program is better than having the same number of commercials at the begining and end	(Not included in 1960)	39	35	42
Base: 100 percent =	(2427)	(1900)	(674)	(873)

1960 in what those things are. "Violence" is still number one, but sex, seminudity, vulgarity, smoking, drinking and drugs have increased as causes of concern. (Table 7.)

Parents are "a bit stricter" than they were about controlling their children's viewing (43% say they have "definite rules" as against 41% in 1960). But better-educated parents, the biggest group in approving of TV for children, are much more inclined to have rules (46%) than grade-school-educated parents (25%), who are most fearful about TV for children. In general, however, "there are about as many parents who look to the children for help in deciding what they (parents) are going to watch as there are parents who try to decide about their children's viewing."

The 1970 study was financed by a grant by CBS, which also underwrote the 1960 study, to the Bureau of Social Science Research, a Washington-based independent nonprofit organization. Based on a national probability sample, some 1,900 adults (aged 18 and over) were interviewed by the Roper Organization, New York, in late winter and early spring of 1970—exactly 10 years after interviewing was done in the 1960 study. In addition there was a separate special study in Minneapolis-St.Paul, where, in cooperation with the American Research Bureau, the researchers were able to measure what viewers said against what they actually watched, corresponding to a similar special study in New York as part of the 1960 work. . . .

The report is by Robert T. Bower, director of the Bureau of Social Science Research, who emphasizes in his preface that CBS had no control over any aspect of the study or report. It is . . . published as a 205-page book titled *Television and the Public* by CBS's Holt, Rinehart & Winston subsidiary, which CBS . . . [distributed] widely to editors, educators and other opinion leaders.

The report ranges over many areas covered in the 1960 study, but the rising role of television as a journalistic force in the public's perception of the medium represents one of the most striking changes of the decade.

It is demonstrated in many ways. In 1960, for example, television had been voted best mass medium in only one of four specified news categories: giving the clearest understanding of candidates and issues in national elections. But by 1970, Dr. Bower reports, "we find television surging ahead of newspapers as the news medium that 'gives the most complete news coverage,' overtaking radio in bringing 'the latest news most quickly,' edging out newspapers in 'presenting the fairest, most unbiased news' and increasing its lead" in the one area where it was ahead in 1960, national political coverage. (Table 5.)

Dr. Bower notes that these findings parallel the results of studies conducted—also by the Roper Organization—for the Television Information Office since 1959. (He also notes at another point that when an Apollo 13 moon-flight emergency occurred during interviewing in Minneapolis-St. Paul, where 52% had rated TV the fastest news medium, 58% got their first word of the emergency from radio, as against 40% from TV. However, he says, TV regained its position as predominant source of information in the remaining four days of the flight.)

Table 5

"Now, I would like to get your opinions about how radio, newspapers, television and magazines compare. Generally speaking, which of these would you say . . ."

		Percent 1960	Percent 1970
"Gives the most complete news coverage?"	Television	19	41
	Magazines	3	4
	Newspapers	59	39
	Radio	18	14
	None or don't know	1	2
"Brings you the latest news most quickly?"	Television	36	54
	Magazines	0	0
	Newspapers	5	6
	Radio	57	39
	None or don't know	2	1
"Gives the fairest, most unbiased news?"	Television	29	33
	Magazines	9	9
	Newspapers	31	23
	Radio	22	19
	None or don't know	9	16
"Gives the clearest understanding of candidates and issues in national elections?"	Television	42	59
	Magazines	16	8
	Newspapers	36	21
	Radio	5	3
	None or don't know	1	9

1960 Base: 100 percent = 2427 (minus NA's which vary from item to item)
1970 Base: 100 percent = 1900 (minus NA's which vary from item to item)

As another evidence of the public's growing perception of TV's news role Dr. Bower recalls that viewers and critics in 1960 were talking primarily about entertainment and cultural values, but in 1970 had shifted their focus to news functions, objectivity, concentration of control and effects of news coverage on audience behavior. And even in the area of TV and children, he notes, much of the violence parents object to their children's seeing is violence that is reported in the news.

He cites Vice-President Spiro Agnew's celebrated Nov. 13, 1969, attack on network news specifically. This was just three months before interviewing was done for the 1970 study—and still TV was voted the fairest and most unbiased medium. . . .

The study looked for bias in a number of directions. In one, 53% of the conservatives, an equal percentage of liberals and a few more middle-of-the-roaders (56%) said they thought newscasters in general "give it

Table 6

"What do you think are some of the main advantages of television for children?"
The advantages of TV for children by respondent's general attitude (pro or con) toward television for children*

Percent who mention:	1960 Parents		Others		1960 Total	1970 Total	1970 Parents		Others	
	Pros	Cons	Pros	Cons			Pros	Cons	Pros	Cons
Education	74	49	72	45	65	80	85	69	85	62
Baby-sitting	34	21	31	13	28	16	17	13	18	9
Entertainment	21	15	23	8	19	22	27	20	21	17
Programs good generally	4	17	6	16	8	2	2	2	2	2
Stimulates socializing	2	—	1	—	1	2	3	—	2	2
Adult supervision necessary	4	2	10	4	6	2	2	1	2	1
Other, general	1	4	1	4	2	4	3	6	2	6
Base: 100% =	(858)	(292)	(781)	(419)	(2350)	(1592)	(589)	(159)	(607)	(237)

*Multiple response item: percentages do not necessarily add up to 100 percent.

straight," while 30% of the conservatives, 26% of the liberals and 25% of the middle-roaders thought newscasters tend to color the news. Republicans were more suspicious (32%) than Democrats (22%). In the total sample, viewers divided about equally as to whether the newscasters they individually watch most are liberal (14%) or conservative (13%); more consider them middle-roaders (36%) and even more can't tell (38%). But overwhelmingly they feel their favorite newscasters give the news straight (78%) rather than let their personal opinions color it (6%).

Dr. Bower offers this summary:

It appears that a sizable proportion (about one-fourth) of the public feels that television news is generally biased in its presentation. A much smaller group of hard-core critics think even their own favorite newscaster colors the news. But the vast majority of people either accept the objectivity of television newscasting in general or find a specific newscaster to watch who is felt to be objective in his reporting. . . . If the public at large were the judge, the medium would probably be exonerated [of bias charges] or at worst be given a suspended sentence.

Table 7

"What do you think are some of the main disadvantages of television for children?"
Disadvantages of television for children by parental status and general attitude
(pro and con) toward television for children.*

	1960						1970			
	Parents		Others		1960	1970	Parents		Others	
Percent who mention:	Pros	Cons	Pros	Cons	Total	Total	Pros	Cons	Pros	Cons
See things they shouldn't:	46	55	48	64	51	52	48	55	50	64
Violence, horror	26	32	28	40	30	30	27	32	30	35
Crime, gangsters	7	8	11	13	10	8	6	10	9	12
Sex, suggestiveness, vulgarity	4	7	4	6	5	11	10	12	11	13
Smoking, drinking, dope	2	2	2	3	2	5	4	5	6	7
Adult themes	2	3	1	3	2	9	6	11	10	12
Harmful or sinful products advertised	1	1	1	—	1	1	1	—	1	1
Wrong values or moral codes	3	5	2	5	3	8	8	11	8	9
Other, general	7	11	8	9	8	2	3	5	2	5
Keeps them from doing things they should	34	51	31	41	36	30	29	40	26	34
Programs bad, general	10	9	8	13	10	2	2	6	2	3
Other, program content	3	9	2	6	4	6	7	10	5	6
Physical harm	3	7	4	8	5	5	3	4	5	7
Advertising too effective	2	3	1	—	1	2	3	3	2	3
Other	2	3	1	3	2	5	6	5	5	3
Base: 100% =	(858)	(292)	(781)	(419)	(2350)	(1583)	(586)	(157)	(604)	(236)

*Multiple response item: percentages do not necessarily add up to 100 percent.

The study also undertook to learn which news medium people think puts most emphasis on "good things" and which puts most on "bad things"— and found that TV was voted number one on both counts. Dr. Bower suggests a possible explanation: "that for a large group of viewers television is simply so dominant a medium in bringing all the news, any sort of news, they see it as emphasizing all things—both the good and the bad—without any sense of contradiction. Yes, it emphasizes the good things; yes, it emphasizes the bad things; it emphasizes everything."

The study found 57% rated TV's performance in presenting 1968 presidential election campaign issues and candidates as good (44%) or excellent (13%); 32% wanted more political programs in the 1970 campaign while 15% wanted fewer, and 43% said TV played a "fairly important" (30%) or "very important" (13%) part in helping them decide whom they had wanted to win in 1968. He doesn't think that last finding should be construed to mean TV caused large numbers to bolt their parties but, rather, that it reflects "a sense of increased familiarity with the candidates and, most likely, a reinforcement of pre-existing tendencies."

At another point Dr. Bower says: "The indications are that television does not tend to favor one faction over another in such a way as to suggest a partisan political influence during a campaign, or even to discriminate among the social groups of which the population is composed. To an amazing degree, the perceived effects of television's political coverage are spread evenly among the public."

In summary, he says:

> The high assessment of television in its journalistic role that has been shown in this chapter certainly represents a general public endorsement, all the more resounding since it occurs at a time when TV news is under attack.
>
> Clearly, this part of television's content has largely been exempted from the trend toward a lower public esteem for the medium as a whole. But the vote is by no means unanimous. TV news presentation is not free of the suspicion of bias that the American public accords to tell all the mass media; and while the improvements in the technology of rapid worldwide coverage of daily events may be roundly applauded, there are those who would prefer less emphasis on the unpleasant and disturbing national conflicts.

THE NEW EMPHASIS

These presumably would be older viewers, for in another section the study found age to be the greatest differentiator of views about social strife such as riots, street protests, race problems and campus unrest. "The young applaud what the old condemn in what would seem to be expressions about the world at large, attributed to television only as the bearer of bad tidings," Dr. Bower observes.

Age also figured in one of the major changes found in viewing patterns in 1970. Ten years earlier, the heaviest viewing had been found among teenagers; in 1970, teenagers watched less than any of the other age groups. They also were the only age group that failed to watch more in 1970 than their counterparts did in 1960. In itself the decline was not considered large—from 26.25 median hours per week in 1960 to 25.33 in 1970—but in a broader context, Dr. Bower suggests, it could be huge.

The 1970 dip might be a transitory one, he says, with the teenagers increasing their viewing as they grow older, as viewers who were 28 or 29 in 1970 watched more than those 18 or 19 in 1960. "But," Dr. Bower cautions, "if it happens to be a way of life that will endure as the generation ages," the uptrend of TV viewing is threatened.

Among other changes found in 1970:

Where 1960 viewers preferred regular series to specials (49% to 32%), 1970's preferred specials (44%) to series (36%).

Despite a somewhat declining esteem for TV as a whole, viewers found more specific programs to applaud. On average, the proportion of all programs rated "extremely enjoyable" rose from 44% in 1960 to 50% in 1970. In addition, or perhaps as a factor in that increase, Dr. Bower reports that 70% of the viewers said they thought there were more "different kinds of programs" in 1970, giving them a broader range to choose from.

As for changes in television itself, reaction was overwhelmingly favorable (55% had only favorable things to say, as opposed to 16% who were solely unfavorable, with the rest neutral, balanced or in the no-answer category).

Generally, they felt neutral about 10-year changes in sports programs and movies, were critical on such morality questions as sex, nudity and vulgarity (10%) and on violence (4%), which they often linked with news, and were favorable toward changes perceived in general entertainment (19%), technical advances such as color and increased numbers of station (23%) and, most of all, changes in news and information (33%).

What they said and what they saw

The Bureau of Social Science Research's special study in Minneapolis-St. Paul, made in conjunction with its national study, confirmed again what many already knew: Viewers don't always watch what they say they want to see on television.

With the cooperation of the American Research Bureau, the researchers interviewed some Minnesotans wha had previously kept ARB diaries, and then compared what they said with what they had watched. One conclusion: "The people who say they usually watch television to learn something do watch news and information programming more than others, but only a little bit more. Those who feel there is not enough 'food for thought' on television watch as many entertainment shows as the rest of the viewers. Those who want television stations to concentrate on information programs spend only slightly more time watching such programs than those who want the 'best entertainment,' despite the fact that a great deal of informative fare is available in the Minneapolis-St. Paul area for those who could just switch the dial to another channel."

The researchers also rated respondents on a "culture scale" and examined their viewing in that context; the "high-culture" people, it turned out, "watched television somewhat less than those who scored lower; when they did watch, their viewing was distributed among program types in almost precisely the same way as the low-culture scorers, hardly a hair's breadth between them except in the news [higher viewing] and sports [lower] categories."

"Live coverage of national events, educational television, more channels, television by satellite and longer news programs are all viewed as changes for the better by 70% or more of the sample," Dr. Bower writes. "At the other end, talk shows, fewer westerns and live coverage of civil disruptions *are* approved by only about a third."

Noting that coverage of space shots and other national events ranked at the top of changes rated for the better, while coverage of riots and protests ranked at the bottom, Dr. Bower assumes that in these cases "people are responding to the message as much as the medium, probably it is the space effort people like and the riots they dislike."

Dr. Bower also cautions that it should not be assumed that "the American television audience has changed in 10 years from a population of entertainment fans to a population of news hawks." Entertainment, he notes, still dominates TV fare and commands most of the viewer's time.

"But," he continues, "there is apparently a general shift in people's perception of what television is and what it means to them, and the new focus on the news and information content of television has undoubtedly altered people's views about various other aspects of the medium's role— from how it affects the 12-year-old to whether it is a benign or malevolent force in society." More than that, he concludes, "the journalistic emphasis may have introduced important new criteria by which TV will be judged in the future."

ENTERTAINMENT

Living rooms of about sixty million homes in the United States are lighted each evening by the glow of the television screen tuned to popular entertainment programs. There is no hiding the fact that both television and radio in this country are used primarily for "getting away from it all." Furthermore, the economic underpinning of the broadcasting industry is based upon its entertainment and advertising functions. While studies by The Roper Organization, Inc. (a series of reports on American attitudes toward broadcasting) consistently reflect our dependency on television for news, the mass audience, barring disasters and spectacular news events, selects entertainment to fill more than 85 percent of the 6 hours and 20 minutes of average viewing time per day per home.

Numerous issues focus on the electronic media's entertainment function. For television, "ageless" criticism such as "bland and repetitive program plots," "inane" situation comedies, "escapist, melodramatic series" continue to be leveled at stations and networks in the seventies. As for radio, the major criticisms focus on the sameness of programming from station to station and the charge that radio is nothing more than a jukebox with headlines and commercials. The most important issues, we feel, concern TV violence, program reality, reruns, and the effects of TV and radio programming—the topics of the next five articles.

Television violence has often been singled out as a contributor to real violence and the latest national study, described in the Eli A. Rubinstein's article, reports a "causal relationship." While Rubinstein's analysis is an accurate report of the Surgeon General's Scientific Advisory Committee on Television and Social Behavior, it should be noted that there were some investigators who were not in total agreement with the findings. For example, psychology professors Robert Singer and Seymour Feshback reported in one volume of the Surgeon General's Report that their research involving boys 8 to 18 showed that "violent program content which these boys observed is not a significant cause of their aggression."

Where is the line between reality and fantasy or dramatic license to be drawn in television programs? Do people take what they see in dramatic shows as reality? Do viewers recognize that most entertainment programs operate in a world created by writers and directors? Robert Daley, a former deputy police commissioner in New York City, has some views about this as it applies to his area of expertise. He also raises questions about possible misrepresentations in television dramas that focus on particular professions. Are there really doctors like Marcus Welby or lawyers like Perry Mason or Owen Marshall?

The problem of reruns is another issue that will receive increasing attention during the last half of this decade. The networks claim it is too expensive to produce more than 22 to 24 original episodes of a series program at today's costs. These programs are run and then repeated beginning sometime in March to fill in the schedule. Some industry figures argue that viewers are being shortchanged because they are getting fewer original episodes a season (in 1960 there were 39 originals and 13 repeats). On the other hand, there are those who believe that viewers appreciate reruns because many miss individual shows the first time around. There also is a segment of the audience that likes the rerun idea because then they can watch one series for six months and when the reruns begin, switch to a series that was scheduled on the same day, same time, but different station. Then there are the anti-rerun groups whose income is tied to the television industry. Most Hollywood craft unions are unhappy because a small number of original programs produced in any year means there are fewer working days. The more originals, the more work. Reruns were even the subject of a White House letter to the networks in which President Nixon urged the networks to reduce reruns through some interindustry arrangement or face regulation to solve the problem. A history and discussion of the rerun issue is presented by Bill Davidson.

One issue in radio centers on the opportunity to provide specialized programming through the many radio outlets. In May, 1974, there were 6932 commercial and FM stations on the air compared to 709 commercial UHF and VHF television stations. Because of this large number of radio stations, there is the opportunity to program for audiences with special needs or interests. For example, at least one commercial classical music station usually thrives (or at least survives) in a medium-to-large metropolitan market. The all-news station is a specialized radio concept, as are Spanish-language stations and those aimed at the black community. While programming specialization may be good for various segments of the audience, there are questions raised about how stations are filling the needs of special audiences. Douglas O'Connor and Gayla Cook criticize black radio because they believe the programming is below standard and is not fulfilling its responsibilities.

Television and radio programming have obviously had their effects on our day-to-day activities, our life styles and our buying habits. An average family, at least sometimes, plans meals and other family activities around the television schedule. Everyone is aware of the seasonal joking about the millions of football widows whose husbands are engrossed in televised college and professional football on Saturday, Sunday, and even Monday evenings during five months of the year. Now the World Football League will extend the playing and viewing season two additional months. Given the 6 hours and 20 minutes of average daily viewing per home, the question is, can we enjoy television without destroying family life?

Television viewing can be accommodated in at least three ways. One is to watch it indiscriminately; watch anything that is on regardless of family routine and interaction. Another is to be selective, choosing those programs we enjoy and feel are the best, then fit this viewing into the family routine, if necessary, thus limiting the disruption of normal family interaction. A final way to handle the problem is to throw the rascal out; do without television entirely. Obviously, the second course of action appears to be the right choice if we feel that television is an intruder into our homes, but that it also has something of value to offer. Applying careful selectivity and planning in our viewing supplements family activities and exposes us to some of the highest quality entertainment and informational programs available. Choosing the third option obviously eliminates the disruptions in the family routine caused by television and provides other family benefits that Colin McCarthy describes in "Ousting the Stranger from the House." The issue he considers is who is in control, the viewer or the television set?

Other issues related to entertainment programming not included in this group of readings are the role of ratings in the broadcast system, the search for better programming to replace the Saturday morning children's cartoon ghetto accused of being too violent, the controversy over the content and treatment of programs about sensitive topics such as the abortion episode on the "Maude" program, and the subtle effects that may be communicated to viewers of ethnic humor programs such as "All in the Family" and "Sanford and Son." The reader is encouraged to explore the bibliography to examine these issues further.

BIBLIOGRAPHICAL ESSAY

Dr. Rubinstein's article on TV violence should be supplemented by the Surgeon General's Scientific Advisory Committee on Television and Social Behavior, *Television and Growing Up; The Impact of Televised Violence*, Government Printing Office, Washington, D.C., 1972. There also are five volumes of research studies which accompany the report. A good, general review of the reports and of the criticism which has surrounded them is a report of the Aspen Institute Conference on the Surgeon General's report. It is titled "A First Hard Look at the Surgeon General's Report on Television and Violence," by Douglass Cater and Stephen Strickland (March 1972), issued by Communications and Society, Palo Alto, Calif. A survey by Dennis Howitt, "Attitudes Towards Violence and Mass Media Exposure," *Gazette* (1972), 208–234, presents a different view to the effects of violence. Related research should be undertaken in sources cited in the following bibliographies: Charles K. Atkin, *et al., Television and Social Behavior: An Annotated Bibliography of Research Focusing on Television's Impact on Children*, National Institute of Mental Health, Washington, D.C., 1971, and John P. Murray, *et al.,* Eds., "Television and the Child: A Comprehensive Research Bibliography," *Journal of Broadcasting* (Winter, 1971–72), 3–20.

Our selection by Robert Daley concerns the effects of television in structuring "reality" through its entertainment programs. An interesting book by Edmund Carpenter, *Oh, What a Blow That Phantom Gave Me!*, Harper & Row, New York, 1974, places the electronic media in the larger context of its impact on culture, particularly traditional cultures. For a specific look at the effects of television entertainment, see Larry Gross "The 'Real' World of Television," *Today's Education* (January/February, 1974), 86, 89–92. For several years scholars and media critics have been concerned about the effects of a popular program such as "All in the Family" on racial and ethnic attitudes of white Americans. For a very personal view, see Laura Z. Hobson, "As I Listened to Archie Say 'Hebe'..." *The New York Times*, (September 12, 1971), sec. 2, 1+. A frightening research report on the possible reinforcement effects of the same program can be found in Neil Vidmar and Milton Rokeach, "Archie Bunker's Bigotry," *Journal of Communication* (Winter, 1974), 36–47.

The tendency for networks to begin their rerun schedule far earlier than was true late in the sixties is discussed by Bill Davidson. While there is a large number of articles available in the trade press on this issue, students should consult a copy of the Office of Telecommunications Policy's study of network reruns, dealing with "An Analysis of the Causes and Effects of Rerun Programming and Related Issues in Prime Time Network Television," issued in 1973. A thorough review of the preliminary report appeared in *Broadcasting* (February 5, 1973), 42–44.

The relationship of racial minorities to American mass media is varied and complex. Many articles criticize the media for their lack of sensitivity to the plight of minority groups; others indicate that the mass media have made great strides. We have chosen to segment our articles on minorities and women in media in what we consider to be appropriate chapters of the book. Thus, the reading suggestions given here deal only with the kinds of programming blacks will find on radio or television. Their ownership of television media (aside from radio, which is discussed in this section), their status as participants in management, news and programming, appear elsewhere in the book. To complement our critical article by Douglas O'Connor and Gayla Cook, students should consult one or more of the following series of studies completed by Stuart H. Surlin of the University of Georgia. Dr. Surlin has published, in chronological order of publication, "Ascertainment of Community Needs by Black-Oriented Radio Stations," mimeograph report (January, 1972), "Percentage of Air Time Devoted to News and Public Service Programming by Black-Oriented Radio," a paper prepared for the Minorities and Communications Division, Association for Education in Journalism Convention, 1972, (both available from author) and "Black-Oriented Radio: Programming to a Perceived Audience," *Journal of Broadcasting* (Summer, 1972), 289–298. The last will be most easily accessible to students. Also related to the black-oriented radio issue is a short piece by Bernard E. Garnett, "A Negro Radio Station Cuts Back Gospel Music, Faith-Healer Ads, Wins Top Rating in Savannah," *The Wall Street Journal* (January 16, 1973), 32. For a caustic comment about television's programming of black entertainment programs, see Eugenia Collier, "TV Still Evades the Nitty-Gritty Truth!" *TV Guide* (January 12, 1974), 6–8+.

Colman McCarthy's brief explanation of why he threw television out of the house might well be augmented, in somewhat the same spirit, by Aljean Harmetz, "Why My Sons Watch 'The Waltons,' " *The New York Times* (February 25, 1973), sec. D, 19.

48

STUDY QUESTIONS

1. Eli Rubinstein points out that "... the mental health and racial development of the child viewer are more vulnerable to negative and positive influences of television viewing precisely because the child is more sensitive to his environment than is an adult." Given this statement, do you agree with him that "society is more responsible for children (vis-à-vis television) because of this vulnerability? What can adult viewers do to exert this responsibility? Does exertion of pressure upon networks and stations to make changes in programming violate First Amendment freedoms?

2. What are some of the reasons for the violence in television programs?

3. In your own viewing of television, what can you point to as distortions of reality that might give viewers erroneous impressions?

4. The networks view the rerun as a way to keep costs down. What is your feeling about the rerun dilemma and the attempt to pass legislation requiring networks to increase the number of original programs per season? Are there precedents for legislation effecting other businesses in a similar manner?

5. Listen to a black-oriented radio station to determine if it appears to be responsive to the real needs of the black community. Is it more or less responsive to community needs than the general audience stations? Explain.

6. Colman McCarthy suggests that we turn off (and throw out) the television set so we can liberate ourselves to read, talk, and, in general, lead a more healthy family existence. What are the positive and negative ramifications of this proposal? Are there alternatives to his approach?

The TV Violence Report: What's Next?

ELI A. RUBINSTEIN

Reprinted from Journal of Communications, vol. 24, 1 (1974), with permission of the publisher and the author. Copyright 1974. Eli A. Rubinstein is Professor of Psychiatry (Behavioral Sciences) at the School of Medicine, State University of New York at Stony Brook. He was Vice-Chairman of the Surgeon General's Scientific Advisory Committee on Television and Social Behavior, and editor of the multi-volume research report to the Surgeon General.

On the morning of March 24, 1972, after three full days of Senate hearings, Senator John Pastore, chairman of the U.S. Senate Subcommittee on Communications, opened the last day of hearings by making the following statement:

> When the Surgeon General appeared to tender the Report of his Committee on televised violence and its impact on children, I said our journey was just beginning. In my judgment, what has taken place in the past few days is nothing less than a scientific and cultural breakthrough. For we now know there is a causal relation between televised violence and antisocial behavior which is sufficient to warrant immediate remedial action. It is this certainty which has eluded men of good will for so long.
>
> Great as this achievement is, I also believe these hearings have underscored what I said at the outset—long and arduous effort is still before us. What has been accomplished will be lost if we do not proceed expeditiously and effectively. For the highest medical authority in the land has told us, "No action in this social area is a form of action. It is an acquiescence in the continuation of the present level of televised violence entering American homes."
>
> I am, therefore, requesting the Secretary of Health, Education, and Welfare, the Surgeon General, and the FCC to establish a method of measuring the amount of televised violence entering American homes —a violence index—so that the Secretary may report to this committee annually the results of his study. That is only part of what we expect to be done. (16)

At one level that certainly sounds impressive: "a scientific and cultural breakthrough." An overgenerous evaluation, perhaps, but this *was* the first time a scientific committee used the term "causal relationship" in evaluating the link between televised violence and subsequent aggressive behavior of children.

However, many concerned parents and sophisticated observers of this whole debate over televised violence and its effect on children's behavior are probably less than overwhelmed that a committee report based on three years' worth of research, five volumes of technical reports, and the expenditure of one million dollars seemingly resulted in nothing more than a request for still another series of reports.

In January 1972, the Surgeon General's Scientific Advisory Committee on Television and Social Behavior issued a report on an examination of research on televised violence and its impact on social behavior. This committee of 12 behavioral scientists had been appointed by the Secretary of the Department of Health, Education and Welfare in June 1969. A large program of research with a budget of one million dollars was initiated to provide the needed evidence. The studies sponsored by the committee's program were published in five volumes of research reports. After assessing the findings of its own research program and other research in the field, the committee reached the following carefully worded conclusion:

> Thus, there is a convergence of the fairly substantial experimental evidence for short-run causation of aggression among some children by viewing violence on the screen and the much less certain evidence from field studies that extensive violence viewing precedes some long-run manifestations of aggressive behavior. This convergence of the two types of evidence constitutes some preliminary indication of a causal relationship, but a good deal of research remains to be done before one can have confidence in these conclusions. (15)

What is of special relevance to public concern in this entire research effort is that a high-level appointed committee of behavioral scientists completed a major research program whose conclusions have policy implications for the television industry. The findings were acknowledged by network officials, who have never before publicly admitted that television programming might negatively influence the behavior of children.

What are the highlights of the findings of this entire research program and what implications do they have for the future of television program content? I will concentrate on the effects of television on children in the United States—not because children alone are influenced by television, but because the mental health and social development of the child viewer are more vulnerable to negative and positive influences of television viewing, precisely because the child is more sensitive to his environment than is an adult. Society is more responsible for children because of this vulnerability.

First of all, we know that children watch a lot of television. The television set is on for an average of more than six hours a day. Most children watch television every day and watch at least two hours a day. However, individual variation is significant and is related to the child's age, sex, and intelligence. Television viewing drops off after the child enters high school. Girls tend to watch more than boys. Blacks view more than whites. The brighter high-school viewer watches less. The brighter sixth-grade student tends to watch more. Before sixth-grade age, few children watch after 9 P.M. The teenage audience continues to watch until 11 P.M. At all age levels about one-quarter of the children watch more than five hours a day on school-days. (10)

Children's program preferences are demonstrated early. Five-and six-year olds have established patterns of both viewing time and program preference. Among preschool children, cartoons have been consistently most popular. Among first-graders, situation comedies begin to be as popular as cartoons. By the sixth grade, the preference for cartoons gives way to adventure programs. In early adolescence, musical variety programs and dramatic shows become more popular. From that age level on, the viewing preferences approach those of the adults. With the exception of *Sesame Street*, viewing of educational programs is relatively low. Viewing of news programs by children is also low.

Perhaps the most extensively and precisely documented aspect of the effect of television on the young viewer is its impact on social learning. Much of the experimental evidence comes from investigators who are more interested in theories of social learning than in the effect of television viewing as such. Nevertheless, the effectiveness of observational learning through viewing films and television programs has now been clearly demonstrated in a variety of laboratory experiments. The results are fairly well summarized in a variety of recent review articles (9, 12, 13, 17). From the pioneering work of Bandura and Walters (2) to the various research studies done for the Surgeon General's research program on television and social behavior, the case for social learning through direct viewing of films and television is no longer questionable. While much of the evidence has concerned itself with the issue of imitation of violence, there is no reason that other types of behavior are not equally susceptible to modeling and imitation.

What about television and the family? While there is some evidence that television viewing is often a group activity, interaction among TV viewers tends to be limited. One of the classic studies on television and the child, by Himmelweit et al. (8), found no evidence that television binds the family together. Recent data collected by Bechtel et al. (3), in which families were observed by video camera while they watched television, showed that the family sat together, but did not interact.

However, programs do provide topics of conversation and sometimes generate conflicts if parents try to control the amount or type of viewing. Two-thirds of the students in the Lyle and Hoffman sample (11) admitted that their parents complained about their viewing. Family quarreling about program selection also was reported.

Some interesting inferences about television and the family can be made from Chaffee and McLeod's data (4). The research attempted to assess parent-child communication patterns and to relate these to television viewing behavior. "Parental example" does not seem to influence adolescent viewing. If anything, "reverse modeling" from child to parent is more consonant with the data. Chaffee and McLeod suggest that adolescents are seen as the TV experts: the parents seek the child's advice more often than vice-versa.

Perhaps of central importance to the examination of violence in television content is the question: why is there so much violence on television? And— make no mistake about it—there continues to be much violence on American network television. In the fifth of a series of annual reports on televised dramatic violence, Gerbner and Gross (6) found that a 1972 composite index of dramatic violence on prime-time network television remained at about the level it has been each year since 1970. The composite index has declined somewhat from 1967 to 1973. However, eight of every ten programs and nine out of every ten cartoons contained some violence in 1972. Furthermore, the actual prevalence of violence (percentage of programs and hours containing violent action) did not change since these studies began in 1967. (The definition of dramatic violence used by Gerbner and Gross has been "the overt expression of physical force, compelling action against one's will on pain of being hurt or killed or actually hurting or killing.")

This lack of change in the level of violence—although admittedly measured by a somewhat crude scale—is not simply explained. One cannot assume that network officials, who are well aware of the public concern about violence in television, have simply ignored scientific evidence and public concern. The relative lack of response is a more complex phenomenon than that.

Aside from the obvious fact that commercial television is a large industry, with all the complex administrative problems of a massive organizational structure, there are particular attributes of the production process which come into play. Baldwin and Lewis (1), who interviewed 48 high-level production people, including producers, writers, directors, and some network censors, show how the pressures of production and the effort to obtain the maximum number of viewers influence the inclusion of violence in program content.

They also point out that the television people are influenced by old clichés about violent content. They believe television is being used as a scapegoat for other more important determinants of violence in our society. They tend to believe the cathartic hypothesis about violent entertainment. In any case, they believe parents should be responsible for their children's viewing habits. The entire sequence of steps ending in the actual production of a television program is a combination of commercial and creative influences. The problems of serving a mass audience seven days a week under constant pressure of production deadlines inevitably produce formula approaches and limited originality. Any effort to modify television programming must take into account these formidable barriers to innovation. How can this situation be modified?

Old arguments that television merely mirrors the world around it or that violence is part of human nature are not nearly so persuasive if one looks at other cultures. A recent study of violence on television in Great Britain, conducted by the British Broadcasting Corporation (5), shows that British television contains less than two-thirds the amount of violence shown on American network programming. More than half of the most violent programs are American imports. The most critical problem, however, is not explaining why there is so much violence, or even reducing the excessive and gratuitous violence that is displayed on many American programs which children watch. It is, rather, how to provide a viable alternative to the present type of programming for children.

It is not enough to admonish the public about the hazards of violence on television. A recent published statement by the former U.S. Surgeon General (14) calls for concrete actions: (a) Parents should refrain from using television as a baby sitter. They must spend more time watching with

their children and simply shutting off the violent programs. (b) We need a system for objectively monitoring the trends in network television violence. (c) The FCC should declare the 7:30 P.M. to 9:00 P.M. slot "family television time" and restrict adult content to later programming.
(d) American parents must demand better TV fare for their children.

Implementing these suggestions is something else again. The data show that parents do not now control their children's viewing activities. Exhorting parents to do so is unlikely to produce significant changes in their behavior. Similarly, telling American parents to demand better TV fare is not likely to lead to anything concrete because the precise steps to the goal are not described. Recommendations for a violence index or for restricted family television time come somewhat closer to possible translation into action, but there are still some serious operational problems.

The theory that public exhortation will have a significant effect on viewing habits is not attractive if we look at the results of the much more extensive and intensive effort to change the smoking habits of the American public. Despite ten years' worth of public education and the clear warning by the Surgeon General on every package of cigarettes, a significant proportion of young people are still smoking.

But television viewing habits are different in one significant way from smoking habits. There is no "good smoking"—at least until all carcinogenic material is removed from tobacco. However, there can be "good TV watching": television can provide stimuli to prosocial behavior, just as well as it can provide a stimulus for aggressive behavior.

The television industry is understandably opposed to any effort which adds new controls or restrictions to its operation. But if the emphasis is on expanding the role of television for positive child development rather than merely restricting the negative influences, this should be an incentive for media participation. *Sesame Street*, by demonstrating a viable alternative for children's programming, has provided the networks with millions of dollars' worth of creative ideas and research information on how to improve television for children.

New research is now needed much beyond the earlier emphasis on the effects of televised violence. The evidence on televised violence is now sufficient to warrant remedial action and does not need further large-scale research. Instead, the issue of televised violence should be pursued by continuing to obtain annual information about the level of televised violence. This can be done through the development of an annual "violence index" as requested by Senator Pastore. Plans for the development of such an index are now under way through the auspices of the National Institute of Mental Health. The larger issue of television and the young viewer needs further examination.

A major research effort should be initiated exploring the impact of television on the very young child. One approach might be an extensive longitudinal study of children from two to five years old, a nursery school setting. We need to know what makes a program appealing, and we need to know what concepts children develop from their earliest exposure to television through the first few years. In what way is the child's concept of reality influenced or modified by the vicarious experience with television?

Research should investigate the ways in which television reinforces social stereotypes: the role of women, the attributes of ethnic groups, the characteristics of people in different social classes. We need to know more about cross-cultural differences in television program practices, in program content, and in responses by children to those differences. We need to know more about family viewing and about how family communication is influenced by those viewing patterns. Methods for educating parents and children on how to watch television need to be developed. Just as there are effective guides to reading books, there should be guides to effective television viewing. This will become increasingly important as technology advances and opportunities and choices for viewing proliferate. Initial efforts will be difficult, but this should become easier and more useful as our knowledge increases.

On the larger issue of social policy, there are now enough facts and enough opinions from various sources (including the 1970 White House Conference on Children, the Congressional hearings, various citizen action groups, and other public and private organizations) to enable us to develop a truly comprehensive and action-oriented national program setting guidelines for children's television.

Efforts should be initiated to establish a long-term instrumentality, preferably outside the government[1] and so organized as to avoid all the

[1]The specter of "government control" can complicate and influence the decision-making process. In the Surgeon General's program a mistake was made in the process of selecting committee members. Officials of the U.S. Department of Health, Education and Welfare, attempting to avoid a presumably adversary position, offered the three commercial television networks "veto power" over those individuals proposed for membership on the committee. The publicity and comment generated by this action tainted the committee's work and affected the reception of its official report.

First Amendment problems, adversary pressures, or special interest influences. The central important attribute of any program is that it be able to continue over an indefinite period of time and that it be organized so as to elicit, where appropriate, involvement of the television industry, the public, advertisers, media specialists, and researchers in the academic community. The government might provide funding and initial planning, but it should not be involved in the formal operation.

The major areas of activity might be: (a) a continuing research program to study ways of enhancing the value of television to the child viewer and to explore the impact of new technology on child development; (b) a clearinghouse and distribution center for periodic progress reports; (c) a public advocate to provide expert testimony on matters relating to children and television.

It is important to see the total task, whether in a single coordinated program or under separate auspices, as a long-term endeavor. The technology yet to be perfected is likely to be as powerful in its potential impact on the viewer, adult as well as child, as anything we have witnessed to date. Cable systems, including the use of two-way communication, portable miniaturized sets, cassettes, and other devices for recording and delayed rebroadcasting, all portend extended and increased use of television.

Perhaps the most challenging long-range implication is not just increased exposure to television but increased access to and participation in television itself. Closed-circuit community television, various devices for two-way interactive communication, the increased use of satellites for educational television experiments—all will modify the whole of television practices. Establishing some instrumentality that can look at the problem in its larger framework will help us to understand and evaluate the impact of these new developments as they come.

Granger (7) invokes a basic principle of medicine in setting guidelines for children's television programming: "First do no harm." Certainly, the mental health implications of children's television should be a major concern of all those involved in its production and evaluation.

It would seem, however, that the emphasis for the future should be to accentuate the positive. What is needed is not so much to purge television of mediocre programs for children. Children *will* watch television. Eliminating what is harmful without offering a viable and positive alternative would be only half a step at best.

The potential of television as a positive socializing influence has not been realized. It is to that purpose that intensive research and policy efforts should be addressed in the future.

REFERENCES

1. Baldwin, T. F., and C. Lewis, "Violence in Television: The Industry Looks at Itself." In G. A. Comstock and E. A. Rubinstein (Eds.) *Television and Social Behavior, Vol I. Content and Control.* Washington, D.C.: U.S. Government Printing Office, 1972.

2. Bandura, A., and R. H. Walters. *Social Learning and Personality Development.* New York: Holt, Rinehart and Winston, 1963.

3. Bechtel, R. B., C. Achelpohl, and R. Akers, "Correlates Between Observed Behavior and Questionnaire Responses on Television Viewing." In E. A. Rubinstein, G. A. Comstock, and J. P. Murray (Eds.), *Television and Social Behavior. Vol. IV. Television in Day-to-Day Life: Patterns of Use.* Washington, D.C.: U.S. Government Printing Office, 1972.

4. Chaffee, S., and J. McLeod, "Adolescent Television in the Family Context." In G. A. Comstock and E. A. Rubinstein (Eds.), *Television and Social Behavior. Vol. III. Television and Adolescent Aggressiveness.* Washington, D.C.: U.S. Government Printing Office, 1972.

5. Emmett, B. P. *Violence on Television.* London: British Broadcasting Corporation, 1972.

6. Gerbner, G., and L. Gross. *The Violence Profile No. 5.* Philadelphia, Pa.: The Annenberg School of Communications, 1973.

7. Granger, R. H. "First Do Not Harm." Yale Alumni Magazine, 1973, 36(5).

8. Himmelweit, H. T., A. N. Oppenheim, and P. Vince. *Television and the Child: An Empirical Study of the Effects of Television on the Young.* London: Oxford University Press, 1958.

9. Liebert, R. M. "Television and Social Learning: Some Relationships Between Viewing Violence and Behaving Aggressively." In J. P. Murray, E. A. Rubinstein, and G. A. Comstock (Eds.), *Television and Social Behavior. Vol. II. Television and Social Learning.* Washington, D.C.: U.S. Government Printing Office, 1972.

10. Lyle, J. "Television in Daily Life: Patterns of Use." In E. A. Rubinstein, G. A. Comstock, and J. P. Murray (Eds.), *Television and Social Behavior. Vol. IV. Television in Day-to-day Life: Patterns of Use.* Washington, D.C.: U.S. Government Printing Office, 1972.

11. Lyle, J., and H. R. Hoffman. "Children's Use of Television and Other Media." In E. A. Rubinstein, G. A. Comstock, and J.P. Murray (Eds.), *Television and Social Behavior, Vol. IV. Television in Day-to-day Life: Patterns of Use.* Washington, D.C.: Government Printing Office, 1972.

12. Siegel, A. "The Effects of Media Violence on Social Learning." In R. K. Baker and S. J. Ball, *Mass Media and Violence: A Staff Report to the National Commission on the Causes and Prevention of Violence.* Washington, D.C.: U.S. Government Printing Office, 1969, pp. 261–283.

13. Singer, J. L. (Ed.) *The Control of Aggression and Violence.* New York: Academic Press, 1971.

14. Steinfeld, J. L. "Television Violence *is* Harmful." *Reader's Digest,* April, 1973. pp. 37–45.

15. Surgeon General's Scientific Advisory Committee on Television and Social Behavior. *Television and Growing Up: The Impact of Televised Violence.* Washington, D.C.: U.S. Government Printing Office, 1972.

16. U.S. Senate Subcommittee on Communication. *Surgeon General's Report by the Scientific Advisory Committee on Television and Social Behavior.* Washington, D.C.: U.S. Government Printing Office, 1972.

17. Weiss, W. "Effects of the Mass Media on Communication." In G. Lindzey and E. Aronson (Eds.), *The Handbook of Social Psychology.* (2nd Ed.) Reading, Massachusetts: Addison-Wesley, 1969, pp. 77–195.

The TV Cops:
Distortions Blur a Real Problem

ROBERT A. DALEY

©1972 by The New York Times Company. Reprinted by permission. Robert Daley, a former deputy police commissioner of New York City, is completing a book about the police department.

This is the season of the cop shows. There are dozens of them.

The only thing they all share is heroes carrying shields and guns—that, plus an incredible collection of half-truths, illusions, stupidities and outright lies.

Are our police departments important to us? If they are, is it not important that we know who our policemen are and how they conduct themselves? Should we really go on watching actors impersonating the way

Daley

59

other actors have always impersonated policemen? Are we in the process of fabricating a police myth via TV that will last for decades to come?

The cop shows do not demand any sort of judgment from the viewer; they make no demands upon his intellect; they do not require his participation in any way. And yet, in real life the police departments all around him are in need of help. The entire criminal justice system is in desperate need of help.

Help comes principally from tax dollars and from the decisions of a few enlightened men. But as long as our ideas and opinions of the police are formed principally by TV cop shows, very little intelligent help can be forthcoming.

How could the country at large suspect that help is needed with so many invincible cops already on hand? How could anybody believe that real evil is loose in the land—or that evil basically is mindless and irrational —when the evil on the TV screen is so neat, so comfortable to watch, so beautifully constructed and motivated?

I have watched one cop show after another lately, taking notes. Here is how the notes read:

The Rookies—Put a young black actor and a young white actor inside cops' suits and seat them in a radio car. Then dab whipped cream all over the plot.

In this one, two very bad white guys (eventually caught by the rookies) force a decent black man (eventually saved by the rookies) to serve as driver of their getaway car. This amounts to several preposterous ideas.

Crooks are racists, too, and tend to keep the color line. Certainly only the very stupidest white crooks would trust an unreliable, chicken-hearted black man to wait for them with engine running outside the store they were about to stick up.

But more important, no patrolman—and especially no rookie patrolman —ever follows a case through from beginning to end. The patrolman makes his arrest or writes a summons for a traffic violation, and then he goes off in some other direction. He does not get involved in the suspect's life.

One other thing. There are some nice shots of the lieutenant's office back in the station house. Above his desk are shelves with lots of books on them. I have never seen books on anybody's shelf in the police department in New York.

On the whole, police offices are among the shabbiest that exist in our world. They are manned 24 hours a day. They are the personal office of nobody. In most cases, the only permanent decorations are wanted posters and maps of sectors of precincts or divisions.

Adam-12—This purports to show the adventures of two young Los Angeles cops in a radio car. It claims to be an authentic portrayal of police at work, and it is produced by Mark VII Ltd., which is Jack Webb's company. It appears to be a uniformed version of "Dragnet."

The two cops handle routine calls as well as the major case of each particular show. Tonight they are flagged down by a girl on a horse, who informs them that a light plane has just landed in a nearby, nearly inaccessible valley.

They go bounding over the ground and immediately come to the conclusion that they have fallen upon a marijuana-smuggling operation. But they're not sure, and there's nothing they can do about it now. They are forced to let the plane take off.

Now, there is real mystery in police work. Every time a cop knocks on a door, he has no idea what is waiting for him on the other side—it could be anything from an abandoned baby to a psychopath about to blow the cop's head off. It could be nothing at all. No cop ever knows.

On TV, the audience almost always knows who the suspect is and whether or not the suspect is guilty, having most likely seen the crime take place. In fact, TV cops are so successful precisely because they appear to have already seen the earliest scenes of the TV play themselves—they know with absolute certitude who's guilty and who is not.

Adam-12 is not perfect. All the detectives wear shirts and ties, which is ridiculous, and all the radio cars are brand-new and shiny, unlike real ones, which are driven 24 hours a day by a variety of drivers and which look exactly as beat-up as taxicabs in a very short time. Nonetheless, it is a pleasure to watch cops coping with they don't know what.

Ironside—Before the opening billboards of this program even began to flash upon the screen, I had already sat through—in a rather stunned silence—60 minutes of *Mod Squad*. The story was about a girl who needed plastic surgery because her face was disfigured. Pete, one of the cops, fell in love with her. The police captain, whose primary responsibility, apparently, is to give free rein to the Mod Squad, was also willing to give all his time and thought to this girl. Now I ask you, which police captain or police anything can afford to get personally involved?

Now on comes Chief Ironside, beginning his sixth season in a wheelchair, from which he personally solves nearly all of San Francisco's interesting crimes.

During this particular show, Chief Ironside goes on a TV program with other so-called experts to explain the mentality of an unknown murderer who has left them an unexplained body.

I offer this item in the interest of truth. It has nothing to do with police work. What does have to do with police work is the simple fact that no chief would put his prestige on the line by attempting to solve a murder during a TV broadcast, which is what Ironside here proposes to do.

Ironside is about to make the murderer, who is safe in his own apartment, crack.

Murderers don't crack. I have never seen a defendant in a murder trial break down on the stand; hardened criminals often become like gifted athletes, who know how to perform under pressure. Nobody cracks, except on TV.

Now I watch this stupid program, and then at last I can't take it anymore; I walk out of the room.

Raymond Burr, who plays Chief Ironside, is just an actor with piercing eyes, trying to make a living. The producers of *Ironside,* like the earlier producers of *Perry Mason,* are just men trying to make money. But what is the idiocy of programs such as this doing to our country?

The Streets of San Francisco—This week Janice Rule portrays a prostitute, the terrified target of some psychopath who already murdered three other prostitutes.

There is good whore dialog. Obviously, whoever wrote this show knows more about whores than about cops. Perhaps I should add: Why have none of us concerned citizens ever thought to become concerned about cops?

Karl Malden, a splendid actor no matter how poor his material, is the star of this show. Michael Douglas, son of Kirk, plays his young assistant. Since Janice Rule is likely to be killed before this show is over, they hide her out in a fleabag hotel that has a phone only at the top of the stairs.

In the New York Police Department, we were often obliged to hide out witnesses. We kept them at the Commodore Hotel, or the Howard Johnson's Motor Lodge or such.

Entertainment

I also suspect that [the San Francisco police], like us, would assign two detectives to watch a prostitute all night. One simply isn't enough. It's not enough should the murderer show up, and it's not enough should the prostitute try anything on the detective. I mean anything.

Young Douglas sits up all night in a hotel room with the prostitute but is still on duty all the next day. Besides having a 100-shot revolver in his belt, he doesn't need sleep. Why have we come this far in police dreams without equipping our hero cops with basic human frailties—such as the need for sleep, such as fear when they are getting shot at?

In this particular show, the psychopath is eventually trapped on a rooftop, where the young detective has a conversation with him instead of grabbing him. If you think cops are rough toward speeders, you should see them behave towards felony suspects.

The guy would be grabbed, frisked and cuffed faster than a fullback can plunge into the line. But in this show, the psychopath doesn't even get handcuffed after his arrest.

In a number of shows, the prisoner doesn't get handcuffed at all, and in others he got handcuffed with his hands in front of him, which is inconceivable. Handcuffs clamped on that way are a deadly weapon in themselves. All the suspect has to do is bring them down on the head of the cop who is attempting to arrest him. This may sound like a small point and not worth mentioning, but it has to do with danger; it has to do with the aura of fear and risk surrounding every cop. A television show that ignores danger and the cop's natural fear is, it seems to me, an important lie in the lives of all of us.

Then, lucky us, *NBC Mystery Movie* presents *McMillan and Wife*. This one starts out with Police Commissioner McMillan himself chasing the suspect up and down Nob Hill on cable cars. When somehow the suspect transfers from an uphill to a downhill car, so does the police commissioner, leaping across at the risk of his life.

This occurs several times, and eventually the police commissioner grabs the suspect, dusts off his hands and remarks: "That closes up the something case." I didn't catch the name of whatever case it closed. I was ready to walk out at once. Police commissioners do not catch suspects with their bare hands.

I suggest that hardly anybody in this country knows what a police commissioner does. One thing he does not do is move through the police world accompanied by his wife, as McMillan does.

REJECTED REALITY

One night my television screen stayed dark. Choosing to miss God knows how many cop shows on TV, I went to the movies to see *The New Centurions*.

This started as a novel by a Los Angeles police sergeant named Joseph Wambaugh, which, though somewhat artless, was an absolutely true book about cops in Los Angeles. The only reviews of the film which I read praised George C. Scott and panned nearly everything else, and I was not prepared for a movie that was as faithful to truth and as accurate as the book had been.

The French Connection was a far more profitable movie, although it purported to tell in blood-stained terms the "true" story of a real narcotics operation. In real life, none of the actual participants was ever so much as scratched by a nail.

The French Connection was full of preposterous scenes, where *The New Centurions* stuck to scenes true to the lives of the men who ride radio cars in Los Angeles and in every other city in this country. The feeling of danger behind every door is in this picture, but the real danger comes when the hero is not prepared for it in any way.

Twice he is shot by guns he doesn't know are there. There is only one shootout, and for the first time in my memory we are allowed to see the faces of every cop afterward—and every single face shows terror.

I left the theater totally satisfied, but in the car my wife said: "It didn't seem believable to me when George C. Scott killed himself."

I said: "Anybody who knows anything about cops would accept that scene as absolutely believable." Cops kill themselves all the time. I can think of three police suicides within a few months that I knew about personally. Inevitably, with every cop owning at least two guns, there are going to be suicides.

But in my heart I felt dismay. The American public has been force-fed so much clap-trap in movies and TV that hardly anyone anymore is able to recognize truth, or to tell the real from the fraudulent. And if it is this bad on the level of cop films and shows, how can we expect it to be better on any other level—politics, for instance?

Those Reruns:
The Facts Behind the Complaints

BILL DAVIDSON

TV Guide, June 9, 1973. Reprinted with permission from TV GUIDE® Magazine. Copyright © 1973 by Triangle Publications, Inc., Radnor, Pennsylvania. Bill Davidson is a contributing editor of *TV Guide*. He was formerly editor-at-large for the *Saturday Evening Post* and an editor for both *Look* and *Collier's*. His most recent of seven books is *The Fifty-Meter Jungle*.

[Eds. note: Costs have gone up since this article was written; the issue remains as current as Davidson reported it.]

One Sunday night in March 1971, an ordinarily mild-mannered, 52-year-old Californian named Bernard Balmuth attained an all-time high in televiewer fury and frustration.

Mr. Balmuth had sat down in his comfortable Los Angeles home to see one of his favorite shows, *The FBI*. He was slippered and bathrobed; a pitcher of cooling liquid and a bowl of potato chips were comfortably within reach. But when the program began, Balmuth uttered a bellow of outrage.

As he recalls the event today, Balmuth says, "I found myself watching a segment of *The FBI* I had seen just a few weeks before. The winter snows still were on the San Gabriel mountains outside my window and there was a blizzard in Chicago, but *The FBI* already had begun its summer reruns.

"I decided to take pen in hand and try what no one is supposed to be able to get away with: fighting City Hall."

Fighting City Hall in Balmuth's case consisted, ultimately, of filing (in May 1972) a single-citizen petition to the Federal Communications Commission. The petition was hand-typed, contained spelling errors, and was based mostly on his examination of 10 years of program listings in a batch of TV GUIDES squirreled away in his garage.

In the hand-typed petition, Balmuth charged the three major networks with bamboozling the public by insidiously increasing the number of repeat shows until they had reached a total of approximately half of the year's prime-time evening hours. Balmuth demanded that the networks cut reruns back to only 13 summer weeks, as had been their practice prior to 1960.

Davidson

65

And he insisted that the networks be forced to label reruns as such, plainly and unmistakably, on the air.

At the time, Balmuth's action seemed akin to Don Quixote's assaults on windmills. But, in the last year or so, the following events have occurred:

(1) The FCC accepted Balmuth's petition as if it had been filed by a giant corporation.

(2) The networks have since spent hundreds of thousands of dollars fighting it.

(3) The Hollywood film and TV unions, and the entire AFL-CIO joined forces to back the Balmuth petition.

(4) Robert Wood, president of CBS-TV, devoted an impassioned hour's speech to attacking the Balmuth proposal, and CBS has had the speech bound for distribution throughout the United States.

(5) The Los Angeles City Council, the California Senate and many members of Congress have officially joined Balmuth's crusade.

And

(6) Richard Nixon, President of the United States, wrote a letter urging the networks to find a voluntary solution of the epidemic of reruns, or else the White House "will explore whatever regulatory recommendations are in order."

No other individual, Ralph Nader included, has ever stirred up such a fuss in the broadcasting industry. Balmuth acquired a lot of help, but only after his first petition had been accepted for possible action by the FCC.

To this day, Balmuth insists he acted as a viewer—a member of the public—rather than as a worker in the industry (he is a movie film editor). Nevertheless, when his own union—and all the others, including the writers' and actors' guilds—joined the fray, his crusade took on a much more professional flavor.

For example, Balmuth's *second* petition to the FCC, last August (in answer to the networks' hundreds of pages of reply to his initial five-page complaint), bears about as much relationship to his first petition as a Henry Kissinger dissertation does to a schoolboy composition. He was assisted in its preparation by union attorneys as highly paid as their network corporate counterparts.

Also, Balmuth had big stars like Charlton Heston and Carroll O'Connor running around gathering citizens' signatures on petitions and lobbying with their Congressmen.

Kathleen Nolan (who did *The Real McCoys* and *Broadside* TV series) made national tours urging housewives to join the antirerun campaign by writing protest letters to Congress and the FCC. Top brains in the Writers Guild constantly are thinking up arguments to support the crusade. One of the most cogent of these is by former Writers Guild president Melville Shavelson, now a movie producer.

Shavelson said, "The networks are flagrantly violating the Government's truth-in-advertising laws. A TV commercial can't advertise a retread tire as a new tire, but NBC, CBS and ABC are allowed to present retread *shows* without labeling them as such."

Like all great controversies in the broadcasting field, the main issues in the rerun flap boil down to a conflict between economics and varying concepts of what is in the public interest.

As with everything else in our economy, TV production costs have soared. Up until 1960 (and in some cases, as late as 1963) nearly every television series consisted of 39 original programs, plus 13 reruns during the summer. Then, a half-hour show cost less than $50,000 to produce; an hour segment rarely ran more than $100,000.

Harris Kalleman, now MGM's vice president in charge of TV, said he made *The Rebel* with Nick Adams for only $40,000 a week, and the then-expensive *Richard Boone Show* for $130,000. "Today," he says, "I couldn't do it for under $100,000 for the half-hour show and considerably more than $200,000 for the hour."

As the labor and production costs of shows rose, the networks began to cut back on the originals and gradually increased the number of reruns. The reason for this, as network economists point out, is that a $200,000 show earns an average of $55,000 a minute in commercials when it is aired. This amounts to $330,000 in revenue, which would seem to give the network a healthy $130,000 profit. Apparently this is not so, however. The networks say that *all* the profit from a show's first airing is eaten up by payments to the local stations, to advertising agencies and to the telephone company for transmission charges.

"Therefore," says NBC Television president Don Durgin, "the only way the networks can come out ahead is to rerun the show, when, with nearly all the production costs already paid, we can clear around $100,000."

The economics go like this: when NBC reruns a variety hour that originally cost $200,000, the production cost of the rerun is only $30,000. Even though advertisers pay lower per-minute rates for commercials on reruns, with other costs remaining the same, the $100,000-or-so profit results.

No one denies that the networks deserve a profit. The question put by the antirerun groups, however, is whether or not the networks have gone too far in maintaining abnormally *high* profits (they rose from $87,000,000 to $145,000,000 in 10 years). Balmuth and his supporters say the three networks have gone "absolutely wild in their lust for gain" by rerunning every show at least once and sometimes *twice* every year.

The Balmuth position is supported [in an] exhaustive study by [former] President Nixon's White House Office of Telecommunications Policy, [then] headed by the controversial Dr. Clay T. Whitehead. The scholarly study on reruns concludes that there exists in the three networks "a cycle of rivalry behavior which has the effect of driving down the quantity of original programming in favor of the maintenance of high profits."

The networks' own rerun schedules appear to support this hypothesis. *The Waltons,* for example, which began on Sept. 14, 1972, went into a complete cycle of "summer" reruns on March 15—before the first crocuses pushed through the snows in New England. Several series even infiltrated reruns during the Christmas holiday week this past year.

Typical of the original-to-rerun ratio is *The Wonderful World of Disney* on NBC. In information supplied to the White House for its report, the network revealed that the Disney series made only 20 original shows last year, whereas there were 28 reruns. This means that not only were the 20 originals shown a second time, but there were eight others that either were shown for the *third* time, or were culled from even *older* Disney seasons.

The White House study proves that the average network series currently airs no more than 22 to 24 original programs per year. Reruns, says the report, actually fill 51.8 per cent of all "prime time."

In his now-famous speech to the Hollywood Radio and Television Society last Sept. 12, CBS Television president Robert W. Wood admitted that such figures probably were accurate, but he contended that reruns are a benefit rather than a detriment to the public. He made the point that only 14 per cent of the people see a given show the first time around and can look forward to viewing a program opposite it when the rerun season begins. Wood also gloomily predicted that if the networks were forced to make even 12 more original shows per series every year, the extra cost of production, $150 million, would wipe out the combined profits of all three networks and cause a loss of up to $65 million in some years—resulting in further unemployment in the industry and the inevitability of cheaper, inferior programming.

Wood's opponents challenge him on both points. Says Mac St. Johns, vice president of the unions' rerun-fighting Film and Television Coordinating Committee, "The problem with waiting for a rerun of a show you've missed because you wanted to watch something else is that it might not be around come rerun season. Suppose, for example, you opted for *All in the Family* last fall and figured on seeing that night's episode of *Alias Smith and Jones* in the spring. Forget it. *Alias Smith and Jones* has been canceled."

Except for the unions, who are interested in more work for their already heavily unemployed members, there is less tendency to dispute, head-on, Wood's contention that 12 extra shows per series would bankrupt the networks. Rather, one finds that most producers, studio heads and even TV stars would prefer to compromise at a lower number of original programs per season than the 39 requested in the Balmuth petition. The most popular figure seems to be 30, which would extend the season for original shows almost until May.

William Self, president of 20th Century-Fox Television, said, "I don't think the cost factor for 30 shows instead of 22 or 24 would destroy or even seriously hurt the networks. It would cost them more, but it's financially feasible. The networks wouldn't make as *much* profit, but they'd still make a *respectable* profit. Hell, I remember when I produced 52 *Schlitz Playhouse* shows a year when everyone else was doing 13 reruns. People drink a lot of beer in the summertime."

Another compromiser is Grant Tinker, whose MTM Productions turns out two stable hits, *The Mary Tyler Moore Show* and *The Bob Newhart Show*. For many years Tinker was an NBC vice president. He says, "I know the network profit picture very well and, believe me, if they had to extend to 30 shows a year, we wouldn't have to throw any benefits for them." Tinker does believe, however, that the quality of writing and acting would suffer if he had to make more than 30 shows a year.

Harris Katleman of MGM-TV has still another idea. He suggested, "I think a better mix would be 26 original shows per season, plus 13 reruns, plus 13 fresh shows in the summer months. The summer shows could be on tape and could be made cheaply, for, say, about $50,000 a week. Such summer shows would keep network costs down, would give a lot of people a lot of work, and would open the door for inexpensive experimentation. ABC tried to do that last summer with *The Super* and *The Corner Bar*. Those particular shows didn't work, but it's basically a good idea and worth trying." (NBC is trying *The Corner Bar* again this summer, with some cast changes.)

Many big stars, too, have joined the chorus for more shows in a series, although none would like to return to the nightmare 39-week schedule of the past. True, they would make more money from such an increase, but the income from those additional weeks of work (considering actors' rerun fees and high tax brackets) would not be all that much more.

Mary Tyler Moore is one of those who would like to move up to 30 episodes a year. She says, "The public deserves it and I like to work. A half-year's vacation for me is too much." *Mannix*'s Mike Connors said, "My show is a tough one to do physically. Twenty-four episodes takes us eight and-a-half months to film. But 30 shows seems to be a realistic figure to me. It would mean 42 extra shooting days, but it still would give me eight weeks off. That's not a hell of a lot, but for the good of the industry and my fellow workers—and for the public—I'd be willing to make the sacrifice and go along."

Lorne Greene agrees. He adds, "Reruns, like a good steak, can be and often *are* overdone, diluting the public's appetite."

What *is* the state of the public's appetite? So far, the overrich diet of reruns does not seem to have caused any mass complaints of indigestion. Many reruns, in fact, get very good ratings.

Only the unions seem to want government intervention. Even those producers who favor compromise do not relish further meddling by the FCC in programming. The Commission did enough damage, they say, by cutting nighttime network shows from 3½ to 3 hours a night with the "Prime-Time Access Rule," which may have to be repealed. This is considered the principal reason the FCC has been dragging its feet on the rerun petition.

The networks, the production companies and the unions will probably work out some compromise. But when you really get down to it, it's the public which holds the ultimate weapon if, indeed, it doesn't like reruns.

It can stop watching them.

Black Radio:
The "Soul" Sellout

DOUGLAS O'CONNOR and GAYLA COOK

Reprinted by permission from *The Progressive*, vol. 37, 8 (August, 1973), 408 West Gorham Street, Madison, Wisconsin 53703. Copyright © 1973, The Progressive, Inc. Douglas O'Connor is field director of the Office of Communications of the United Church of Christ. Gayla Cook teaches courses in communications at Rutgers University.

What is black, has an affinity with some twenty million people, and has abdicated its responsibility for a fast dollar? The answer is black radio.

According to the 1972 Broadcast Yearbook, there are 330 radio stations across the United States which devote all or a portion of their air time to black programming. [Eds. note: *1974 Broadcast Yearbook* listed 456 radio stations carrying various amounts of black programming.] Blacks, however, own only twenty-two of these community outlets. This is almost twice the black ownership listed in 1970—an encouraging sign compared to the wasteland of television, where blacks own nothing.

A meeting in November, 1972, of the National Association of Broadcasters was devoted to discussion of the myriad difficulties that face minorities in their attempts and aspirations relative to broadcast ownership. The basic question is, what is being done with the existing facilities to serve the culturally distinct needs of black people?

The answer is that black radio has a record of dismal failure in servicing its primary audience. White ownership has set a low standard, but must black owners follow the bouncing ball? With pitifully few exceptions they have been as cruelly exploitative and as unstinting in their misconceptions as their white brethren. If we live in a ripoff society, black radio stands as a prime illustration.

The early dreams of broadcasting as set forth by the architects of the Communications Act of 1934 were based on the proposition that this medium could use its great potential to educate as well as to entertain. It was hoped that the unique partnership encompassing the Government, the broadcasters, and the public would assure a positive quality of life through implementation of this marvel of communication. Mere geographical location would no longer mean isolation from the mainstream of American thought and endeavor. Nation and community would be bonded together and informed through the news, diversity in programming, and emphasis on local matters of interest.

Unfortunately, those dreams have been deferred by many broadcasters in their concern for profit at the expense of their public trust. The broadcast licensee receives on his investment the highest return of any American businessman. He tries to reach the largest audience he can to sell the most advertising possible for the maximum financial profit. His coat of arms is the dollar sign, and his motto is, "The public be damned."

The Federal Communications Commission (FCC) is supposed to regulate the industry to safeguard the rights and interests of the public in broadcasting. However, the FCC's record of enforcement is one of general inefficiency. Indeed, without the pressure of various citizen's groups which insist on enforcement of existing laws, that agency would be content to be merely an issuer of broadcast licenses.

The Communications Act was, among other things, structured to secure a close relationship between the broadcaster and his area of service. The broadcaster presumably would share the problems of his area and present a considered and empathetic body of fact and opinion relative to pertinent issues within the community. Somehow it did not work out that way. The impulse for profit attracted the entrepreneur whose quest for the dollar led to the quixotic ownership pattern which afflicts the industry today.

The voice of black radio conforms to type wherever one may travel in this nation. What exists is a formula that presumes black Americans are monolithic in taste and viewpoint. This packaged formula consists of soul music—rhythm and blues—to the almost total exclusion of other black musical and dramatic expression. News, if any, is usually of the "rip 'n read" variety pulled off the ticker and read by a disc jock to the accompaniment of sounds to simulate a newsroom. This news is of a quasi-national or regional nature and no more informs the local community about neighborhood happenings than does Walter Cronkite.

Ironically, news of the local black community generally goes unreported unless the white-owned wire services pick it up first and feed it to the reporterless soul station. Since most black stations are unable to compete with major networks and television in depth and detail of news coverage about world events, one can wonder why these outlets have not developed black local news coverage as their own purview. However, that would mean spending money. Instead of spools of tape and few low paid "personalities," as the jocks are called, a station might need some trained reporters, a news staff, and perhaps a mobile truck.

An electronic Trojan Horse has been wired into the black community. It is concealed by a thin veneer of cultural compatibility and amplified shouts of "Right on, brothers and sisters" from "personalities" whose unabashed huckstering often borders on hysteria. This method of selling often overpriced and sometimes inferior products to black audiences is an insidious maneuver to extract dollars from those very persons who live at or near basic poverty levels. In this packaged "black style" even the most blatant bait and switch advertising is given in terms of black involvement.

For those unfamiliar with this sort of come-on, the sample which follows illustrates style and content: Imagine a somewhat husky voice laden with urban street accents saying,

> "Hey, looka here, brothers and sisters. I got some news for you. Things kind of rough out there, right? I mean job situation ain't too tough and credit ain't too cool? Uh-huh. Well, dig what John Brothers is puttin' down. A brand new color television set for just your signature on a piece of paper. That's right. Just your signature. John Brothers don't care about your credit ratin'. If you got a job and have been working for three months or more, John Brothers will let you have this beautiful color TV for no money down and up to three years to pay. Can you dig it? Now get this, my fine black brothers and my beautiful black sisters, if y'all hurry down to John Brothers and tell 'em that I, your main man, Willie B., sent you, they will give you a free gift—along with that pretty, pretty color TV. Ain't that somethin'? It's yours at outasight John Brothers. Can you dig it? John Brothers."

The signatures thus collected will often be used in selling the credit list to a factoring agent—one who buys accounts receivable and then collects them—who will pay the dealer a lump sum for each television set so assigned, after the verification of the consumer's current employment status and a history of at least three months of employment. The factor will then sometimes act as a collecting agency, often disregarding the terms of payment indicated in the original contract and will then demand either an increased schedule of payment, a higher rate, or payment in full. This forces the purchaser of the set to speed up payments for the benefit of the factor's bookkeeping or suffer garnishment of salary or—happiest of worlds in the view of the factor—return the set and forfeit the money already paid. The factor is then able to sell the television set at cost back to John

Brothers or some other merchant. The sets will be refurbished and sold once more at top prices to the unwary customer—as the beat goes on and on over the black-oriented station with its black shills selling the same old patent medicine in the sweet soul style.

Now, let's take a look at the employment patterns of the white-owned black stations. For years blacks occupied the role of station "personality." This person came in the morning to do the sign-on and remained throughout the day till sign-off. His pay was low, and he depended upon the ads he could attract and the promotion of dance events in which his name and that of the station were featured. The station usually financed the production and allowed him to "plug" the show on the air. Based on his drawing power, he sometimes might be given a percentage of the gate.

When the social pressures of the Sixties forced reexamination of these antique hiring practices, some stations discovered new methods to operate the old game of "nigger, hide behind the door." They gave blacks an opportunity to "train" for executive positions. Titles such as "program director" were bestowed on switchboard operators or clerks. Pay was not commensurate with titles and these "directors" had no hand in decision making.

Moreover, they maintained their former duties. Thus, the station, through mistitling, satisfied those blacks who might raise embarrassing questions and the FCC's stated concerns about upgrading minorities. There have been some jarring examples of improper use of titles. In South Carolina one disc jockey found his name listed as "program director" when a local citizens group showed him the application his employer had tendered for license renewal. This same application named another part time black employe as "news director."

Conditions have generally changed for the better, but many stations continue to maintain the old traditions in the hiring of black executives and in the decision-making process. In short, there have been gains, some of them major in character, but these have come about much too slowly and painfully.

One turns the dial fruitlessly to find informed black opinion about the large and small issues affecting black America, finding instead that the entire spectrum of news coverage is encompassed within three minutes of headline reading. This is not surprising when one takes into account a 1970 survey by Bernard Garnett and the Nashville Race Relations Information

Center in which twenty-five major black-oriented stations were polled about black executives on the staff at each facility. The findings disclosed that there were nineteen full time news directors, three of whom were white, plus one part time news director. Six stations had extremely limited news gathering personnel or no news department at all. The bulk of full time personnel other than news directors were located in just five of the stations. In most stations the news director had no support staff. For the twenty-five stations overall there were but twenty-one full time news people.

These statistics underline the almost tragic state of news reporting in black radio. Black radio, in placing its emphasis on the soul package formula, has misused its position and has obviated any right to be trusted by the black community. What is worse, black radio has become a third rate channel of information.

There is virtually no hard information or news or interpretation about political procedure or how legislation passed at the Federal, state, and city levels affects blacks. In Dallas, Texas, blacks who owned houses located in a slum area which major business interests coveted were misinformed about their rights by speculators. It soon became a major topic of conversation in the black community, but the local black stations did not inform the community in any fashion. The local black newspaper did its best, without avail, to get the stations to address these issues. Here was a classic example of black radio avoiding its responsibilities.

The guiding philosophy behind the soul package formula is that blacks are easily satisfied with any offering that can be given a black label. The cynicism which represents this philosophy was expressed, ironically enough, by a black executive in an advertising agency which specializes in "black" products marketed by white firms. It was not the first instance of a "house nigger" being cavalier about the institution which feeds his belly and washes his mind. "Baby," he told us, "all you need to do to sell niggers is put up a picture of Martin Luther King to sell half the population and a black chick with an Afro to get the other half, and whatever else you do, show plenty soul. See, niggers never question their leaders or their institutions."

The most common excuse for the soul package formula is that old chestnut: "We give the public what it wants." According to that theory one must suppose that blacks listen only to rhythm and blues since not enough of them like other kinds of music, that the black attention span is too limited to deal with more than a scanning of headlines, and that black performers are found only in the world of rhythm and blues.

In black radio, as in black film and the social communication of the black body politic, one discerns a model that quite often utilizes the current "hipness" or "black English" expressions and metaphors. This communications model is easily copied.

The more vital part of the black communications model is best exemplified in the institution that has the longest existence in the black experience in America, the black church. In the black church the medium is indeed the message and the message is the manner of sermon delivery. The black sermon begins slowly, with profound emotion. It beckons the audience to participation. Parishioners are drawn into participation by a technique that calls for response and even physical involvement through percussive utilization of music and speech. Chants abound, and texts are read with increasing speed and heightened with drama until the audience is whipped into a climactic urgency. There is a sheer emotional and physical involvement, brief and intense, which at its end leaves the audience satiated.

One observes the same principle in those exhortations between black politicians and their black constituents. Adam Clayton Powell called out, "Am I right or wrong?" The answer: "Right on!" Jesse Jackson, his handsome face sternly masculine, demands seductively, "Do you love your Jesse?" and the sisters down front make it obvious that they do. The politician skillfully orates and is answered by slogans and chorusing. The audience so neatly manipulated sometimes leaves such gatherings only to realize later that this emotional presentation is often less than significant. It is not without reason that so many black community leaders are clergymen.

Others besides blacks are manipulated emotionally by gifted demagogues who can turn a phrase, but the black communications model in America is singular in historical antecedent. During slavery the black church was the principal means of social and political communication. Slaves were otherwise prohibited from congregating, and communication through the medium of the church was learned at the same time they learned English.

While the black disc jockey has an audience which rivals that of the black clergy, black radio seldom manifests black philosophy or black control, even in those rare instances where it is black-owned. Radio must serve as purveyor of education, information, and entertainment. By concentrating on entertainment, and in general only one facet of that broad field, black radio has failed its responsibility to communicate properly the aspects of social and political education characteristic of electronic or other media in a developed society.

When one considers the audience power of black radio in comparison to the nation at large, the chasm between potential and performance is even more deplorable, especially if viewed from a standpoint of politicization. According to the latest figures available, black-oriented stations have the potential to reach seventy-eight per cent of the U.S. black population. In 1963 the Center for Research in Marketing estimated that nine out of ten in the potential black audience listened to black-oriented radio and that six out of ten listened to black stations more than, or to the exclusion of, white radio. In 1970 the rating figures corroborated similar listening patterns among the black audience.

In the 1969 study by C. E. Harper, Inc., which focused on the advertising recall of radio listeners, black-oriented listenership had the highest advertising recall (18.1 percent) of any kind of radio. This figure was only slightly lower than the percentage of recall (19.4 per cent) reported for prime time television's general audience sample. This means that black listeners are generally more attentive to commercial messages especially designed to reach them.

Advertisers are quite aware of the consumer habits of this large and responsive audience and, naturally enough, try to exploit the situation. This is another reason why those organized and enlightened groups of black citizens who have or should have an interest in media must begin to examine critically the full content of black radio and instigate the steps necessary for reform and public inquiry into dubious practices in radio advertising.

Advertisers have noted that American blacks, as a totality, control the ninth largest amount of disposable income in the world. This knowledge prompted Jack Davis, executive vice president of Bernard Howard and Company, to state last year in the trade publication, *Broadcasting,* "A major advertiser today probably cannot achieve success or a number one position in most urban areas without seeking the support of the black market."

Black radio, then, has more potential to be a liberating, educational, and socially responsible medium, in relation to its special audience, than virtually any other among the mass media. What is needed is imaginative, analytic, and responsible programming. It would seem to be a moral responsibility for both black and white ownership of black radio to bring this about. Some broadcasters dissent from this view; they claim that moral obligation is to broadcasting what "message" movies are to the film industry. It does not sell. However, a new breed of black broadcasters has lately swelled the ranks of black ownership. Their outlook and vision for the future of black broadcasting are completely at odds with the exploitation and the negative philosophy toward reform so often encountered in the industry.

The Reverend H. Carl McCall, one of the new owners of WLIB-AM, New York, when asked how black leadership would make a difference in the station's communication with its audience, replied:

> "The real thing that will make it different is the fact that it is a black-owned station. I think black people are going to have to be more sensitive to the needs of the black community and not exploit that community. We know what black-oriented radio has been and it's been that way because the people running it and controlling it have been interested in profits rather than service.
>
> "Now, this doesn't mean that when black people get into industry that they are not going to be concerned about profit. But profit for us is not the major issue. I think we can make a profit and at the same time provide this important service and educate, inform, and entertain the community in a quality fashion. We can make even more money than those people who acted exploitatively in the past. As blacks, we come to black-oriented radio as critics—as people who have been offended by it. Those offenses are still very evident to us and we have had time to think about methods of change."

The Reverend McCall is representative of some of the new black influx into broadcasting. This commitment to enlightenment offers broader access to the community which, in turn, through responsible criticism, can inform the media about its needs. This concerned black approach could help provide material for the social and political development of the community.

In speaking for pertinent black voices in philosophic, social, and political concerns we must remember that radio is not only a forum for ideas but is also a vehicle for entertainment. Essentially, the word entertainment signifies variety which, in the area of music, has been lacking in black-oriented radio. In this medium it has been enough simply to do the "soul chart" without references to the wide variety of black taste. The assumptions guiding this viewpoint spring from the same racist kind of thinking that causes some whites to believe that each black person they meet is exactly the same as every other black they have not met.

The falsity of this presumption about blacks is indicated by the experience of black-oriented WBLS-FM. Operating in the highly competitive market of New York City, in early 1971, the station, then known as WLIB-FM, was rated fifth, a creditable position. The broadcast format had little variety and had gained its high ratings through its strong pull on the black audiences. It should be noted here that while most black stations are white-owned, white listenership is sparse. Therefore, it took some courage on the part of ownership to depart from a successful format and attempt to change a monolithic approach.

Frankie Crocker, a well known black disc jockey, was allowed to introduce what he called the "Total Black Experience in Sound." "TBEIS" brought the dizzying variety of black musical contribution to the fore. Afro-Cuban, blues, black rock, jazz in its many forms, black Latin, and rhythm and blues became the format. This program acted as a lead-in to Del Shield's articulate and tasteful midnight jazz show. The combination was dynamite. In less than ten months the station jumped to third place in a major market survey. The point that black audiences are ripe for diversity in approach and do not have to be huckstered or insulted intellectually was proven conclusively.

Imaginative, analytical, and responsive programming that entertains, informs, and educates does not simply happen. It is part of a process which should relate the broadcasters more closely to the audience. The process, ideally, could enunciate the broad range of human identity and concern and could speak to the enlightened self-interest of the listener. In this fashion the medium could give thoughtful consideration to the events of the day, and by dealing with these often controversial issues it could inform the public.

The audience, in its turn, could feed back, through comment and responsible criticism, a majority point of view which might direct the medium to deal more constructively with the full extent of public interest. Alas, this does not appear to be the objective of the so-called free enterprise system.

Given the lackluster performance which has become the broadcasting norm, the community has little to which it can respond. "Keep it bland" seems to be the motto. Not long ago Clay T. Whitehead, director of the White House Office of Telecommunications Policy, proposed blandness and non-criticism of Government institutions. While the thrust was directed mainly against television, it will have a deleterious effect on both electronic and print media. It therefore becomes essential that citizens be educated to awareness of their power potential in the form of citizen groups concerned about media.

In the area of broadcasting, such diverse groups as the Office of Communication of the United Church, Black Efforts for Soul in Television, and the Citizens Communications Center have been in the vanguard in the effort to protect citizen and community rights. Their continuing campaign to give technical and legal assistance free of charge, and to lobby in behalf of the public interest, combines with the informative literature they publish to bring a warming ray of sun to these times of Administration repression.

Given the failure of the FCC to regulate and enforce its own rulings, it becomes the concern of citizen groups to keep the industry honest. That such citizen groups have performed successfully in behalf of all of us is easily documented. Obviously, the challenge is not at an end. FCC Commissioner Richard E. Wiley has recently proposed "deregulation" which would eventually remove most, if not all, public service obligation in radio. Such moves allow the industry to ignore service in favor of profit and close the books on an era of hard won progress. Legislation presently in Congress is designed to make the process of license renewal easier for the broadcaster and challenges more difficult for citizen groups.

That such proposals, which implicitly maneuver the public out of an effective role in the medium, could be seriously considered is evidence of the fact that citizen power can be short circuited unless the public stands ready to protect itself.

If the public interest is to be protected, it will be done by an informed and concerned citizenry. Blacks and other minorities, including women, have pioneered in seeking access to the media in programming and employment. Their example has been a successful one. Organized coalitions of grass roots and established groups having a broad base in the community at large have been singularly effective in signing agreements with individual broadcasters, and in some instances they have been able to effect legislative

Entertainment

changes. It is possible that such groups may come together on a national basis to serve as a citizens' lobby and industry watchdog. This constituency could be an aggressive and pertinent factor in reminding the broadcasters and the FCC alike that the airwaves belong to the people.

Ousting the Stranger
from the House

COLMAN McCARTHY

Copyright Newsweek, Inc. 1974, reprinted by permission. Colman McCarthy is a columnist and editorial writer for *The Washington Post*. His recent book is *Disturbers of the Peace*.

When I turned off the television for the last time about a year ago and dumped the set for good, some friends, relatives and unasked advisers on the block predicted I would not last long without it. Few disputed the common gripe that TV is a wasteland, with irrigation offered only by the rare trickle of a quality program. Instead, they doubted that the addiction of some twenty years before the tube could be stilled by this sudden break with the past. It is true that an addiction had me, my veins eased only by a fix of 30 to 35 hours a week; my wife's dosage was similar, and our children—three boys under 7—already listened more to the television than to us.

Now, a year later—a family living as cultural cave men, says an anthropologist friend—the decision we made was one of the wisest of our married life. The ratings—our private Nielsens—during this year of setlessness have been high, suggesting that such common acts as talking with one's children, sharing ideas with one's wife, walking to the neighborhood library on a Saturday morning, quiet evenings of reading books and magazines aloud to each other, or eating supper as a family offer more intellectual and emotional stimulation than anything on television.

McCarthy

81

THE DEADLINE GUILLOTINE

The severity of an addiction to TV is not that it reduces the victim to passivity while watching it but that it demands he be a compulsive activist to get in front of it. If I arrived home at 6, for example, and dinner was ready at 6:25—my wife's afternoon movie had run late, so dinner was late—I would shove down the food in five minutes. The deadline, falling like a guillotine, was at 6:30. Chancellor came on then, Cronkite at 7; if CBS was dull, Smith and Reasoner were on ABC. If I hadn't finished dinner, I would sprint back to the table during the commercials for short-order gulps, then back to cool John, Uncle Walter or wry Harry. My wife, desperate May, was left at the table to control the bedlam of the kids, caused by my in-and-out sprints. The chaos I heard coming from the dining room was fitting: it was matched by the chaos in the world reported on the evening news, except the latter, in the vague "out there," was easier to handle.

With the set gone, these compulsions and in-turnings have gone too. We eat dinner in leisure and peace now. We stay at the playground until the children have had enough fun, not when I need to rush home to watch the 4 P.M. golf. Occasionally, my wife and I have the exotic experience of spending an evening in relaxed conversation, not the little half-steps of talk we once made in a forced march to Marital Communication. In those days, we would turn off the set in midevening and be immediately oppressed by the silence.

What had been happening all those years of watching television, I see now, was not only an addiction but also, on a deeper level, an adjustment. All of us had become adjusted to living with a stranger in the house. Is there any more basic definition of a television set than that? More, the stranger in the house was not there to entertain us, a notion the televisers would like to serve. The stranger was present to sell us products. The person before a set may think he is a viewer but the sponsors who pay for broadcasts know better: he is a buyer. It is a commercial arrangement, with the TV set a salesman permanently assigned to one house, and often two or three salesmen working different rooms. It is a myth that TV is free entertainment.

I was not only paying personally for the stranger-salesman in my house but he was often manipulating or lying to my children. I saw the effects in such places as the supermarket aisles, when the boys would loudly demand a sugared cereal, junk-snack or six pack of soda, all of these items only high-priced garbage that helps rot the teeth and keeps children from fruit and other nutritious food. My kids had been conditioned well by the sellers on TV, predatory strangers as menacing in one way as street predators are in another. But, someone told me, that's only commercial television, suggesting that programs like "Sesame Street" and its mimics are different. They are, perhaps, but no more worthy.

THOSE "QUALITY" SHOWS

If the televisers want to teach my children something, I suggest such subjects as obedience to parents, sharing toys with brothers and sisters, kindness to animals, respect for grandparents. These kinds of lessons were strangely missing from the "quality" childrens' shows I looked in on. It is true that these concepts must be taught by the parents but it is insufferable to note the preachings of the "Sesame"-type producers, hearing them blat about how they care for children. I see their programs as a moral hustle, conning parents into thinking it's a high educational experience to dump the kids before the tube. In the end, the yammering about letters, shapes, numbers does not liberate the child's imagination. It captures it, a quick-action lariat that ropes in the child's most precious resource, his creativity.

Occasionally I have feelings that I may be missing an event of special value, a feeling that the televised truth goes marching on without me. But in my straggler status I have never failed to catch up eventually with the essence of what I missed, mostly by reading the newspapers or magazines— say a Presidential press conference or the Watergate testimony.

THE COLD-TURKEY GAMBIT

The stranger is gone now. Our lives are fuller and richer. Cold turkey worked. The kids don't run to neighbors' houses to watch TV, as I had feared. As for whether we [will] ever invite the stranger back to our house, it isn't likely unless the industry learns new manners.

A first sign of the kind of manners I'm thinking about would be revealed if, say some evening this announcement was beamed into the 97 per cent of America's electrically wired homes that have TV's:

"Ladies and gentlemen, until further notice we are ceasing our broadcasts. The programs we had planned are now seen to be dull, banal,

McCarthy

83

pointless, not worth your time and not ours. Don't turn to another channel, because you will only be insulted there too—insulted by the programs and by the corporate advertisers who want to gull you into buying products you can live well, even better, without.

"Come forward and turn off your set. When the die-out dot appears, get up and take a walk to the library and get a book. Or turn to your husband and wife and surprise them with a conversation. Or call a neighbor you haven't spoken with in months. Write a letter to a friend who has lost track of you. Turn off your set now. When we devise you some worthwhile programming, we'll be back on the air. Meanwhile, you'll be missing almost nothing."

NEWS

The informational function of television is clearly its most important benefit in a democratic society where people must make informed decisions. It is true that the amount of television time devoted to entertainment and to advertising far exceeds the amount of time spent to inform or educate the public. However, the time spent on certain types of broadcast programming, for instance, news programs, has never been a good indicator of the importance of that programming to society; this has been especially true in television programming.

Network and station managements point with pride to their news programs, which serve a vast audience; people in America get more of their news from television than from any other medium. Networks have increased their news programs from 15 minutes in the fifties to 30 minutes in the seventies and are considering enlarging that time segment. Local stations have lengthened their programming from a 15-minute slot to one hour newscasts in several markets today. A few stations already have extended local news programming to two hours nightly.

The increased importance of television news in our society has been a mixed blessing to the industry. On the one hand, station owners use the increased audiences to prove that their public service responsibilities are being met through news programs. On the other hand, the increased importance of news to society has caused some critics to focus their attention upon news. They have criticized especially its pictorial violence and the seemingly biased nature of its coverage. This criticism became more vigorous during the sixties, when racial and student activists found television cameras able and willing to take their actions and their grievances into every American home via the six o'clock news. Viewers reacted to the message and to the messenger by heaping criticism upon television news for its extensive coverage of antisocial groups and events. The messenger was blamed for the bad news.

The traditional response of newsmen to this kind of criticism has been that their reports just mirror society. The question of whether that is true is the central issue in news broadcasting today. For only when we understand the human and institutional values that go into the news-gathering and newscasting processes can we realistically deal with what may be a bias in news. Not a political bias, as some have alleged, but an institutional bias that shapes the kinds of news we receive, giving us an agenda of news items each evening that is devoted to violence, conflict, and action, all presented in living color. This process is particularly critical at the network level because our view of the world and of our society is shaped, in large part, by the slice of "reality" that appears in network news. Three articles shed some light on this issue. Edward Jay Epstein discusses the process of the selection of news, emphasizing the economic and professional values that are involved. George A. Bailey and Lawrence W. Lichty present a case history of one important news-gathering incident—the Tet offensive—which clearly illustrates many of the processes described by Epstein. Dan Rather adds yet another example in his article on television's role (or lack of it) in uncovering the Watergate affair. Read together, the three articles provide an unusual insight into the news-gathering process at the network level.

The "herd instinct" in journalism, which means that newsmen flock together to cover the same stories, the same news conferences, speeches, and announcements, has been a problem for years. The coming of radio and then of television simply added to the number of reporters covering the same stories. Television increased the numbers significantly because the medium usually requires a three-man team to cover a story. One of the outgrowths of this massive waste of money, time, and talent has been the concept of *pooled coverage*, where one or only a few reporters may be selected to cover a story for all of the news media. The reason for pooled coverage usually is that there is not room enough for all of the reporters or correspondents, and its use has been limited, for the most part, to important news stories such as trips by the president. It has not been applied to routine stories and conferences, the daily diet of journalism. Fred W. Friendly's article, which suggests nationwide electronic pooled coverage of daily news events, deserves careful thought as a solution to "herding" newsmen for routine coverage.

The distinction between newspaper journalism and broadcast journalism is not always clear, especially to the consumer of news. Practices that apply in one medium do not apply in the other because of technological differences. One of these practices is "editing"—the selection of material for inclusion in an article or broadcast. *The Selling of the Pentagon,* a 1971 CBS documentary that became a *cause célèbre* because of congressional reaction, is an example of the differences in media practices. Following the broadcast of the program, which was an attack on the Pentagon's public relations program, a congressional investigation was made. During the investigation, a House committee headed by Rep. Harley O. Staggers requested "outtakes" (filmed and taped material that did not appear in the broadcast); CBS President Frank Stanton refused to give any of this to the committee. Staggers sought, but failed to get, congressional approval for contempt of Congress by the network, thus ending this brief free press crisis. The incident attracted national attention and a large number of articles, editorials, and studies were published dealing with the issues. We have selected the issue of CBS' editing practice for inclusion here. Richard Salant, CBS News' president at the time, defends the network's editing policy. That same policy is criticized in an editorial from the *Washington Post.*

Local news also has become a more important element in television programming in the past few years. Today, some local stations are undertaking vigorous investigative reporting, consumer reporting, and community interest campaigns. Geraldo Rivera of WABC-TV in New York has produced outstanding documentary coverage of local conditions. One of his documentaries, *The Littlest Junkie* (dealing with drug-dependent babies born to drug-addicted mothers), was considered responsible for a bill introduced in the New York state legislature. Jack Cato, of KPRC-TV in Houston, was the first reporter on the scene when police began digging up the bodies of the 27 Houston youths killed in homosexual orgies. Thus, some local television news programs have become more important to the viewer because of vigorous, active reporting.

Other stations, however, are following another news programming trend, one that is not necessarily in the public interest. That trend deals with what is called, often derisively, "happy talk" programming. WABC's

Eyewitness News in New York was one of the earlier news programs to try the new format, where on-camera correspondents report the news and then "act human" by throwing one-liners, flip rejoinders, and wisecracks at other newscasters on the program. A perennial third-place finisher in New York rating races, WABC moved into first place with the new format. According to Richard Townley, a former investigative reporter in New York television, the ratings made WABC so popular that an ABC network source claimed the 11 P.M. *Eyewitness News* brought in "more [revenue] than a one-minute commercial on the ABC coast-to-coast network news in 1971." The success WABC and other stations have had with the format has fostered a trend throughout the United States, with stations in over fifty markets adapting the format to local conditions. The issue growing out of this trend is not whether ratings are desirable for news broadcasts; in our commercial environment they clearly are. The issue is whether the change to the "happy talk" format is in the public's interest. That is, does the emphasis on "personalities" who can relate to each other on camera in a relaxed, conversational way mean that *less* hard news will be covered in what already is a time-bound medium? If more and more people are getting most of their news from television, what does this trend mean to society? Walter Cronkite has said, "If there are any benefits at all in the format, the dangers are much more explicit—mainly the danger in creating the impression that news is just another facet of entertainment." Are we going to see the television equivalent of the sensational human interest tabloid newspaper of the twenties? The article by Halina J. Czerniejewski and Charles Long clearly illustrates the problems created by the "happy talk" format.

Beginning in the sixties, black groups across the country began making white America aware of certain deficiencies in broadcasting, namely that most of the people reporting the news were white and did not reflect the large racial and ethnic minorities that exist in our society. These groups also pointed to what they considered to be a programming bias, a bias that showed particular minority groups in racist terms. No segment of broadcast programming escaped minority censure: entertainment, news, and advertising were criticized severely. The article by Edith Efron is part of a larger series she wrote on blacks in broadcasting.

Similarly, women in news positions (as representative of women in business) have been cast in the role of a minority group by their employers. This lower ranking of women is explored in the article by Barbara Riegle, a radio news reporter concerned with the part (or the lack of a part) played by women in broadcasting.

One of the major concerns in broadcast journalism is how to establish a high level of news performance and credibility without government interference. We discuss the relationship between government and broadcasting in a later section, but it is pertinent here to mention some of the issues growing out of this concern for quality performance. In 1973 the foundation-supported National News Council began its work of evaluating the performance of the national mass media. The Task Force, which recommended the establishment of a News Council, suggested

> That an independent and private national news council be established to receive and to examine and to report on complaints concerning the accuracy and fairness of news reporting in the United States, as well as to initiate studies and report on issues involving the freedom of the press. The council shall limit its investigations to the principal national suppliers of news—the major wire services, the largest "supplemental news services, the national weekly news magazines, national newspaper syndicates, national daily newspapers, and the national broadcasting networks.

Those who supported the establishment of the council suggested that it "might contribute to better public understanding of the media and [would] foster accurate and fair reporting and public accountability of the press." The News Council was just one proposal made in recent years concerning ways of improving broadcast news accuracy and fairness. Our selection from Harry J. Skornia outlines the problems as well as some of the possible solutions; it bears careful and critical reading.

These, then, are some of the issues dealing with broadcast news; they do not exhaust the possibilities, of course. For instance, there still is the issue of deceptive practices in news programming, or, to put it less politely, faked news. Charges, many of them never proven before the FCC, frequently have been made against the networks for news practices that allegedly involved staging of a news story. Networks responded to these charges with denials and by changing certain news-gathering practices. Stations also have been accused. WPIX-TV, the New York *Daily News*–owned station, was severely criticized by the FCC's Broadcast Bureau for alleged "falsification and misrepresentation" of the news. The 225-page report by the bureau specifically dealt with station news practices from August to December in 1968. The recommendation of the bureau was that WPIX should lose its license. Hearings on the renewal of the WPIX-TV license were held in New York and Washington intermittently from May, 1970 to January, 1973, when they finally closed. As of November, 1974, the Hearing Examiner had not released his decision for or against renewal. The station's license status is still in question.

Another issue that may receive Federal Communications Commission action concerns conflicts of interest by broadcasters or by station management. The classic case involved the late Chet Huntley, NBC co-anchorman with David Brinkley in the sixties. Congress had passed the Wholesale Meat Act of 1967, which brought approximately 15,000 additional meat packing and processing plants under Federal inspection standards. Huntley broadcast several attacks against the act without indicating to his viewers that he himself was the owner of a cattle ranch in Montana and was executive-president of a group engaged in the purchase and sale of cattle. In his deposition to the FCC, Huntley denied having substantial holdings or being affected in any way by the act. The issue, however, is whether broadcast newsmen should be required to reveal possible conflicts of interest when they editorialize.

Conflict of interest also concerns station news practices. There is concern that some news stations "slant" their coverage because of "corporate benefits," as was charged in the KRON-TV case in San Francisco. The licensee of KRON is the Chronicle Publishing Co. A KRON cameraman, Albert Kihn, initiated the complaint against the station, charging that management slanted and suppressed news in reporting newspaper strikes and consolidations of the San Francisco newspaper business over several years. After a long hearing, in which many of the charges were substantiated, the Commission renewed the KRON license.

Students are encouraged to seek out further information on these issues in the bibliographical essays that follow.

BIBLIOGRAPHICAL ESSAY

Television news has come in for great criticism over the years; some of it has been directed at its relationship to government. We cover that issue later in the book. Here, as the readings for this chapter indicate, we concentrate on the issues of television news and its shaping of reality, of its natural or political bias, of the relationship of blacks and women to broadcast news reporting and of the professionalization of broadcast news.

Edward Jay Epstein's article should be read in conjunction with the case study of a televised report from Vietnam by George A. Bailey and Lawrence Lichty. For a more detailed look at the issues outlined by Epstein, consult the full article in the *New Yorker* from which our selection was excerpted, or *News From Nowhere: Television and the News,* Random House, New York, 1973.

For a look at the "political bias" of network newsmen, see Epstein's "The Values of Newsmen," *Television Quarterly* (Winter, 1973), 9–20, which emphasizes the view newsmen have of themselves and of their role in society; two books by Edith Efron, *The News Twisters*, 1971, and *How CBS Tried to Kill a Book*, 1972, which recounts her view of CBS' attempt to discredit her earlier book, both published by Nash, Los Angeles; Joseph Keeley, *The Left Leaning Antenna: Political Bias in Television*, Arlington House, New Rochelle, N.Y., 1971. See Paul H. Weaver, "Is Television News Biased?" *The Public Interest* (Winter, 1972), 57–74, where he agrees basically with Ms. Efron's discovery of bias but not with her conclusions as to why the bias exists, and Robert L. Stevenson, *et al.*, "Untwisting *The News Twisters:* a Replication of Efron's Study," *Journalism Quarterly* (Summer, 1973), 211–219, where the authors totally disagree with Ms. Efron, based largely on the same data. Ms. Efron disputes their conclusions in the Spring, 1974, *JQ*. In 1972 the American Institute for Political Communication, Washington, D.C., published a booklet *"Liberal Bias" As a Factor in Network Television News Reporting*, a report which monitored the three network evening news shows during the 1972 primary election campaign. The study concluded that there was a substantial amount of bias exhibited by the networks in a few particulars, but that there was a decline toward the end of the period. Finally, see Paul H. Weaver, "The Politics of a News Story," in *The Mass Media and Modern Democracy*, Rand McNally, Chicago, 1974, edited by Harry M. Clor. Weaver returns to his theme of political bias in news reporting. (Most of these articles deal with both print and electronic journalism.)

Several excellent books are available that discuss the methods and limitations of television news. They are, in chronological order of publication, Fred W. Friendly, *Due to Circumstances Beyond Our Control*, Random House, New York, 1967; Harry J. Skornia, *Television and the News*, Pacific Books, Palo Alto, Calif., 1968; Maury Green, *Television News: Anatomy and Process*, Wadsworth, Belmont, Calif., 1969; Alexander Kendrick, *Prime Time: The Life of Edward R. Murrow*, Little, Brown, New York, 1969; William Small, *To Kill A Messenger: Television News and the Real World*, Hastings House, New York, 1970, and Irving E. Fang, *Television News*, 2nd ed., Hastings House, New York, 1973. An interesting group of essays have been brought together on the subject of news in David J. LeRoy and Christopher H. Sterling, Eds., *Mass News: Practices, Controversies and Alternatives,* Prentice-Hall, Englewood Cliffs, N.J., 1973. While there have been a large number of books available on the role of television in communicating information to Americans about Vietnam, perhaps the most insightful book, especially as it relates to our article by Bailey and Lichty, is Don Oberdorfer's *Tet!*, Doubleday, New York, 1971. A good, general view of the Vietnam war coverage is Dale Minor, *The Information War*, Hawthorn, New York, 1970. Epstein also published an insightful three-part series on "The War in Vietnam: What Happened vs.

What We Saw," *TV Guide*, beginning September 29, 1973. Dan Rather's article emphasizes one of the limitations of television in attempting to cover Administration-related stories such as Watergate. The conflict between the presidency and the press is shown well in David Wise's, *The Politics of Lying: Government Deception, Secrecy and Power*, Atlantic, Boston, Mass., 1973, which discusses the relationship between the press, broadcasting, and all presidents since Eisenhower. An excerpt from the book appeared in *The Atlantic* (April, 1973). Edwin Diamond, "TV and Watergate: What Was, What Might Have Been," *Columbia Journalism Review* (July/August, 1973), 20, gives a negative view, largely in support of Dan Rather's article. See also the special section in *Columbia Journalism Review* (November/December, 1973), which was devoted to the press and the Watergate hearings.

Fred Friendly's suggestion for pooled coverage is outstanding because of its seminal qualities, yet the need for such coverage is expressed in those books previously cited. The issue over editing practices in *The Selling of the Pentagon*, the CBS documentary, receives severe criticism in one chapter in Mayer's *About Television*, Harper & Row, New York, 1972. Virtually the same article appeared first as "Television," *Harper's Magazine* (December, 1971), 40+. For a review of network documentaries for one season, see Patrick D. Maines and John C. Ottinger, "Network Documentaries: How Many, How Relevant?" *Columbia Journalism Review* (March/April, 1973), 36–42. For a rather complete view of the entire controversy, see National Association of Broadcasters, *CBS and Congress: The Selling of the Pentagon Papers*, a special issue of *Educational Broadcasting Review* (Winter, 1971–1972). This special issue records all of the important documents in the controversy, including background materials on "appropriate" operating standards for news and public affairs programming.

Edith Efron's article focuses on the involvement of blacks in news programming. It is one article from a three-part series that began in the August 19, 1972 issue of *TV Guide*. The figures she reports in this series should be supplemented by a report issued from the Office of Communication of the United Church of Christ in November, 1972. For a brief summary of the findings of the report, see John J. O'Connor's article in *The New York Times* (December 3, 1972), sec. 2, 17. Dorothy Gilliam seeks to answer the question "What Do Black Journalists Want?" *Columbia Journalism Review* (May/June, 1972), 47–52, in an article dealing with newspapers, magazines, and television. A brief report giving a local slant to the issue is "Latinos & the Media: Brown-Out," *San Francisco Bay Guardian* (July 20, 1974), 19.

Barbara Riegle's article on women in broadcasting can be supplemented by a large number of articles dealing with the role of women in broadcasting, their responsibilities and how they are portrayed in programs and advertising. A positive article gives a sketch of Barbara Walters of NBC's "Today" show in Chris Chase, "First Lady of Talk," *Life* (July 14, 1972), 51+. The National Organization for Women (NOW) has been active in recent years in trying to bring change to the television industry by filing petitions to deny relicensing of stations or by attacking the portrayal of women in commercials. For two insightful articles on these issues, both written by Judith Adler Hennessee and Joan Nicholson, see "The Feminists v. WABC-TV," (*More*) (June, 1972), 10–11, and "NOW Says: TV Commercials Insult Women," *The New York Times Magazine* (May 28, 1972), 12–13+. To keep abreast of the news on women in media, read *Media Report to Women*, a monthly magazine issued out of Washington, D.C.

Harry Skornia's article on professionalization in broadcast news emphasizes many of the problems found in the readings listed above. His proposal summarizes, in one respect, many of the criticisms and responses to many of the proposals for improving the field and the practitioners in the field. There is very little that deals specifically with the proposal for professionalization in broadcast news, but Skornia has written a short book, *Television and Society: An Inquest and Agenda for Improvement*, McGraw-Hill, New York, 1965, that gives a more extended treatment to some of his ideas. It is well worth consulting.

STUDY QUESTIONS

1. Discuss the value of the "mirror image" concept of television news. Does this analogy hold up for the local TV news coverage that you watch?

2. What are some of the inherent qualities of network television news that prevent a truly realistic and faithful reflection of society?

3. Do television news departments have a greater responsibility to "taste" or to "realism" in what they show viewers on newscasts?

4. If the pooled national news coverage idea had been in existence in Vietnam during the Tet offensive, how might the General Loan story been improved or harmed? In what ways would stories such as this be affected?

News

5. CBS White House Correspondent Dan Rather believes that television news was not as effective as newspapers in reporting the Watergate story. What are his reasons for this? Do you agree or disagree with him? Why?

6. What is your position on the question of journalistic editing? Two arguments are presented in "Editing in the Electronic Media: A Documentary Dispute." Do you side with Richard Salant, president of CBS News, or with the editor of the *Washington Post*? Why?

7. How do the newscasts in your city fit into the descriptions of local television news? Is "happy talk" or "tabloid news" the way to go for ratings?

8. Are blacks and women a part of the broadcast news team on the stations in your city? Do they have major or secondary roles in the program?

9. Does broadcast news need professionalizing? Why or why not?

10. Which of Dr. Skornia's proposals for improving the state of broadcast news do you favor? Explain.

11. Should broadcast newsmen be licensed? If yes, who should be the licensing agent?

The Selection of Reality

EDWARD JAY EPSTEIN

From *News from Nowhere: Television and the News,* by Edward Jay Epstein. Copyright © 1973 by Edward Jay Epstein. Reprinted by permission of Random House, Inc. Originally appeared in *The New Yorker.* Edward Jay Epstein is a media critic who earned his credentials with the much discussed book from which this selection is taken. He has written extensively on mass media topics.

Each weekday evening, the three major television networks—the American Broadcasting Company, the Columbia Broadcasting System, and the National Broadcasting Company—feed filmed news stories over lines leased from the American Telephone & Telegraph Co. to the more than six hundred local stations affiliated with them, which, in turn, broadcast the stories over the public airwaves to a nationwide audience. The CBS Evening News, which is broadcast by two hundred local stations, reaches some nineteen million viewers; the NBC Nightly News, broadcast by two hundred and nine stations, some eighteen million viewers; and the ABC Evening News, broadcast by a hundred and ninety-one stations, some fourteen million. News stories from these programs are recorded on videotape by most affiliates and used again, usually in truncated form, on local news programs late in the evening. Except for the news on the few unaffiliated stations and on the noncommercial stations, virtually all the filmed reports of national and world news seen on television are the product of the three network news organizations.

The process by which news is gathered, edited, and presented the public is more or less similar at the three networks. A limited number of subjects —usually somewhere between twenty and thirty—are selected each day as possible film stories by news executives, producers, anchor men, and assignment editors, who base their choices principally on wire-service and newspaper reports. Camera crews are dispatched to capture these events on 16-mm. color film. The filming is supervised by either a field producer or a correspondent—or, in some cases, the cameraman himself. The film is then shipped to the network's headquarters in New York, or to one of its major news bureaus—in Chicago, Los Angeles, or Washington—or, if time is an important consideration, processed and edited at the nearest available facilities and transmitted electronically to New York. Through editing and rearranging of the filmed scenes, a small fraction of the exposed film— usually less than ten per cent—is reconstructed into a story whose form is to some extent predetermined. Reuven Frank, until two months ago the president of NBC News, has written:

> Every news story should, without any sacrifice of probity or responsibility, display the attributes of fiction, of drama. It should have structure and conflict, problem and denouement, rising action and falling action, a beginning, a middle and an end.

After the addition of a sound track, recorded at the event, the story is explained and pulled together by a narration, written by the correspondent who covered the event or by a writer in the network news offices. Finally, the story is integrated into the news program by the anchor man.

Network news organizations select not only the events that will be shown as national and world news on television but the way in which those events will be depicted. This necessarily involves choosing symbols that will have general meaning for a national audience. "The picture is not a fact but a symbol," Reuven Frank once wrote. "The real child and its real crying become symbols of all children." In the same way, a particular black may be used to symbolize the aspirations of his race, a particular student may be used to symbolize the claims of his generation, and a particular policeman may be used to symbolize the concept of authority. Whether the black chosen is a Black Panther or an integrationist, whether the student is a militant activist or a Young Republican, whether the policeman is engaged in a brutal or a benevolent act obviously affects the impression of the event received by the audience. When the same symbols are consistently used on television to depict the behavior and aspirations of groups, they become stable images—what Walter Lippmann, in his classic study "Public Opinion," has called a "repertory of stereotypes." These images obviously have great power; public-opinion polls show that television is the most believed source of news for most of the population. The director of CBS News in Washington, William Small, has written about television news:

> When television covered its "first war" in Vietnam, it showed a terrible truth of war in a manner new to mass audiences. A case can be made, and certainly should be examined, that this was cardinal to the disillusionment of Americans with this war, the cynicism of many young people toward America, and the destruction of Lyndon Johnson's tenure of office. . . . When television examined a different kind of revolution, it was singularly effective in helping bring about the Black revolution.

And it would be difficult to dispute the claim of Reuven Frank that "there are events which exist in the American mind and recollection primarily because they were reported on regular television news programs."

How were those events selected to be shown on television, and who or what determined the way in which they were depicted? [Former] Vice-President Spiro Agnew believes the answer is that network news is shaped "by a handful of men responsible only to their corporate employers," who have broad "powers of choice" and "wield a free hand in selecting, presenting, and interpreting the great issues in our nation." Television executives and newsmen, on the other hand, often argue that television news is shaped not by men but by events—that news is news. Both of these analyses overlook the economic realities of network television, the effects of government regulation on broadcasting, and the organizational requirements of the network news operations, whose established routines and procedures tend to impose certain forms on television news stories.

David Brinkley, in an NBC News special entitled "From Here to the Seventies," reiterated a description of television news that is frequently offered by television newsmen:

> What television did in the sixties was to show the American people to the American people. . . . It did show the people, places and things they had not seen before. Some they liked, and some they did not. It was not that television produced or created any of it.

In this view, television news does no more than mirror reality. Thus, Leonard Goldenson, the chairman of the board of ABC, testified before the National Commission on the Causes and Prevention of Violence that complaints of news distortion were brought about by the fact that "Americans are reluctant to accept the images reflected by the mirror we have held up to our society." Robert D. Kasmire, a vice-president of NBC, told the commission, "There is no doubt that television is, to a large degree, a mirror of our society. It is also a mirror of public attitudes and preferences." The president of NBC, Julian Goodman, told the commission, "In short, the medium is blamed for the message." Dr. Frank Stanton, vice-chairman and former president of CBS, testifying before a House committee, said, "What the media do is to hold a mirror up to society and try to report it as faithfully as possible." Elmer Lower, the president of ABC News, has described television news as "the television mirror that reflects . . . across oceans and mountains," and added, "Let us open the doors of the parliaments everywhere to the electronic mirrors." The imagery has been picked up by critics of television, too. Jack Gould, formerly of the *Times,* wrote of television's coverage of racial riots, "Congress, one would hope, would not conduct an examination of a mirror because of the disquieting images that it beholds."

The mirror analogy has considerable descriptive power, but it also leads to a number of serious misconceptions about the medium. The notion of a "mirror of society" implies that everything of significance that happens will be reflected on television news. Network news organizations, however, far from being ubiquitous and all-seeing, are limited newsgathering operations, which depend on camera crews based in only a few major cities for most of their national stories. Some network executives have advanced the idea that network news is the product of coverage by hundreds of affiliated stations, but the affiliates' contribution to the network news program actually is very small. Most network news stories are assigned in advance to network news crews and correspondents, and in many cases whether or not an event is covered depends on where it occurs and the availability of network crews.

The mirror analogy also suggests immediacy: events are reflected instantaneously, as in a mirror. This notion of immediate reporting is reinforced by the way people in television news depict the process to the public. News executives sometimes say that, given the immediacy of television, the network organization has little opportunity to intervene in news decisions. Reuven Frank once declared, on a television program about television, "News coverage generally happens too fast for anything like that to take place." But does it? Though it is true that elements of certain events, such as space exploration and political conventions, are broadcast live, virtually all of the regular newscasts, except for the commentator's "lead-ins" and "tags" to the news stories, are prerecorded on videotape or else on film, which must be transported, processed, edited, and projected before it can be seen. Some film stories are delayed from one day to two weeks, because of certain organizational needs and policies. Reuven Frank more or less outlined these policies on "prepared," or delayed, news in . . . [an internal] memorandum he wrote when he was executive producer of NBC's Nightly News program. "Except for those rare days when other material becomes available," he wrote, "the gap will be filled by planned and prepared film stories, and we are assuming the availability of two each night." These "longer pieces," he continued, were to be "planned, executed over a longer period of time than spot news, usable and relevant any time within, say, two weeks, rather than that day, receptive to the more sophisticated techniques of production and editing, but journalism withal." The reason for delaying filmed stories, a network vice-president has explained, is that "it gives the producer more control over his program." First, it gives the producer control of the budget, since shipping the film by plane, though it might mean a delay of a day or two, is considerably less expensive than transmitting the film electronically by satellite or A.T. & T. lines. Second, and perhaps more important, it gives the producer control over the content of the individual stories, since it affords him an opportunity to screen the film and, if necessary, reedit it. Eliminating the delay, the same vice-president suggested, could have the effect of reducing network news to a mere "chronicler of events" and forcing it "out of the business of making meaningful comment." Moreover, the delay provides a reserve of stories that can be used to give the program "variety" and "pacing."

In filming delayed stories, newsmen are expected to eliminate any elements of the unexpected, so as not to destroy the illusion of immediacy. This becomes especially important when it is likely that the unusual developments will be reported in other media and thus date the story. A case in point is an NBC News story about the inauguration of a high-speed train service between Montreal and Toronto. While the NBC crew was filming the turbotrain during its inaugural run to Toronto, it collided with —and "sliced in half," as one newspaper put it—a meat trailer-truck, and then suffered a complete mechanical breakdown on the return trip. Persistent "performance flaws" and subsequent breakdowns eventually led to a temporary suspension of the service. None of these accidents and aberrations were included in the filmed story broadcast two weeks later on the NBC evening news. David Brinkley, keeping to the original story, written before the event, introduced the film by saying, "The only high-speed train now running in North America has just begun in Canada." Four and a half minutes of shots of the streamlined train followed, and the narration suggested that this foreshadowed the future of transportation, since Canada's "new turbo just might shake [American] lethargy" in developing such trains. (The announcement of the suspension of the service, almost two weeks later, was not carried on the program.) This practice of "preparing" stories also has affected the coverage of more serious subjects—for instance, many of the filmed stories about the Vietnam war were delayed for several days. It was possible to transmit war films to the United States in one day by using the satellite relay, but the cost was considerable at the height of the war—more than three thousand dollars for a ten-minute transmission, as opposed to twenty or thirty dollars for shipping the same film by plane. And, with the exception of momentous battles, such as the Tet offensive, virtually all of the network film was sent by plane. To avoid the possibility of having the delayed footage dated by newspaper accounts, network correspondents were instructed to report on the routine and continuous aspect of the war rather than unexpected developments, according to a former NBC Saigon bureau manager.

The mirror analogy, in addition, obscures the component of "will"—of initiative in producing feature stories and of decisions made in advance to cover or not to cover certain types of events. A mirror makes no decisions; it simply reflects what takes place in front of it. . . .

The search for news requires a reliable flow of information not only about events in the immediate past but about those scheduled for the near future. Advance information, though necessary to any news operation, is of critical importance to the networks. For, unlike newspapers and radio stations, which can put a news story together within minutes by means of telephone interviews or wire-service dispatches, a television network usually needs hours, if not days, of "lead time" to shoot, process, and edit a film story of even a minute's duration. The types of news stories best suited for television coverage are those specially planned, or induced, for the conveniences of the news media—press conferences, briefings, interviews, and the like—which the historian Daniel J. Boorstin has called "pseudo-events," and which by definition are scheduled well in advance and are certain to be, if only in a self-fulfilling sense, "newsworthy." There are also other news events, such as congressional hearings, trials, and speeches, that, although they may not be induced for the sole purpose of creating news, can still be predicted far in advance. The networks have various procedures for gathering, screening, and evaluating information about future events, and these procedures to some degree systematically *influence* their coverage of news.

Most network news stories, rather than resulting from the initiative of reporters in the field, are located and assigned by an assignment editor in New York (or an editor under his supervision in Washington, Chicago, or Los Angeles). The assignment desk provides material not only for the evening news program but for documentaries, morning and afternoon programs, and a syndicated service for local stations. Instead of maintaining —as newspapers do—regular "beats," where reporters have contact with the same set of newsmakers over an extended period of time, network news organizations rely on ad-hoc coverage. In this system, correspondents are shunted from one story to another—on the basis of availability, logistical convenience, and producers' preferences—after the assignment editor has selected the events to be covered. A correspondent may easily be assigned to three subjects in three different cities in a single week, each assignment lasting only as long as it takes to film the story. To be sure, there are a number of conventional beats in Washington, such as the

White House, but these are the exception rather than the rule. Most of the correspondents are "generalists," expected to cover all subjects with equal facility. And even in fields for which networks do employ special correspondents, such as sports or space exploration, better-known correspondents who are not experts in those fields may be called on to report major stories. The generalist is expected not to be a Jack-of-all-trades but simply to be capable of applying rules of fair inquiry to any subject. One reason network executives tend to prefer generalists is that they are less likely to "become involved in a story to the point of advocacy," as one network vice-president has put it. It is feared that specialists, through their intimate knowledge of a situation, would be prone to champion what they believed was the correct side of a controversy. But perhaps the chief reason that generalists are preferred to specialists is that, being able to cover whatever story develops, they lend themselves to an efficient use of manpower. The use of ad-hoc coverage leads to the constant appearance "on camera" of a relatively small number of correspondents. One network assignment editor has suggested that it is "more for reasons of audience identification than economy" that a few correspondents are relied on for most of the stories. The result, he continued, is a "star system," in which producers request that certain leading correspondents cover major stories, whatever the subject might be. Another consequence of having small, generalist reporting staffs is that the networks are able to do relatively little investigative reporting. . . .

What is seen on network news is not, except in rare instances, the event itself, unfolding live before the camera, or even a filmed record of the event in its entirety, but a story about the event which has been constructed on film from selected fragments of it. Presenting news events exactly as they occur does not meet the requirements of network news. For one thing, the camera often is not in a position to capture events while they are happening. Some news events are completely unexpected and occur before a camera crew can be dispatched to the scene. Others cannot be filmed either because of unfavorable weather or lighting conditions (especially if artificial lighting is unavailable or restricted) or because news crews are not permitted access to them. And when institutions, such as political conventions, do permit television to record their formal proceedings, the significant decisions may still take place outside the purview of the camera. But even if coverage presents no insurmountable problems, it is not sufficient in most cases simply to record events in their natural sequence, with all the digressions, confusions, and inconsistencies that are an inescapable part of any reality, for a network news story is required to have a definite order, time span, and logic.

In producing most news stories, the first necessity is generating sufficient film about an event, so that the editor and the writer can be assured of finding the material they need for the final story. Perhaps the most commonly used device for producing this flow of film is the interview. The interview serves several important purposes for television news. First, it enables a news crew to obtain film footage about an event that it did not attend or was not permitted to film. By finding and interviewing people who either participated in the event or have at least an apparent connection with it, the correspondent can re-create it through their eyes.

Second, the interview assures that the subject will be filmed under favorable circumstances—an important technical consideration. In a memorandum to his news staff, Reuven Frank once gave this advice about interviewing:

> By definition, an interview is at least somewhat controllable. It must be arranged; it must be agreed to. . . . Try not to interview in harsh sunlight. Try not to interview in so noisy a setting that words cannot be heard. Let subjects be lit. If lights bother your subject, talk to him, discuss the weather, gentle him, involve his interest and his emotions so that he forgets or ignores the lights. It takes longer, but speed is poor justification for a piece of scrapped film.

To make the subjects appear even more dignified and articulate, it is the customary practice to repeat the same question a number of times, allowing the respondent to "sharpen his answer," as one correspondent has put it. At times, the person interviewed is permitted to compose his own questions for the interviewer or, at least, to rephrase them. Rehearsals are also quite common.

Third, interviews provide an easy means of presenting an abstract or difficult-to-film concept in human terms, as Reuven Frank has explained:

> The best interviews are of people reacting—or people expounding. . . . No important story is without them. They can be recorded and transmitted tastefully . . . nuclear disarmament, unemployment, flood, automation, name me a recent major story without its human involvement.

Although the networks have instituted strict policies against misleading "reenactments" and "staging," film footage is sometimes generated by having someone demonstrate or enact aspects of a story for the camera. Bruce Cohn, a producer for ABC News at the time, explained the practice last year to the House Special Subcommittee on Investigations during hearings on "news staging." Describing the difference between hard news and feature stories, Cohn said, "Generally speaking, a feature story is only brought to the public's attention because the journalist who conceived of doing such a report thinks it would be of interest or of importance. Therefore, a feature story must be 'set up' by a journalist if it is to be transformed into usable information. There is no reason why this 'setting up' cannot be done in an honest and responsible manner . . . people involved in feature stories are often asked to demonstrate how they do something . . . in fact, by its very nature, a feature story may be nothing but what the subcommittee negatively refers to as 'staging. . . .' "

Since network television is in the business of attracting and maintaining large audiences, the news operation, which is, after all, part of the networks' programming schedule, is also expected to maintain, if not attract, as large an audience as possible. But a network news program, unlike other news media, apparently can't depend entirely on its content to attract and maintain an audience. To a great extent, the size of its audiece is determined by three outside factors. The first is affiliate acceptance. If a program is not carried, or "cleared," by the affiliates, then it simply is not available to the public. (ABC has significantly increased the audience for its evening news program since 1969 by increasing the number of stations that clear it from a hundred and twenty to a hundred and ninety-one.) The second is scheduling. A program that is broadcast at 7 P.M., say, stands a good chance of drawing a larger audience than it would at six-thirty, since more people are usually watching television at the later hour. (The television audience increases all day and reaches a peak at about 9 P.M.) The third factor is what is called "audience flow." Network executives and advertisers believe that a significant portion of the audience for any program is inherited, as they put it, from the preceding program. According to the theory of audience flow, an audience is like a river that continues in the same direction until it is somehow diverted. "The viewing habits of a large portion of the audience—at least, the audience that Nielsen measures—are governed more by the laws of inertia than by free choice," a network vice-president responsible for audience studies has remarked. "Unless they have a very definite reason to switch, like a ballgame, they continue to watch the programs on the channel they are tuned in to."

Many network executives believe that network news is even more dependent on audience flow than are entertainment programs, or even local newscasts featuring reports on local sports and weather conditions. Richard Salant, the president of CBS News, has said that "you'll find a general correlation between the ratings of the network news broadcast and the local news broadcast—and probably the local news is the decisive thing." But what of the selective viewer, who changes channels for network news? Network executives, relying on both audience studies and personal intuition, assume, first, that there is not a significant number of such viewers, and, second, that most of them choose particular news programs on the basis of the personalities of the commentators rather than the extent of the news coverage. Acting on these assumptions about audience behavior, the networks attempted to improve the ratings of their news shows by hiring "star" commentators and by investing in the programs that precede the network news. For example, in a memo to the president of NBC several years ago, a vice-president responsible for audience analysis made this suggestion for increasing the ratings in Los Angeles of the network's evening news program:

> It seems to me the only surefire way to increase our audience at 3:30 P.M. (and actually win the time period) is with Mike Douglas [a syndicated talk show, which NBC would have had to buy from Group W Productions, a subsidiary of the Westinghouse Broadcasting Company]. At 5-6 P.M. our news then should get at least what KABC is getting (let's say a 7 rating).
>
> Coming out of this increased lead-in—and a *news* lead-in, at that —I believe that [the evening news] at 6 P.M. will get a couple of rating points more. . . .

Similarly, a network can invest in the local news programs that precede or follow the network news on the five stations it owns. NBC concluded from a detailed study that it commissioned of the Chicago audience that local news programs, unlike network news, which builds its audience through coverage of special events, can increase their ratings through improved coverage of weather, sports, and local events. The study recommended, for example, that the network-owned station in Chicago hire a more popular local weathercaster, since "almost as many viewers look forward to seeing the weather as the news itself." The networks also assist the affiliated stations with their local news programs, by providing a news syndication service. This supplies subscribing stations with sports and news stories through a half-hour feed, from which the stations can record stories for use on their own news programs.

Implicit in this approach to seeking higher ratings for network news programs is the idea that it doesn't make economic sense to spend large amounts on improving the editorial product. Hiring additional camera crews, reporters, and researchers presumably would not increase a news program's audience, and it definitely would be expensive. For instance, not only does each camera crew cost about a hundred thousand dollars a year to maintain, in equipment, salaries, and overtime, but it generates a prodigious amount of film—about twenty times as much as is used in the final stories—which has to be transported, processed, and edited. NBC accountants use a rule-of-thumb gauge of more than twenty dollars in service cost for every foot of film in the final story, which comes to more than seven hundred and twenty dollars a minute. And it is the number of camera crews a network maintains that defines, in some ways, the scope of its news-gathering operation. "The news you present is actually the news you cover," a network news vice-president has said. "The question is: How wide do you fling your net?"

In 1968, when I had access to staff meetings and assignment sheets at the three networks, NBC covered the nation each day with an average of ten camera crews, in New York, Chicago, Los Angeles, Washington, and Cleveland, plus two staff crews in Texas and one staff cameraman (who could assemble camera crews) in Boston. (In comparison, CBS's local news operation in Los Angeles, according to its news director, uses nine camera crews to cover the news of that one city.) Today, NBC says it has fifty domestic camera crews, but this figure includes sports, special events, and documentary crews, as well as local crews at the network's five stations. CBS says it has twenty full-time network news crews, in New York, Chicago, Los Angeles, Atlanta, and Washington, and ABC says it has sixteen, in New York, Chicago, Los Angeles, Washington, Atlanta, and Miami. Each of the networks also has camera crews in nine cities overseas. To be sure, when there is a momentous news event the networks can quickly mobilize additional crews—those regularly assigned to news documentaries, sports, and local news at network stations, or those of affiliated stations—but the net that is cast for national news on a day-to-day basis is essentially defined by the crews that are routinely available for network assignment, and their number is set by the economic logic of network television.

Another element in the economics of network news is the fact that it costs a good deal more to transmit stories from some places than it does from other places. The lines that connect the networks and their affiliates across the country can normally be used to transmit programs in only one direction—from the network's headquarters in New York to the affiliates. Therefore, to transmit news reports electronically from any "remote" location—that is, anywhere except network facilities in a few cities—to the network for rebroadcast, a news program must order special "long lines" between the two points from the American Telephone & Telegraph Co. The charges for the "long line" are now fifty-five cents a mile for up to an hour's use and seven hundred and fifty dollars for a "loop," which is the package of electronic equipment that connects the transmission point (usually an affiliated station) with the telephone company's "long lines." It is even more expensive to order stories sent electronically by means of the satellite-relay system—eighteen hundred and fifty dollars for the first ten minutes of a story from London to New York and about twenty-four hundred dollars for the first ten minutes of a story from Tokyo to New York—and these costs are charged against the program's budget. The weekly budget for the NBC Nightly News is in excess of two hundred thousand dollars, and that of the CBS Evening News is almost a hundred thousand dollars, but more than half of each is committed in advance for the salaries and expenses of the producers, editors, writers, and other members of the "unit," and for the studio and other overhead costs that are automatically charged against the program's budget. (Differences in the billing of these charges account for most of the difference in the budgets of the NBC and CBS programs.) At CBS, about forty-nine thousand dollars a week, or eight thousand dollars a program, is left for "remotes." Since a news program needs from six to eight film stories a night, and some satellite charges can be as high as three thousand dollars apiece, the budget, in effect, limits the number of "remote" stories that can be transmitted in an average week.

Because of differences in transmission costs, producers have a strong incentive to take news stories from some areas rather than others, especially when their budgets are strained. The fact that networks base most of their camera crews and correspondents in New York, Washington, Chicago, and Los Angeles reinforces the advantage of using news stories from these areas, since they involve less overtime and travel expense. It is not surprising, then, that so many of the film stories shown on the national news programs originate in these areas. Although the geographical distribution of film stories varies greatly from day to day, over any sustained period it is skewed in the direction of these few large cities. It is economically more efficient to consign news of small-town America and of remote cities to timeless features such as Charles Kuralt's "On the Road" segments on the CBS Evening News. This suggests that if network news programs tend to focus on problems of a few large urban centers, it is less because, as former Vice-President Agnew argued, an "enclosed fraternity" of "commentators and producers live and work in the geographical and intellectual confines of Washington, D.C., or New York City . . . [and] draw their political and social views from the same sources" than because the networks' basic economic structure compels producers, willy-nilly, to select a large share of their filmed stories from a few locations.

The Fairness Doctrine requires broadcasters to provide a reasonable opportunity for the presentation of "contrasting viewpoints on controversial issues of public importance" in the course of their news and public-affairs programming. Unlike the "equal time" provisions of Section 315 of the Communications Act—which applies only to candidates running for a public office and requires that if a station grants time to one candidate it must grant equal time to other candidates, except on news programs—the Fairness Doctrine does not require that opposing arguments be given an equal number of minutes, be presented on the same program, or be presented within any specific period. It is left up to the licensee to decide what constitutes a "controversial issue of public importance," a "fair" reply, and a "reasonable time" in which the reply should be made. Moreover, broadcasters are apparently not expected to be equally "fair" on all issues of public importance; for example, the Commission states in its time available to Communists or to the Communist viewpoints." "Fairness Primer" that it is not "the Commission's intention to make

Although no television station has ever lost its license because of a violation of the Fairness Doctrine, the doctrine has affected the form and content of network news in a number of ways. Most notably, the Fairness Doctrine puts an obligation on affiliates to "balance" any network program that advances only one side of an issue by themselves providing, in the course of their own programming, the other side, and the affiliates, rather than risk having to fulfill such an obligation, which could be both costly and bothersome, insist, virtually as a condition of taking network news, that the networks incorporate the obligatory "contrasting viewpoints" in their own news report. The networks, in turn, make it a policy to present opposing views on any issue that could conceivably be construed as controversial.

This pro-and-con reporting is perfectly consistent with the usual notion of objectivity, if objectivity is defined, as it is by many correspondents, as "telling both sides of a story." It can, however, seriously conflict with the value that journalists place on what is now called investigative reporting, or simply any reporting the purpose of which is "getting to the bottom" of an issue, or "finding the truth," as correspondents often put it. A correspondent is required to present "contrasting points of view" even if he finds the views of one side to be valid and those of the other side to be false and misleading (in the Fairness Doctrine, truth is no defense), and therefore any attempt to resolve a controversial issue and "find the truth" is likely to be self-defeating. . . .

A frequent criticism of television news is that it is superficial—that it affords only scant coverage of news events, lacks depth or sufficient analysis of events, and engages in only a minimum of investigative reporting. The assumption of such criticism is that television newsmen lack journalistic credentials, that producers and executives are lax or indifferent toward their responsibilities, and that changing or educating the broadcasters would improve the news product. But the level of journalism in network news is more or less fixed by the time, money, and manpower that can be allocated to it, and these are determined by the structure of network television. Any substantial improvement in the level of network journalism, such as expanding coverage of events to a truly nationwide scale, would therefore require a structural change in network television that would effectively reorder its economic and political incentives, rather than merely a change of personnel.

Another common criticism is, again, that network news is politically biased in favor of liberal or left-wing causes and leaders, because a small clique of newsmen in New York and Washington shape the news to fit their own political beliefs. In this critique, network news is presumed to be highly politicized by the men who select and report it, and the remedy most often suggested is to employ conservative newsmen to balance the liberal viewpoints. Since, for economic reasons, much of the domestic news on the network programs does in fact come from a few big cities, and since in recent years many of the efforts to change the distribution of political values and services have been concentrated in the big cities, the networks perhaps have reported a disproportionately large share of these activities. The requirement that network news be "nationalized" further adds to the impression that networks are advancing radical causes, for in elevating local disputes to national proportions newscasters appear to be granting them uncalled-for importance.

Left-wing critics complain that network news neglects the inherent contradictions in the American system. Their critique runs as follows: Network news focuses not on substantive problems but on symbolic protests. By overstating the importance of protest actions, television news invites the audience to judge the conduct of the protesters rather than the content of the problem. This creates false issues. Popular support is generated against causes that, on television, appear to rely on violent protests, while underlying economic and social problems are systematically masked or ignored. Broadcasters can be expected to help perpetuate "the system," because they are an important part of it. Thus, one critic writes, "The media owners will do anything to maintain these myths. . . . They will do anything to keep the public from realizing that the Establishment dominates society through its direct and indirect control of the nation's communication system." In fact, however, the tendency to depict symbolic protests rather than substantive problems is closely related to the problem of audience maintenance. Protests can be universally comprehended, it is presumed, if they are presented in purely symbolic terms: one group, standing for one cause, challenging another group and cause. The sort of detail that would be necessary to clarify economic and social issues is not easily translated into visual terms, whereas the sort of dramatic images that can be found in violent protests have an immediate impact on an audience. Newsmen therefore avoid liberal or radical arguments not because they are politically committed to supporting "the system" but because such arguments do not satisfy the requisites of network news.

Epstein

109

Finally, in what might best be called the social-science critique, network news is faulted for presenting a picture of society that does not accurately correspond to the empirical data. Spokesmen selected by television to represent groups in society tend to be statistically atypical of the groups for which they are supposedly speaking; for example, militant students may have appeared to be in the majority on college campuses in America during the nineteen-sixties because of the frequency with which they were selected to represent student views, when in fact data collected by social scientists showed that they constituted a small minority. It is generally argued that such discrepancies stem from a lack of readily usable data rather than any intent on the part of journalists to misrepresent situations. The implication in this critique is that if network news organizations had the techniques of social scientists, or employed social scientists as consultants, they would produce a more realistic version of the claims and aspirations of different segments of society. However, the selection of spokesmen to appear on television is determined less by a lack of data than by the organizational needs of network news. In order to hold the attention of viewers to whom the subject of the controversy may be of no interest, television newsmen select spokesmen who are articulate, easily identifiable, and dramatic, and the "average" person in a group cannot be depended on to manifest these qualities. Moreover, the nationalization of news requires that spokesmen represent the major themes of society rather than what is statistically typical. Given the organizational need to illustrate news stories with spokesmen who are both dramatic and thematic, network news cannot be expected to present a picture that conforms to the views of social scientists, no matter how much data or how many technical skills the social scientists might supply.

As long as the requisites remain essentially the same, network news can be expected to define American society by the problems of a few urban areas rather than of the entire nation, by action rather than ideas, by dramatic protests rather than substantive contradictions, by "newsmakers" rather than economic and social structures, by atypical rather than typical views, and by synthetic national themes rather than disparate local events.

Rough Justice on a Saigon Street

GEORGE BAILEY and LAWRENCE LICHTY

Reprinted from *Journalism Quarterly*, vol. 49, 2 (Summer, 1972), with permission of the publisher and the authors. Copyright 1971 by George A. Bailey and Lawrence W. Lichty. George Bailey and Lawrence Lichty are at work on a book about television coverage of the Vietnam War. Lichty is a professor in the department of communication arts at the University of Wisconsin in Madison. Bailey is an assistant professor in the department of mass communication at the University of Wisconsin in Milwaukee.

The Viet Cong had announced a Tet truce but on January 29, 1968, and for the next few days, the VC and NVA attacked nearly every city and many villages in South Vietnam.[1] Heavy fighting followed for several weeks in Saigon and Hue. The first film reports of the attack were seen on American television January 30.

On Wednesday, January 31, the *Huntley-Brinkley Report* switched via satellite to Jack Perkins live in Tokyo. Perkins announced that he would show unedited film of fighting in and around the U.S. Embassy. The film had just been developed and Perkins narrated the story partly from information he was receiving at that time talking by telephone with Executive Producer Robert Northshield in New York. In other reports the networks covered the war in the cities along with reaction at home.

On Thursday, February 1, David Brinkley introduced John Chancellor who narrated seven still photographs from the wire service. Part of his narration follows:

> There was awful savagery. Here the Viet Cong killed a South Vietnamese colonel and murdered his wife and six children. And this South Vietnamese officer came home during a lull in the fighting to find the bodies of his murdered children. There was awful retribution. Here the infamous chief of the South Vietnamese National Police, General Loan, executed a captured Viet Con officer. Rough justice on a Saigon street as the charmed life of the city of Saigon come to a bloody end.[2]

The last picture was the now-famous photograph by Eddie Adams of the Associated Press. That picture won the Pulitzer Prize for spot news photography and many other awards.

Broadcasting those stills, the Huntley-Brinkley newsmen in New York

Bailey/Lichty

did not yet know that an NBC film crew in Saigon had color motion pictures of the Loan execution and those pictures could be available for the next day's program. That next day, February 2, 1968, would be the most sensational day of broadcast coverage in that sensational week of the Tet offensive, and to many observers the turning point in American opinion and policy toward the Vietnam war.

REPORTING THE LOAN STORY

By Thursday morning, Saigon time, the fighting was fierce all over the city. Particularly hard hit was Cholon, the Chinese quarter of Saigon where the Viet Cong had set up a headquarters in the Buddhist An Quang Pagoda. An NBC news crew and AP photographer Eddie Adams decided to share a car into Cholon. (The AP and NBC bureaus were adjacent on the fourth floor of the Eden building.) The NBC correspondent was Howard Tuckner, the cameramen were two Vietnamese brothers, Vo Huynh and Vo Suu, and the sound man was Le Phuc Dinh. Huynh took an Arriflex to shoot silent film. Suu carried an Auricon sound-on-film camera.

The Tuckner crew and Adams were standing in a street near the Pagoda before noon. At the far end of the block they saw several South Vietnamese Marines with a prisoner in civilian clothes. The Marines walked up toward the newsmen to present the prisoner to Brigadier General Nguyen Ngoc Loan who had taken charge of the Pagoda action. The cameramen began filming, one Vo brother on each side of the street. Huyn shot a close-up of a pistol being carried by an ARVN Marine which had been taken from the prisoner who appeared to have been beaten. Tuckner later described what happened:

> He [the captive] was not scared; he was proud. I will never forget that look when he walked up the street. General Loan took one look at him and knew he was going to get no information out of him. Loan had been through this with many prisoners. There was not one word. Loan did not try to talk to him nor to scare him. He did not wave his gun at his face or his head. He did not put the gun to his temple. He just blew his brains out.[3]

During that time Tuckner kept whispering into Suu's ear, "keep rolling, keep rolling." Eddie Adams was snapping many photographs. Later Adams wrote that as Loan's hand came up so did his camera and he just snapped by instinct.[4] The prisoner dropped to the street with blood spurting out of his head. An ARVN Marine placed a small red Viet Cong propaganda leaflet over the corpse's face. Tuckner and Adams were the only Westerners in sight. Tuckner feared that their film would be confiscated or worse. He signaled Suu to quickly change film magazines and hide the exposed footage. Tuckner stood silent as Loan walked up to him and said:

> Many Americans have been killed these last few days and many of my best Vietnamese friends. Now do your understand? Buddha will understand.[5]

The NBC crew walked away and continued shooting scenes around the Pagoda. The corpse was lifted off the pavement and thrown on a flatbed truck. The South Vietnamese forces cleared the Pagoda of Viet Cong and their hostages as the Tuckner crew filmed the action. Later Tuckner took time to write a "stand-upper" for the execution story, and his crew filmed him as he read the stand-up summary to the camera. Tuckner's summary was written to be shown after the execution film. In that stand-upper he related what Loan had said.

In the afternoon, Thursday, February 1, Tuckner and the crew returned to NBC's Saigon bureau. Ron Steinman, the bureau chief, debriefed each crew member individually. Vo Suu was sure that he had recorded the shooting on the film; Tuckner was not convinced. Steinman also talked with Eddie Adams. Now it seemed that the film report would best end with the execution and the "stand-upper" would be anticlimactic. Tuckner wrote a simple substitute narration—with several variations to provide for the possibility that not all the film was good. This narration was recorded on audio tape at the bureau. In this script the story of the pagoda fighting is played first, before the execution, in a re-ordering of actual events. Cameraman Suu wrote out captions for the film describing the material shot by shot and various technical matters for developing and editing.

Meanwhile in the next office, under the direction of Horst Faas, AP developed, printed and transmitted the Adams photo to New York. At 8:16 A.M. Thursday morning New York time it was sent out to newspapers around the country—about 11 hours after the shooting. The NBC film was still in Saigon, undeveloped.

During this period of the war, film was ordinarily sent by plane to New York for developing and editing but alternatively could be received in San Francisco, Los Angeles or less frequently Seattle or Chicago for editing and subsequent transmission via land lines if this would make a deadline for one of the evening or morning network programs. For faster transmission, the film could be sent to Tokyo, developed and edited there, and sent via Pacific satellite to New York for broadcast live or video taped. Each network had an arrangement with a Japanese broadcasting company to use Tokyo studios to originate the live and film transmissions.

Thursday the Tan Son Nhut airport was closed to commercial planes. The next flight out, a medevac taking wounded men to Japan or the U.S., would be Friday. During Tet the military provided special cars or jeeps to carry newsfilm to the airport. NBC newsmen had prepared six film stories for shipment. The undeveloped film and audio tape was in cans with scripts and additional instructions. The material was placed in the standard red burlap bags marked "NBC" in big white and black letters. By one o'clock Friday afternoon in Saigon—about 28 hours after the shooting—the Loan film was still at the bureau.

Cable connections between Saigon and Tokyo were always poor. During Tet they were worse. NBC usually had fairly good TELEX connections between Saigon and New York. Steinman sent a TELEX message to New York advising the availability of the six film stories. New York would relay the information to Tokyo. Steinman did not want to overemphasize the shock nature of the film since he was convinced that if it was as Suu insisted, the impact would be obvious. Further, he feared that the TELEX might be monitored and there was still a chance that the film might be confiscated. The following is part of his TELEX to NBC New York sent at 0537 GMT—1:37 P.M. Friday afternoon in Saigon; 12:37 A.M. Friday morning in New York.

> THE FOLLOWING IS THE SHIPPING ADVISORY. FILM HAS NOT YET BEEN SHIPPED. WHEN SHIPPED WE WILL CONFIRM FASTEST AND BEST WAY POSSIBLE. HOPEFULLY THE TELEX WILL STILL BE WORKING. SHIPPED IN THREE SEPARATE BAGS ARE FILM NUMBERS 456, 457, 458, 459, 460, AND 461.
>
> FILM NUMBER 456 IS TUCKNERS PAGODA FIGHTING. GOVERNMENT TROOPS WENT INTO THE AN QUANG PAGODA, SEAT OF BUDDHIST MILITANCE AND TRIED TO CLEAN OUT THE VIET CONG WHO HAD TAKEN IT OVER. THIS STORY IS COMPETITIVE. CBS AND ABC WERE THERE BUT WE ARE THE ONLY ONES WHO HAVE FILM ON THE EXECUTION. TUCKNER HAS WRITTEN PRODUCTION NOTES AND SCRIPT TO GO WITH SUU AND HUYNHS 720 SOF 360 SIL NORMAL. DINH WAS SOUNDMAN. NARRATION ON FULL COAT AND AUDIO TAPE. ONE WILDTAPE. CLOSER ON FILMROLL ONE AND TWO BUT READ TUCKNERS DETAILED NOTE FOR EXACT

CLOSER WE PREFER AND THINK SHOULD BE USED. THIS IS IM-
PORTANT BECAUSE WE ARE DEALING WITH A DELICATE PROB-
LEM.[6] . . . VIET CONG OPEN UP ON MARINES. THEN THE LOAN
SEGMENT. THIS IS ON SUUS SOUNDROLL AND HE THINKS HE GOT
MOST OF IT. HIS CAPTIONS IN BRIEF READ AS FOLLOWS: A VC
OFFICER WAS CAPTURED. THE TROOPS BEAT HIM, THEY BRING
HIM TO LOAN WHO IS HEAD OF SOUTH VIETNAMESE NATIONAL
POLICE. LOAN PULLS OUT HIS PISTOL, FIRES AT THE HEAD OF THE
VC, THE VC FALLS, ZOOM ON HIS HEAD, BLOOD SPRAYING OUT.
IF HE HAS IT ALL ITS STARTLING STUFF. IF HE HAS PART OF IT
ITS STILL MORE THAN ANYONE ELSE HAS. TUCKNERS COPY COV-
ERS IT IN STRAIGHT NARRATIVE WITH SOME ALTERNATIVE COPY
JUST IN CASE SOME OF THE SHOTS MAY BE DIFFERENT OR NOT
ALL THERE. I SUGGEST YOU DEVELOP ALL OF THE FOOTAGE.[7]

Just over two hours later New York sent Steinman's message on to the
Tokyo bureau. The five other stories were each described as was the Loan
story. That is, for each piece Steinman gave technical data, crew names,
synopsis, suggestions for editing, and whether the other networks had
similar film. A total of more than 4,000 feet of film was readied for
shipment, a running time of nearly two hours. From all that, less than eight
minutes would finally be broadcast on that day's *Huntley–Brinkley Report.*
This ratio of 15 to one is typical for NBC (see Table 1).

Table 1
Newsfilm from Vietnam for the Huntley-Brinkley Report of February 2, 1968

Title of Story	Film Exposed (Feet)	(Time)	Film Broadcast (Time)	Ratio (Exposed/ Broadcast)
Tuckner's Pagoda/Loan	1080	30:00	3:55	7.7 to 1
Hall's Cholon Fighting	590	16:24	——	——
Nessen's Hue Fighting	350	9:44	2:30	3.9 to 1
Arndt's Ban Me Thuot	930	25:50	1:25	20.7 to 1
Nessen's Da Nang	100	2:47	——	——
Westmoreland Briefing	1100	30:34	——	——
Totals	4150	115:19	7:40	15.0 to 1

NBC correspondent Ron Nessen had filed two of the other stories. One
was film of fighting at Hue where the enemy was holding much of the city,
and the other film of a Da Nang napalm dump destroyed by rockets.
Wilson Hall had covered the heavy fighting in the streets of Cholon and
narrated a silent film story of aftermath in the provincial capital of Ban Me

Bailey/Lichty

115

Thout shot by soundman Arndt. The last film was unnarrated footage of a news conference by General Westmoreland in which, according to the New York *Times*, he said the enemy's main effort still was to be an attack on the Marines at Khe Sanh.

At this time there was only one color film processing lab in Tokyo and it was used by the three networks. The film was processed in the order it arrived at the lab. During Tet NBC hired a grand prix motorcycle racer to speed the NBC film to the lab first.

EDITING AND BROADCAST TO THE NETWORK

Robert Northshield, executive producer of the *Huntley–Brinkley Report*, arrived at the New York office that Friday about 10 A.M. The night before he had broadcast the Adams stills. That morning he saw most of the major newspapers consensually validate his assessment of the stills. The New York *Times* printed the moment-of-death picture on the front page and reprinted it with others on page 12. The Washington *Post* printed it across five columns of the front page. The Chicago *Tribune* printed three Adams photos, but on the third page. The Los Angeles *Times* filled the three front page columns. The New York *Daily News* filled the bottom half of its front page. Several papers printed another photo nearby the Loan shot. That photo showed an ARVN officer carrying the body of one of his children murdered by the Viet Cong. The *Huntley–Brinkley Report* had broadcast that one also Thursday evening.

Northshield read the overnight cables and learned that NBC had color film of the Loan incident that might include the moment of the execution. He then placed a phone call to talk with those who could view the film.

At the Tokyo bureau were Jack Reynolds, news manager and satellite producer, and several part-time editors used regularly by the bureau. Also reinforcing the staff for the Tet and *Pueblo* stories were Ray Weiss, sent from New York to help coordinate the bureau; Fred Rheinstein, an NBC staff director and editor; and correspondent David Burrington, who had previously reported from Vietnam. Correspondent Jack Perkins, producer Bill Wordam, cameraman Grant Wolfkill and soundman Waku, just returned from Korea, also took part in the discussion.

In the discussion Northshield said that the TELEX from Saigon mentioned a zoom to a close-up of the corpse's bloody head and that would probably be in bad taste for television. Wordam assured Northshield that the film was "quite remarkable," and there was enough time "for the director to cut away before the zoom at the end of the film." He referred to the video director of the program in New York. So the film was deliberately edited long so that a final decision could be made in New York.

Another member of the NBC staff working on the film later said he thought some of the close-up should have been shown, for Americans were getting a "too sanitized" picture of the war and they should have had "their noses rubbed in" the violence and gore.

Northshield authorized use of the satellite to transmit the film to the States. The bill would be about $3,000 for a 10 minute minimum. After a late lunch Northshield called Tokyo again. The Loan film had been edited to 4:12 and was set for transport to the NHK studio along with two of the other Saigon-oriented stories. Ron Nessen's Hue report and Wilson Hall's narration of Ban Me Thuot fighting and aftermath had been selected.

The *Huntley–Brinkley Report* was fed over the NBC network twice each day. The first show was live at 6:30 P.M. Eastern time. If it went well, then a video tape was fed at 7 P.M. Changes could be made for the second feed if necessary. Northshield recalled the Friday broadcasts:

> The film came in over satellite between 6:20 and 6:30 P.M. before air-time and it was recorded routinely on tape. I saw the picture then and heard what was said over the pictures. John Chancellor happened to be in the studio that day. He saw it with me. We were both stunned, because the way it came in the general took the gun, shot him in the head, the man fell down, and we held the picture while Loan rehol-stered the gun and walked through the frame. You still see the corpse from whom blood is now gushing. So it was too much for me. Now here the interesting point is that those men in Tokyo had been looking at the rawest, roughest film anyone has ever seen. They saw it differ-ently than I did in an airconditioned control room in New York. It was too rough for me. So I said to Chancellor, "I thought that was awful rough." He could hardly speak. I said I was going to trim it off a little. So when it went on the air you saw less than what I have described. That is, as soon as the man hits the ground we went to black. It had already been established between me and the director that we would go to black after the film, which is unusual for our show. Usually we go right to the Huntley–Brinkley slide. This time we went to black for three seconds and then to the slide.

The *Huntley–Brinkley Report* typically used a title slide (logo) between a film story and a commercial break.

The program that day presented Chet Huntley with Vietnam news. He said that the Tet offensive was now five days old and heaviest fighting was at Hue. He introduced the Nessen film from there. After that, Huntley read some copy about fighting in provincial cities and introduced the Hall film from Ban Me Thout. Then Huntley was framed in the lower left of the screen with a map of Saigon at his back. He read this introduction:

A pall lay over Saigon where American and South Vietnamese forces struggle to eliminate stubborn pockets of Viet Cong resistance. The Americans even battled the enemy near the Saigon home of General Westmoreland, the American commander. There was fighting in the Cholon section, where the city's Chinese live. But the conflict was the sharpest at the An Quang Pagoda near the Saigon race track. Here via satellite is a report from NBC News correspondent Howard Tuckner on the battle for Saigon.

Tuckner's report as edited by the program's director in New York for the first feed ran 3:55. The last 17 seconds of the Tokyo-edited version were trimmed off, excluding the zoom to a close-up of the victim's head. The first 3:03 of the report was the clearing action at the Pagoda which had actually taken place after the execution. The Loan sequence itself ran only 52 seconds. The following is the narration Tuckner read over the first part of the film. Taped sounds of gunfire, shouting and other battle sound were included:

In this part of Saigon government troops were ordered to get as much revenge as possible. The fighting was only one block from the An Quang Pagoda, a Buddhist church the Viet Cong had been using as their headquarters with the reported approval of the militant Buddhist monk Tri Quang. An hour earlier Viet Cong flags had flown from these rooftops. Now snipers were up there and government troops were trying to locate their positions. Crack South Vietnamese Marines considered all civilians potential enemies. No one was above suspicion. The Viet Cong were working their way to the An Quang Pagoda and now the government troops had to clear the area no matter how high the risk. The Viet Cong were now firing from the roof of the Pagoda. For half an hour it was like this. The Viet Cong fled through the back of the Buddhist church but many others were there. Some of these are undoubtedly Viet Cong sympathizers; some are undoubtedly religious Buddists who felt the temple was the safest place to be in times like these in Saigon. The bullets had wounded at least twenty of them.

The government Marines knew that the night before the Viet Cong had held a meeting and that the Buddhists had cheered when they were told the Viet Cong were in the city to liberate Saigon.

The execution sequence followed directly. Tuckner recorded very little narration relative to that recorded above. In the first scene the prisoner was marched down the street toward NBC cameras while the ARVN Marines questioned the captive. Tuckner said, "Government troops had captured the commander of the Viet Cong commando unit." During a medium close-up of the prisoner Tuckner said, "He was roughed up badly but refused to talk." The camera tilted down to show a pistol carried by one of the Marines. Tuckner said, "A South Vietnamese officer held the pistol taken from the enemy officer." A camera angle from behind Loan, a wide angle view, showed the general drawing his own revolver and waving it to shoo away onlookers. Tuckner said, "The chief of South Vietnam's National Police Force, Brigadier General Nguyen Ngoc Loan, was waiting for him." That was the last line of narration. Loan moved around to the side of the captive and shot him directly in the side of the head. The corpse dropped to the pavement while blood spurted out his head. The time between the gun shot and the end of the film broadcast was six seconds.

If the film had been broadcast in its complete Tokyo-edited version, then the time allotted to showing the bleeding corpse dropping and on the pavement would have been 23 seconds.

The interval from the execution in Saigon to its broadcast by NBC was 46 hours.

Robert Northshield viewed the first feed of the *Huntley–Brinkley Report* that day and decided to trim another two seconds from the film for the second feed at 7 P.M.

LATER BROADCASTS OF THE FILM

Some NBC affiliate stations videotaped segments of the network newscasts for use in local news programs. There was no practical way to determine how many local stations replayed the Loan film that day. To our knowledge, the film was broadcast nationally only two other times. The first was a special edition of the *Frank McGee Report* on March 10, 1968. That broadcast reviewed Tet and introduced an upcoming series of such news summaries, *Vietnam: The War This Week*. The McGee broadcast included the following added narration:

South Vietnam's national police chief had killed a man who had been captured carrying a pistol. This was taken as sufficient evidence that he was a Viet Cong officer, so the police chief put a bullet in his brain. He's still the chief of police.

Nineteen months later, on October 7, 1969, NBC broadcast a special produced by Northshield, *From Here to the 70s*. It presented the Loan film without introduction or comment spliced among many other pieces of newsfilm from the decade.

The Adams photograph has been reprinted in many newspapers, magazines, books, posters, and broadcast on television all over the world.[8] The award of the Pulitzer Prize in spring 1969 stimulated another wave of reproduction of the Adams photograph. It is certainly one of the most widely circulated photographs in history.

One reason the NBC film of Loan was not circulated as widely as the Adams photograph was, of course, the differential natures of the print and cinematographic media. The motion film could not be presented in books or magazines.[9] Both ABC and CBS were to later refer to the Loan story on television newscasts and both displayed the AP photo.[10]

A CYBERNETIC GATEKEEPING MODEL

The production of the Loan story by NBC News provides an opportunity to apply various gatekeeping models to the process of network journalism.

In early models—best described as linear—the news editor was the object of analysis. He made private, binary, irrevocable decisions allowing portions of the news content arriving at his desk further passage toward publication. Generally, he acted on one story at a time and usually only once. Case studies and experiments often ignored even the most popularized concepts of the organization man whose behavior is a function of his position in a bureaucracy. Later studies introduced intervening variables which influenced gatekeeper behavior and noted the effect of peer groups, reference groups, formal training, informal socialization and the like— concession that the journalist was a human being after all with social and psychological determinants of his actions.

A cybernetic model, such as suggested by Robinson,[11] takes the news organization as the object of analysis. The *Huntley–Brinkley Report* was the output of formal and informal organizational processes centered at NBC News, a complex communication-decision network populated by members of a trained and socialized subculture. Input included all the events within the surveillance of the organization's reporters, cameramen, bureau managers and assistants, news and film editors.

Decisions by NBC personnel which may have appeared to be personal, individual acts were in fact governed by powerful norms. Being members of the journalistic subculture, NBC gatekeepers assessed the newsworthiness of the Loan story along traditional, identifiable standards. For example, on the exclusivity of the story, Northshield said, "We alone had the story . . . we were way ahead of the competition." This attention to the story as a scoop was reflected throughout the organization. Steinman had cabled, "CBS AND ABC WERE THERE BUT WE ARE THE ONLY ONES WHO HAVE FILM ON THE EXECUTION."

Another traditional standard of newsworthiness is a story's significance, often measured by the importance of persons involved. Northshield said:

> The one thing that matters on this program is the significance of the story. This was, in my view, a significant event. That the chief of the security police, at a time like this, in the view of certainly hundreds and eventually millions, chose to a kill a man. I think the fact that this is significant is unarguable, without question.

Northshield's judgment conformed to traditional criteria.

The journalistic subculture crosses formal organizational boundaries to influence gatekeeping decisions. Consensual validation of the newsworthiness of the film was provided by the New York *Times*, which ran the picture twice. Those editors functioned as a reference group for NBC gatekeepers.

Informal communication-decision networks operated within NBC to reduce the individuality of decision. As one example of peer influence, John Chancellor happened to view the film as it came into New York before airtime. Northshield and Chancellor had great mutual respect. They had worked together on the *Today Show* and on a Chicago newspaper years before. The two had a short conversation about the film before Northshield made his decision to edit it. While that decision was formally the executive producer's alone, the judgment of a highly respected peer worked to reduce the individuality of Northshield's action.

More formal communications-decision networks also influenced individuals in the organization. Involved in the production of this story were such matters as the organizational decision more than three years earlier to maintain a large Saigon bureau, the daily assignment made by the bureau chief, and the interaction of the reporter-cameramen-soundman— even before the event. The film editor might seem the classic gatekeeper, but this case does not support that simplistic interpretation. The Loan film story was edited by a group. *The organization was the gatekeeper.* When the story was transmitted to New York little time remained to change it before going on the air. It was possible to shorten the film, and shorten it still more for a second feed. The range of possibilities in New York were small—go or no go. Yet, this should not be perceived as a simple "gate." New York had participated in the decision-making many times. The power of the executive producer is great. This complex matter cannot be fully discussed here, but reporters, editors, producers, others know which stories are most likely to be broadcast. Each "gatekeeper" has to estimate how the program's executive producer—and even his superiors—will receive the story. A cybernetic organization functions with consideration to its environment—in this case the audience. The one standard news judgment overtly applied throughout the production of the Loan story was that of taste.[12] The film included full-color shots of spurting blood and a close-up of the dead man's face. NBC edited the film according to its estimate of the taste standards of the audience. Feedback on the audience's reaction would come only later. But the cybernetic organization functions with the help of memory—knowledge of past reactions from its audience. This conception of audience thus influences gatekeeping decisions.

What then of the possible influence of an individual journalist's political or moral value system on his decision making in the Loan case? Much has been written arguing that the professional journalist is one who controls his prejudices aiming at a goal of objectivity. Correspondent Tuckner recorded his narration to play with the film. That narration was sparse, not much more than an identification of the principals in the film and the setting. The narration ended before the execution was actually seen. Later, off the air, Tuckner freely revealed his strong personal point of view on General Loan:

> It was the responsibility of the network to broadcast that film. The film showed, at a time when all eyes were on Saigon, that although the United States went over there ostensibly to keep South Vietnam free from Communism and the Communists were accused of atrocities, that a leading figure of the Saigon government killed a man in the street without a trial.

No similar comment or interpretation had been offered by Tuckner or the anchormen on the program.

AUDIENCE REACTION

According to audience research services about 20 million people might have seen the execution film on NBC that night. Viewers from 31 different states sent 90 letters to NBC about the Loan film story.

NBC was accused of bad taste in 56 of the letters. The next most often mentioned criticism was that children might have seen the film, and more than a third of the letters were from parents of young children who had seen the film.

A questionnaire sent the letter writers in April 1968 was returned by 69 respondents. Those who wrote were more likely to be politically active—as judged by membership in organizations, the signing or circulation of petitions, campaigning for political candidates, and other measurements. Of the respondents 61% said that the Vietnam war was a mistake—the same figure for the U.S. reported by Gallup in May 1968.

The analysis of the NBC gatekeeping decisions in preparing this film indicates most discussion was about taste in editing the film. An analysis of letters written to NBC, and questionnaires returned by the letter writers, shows that viewers objected most often to the film as being in bad taste.

Interestingly few persons referred to the Vietnam war in their letters or in responding to the questionnaire. Only four said that the film showed a "true picture" of the war but no one questioned the truthfulness of the NBC film.

NOTES

1. For a detailed analysis of Tet and its impact on American opinion and policy, see Don Oberdorfer, *TET!* (New York: Doubleday, 1971). Oberdorfer calls the Loan story "one of the most powerful ever shown by television news." His section entitled "The Flight of a Single Bullet," pp. 161–171, is based in part on the manuscript for this article.
2. *Webster's Seventh New Collegiate Dictionary* defines "rough" as (2b) "characterized by harshness, violence, or force" and (4b) "executed hastily, tentatively, or imperfectly."
3. Unless otherwise noted, all quotations are from personal interviews or correspondence as follows:
   Howard Tuckner, ABC News—earlier NBC News—interviewed by Bailey and Lichty, Madison, Wisconsin, June 26, 1969.

Robert Northshield, John Chancellor and Jack Perkins, all NBC News, interviewed by Bailey, Milwaukee, Wisconsin, March 31, 1968.

Vo Suu, Vo Huynh, and Ron Steinman, all NBC News, interviewed by Lichty, Saigon, Vietnam, July, 1968.

Jack Reynolds, NBC News, and Roger Peterson, ABC News, interviewed by Lichty, Tokyo, Japan, July, 1968.

David Burrington and Jack Perkins, both NBC News, interviewed by Lichty, New York, June, 1969.

Bill Brannigan, ABC News, letter to Lichty, January, 1970.

Edward Adams, Associated Press, New York, reply to letter from Lichty, August, 1970.

Harold Buell, executive newsphoto editor, Associated Press, letter to Lichty, September 2, 1970.

Ron Steinman, NBC News, London, letters to Lichty, September 3, 1970 and August 10, 1971.

Jack Reynolds, NBC News, Hong Kong, letter to Lichty, September 17, 1970.

Roger Peterson, ABC News, interviewed by Lichty, Washington, D.C., November 6, 1970.

4. Eddie Adams, "They Had Killed . . . Many of My Men," *Editor & Publisher,* February 10, 1963, p. 9.

5. Tuckner provided the quotation to the wire services that day and it was printed in several slightly varying versions. The version here is as remembered by Tuckner several months after the event.

6. Some technical jargon may need explanations: 720 and 360 are numbers of feet of film. SOF means sound-on-film, that is, taping sound and exposing film simultaneously on the strip of magnetic-coated film. A wildtape is an audio tape of sounds not synchronized with particular film footage.

7. TELEX, NBC News Saigon to NBC New York, 0537 Greenwich Mean Time, February 2, 1968. Provided by NBC. We are especially grateful for the cooperation of Robert Northshield in obtaining this correspondence and much other material.

8. The NBC film was distributed to foreign news organizations. The BBC chose to not show the film but televised the AP still. A frame-by-frame analysis of the Loan film shows that the precise instant of the gun shot is *not* on film. Just as Loan raised his arm to fire, someone stepped across the front of the camera lens. The view was blocked for seven frames (about ¼ of a second). In motion, however, the film does appear to show the complete action of the shooting.

9. An interesting example of this is Erik Barnouw, *The Image Empire: A History of Broadcasting in the United States from 1953,* (New York: Oxford University Press, 1970). The Adams still is shown and it is noted that "some Congressmen considered television use of photo in bad taste." There is no mention of the NBC film.

However, the NBC film has been widely shown within at least two fiction films. in Ingmar Bergman's *Passions of Anna* a man and a woman are watching television when the NBC story is broadcast. The Loan sequence is shown, including parts edited out of the network newscast. Later in his film Bergman builds parallels to the NBC footage.

The Peter Sellers/Ringo Starr film *Magic Christian* also makes use of the newsfilm: a character is watching television, and a whole series of violent footage is shown. The Loan sequence is included in that footage, but only the few seconds showing the actual shooting.

Other artists have adapted the news story for their purposes. Elliott Baker's novel *Pocock & Pitt* (New York: Viking, 1969), includes an episode beginning, "Wendell Pocock had his first heart attack on the second day of February, 1968, while watching the seven o'clock news." The character had become hardened and insensitive to Vietnam news, but the Loan film triggers his heart attack.

And General Loan himself was caught up in this ripple effect in the mass media. He became a celebrity of sorts, his actions newsworthy however slight their significance. For example, in December of 1972 the AP reported that Loan was seen visiting crippled children in orphanages. See especially Tom Buckley's "Portrait of An Aging Despot," *Harper's* April 1972, p. 68.

10. ABC did not have a correspondent at the scene but did have a film cameraman. That film was edited in Tokyo by bureau chief Roger Peterson. The film ran 1:55 and with voice over narration by Peterson was sent via satellite. ABC did not have the moment of the gun shot on the film—only the walk leading up to it, and the bleeding corpse on the ground and then thrown on a truck. At the point in the film where the shot occurred ABC-TV in New York cut from the color motion picture film to the AP photo, and then back to film. The ABC cameraman said he was afraid of General Loan and stopped filming.

CBS had no film of the shooting, although correspondent Don Webster, and a film crew were nearby and filed a report of the Pagoda action.

11. Gertrude J. Robinson, "Foreign News Selection Is Non-Linear in Yugoslavia's Tanjug Agency," *Journalism Quarterly*, 47:340–51 (Summer 1970). Robinson also provides review of many of the major earlier gatekeeping studies.

12. Gans notes that much of TV news is on matters of taste. Herbert J. Gans, "How Well *Does* TV Present the News?" *The New York Times Magazine,* Jan 11, 1970, p. 31.

Why TV Gave a Lackluster Show in Unraveling the Watergate Mystery

DAN RATHER

Reprinted from *Los Angeles Times,* December 30, 1973. Copyright by Dan Rather. Used by permission. Dan Rather, former chief CBS White House correspondent, is now chief correspondent for *CBS Reports.* He is co-author of *The Palace Guard* published by Harper & Row in 1974.

Broadcast journalism's performance in the investigation of Watergate and related crimes was poor. But the coverage of the Senate's Watergate hearings was excellent. We in the profession are still searching for the reasons why.

Rather

125

It is not true that television and radio were slow to get onto the Watergate story. The day police arrested burglars at Watergate, CBS News recognized it as a story, as a possible major story, and that day we jumped all over it. The break-in was a lead story in the CBS Saturday news.

Wire services carried a few short reports, but they were playing it down. The *Washington Post* printed nothing about the break-in that morning. The *Post* later covered itself in glory on the story, badly beating us and everyone else in the business, but the day of the break-in, the *Post* didn't have a line. Neither did most other papers. None of our competing networks led with the story.

After all was said and done, CBS News won two Emmy awards for its Watergate coverage. But we knew we were a distant second-best to the *Post* and that what we had done wasn't nearly as good as it could and should have been.

We delivered a little that summer but not much. We worked our tails thin. But facts and people who knew anything remained, for us, scarce.

By September, the feeling of frustration led to formation of a special unit to coordinate efforts to come up with new ways of attacking the story. Money was set loose from the budget and personnel added to make the unit what Walter Cronkite wanted it to be.

Still, as September faded into October, we were able to turn up little. Many rumors, few facts. CBS News was putting some stories about Watergate on the air, more than our broadcast competitors, but pitifully few compared to what we were spending in money, time and effort.

So why were we failing? Looking back on it, these are some of the reasons:

1. The deadly daily diet of deceit sent us from the White House. Those dishing this out believed that if the Watergate story could be limited to the *Post*, it could be contained and kept from spreading. They knew that if the networks ever really got onto this story and started running with it, the jig would be up. They lied, schemed, threatened and cajoled to prevent network correspondents from getting a handle on the story. And they succeeded.

2. The average network news correspondent has a heavy load of built-in daily broadcast responsibilities: hourly radio reports and television inserts for which preparation, including writing and technical logistics, eats up an incredible amount of time. Newspapermen usually have deadlines once a day. Broadcast reporters often have them one an hour or more. This tends to make us best at covering breaking

stories, i.e., events as they happen. It tends to make us less than best at piecing together complicated exposés.

3. None of us had the sense, the luck or the courage early enough to remove ourselves from the hully-gully of hour-by-hour daily coverage of our usual run of stories to concentrate—gamble might be the better word—upon the Watergate story actually being what we suspected it could be.

4. We didn't have reporters with long-standing contacts in the local police beat, and even as the story began unfolding, not enough effort was made to develop police department contacts.

5. What we do the most of, and in many ways what we do best, is provide a national headline service for radio and television. We do other things—try to tell stories in depth with documentaries, for example—and sometimes we do these other things well. But by and large, we are a headline service. Getting news that people need and want to know fast and right is the first general order. Getting all the news, digging really deep and long behind the headlines, ranks below that.

But even had CBS News or any other network done the digging that the *Post* did, we perhaps could not have communicated the story itself so well. It might have been possible in a series of documentaries, but the day-to-day labyrinthine developments were too much for a regularly scheduled radio and television newscast to handle.

Newspapers and magazines simply are superior to television and radio in some forms of communication, and one of those forms is lengthy exposé.

6. Finally, and most damnably, we were not skeptical enough. I for one simply had difficulty believing that so many people in positions of high trust could and would lie so flatly about so much, so effectively, for so long.

And some of us, bred in the cautious journalistic tradition of being able to prove beyond a reasonable doubt all you print or broadcast, may have been too cautious and may have demanded too much proof.

As the '72 campaign droned into its final weeks, many of us at CBS News were increasingly wary of being sucked into televising stories about Watergate that did not meet our minimum standards for proof.

What we wanted on the Watergate story were facts and confirmed testimony developed on our own. Try as we did, for all the reasons I have outlined—and more—we still did not in mid-October have much of either.

Taking what we had developed on our own plus what the *Post* and others had reported, we finally put together two "documentaryettes" for the evening news during the last two weeks of October.

Since neither of the other two networks was doing anything on the air with the story and White House pressure was tremendous against us, the airing of these two segments took guts.

Charles (Chuck) Colson was furious at CBS for broadcasting the two Watergate story reviews on the evening news before the election. He, John Ehrlichman, Bob Haldeman, Dwight Chapin, and Ronald Ziegler, among others, had tried their best to lead us away from the story.

By late 1972, CBS News decided to redouble its efforts to do more investigating of the whole Watergate affair. Many of us felt humbled by what we now know to have been a successful campaign of lying and cover-up by somebody very high in government. But it wasn't until live broadcast coverage of the Senate Watergate hearings began in mid-1973 that we began to feel good about what we were doing.

Coverage of live events is one of the things television and radio does best. Putting viewers and listeners there on the scene at a nominating convention, a moon landing, on the top of a hurricane or even in the street after a presidential assassination, this is what television does incomparably.

The *Washington Post* or any other newspaper can devote page after page to what it is like and what people say at a Senate hearing and still miss the essence of what happened, still fail to convey the tone, mood and nuance of the event.

The live television Senate Watergate hearings were a gradual course in civics and political science. They're among television's finest hours. They are broadcast journalism at its prime; no less, and in some ways more, than the Army-McCarthy hearings of the '50s.

So what have we learned, those of us in and out of journalism?

That although we need to pay no less attention to being a headline service, we need to pay more attention to the ways and means of reporting important stories in depth.

That we need to think less about our roles as microphone and camera stars and more about being investigators. A reemphasis on reporting fundamentals all around would be a start.

That organizationally we need more thought about how better to spend our time—how to have reporters less involved in technical arrangements and logistics, and more involved in actual reporting.

That more skepticism should be encouraged in every reporter on the payroll—not cynicism, but skepticism, especially when dealing with people in power.

Pooled Coverage: Small Step to TV News Breakthrough

FRED W. FRIENDLY

Reprinted with permission of Fred W. Friendly. Speech delivered as University Lecturer at the University of Michigan, March 10, 1971. Fred W. Friendly, former president of CBS News, is Edward R. Murrow professor of broadcast journalism at Columbia and television adviser to the president of the Ford Foundation.

Broadcast news, in its frenetic drive to cut costs, is in danger of cutting away vital bone structure rather than fatty tissue. To discharge veteran correspondents, producers, and cameramen, to cut back on documentaries while lumbering along with outmoded and sluggish methods of newsgathering is not only costly; it ignores the experiences of a decade.

That television news suffers from overexposure and underdevelopment is certainly not due to any professional inadequacy. It is due to an awkward and often archaic system of newsgathering which favors bulk footage and costly duplication, frequently at the expense of interpretive and investigative reporting. Overkill in journalism, as in war, is counterproductive.

The spectacle of a half dozen camera crews and a dozen microphones, several from the same organization, standing tripod to tripod at Andrews Air Force Base to witness the Secretary of Defense's routine departure for a NATO meeting, or to cover S. I. Hayakawa's, Abbie Hoffman's, or George Wallace's latest news conference, often says more about the newsgatherers than it does about the news makers. Such events have news value more because they illustrate the fact that the profession must repeatedly commit its best troops to the urgent rather than to the important

Friendly

129

in order to avoid being scooped. The price for such overkill is often paid by missing truly significant stories.

I do not believe that most news directors are afflicted with an unquenchable thirst for violence, or that they are addicted to what Vice President Agnew calls "the irrational driving out the rational in pursuit of controversy." What haunts news directors in their decision-making is the cruel reality that the editor who travels the high road risks being upstaged by the sensational or the bizarre. There are just too many newsworthy events for the available news teams. Duplication in the illusion of competitiveness is a luxury that is sapping the profession of its noblest efforts, depriving the public of its right to know and providing broadcast critics with an exploitable issue.

My purpose is to stimulate a dialogue that may result in a serious study of a more effective use of the manpower, equipment, and funds now available to broadcast news organizations. My proposal is to study the feasibility of creating a nationwide electronic news service. Such a news service would not stifle competition anymore than it did in 1848 when AP wigwags told its members that General Zachary Taylor had won the Whig nomination from Henry Clay. An electronic news service would provide broader and deeper coverage. Joint coverage of noncompetitive events would free the correspondents and cameramen for those enterprise assignments which are the very essence of comprehensive, truly competitive journalism. It would free journalists to report news rather than just cover events whose agenda is so often set by publicists. It would make them explainers of complicated issues rather than what a veteran Washington news hand calls journalistic stenographers.

The weekly news budget for Washington, D.C., provides a useful example of the problem, the challenge, and the opportunity. The daybook of assignments for Feb. 24 [1971] in Washington shows an average of about thirty-eight reasonable assignments. They range all the way from fifteen Congressional hearings, two White House briefings, a John Mitchell news conference on drugs, and a Melvin Laird news conference on Vietnam to one with Ralph Abernathy of the Southern Christian Leadership Conference. The daybook also included a news conference with the president of the National Farmers Union, a speech by Congressman Charles Rangel, and the opening session of the National Governors Conference.

The three major networks, with five to seven available crews, plus UPI, which serves some nine independent TV stations, must each evening determine which ten to twelve stories they will cover. That decision automatically eliminates some twenty-five or thirty stories. A correspondent, often doubling as arranger-producer, accompanies the crew. Although his assignment is every bit as challenging as that of his newspaper and magazine rivals, his additional production obligations are sometimes undertaken at the cost of content. How much more effective and efficient it would be if the major news organizations set up a common assignment desk utilizing a combined resource of fifteen crews to cover twenty or twenty-five different events. Each news organization would be protected from the embarrassment of missing that routine story which suddenly becomes vital, and various correspondents would be freer to dig, to investigate, to report.

Of course there could and should be unilateral coverage. Just because the point of view of the camera lens is the same does not mean that the reporting must be uniform. The camera coverage of the John Mitchell news conference on drugs and Melvin Laird's display of the pipeline liberated from the Ho Chi Minh trail ostensibly during the recent incursion was interpreted differently on all three networks even though the pictures were virtually the same. A network with a special interest in a particular story would have more equipment and more staff available for that interview or that special coverage.

One major Washington broadcast news bureau (not the one I used to work with) has an annual film budget of more than $2 million. I am told that less than 25 per cent of it is earmarked for enterprise, nonroutine coverage.

Film coverage will continue, but more and more the state of the technological art indicates that electronic videcon cameras, live and taped, will be the method of news collection. Senate and House hearings particularly lend themselves to pooled electronic coverage. There is every reason to believe that, as miniaturization and true mobility of equipment improve, a half dozen or more daily videotape remotes may be on the Washington assignment list. And public television, with its implicit virtue of additional and more flexible air time, will provide an increasingly valuable outlet in the utilization and production of some of these pooled Washington happenings. As more and more House hearings open up for

TV coverage—as, in fact, coverage of actual Senate and House chamber hearings become a reality—some kind of Washington joint production and distribution will become mandatory.

I am not proposing establishment of a super news agency, but rather a coordinator of assignments who would daily commit available camera crews to the widest variety of news happenings. Maximization of coverage and minimization of duplication would be his chief goal. Wire services by themselves never made a great newspaper, and may have even sapped a few of their vigor. Should broadcast news organizations depend exclusively on such a service, the whole concept would be counterproductive. What is required are more voices—more stories covered comprehensively—not mountains of film magazines of virtually identical footage.

Should a Washington experiment be judged successful, the concept then could be projected regionally and nationally. In addition to Washington, CBS News has bureaus only in New York, Atlanta, Chicago, and Los Angeles; NBC in New York, Cleveland, Chicago, Los Angeles, and Washington; ABC in New York, Washington, Chicago, Atlanta, Miami, and Los Angeles. Each network, of course, has local, affiliated news organizations, but performance varies, and the method of transmission to New York is cumbersome and expensive.

At the network bureau level the duplication in major cities is costly, not only in assignments unattended but also in the triplication of long lines to pipe what is basically the same story over the same expensive telephone lines to New York. For example, Mayor Daley, announcing that he is or is not going to run a fifth term as Mayor, would probably have six NBC, CBS, and ABC camera crews, plus an even larger number of radio tape crews all covering his news conference. Under present practices they would use three overpriced electronic lines to New York, while a half dozen or more important Midwestern stories went uncovered. An electronic news service could provide the network news divisions and independent stations with an even broader selection of raw material than now.

As the major wire services are now connected by a network of high-speed teletype machines, the Broadcast News Service or Television News Service or whatever its name would be connected for an hour a day, perhaps two hours some days, with microwave or satellite circuits. At a given time—perhaps at 4 every afternoon and 9:30 every evening—a daily budget of film and electronic pieces, including the choice of perhaps a dozen Washington stories, would be fed into the service. The feeds would not be one- or two-minute takes of the Secretary of State or the Armed Forces hearing, but conceivably four or five different segments or a ten-minute highlight from which each news producer could make his own selection.

This technique of shared time is now used on international satellite transmissions from Vietnam and the Middle East. In Europe, member broadcasters of the European Broadcasting Union have a daily news transmission. Generally, this is among a consortium of noncompetitive, often state-funded news organizations, and the land distances are much shorter. But there are many lessons in the activities of EBU, and they should be analyzed.

Should a North American news service be successful it could have daily exchanges with similar organizations in Europe and on other continents. The advantages and opportunities for foreign news coverage are, of course, obvious. Currently each of the three American networks has limited coverage in five or six different capitals—generally the same five or six. By pooling camera crews it could double or triple the nations covered; it might even enable the networks to have bureaus in Africa and South America.

Who would operate such a system? How would it be financed? Preliminary judgment suggests a consortium of users who would form a nonprofit organization similar to Associated Press or the News Election Service. They might include the major commercial networks, public television, and those independent stations which desire to fulfill their public service requirements, possibly together with UPI-TN, and Viz. News, the British Commonwealth News Service which exchanges with NBC News.

The current organization of NES might provide a useful model. NES came into being after the 1964 Goldwater-Rockefeller California primary when CBS, NBC, and ABC, in the name of competition and gamesmanship, permitted vote-counting machinery to escalate to the point where each was employing 22,000 to 24,000 workers to count some 25,000 precincts. Two days after that election, representatives of the three networks and AP and UPI met in my office. The result was the Network Election Service, now called News Election Service, which in every major election since then has provided swift, effective coverage.

Some lawyers raised the alarm then, as they may now, of the danger of antitrust action from the Justice Department or of reservations on the part of the Federal Communications Commission. The Justice Department's initial reaction and its ultimate conclusion after study was that the American electorate would be better served and that, far from restricting competition, pooling of noncompetitive services would free news organizations, their correspondents, and producers for that crucial journalism where competition *could* make a difference. History has continued to be on the side of NES; I think history and the law will be on the side of the broadcasters news service for the same reasons, including the stipulation that no one willing to pay his share would be excluded.

There may be early opposition from some unions. But I am convinced an economic study will reveal that, although there might be some reassignment of contracts and responsibilities, the more effective distribution of manpower would in the long run better serve all.

Changes and improvements in broadcast journalism have never come easily. In the thirties CBS and NBC News were really born when the wire services made the grievous error of shutting off their service to broadcasters. A decade later the ban on recordings that so restricted World War II combat coverage was finally broken, not because of the protest of Ed Murrow, who always had to work live with a censor beside him, but because Bing Crosby wanted to be free to record Kraft Music Hall broadcasts in advance. Then there were those excesses of election night which ended several years later than necessary, and then the pool coverage of some of the noncompetitive portions of space broadcasts.

The opportunity for an electronic news service exists now because the technology is right; because there is a restiveness among some serious observers about the price we may be paying for overkill in the name of Front Page competition; and because the broadcast industry, no longer the fat cat it once was, cannot afford to waste either its resources or time.

The place to begin is Washington. Bill Small called his book about broadcasting from the capital *To Kill a Messenger*. This proposal is intended to liberate that messenger, to get him off that ancient motorcycle caught in a traffic jam racing his rivals to the airport—and permit him to concentrate on the content of his mission.

Editing in the Electronic Media: An Exchange of Opinion

RICHARD S. SALANT (CBS) and
THE WASHINGTON POST STAFF WRITERS

Reprinted with permission of copyright holder *The Washington Post* from Laura Longley Babb, ed., "Editing in the Electronic Media: A Documentary Dispute," *Of the Press, by the Press, and For the Press (And Others, Too)*, The Washington Post Company, 1974, Dell edition. Richard S. Salant is president of CBS News in New York.

CBS COMMENTS–Letter to the POST from Salant

This letter is in response to your editorial of March 26, in which you start by calling the CBS News documentary, *The Selling of the Pentagon*, a "highly valuable and informative exposition of a subject about which the American people should know more," and then proceed to examine in some detail the specific editing of that film and general practices of television news editing technique.

The editorial was obviously written by one who has long labored on the editorial page—and not on the news pages.

You conclude that in some measure (not specified) public confidence and credibility are undermined by our editing techniques "innocent or not."

The question of how a news or documentary broadcast is edited is at least as important as you obviously consider it. It is precisely as important as, and possibly no more complicated than, questions pertaining to editing in the print medium (newspapers and news magazines)—the process by which any journalist rejects or accepts, selects and omits, and almost always compresses material available to him. You do not question the right, indeed the professional obligation of your reporters to do this, nor of your editors to continue the process once the reporter has done his job, nor indeed, of your senior editors to impose their professional judgment upon this same piece of work when or if it comes to them.

But you question not only our right to do the same thing, but also the methods by which we edit, and even our motives ("innocent or not"). You do not, in other words, grant us the right to do precisely what you do—and must do if you are journalists as distinguished from transmission belts.

Why?

Salant/Post Staff

135

The key to why you feel this way is spelled out in your editorial: "People who work in the nonelectronic news business know how readily they themselves may distort an event or a remark . . . these dangers are of course multiplied in the production of a televised documentary."

You are saying that good reporting—fair reporting—is a difficult business, with many pitfalls along the way, that television reporting is a more difficult business with more pitfalls. Fair enough.

Then you go on to suggest, indeed recommend, that our rules should be different than your rules, that sound journalistic ethics and the First Amendment are somehow divisible between rights granted to journalists whose work comes out in ink and somewhat lesser rights for journalists whose work comes out electronically. You say we should go out of our way to "preserve intact and in sequence" the response of those we interview. We both "go out of our way" to be fair and accurate, but we both have limitations of space, and we both seek clarity. Except in verbatim transcripts, neither medium preserves intact or in sequence everything it presents. You say at the very least we should indicate that something in the interview has been dropped. If we asked you to do this, you would properly respond that readers know, without a blizzard of asterisks, that material in your paper is edited, that these are not the complete remarks. Our viewers know it, too. And so do those whom we cover.

But most astonishing of all, you propose that we should give the subject of the interview an opportunity to see and approve his revised remarks. Is that now the policy at the *Washington Post*? Of course not. You know and I know that this strikes at the very core of independent and free journalism. To grant a subject such a right of review is to remove the basic journalistic function of editing from the hands of the journalist and place it—in the case of the documentary in question—in the hands of the Pentagon. I almost wrote—"tell you what, we'll do [it] if you'll do it." Then I had a second thought: No, we won't do it even if you should do it.

We are all after the same thing: to be fair, to inform the public fairly and honestly. We do not suggest that we—or any journalistic organization —are free from errors, but nothing in the First Amendment suggests that we must be perfect, or that we are not human. And nothing suggests that if our responsibility is larger, our job tougher or our coverage broader there should be some new set of rules for our kind of journalism, as if to say the First Amendment is fine so long as it doesn't count for much. You don't seem to mind if our end of the dinghy sinks, so long as yours stays afloat.

Fairness is at the root of all this, and fairness can be and always will be debated.

But I submit that we are as careful about editing, as concerned with what is fair and proper and in balance, as rigorous in our internal screening and editorial control processes as any journalistic organization.

The job of ensuring that fairness, that balance and that sense of responsibility is difficult. It is the subject of our constant review and concern. It is not a question that can be solved by a single statement of policy or staff memorandum. It must be, and it is, the daily concern of our working reporters, editors and management.

We believe, as I have said publicly before, that *The Selling of the Pentagon* was edited fairly and honestly. Long after the useful and valuable debate on this broadcast has subsided and perhaps been forgotten, we shall be editing other news broadcasts and other documentaries as fairly and as honestly as we know how, and in accordance with established journalistic practice—just as you shall be so editing.

The POST Comments

In time the U.N. may have to be called in to arbitrate the burgeoning dispute over the CBS documentary *The Selling of the Pentagon,* but for now we would like, in a unilateral action, to respond to the complaint of Richard Salant of CBS News.

We think it is off the point. And we think this is so because Mr. Salant invests the term "editing" with functions and freedoms well beyond anything we regard as common or acceptable practice. Mr Salant taxes us with unfairly recommending two sets of standards in these matters, one for the printed press and another for the electronic. But he reads us wrong. We were and are objecting to the fact that *specifically, in relation to question-and-answer sequences,* two sets of standards *already* exist—and that what he and others in television appear to regard as simple "editing" seems to us to take an excess of unacknowledged liberties with the direct quotations of the principals involved.

Before we go into these, a word might be of use about the editorial practices (and malpractices) common to us both. When a public official or anyone else issues a statement or responds to a series of questions in an interview, the printed media of course exercise an editorial judgment in deciding which part and how much of that material to quote or paraphrase or ignore. The analogy with TV's time limitations, for us, is the limit on space: deciding which of the half million words of news coming into this paper each day shall be among the 80,000 we have room to print. Thus, "Vice President Agnew said last night . . . Mr. Agnew also said . . ." and so on; it is a formulation basic to both the daily paper and the televised newscast.

That bad and misleading judgments can be made by this newspaper in both our presentation and selection of such news goes without saying—or at least it did until we started doing some public soul-searching about it in this newspaper a good while back. There is, for example, a distorting effect in failing to report that certain statements were not unsolicited assertions but responses to a reporter's question. But that we do not confuse the effort to remedy these defects with a waiving of our First Amendment rights or a yielding up of editorial prerogatives should also be obvious to readers of this newspaper—perhaps tediously so by now. What we have in mind, however, when we talk of the license taken by the electronic media in the name of "editing" is something quite different, something this newspaper does not approve and would not leap to defend if it were caught doing. It is the practice of printing highly rearranged material in a Q-and-A sequence as if it were verbatim text, without indicating to the reader that changes had been made and/or without giving the subject an opportunity to approve revisions in the original exchange.

It is, for instance, presenting as a direct six-sentence quotation from a colonel, a "statement" composed of a first sentence from page 55 of his prepared text, followed by a second sentence from page 36, followed by a third and fourth from page 48, and a fifth from page 73, and a sixth from page 88. That occurred in *The Selling of the Pentagon*, and we do not see why Mr. Salant should find it difficult to grant that this type of procedure is (1) not "editing" in any conventional sense and (2) likely to undermine both the broadcast's credibility and public confidence in that credibility.

The point here is that *The Selling of the Pentagon* presented this statement as if it were one that had actually been made—verbatim—by the colonel: TV can and does simulate an impression of actuality in the way it conveys such rearranged material. Consider, again from the same documentary, a sequence with Daniel Z. Henkin, Assistant Secretary of Defense for Public Affairs. This is how viewers were *shown* Mr. Henkin answering a question:

138

Roger Mudd: What about your public displays of military equipment at state fairs and shopping centers? What purpose does that serve?

Mr. Henkin: Well, I think it serves the purpose of informing the public about their armed forces. I believe the American public has the right to request information about the armed forces, to have speakers come before them, to ask questions, and to understand the need for our armed forces, why we ask for the funds that we do ask for, how we spend these funds, what are we doing about such problems as drugs—and we do have a drug problem in the armed forces; what are we doing about the racial problem—and we do have a racial problem. I think the public has a valid right to ask these questions.

This, on the other hand, is how Mr. Henkin *actually* answered the question:

Mr. Henkin: Well, I think it serves the purpose of informing the public about their armed forces. It also has the ancillary benefit, I would hope, of stimulating interest in recruiting as we move or try to move to zero draft calls and increased reliance on volunteers for our armed forces. I think it is very important that the American youth have an opportunity to learn about the armed forces.

The answer Mr. Henkin was *shown* to be giving had been transposed from his answer to another question a couple of pages along in the transcribed interview, and one that came out of a sequence dealing not just with military displays but also with the availability of military speakers. At that point in the interview, Roger Mudd asked Mr. Henkin whether the sort of thing he was now talking about—drug problems and racial problems—was "the sort of information that gets passed at state fairs by sergeants who are standing next to rockets." To which Mr. Henkin replied:

Mr. Henkin: No, I didn't—wouldn't limit that to sergeants standing next to any kind of exhibits. I knew—I thought we were discussing speeches and all.

This is how the sequence was *shown* to have occurred, following on Mr. Henkin's transposed reply to the original question:

Mr. Mudd: Well, is that the sort of information about the drug problem you have and the racial problem you have and the budget problems you have—is that the sort of information that gets passed out at state fairs by sergeants who are standing next to rockets?

Mr. Henkin: No, I wouldn't limit that to sergeants next to any kind of exhibit. Now, there are those who contend that this is propaganda. I do not agree with this.

The part about discussing "speeches and all" had been omitted; the part about propaganda comes from a few lines above Mr. Henkin's actual answer and was in fact a reference to charges that the Pentagon was using talk of the "increasing Soviet threat" as propaganda to influence the size of the military budget.

Surely, something different from and less cosmic than a challenge to CBS's First Amendment rights is involved in the question of whether or not the subject of such a rearranged interview should not be given a chance to see and approve what he will be demonstrated to have said. And surely this "editing" practice must be conceded—with reason—to have damaging effects on public confidence in what is being shown to have happened— shown to have been said. We agree with Mr. Salant's premise that we are all in the same dinghy. That is why we are so concerned that neither end should sink.

Local Television News in 31 Different Flavors

HALINA J. CZERNIEJEWSKI
and CHARLES LONG

Reprinted from *The Quill,* vol. 62, 5 (May, 1974), published by The Society of Professional Journalists, Sigma Delta Chi, with permission of the publisher. Copyright 1974 by *The Quill.* Halina J. Czerniejewski is news editor of *The Quill;* Charles Long is editor.

THE HAPPY MEDIUM

Early this year, a curious phenomenon made its way into the homes of television viewers in Columbus, Ohio. It had happened in New York, Chicago, San Francisco, Los Angeles—where strange things are supposed to happen. But now, it was in Middle America City, U.S.A.

WLWC decided to make a go of it with its own version of the misnomered "happy talk" news format. It was presenting The DeMoss Report with anchorman Hugh DeMoss, sportscaster Jimmy Crum, weatherman Jerry Rasor and his buddy, a bear.

It was Rasor's idea to get the bear. One evening, led by his trainer, the bear ambled up to the anchordesk, put his paws up and introduced himself to the startled DeMoss and Crum. They say Rasor's a pretty funny guy. But he didn't invite the bear back. Instead, on another night, a leprechaun followed Rasor around while he did the weather report. And not too long ago, the Golddiggers helped him give the highs and lows and predict the probability of precipitation.

Rasor and company were not the only ones getting into the act. The usually straight, no-nonsense DeMoss was no longer following the script. He was making conversation with Crum, Rasor and others on the set. The newscast was peppered with a few humorous and not so humorous remarks, some embarrassed and embarrassing pauses, and a few bad starts.

Was this the return of the "Amateur Hour?" The cards and letters were coming in. And the critics were aghast. No, it was just Avco Broadcasting's attempt to snatch some of the elusive, fickle Nielsen points. And executive news producer Scott Lynch was pleased because it was working.

Although the latest Nielsen ratings indicated WLWC was still No. 2, "we are now in an extremely competitive position with the No. 1 station," Lynch said.

This called for a toast. Nielsen ratings are the bread and butter of a television station. The higher a rating a station has, the more viewers it has, the more advertisers will want to advertise, the more a station can get for the advertisements, and hopefully, the more the station can pour back into its news operation.

Lynch was one of many television producers finding out what some of the larger markets had already known—the viewers were ready for a new television news format.

As *Chicago Tribune* television critic Gary Deeb wrote in a recent column: "TV was long overdue for a change from the tired local news format that found a somber, granite-faced anchorman delivering the news as if he were reading it off stone tablets. There was a godlike, Doomsday quality attached to many local anchormen that was patently ridiculous."

"Viewers are not going for the formality or staginess of the past," says

Sam Zelman, CBS vice president for the network's owned-and-operated (O&O) stations. "They want people to level with them."

There are different ways a news team levels with the viewers, producers decided. One way was Eyewitness News.

"In New York, the Eyewitness News concept began in November 1968. Nobody came into the situation with a format in his backpocket," says Al Primo, vice president of news for the ABC O&O stations and a pioneer in Eyewitness format when he was news director for WABC, New York.

"What we were trying to do was to allow these reporters to come in and tell their own stories, to appear live." Primo's idea is that "the best way to do a news program is to have the reporter who covers a story tell that story to an audience, eliminating all of the middle men in the process. What I knew we didn't want to have was reporters going out, preparing a story, sending the film in, turning it over to a writer who was never at the scene, who then re-edited it, rewrote it, and gave it to the anchorman who read it.

"What we in effect were doing was telling our audience that we had more than three people covering New York. The audience suddenly knew that we were going to send our people out to cover a story and come back and tell them that story directly," Primo says.

The idea caught on. Many ABC affiliates took up the format and got their reporters on the air. And they entitled their program "Eyewitness News." Viewers all over the country were seeing field reporters who were saying, "I was there and here's what happened."

Other stations took a different tack—the Walter-Cronkite-in-the-newsroom-where-we-get-the-reports-on-what's-been-happening approach. Some stations used an on-air set that resembled a newsroom. But the purists took the cameras directly into the clatter, clutter and chaos of the womb of journalists.

"It gives the viewer the feeling of being close, not to where the news is made but to where it is put together," Columbus' Lynch says.

It's all part of using television's many potentials. TV, after all, is a very personal medium. And now, the viewers not only could get the reports and hear the reporters themselves, they could see them and where they worked. And soon, they would be seeing *how* they worked together.

NBC Vice President Robert Mulholland says it stemmed from the *Huntley–Brinkley Report*—"two people who said 'good evening' to each other and said each other's names. Most of the viewing public think that those two guys ad-libbed to each other, talked back and forth. The fact of the matter is, Chet Huntley and David Brinkley never ad-libbed to each other. Yet, in the viewer's mind, the relationship of warmth, friendliness, interest in each other, grew."

It is difficult to say whether the network or local news stations had the first on-air interaction among on-air personalities. Credit or blame for the innovation has been placed randomly throughout the country. It may have sprung up simultaneously and accidentally at several television stations.

"The casual approach developed naturally," according to Primo. "If there are more than three people in the room, you tend to develop a sort of rapport or informality with those people after a certain period."

Joel Daly, who is with the No. 1 station in Chicago, says that's the way he fell into it. When he was with a station in northern Ohio, Daly says, he and another newsman developed a friendship outside the station and their rapport became evident on the air. They would exchange comments during the newscast, or Daly would poke fun at his partner. "It was natural," he says. And the idea went over well.

Later, he and his partner were asked to go to Chicago as a team. They would carry their informal, unusual format into a larger market, the station said. Daly went. But his friend did not. The station, which wanted co-anchormen, had a problem. Could WLS find a partner for Daly who could develop a natural rapport and informality? The station finally did. But it wasn't a simple task.

"The idea is that the interaction has to be 'real,' " says Clayton Vaughn, news director for KOTV, Tulsa, Okla. "The audience is going to know if you're putting them on. They're just not going to buy it."

He says they're not buying it at KABC in Los Angeles, where Vaughn was an on-air newsman.

But KABC will keep on bringing in various persons, plugging them into the co-anchor spots until something clicks. The station is lucky, he says, because it has the money to spend to find the right combination of personalities. "If you don't have the budget . . . go with one anchor. You get rid of 80 percent of your problems that way."

Some stations, Daly says, are going about the process of personalizing their news programs the wrong way. "They look at us and they think you have to have the fatherly figure, a younger guy, a nutty weatherman and an amiable sportscaster." But, there is no formula to the personalities, he says.

Others agree. What you should have, they say, are four persons who can relate to each other on the air. But it's not a bad idea to get some people

Czerniejewski/Long

143

Your guide to happy viewing

By now you've noticed that local television news programs aren't what they used to be—carbon copies (or videotape recordings, for that matter) of each other. Knowing you might like to discuss this phenomenon at future cocktail parties or other gatherinigs journalists attend, we give you this glossary of terms to facilitate discussion. It is by no means complete, since producers could come up with something revolutionary at any time. It also does not suggest that every news program will fall neatly into one category because (1) journalists hate labels, (2) some stations think a combination of previously successful formats have a synergetic effect, (3) some stations haven't decided they want to go with any of them, or (4) all of the above. If you find none of the terms suffice, make something up.

FORMAL FORMAT (nearly obsolete)—(1) Godlike, Doomsday (2) Olympian (3) Format in which the anchorman sits in front of the camera and reads the news, the sportscaster and weatherman do same (4) No conversation between on-air personalities (5) No nonsense (6) No off-the-cuff or scripted remarks about recent haircuts, vacations, cute stories, etc.

EYEWITNESS NEWS—(1) Format in which station proves it had a reporter on the scene and the news did not come from wire services or the newspaper (2) Reporter has two minutes on camera to tell the story, preferably with appropriate background (on berm of highway for road construction story, knee-deep in water on floods, on street during lunch hour if interviewing the mayor, etc.); or reporter can be brought on newsroom set to tell anchorman the story (*see In-the-Newsroom Set*)

IN-THE-NEWSROOM SET—(1) On-air personalities reporting from their natural working habitat—the busy newsroom; include cluttered desks, ringing phones and clacking wire machines (2) Appears to the viewer to be actual newsroom, but can be staged.

INFORMAL FORMAT—(1) On-air personalities may show they have personality (2) On-air personalities permitted to look at each other and exchange comments (3) Weatherman may wear appropriate clothing to aid viewers in choosing proper garb should they wish to dash outdoors midway through the broadcast; discretion is urged when reporting on extremely warm weather (4) Weatherman must also qualify as fall guy.

HAPPY TALK (derogatory)—(1) Of the ha ha school of journalism (2) Jokes, slap-stick and other comedy spiced up with occasional reports (3) More good news than bad with marshmallow commentaries and vaudeville atmosphere.

TABLOID NEWS (very derogatory)—(1) Story or film value based on sex, sin, blood, vulgarity or deviance (2) Variation of Happy Talk whereby jokes are written by former burlesque comedians (3) No news makes good news.
—HJC

the viewers can relate to—some age and experience, some youth and idealism, friendliness, and the ever-popular "fall guy."

YUKKY WEATHER

This is usually the weatherman. He's the one who usually takes the blame for the bad news, Daly says. Daly's news director John Mies says, "Weather is not hard news. And a weatherman is not a newscaster." So John Coleman can yuk it up, but only when the weather isn't serious, Daly says.

Since the weather in Chicago is seldom good, often bad, but not serious, Coleman's got a job on his hands. To make his presentation more palatable, he's been known to stand on his head during the weather. Or, just to break up the tension, he might whip wads of paper around the studio. He has a lot of fun.

And so do other weathermen. Vaughn's forecaster in Tulsa exchanges pleasantries with a puppet. Another Chicago weatherman plays the straight man to a videotape version of himself as a fall guy. And Rasor, in Columbus, has his guest assistants. A weatherman in Albuquerque is known there for his colorful barnyard set which at one time was complete with live chickens and pigs.

What Daly and Vaughn and many others using the informal approach are concerned about is that the "real," "personal" or "human" news show presentations will inadvertently be twisted into the so-called "happy talk," or worse yet, tabloid formats.

"Happy talk" is a difficult term to define. Morry Roth is said to have coined the term when he first made observations on the new television formats for *Variety.* Television newsland was not pleased.

"The man," says Primo of Roth, "is not to be criticized for inventing it, because that magazine uses that kind of jargon. It's a show business magazine. The unfortunate thing is that it has been picked up . . . and used unsparingly."

Critic Deeb writes that "happy talk" was designed "to appeal to viewers who'd rather see more good news than bad, with a vaudeville show on the side." And he accuses Daly's station of falling into the format with "slapstick boorishness" and "marshmallow commentaries."

News Director Mies replies, "We try to make the news understandable and appealing to the audience in terms of what it means to them. . . . The audience responds to our people because we talk *to* them rather than *down* to them."

Daly says it's the dilemma of hanging onto an audience while trying to present the news.

"Television is primarily an entertainment medium," Daly says. "The news portion is 10 percent of local programming time. It exists in this environment of trivial entertainment—escape dramas, situation comedies, etc. We have to coexist in the milieu. We have to hold the viewer's attention."

Relating to the audience, he says, is a way to hold that attention. "If something human happens within the format, we should be able to react as humans—to smile, to use an aside."

"But," says Don Alloway, of the publicity department for ABC network news, "at certain times and at certain places you get out there and walk a very, very fine line between news and show biz. You've got to have a good news director and a good news team to keep the two separate."

Daly admits that sometimes the situation gets out of hand on the air. He says he didn't particularly care for the tuxedoed on-air celebration of a sixth anniversary. And there are jokes that might be unnecessary, he says. And sometimes the team has a bad night and the exchanges fall flat. But, "we try to act as we would when we are invited into someone's home—with responsibility," he says.

A PUBLIC MISUNDERSTANDING

ABC's Primo says some of the criticism of the informal format may lie with the audience. "The informality tends to come more with the sports person and the weatherman. That has been the damaging aspect. People don't distinguish this from the more serious part of (the) news program." Primo was referring to the audience, but Daly and Vaughn say there are local news producers who don't understand the purpose or design of the informal news broadcast. They are the "happy talk" stations which are giving the others a bad name, they say.

"They see us," says Daly, "and they think they've got the formula. They think they have to script it . . . that they *have* to do some jokes and gimmicks."

Lynch says when WLWC first began the new format, "we sort of overreacted." The on-air personalities felt they had to say something—

make a comment, tell a joke or one-liner. It was an uncomfortable situation, he says. "We're doing less of that now."

WLWC and other stations like it are learning what the "informality" purists are screaming about. There apparently is hope for them. But Lee Hanna, vice president of news for NBC O&O stations is worried about something else.

"The thing that disturbs me is the headlong rush to emulate, duplicate," he says. NBC O&O's are the holdouts in the trend toward informality. They have retained the formal format.

"The thing that *really* disturbs me is the proliferation of stations who depend on style rather than substance. That goes directly to this business of consultants—to go into a market to say here's a formula designed by geniuses to be carried out by idiots. Because they can say: *you* do 60 stories in 30 minutes, and *you* do this little package of film clips to be glued together with a chuckle, and make sure the chit-chat between the anchorman and the weatherman lasts 15 seconds," Hanna says.

The two major consulting firms are Frank N. Magid Associates, Iowa, and McHugh and Hoffman, Inc., Washington. They are hired by local news stations to determine what sort of audience the station has, what sort of audience it would like to have and how it can get it. Their recommendations often are based on how other stations in similar circumstances succeeded in other cities.

The consultants contend they never make any recommendations on the content of the news program—merely the packaging.

ABC's O&O's use both consulting firms, Primo says. "On our five stations, no consultant gives journalistic advice—offers none, none is taken. The job of an outside consultant is to measure the impact of your news program on the audience it serves . . . to try to question a sample of people in your audience as to their impressions of what you're doing on the station. And to try to help determine for us what they consider to be the most important problems of the community."

Primo says he doesn't think a consultant should tell a station how to make its news more entertaining. "There are some charges, perhaps well-founded, by smaller stations that consultants do in fact get involved with journalistic judgment," Primo says. "If they do, I think that's a terrible mistake. There's a fine line, here. All of us here guard very jealously our dealings with them. We do not use consultants as news directors."

GETTING TO MANAGEMENT

NBC's Hanna has no use for the consulting firms. "I have one of these monitoring reports from one of these so-called consultants, and you read that and I challenge you to find one reference to good journalism. No, it's simply the business of sort of slavishly following a formula."

Then Hanna recites a typical formula.

"The opening story must run 45 seconds, and it must be followed by three stories that run 15 seconds each, followed by something in the fast film section, then there's got to be a laugh, then there's got to be. . . . That's sickening. A client of one of these consultants will spend $40,000 or $50,000 for one of these reports. If they would spend that much on just their own operations, think about how much more they could accomplish. But this is a quick-buck sort of situation. These things don't last. I'd say it's like a Chinese meal, except I don't want to give Chinese food a bad name.

"The kind of thing Mike Wallace did on *60 Minutes,* the kind of thing Rick Townley did in *TV Guide,* those are things that might come through to station management—that they are involved in a quick, slick, fast-buck type of situation. There is no way to build a valuable, interesting, vital news operation by cosmetic kinds of solutions. You do it with good reporters, smart news directors and with film. There is a lack of enterprise, and that is what is sad."

Station WBRZ in Baton Rouge, La., used the services of Magid not too long ago. Their complaint was not that the firm was involving itself with the news.

"We got away from the formula because we found we were getting more into the 'happy talk' than into the journalism aspect," says investigative reporter John Spain. "Magid says say it even if you don't have anything to say."

That attitude is disturbing to many on-air journalists. Pity the personality who finds he or she has read through the news too quickly and is left with 12 seconds to ad-lib and nothing to say.

"The occasion has happened, yes," says Roger Grimsby, co-anchorman for New York City's top-rated station, WABC. "I've made mistakes that could be criticized as far as taste or judgment are concerned. There has been something flipped through the back of my mind and I spit it out before realizing its full implication."

Grimsby feels there is an ever-present compulsion in TV newsrooms to play "can you top this."

"A person should always remind himself that you don't have to be funny to do a good news program. If there is any humor in a program, it should be the frosting not the cake. And what was happening here (at WABC) for awhile was that even the assignment desk was trying to think funny. . . .

"However, unlike some of those who have emulated the Eyewitness News show in New York, the people on our program rarely talk to each other," Grimsby says. "It's very presumptuous, I think, that anybody at home would be interested in what your private life is like or whatever those other news people talk about. But occasionally I'll throw in a one-liner about what one of the reporters may have reported or something my co-anchorman may have said. If the line doesn't work, it's still over in such a hurry that you don't dwell on it, and it doesn't seem contrived."

But "forget all that," Grimsby says. "We should cover the news better than anyone else—and then do it differently."

The combination of the two is going to grab the audience.

"We still look upon news as something a television station does as a public service," Primo says. "That's still the basic philosophy of why we do news programs. It has never changed. . . . The other thing that has not changed is that the basic principles of journalism applied then also apply now. What has changed, and I think changed for the good, is the method of presentation.

"What we try to do is never compromise our essential product," he says.

"The primary job is to give the news," says Daly. The ha-ha school of journalism is not going to make it. "If all you have are jokes, you won't last. To think you can do it with one-liners is demeaning to the audience."

AT THE TOP OF THE HILL

Then station KGO in San Francisco must be the exception to the rule. It has the top-rated news program in the city. In fact, it has a higher rating than the other two stations put together. Saying KGO is doing it "differently" is an understatement.

Mike Wallace, on the CBS program *60 Minutes*, recently sampled KGO's format and news content. These are excerpts: "And the latest on the little old lady who looked at the male nude foldouts of Jim Brown and John Davidson and said, . . . the congressman's bill, by the way, would not outlaw massaging arms, hands and legs, but would prohibit those ladies from tickling your fancy . . ."

Wallace said, "On Thursday, January 24th, viewers who watched KGO didn't get much of what was happening in the world that day. KGO had only 58 seconds of national news, no foreign news. What they did have time for was the nude centerfold in *Cosmopolitan* magazine, the *Playgirl* mother of the month with another nude male, nudity on the beach, and the 'Nashville Stomper'—a man who had a fetish about stepping on women's insteps."

The station manager responded to Wallace's criticism of KGO's tabloid format. "The easiest thing to criticize is the news. We could sit around and do pontifical kinds of news day in and day out and we'd be back where we were in the old days when we were trying to be very clever and profound about news and died since nobody ever watched us."

The new format was killing the competition, and one of them, KPIX, turned with the tide, according to Wallace. News Director Jim VanMessel told him, "You don't save souls in an empty church."

But the city's cellar-dwelling station, KRON, retained its formal format. It was detrimental to resist the urge to compete. According to the news director, the station was "not going to bastardize our news for ratings."

San Francisco is an example of the extreme lengths a television station might go to grab an audience. The attitude is a throwback to the beginning of tabloid newspapers—screaming headlines, sex-sin-blood. Critics called it pandering to the baser instincts. The style sold newspapers and built empires. And it killed off some good, "straight" newspapers. But some of them survived. And NBC's Lee Hanna thinks some of the "straight" news broadcasts will survive, too.

Fifteen months ago, WNBC in New York was at the bottom of the charts, Hanna says. "We had an asterisk for a rating. Do you know what an asterisk means? No measurable audience. Our average rating was 2.3.

"Last week (late March) we had a share of about a 15, CBS had a share of 19, and ABC had a share of 19," Hanna says. "So you can see we're still far behind. But we have had a 300 per cent increase in our audience, and we haven't done it with laughter, jokes or gags or cosmetics. You don't have to be steamrolled into duplicating what the other guy is doing simply because he is doing it successfully."

But, he says, that doesn't mean the other formats shouldn't exist—even the tabloid format. "There's room for all—just as there's legitimate reason for the New York *Daily News* to sit side by side with *The New York Times*. There are different audiences. Why isn't there room for a tabloid-style newscast to go along with a more conservative newscast?"

REASONER'S REASONING

ABC's Harry Reasoner hopes television will continue to develop a style as newspapers did. "Occasionally, I see some revolting examples around the country of other stations doing the same kind of thing. I don't think it's the final corruption of journalism, nor do I think it's the final solution to journalism's problems.

"*The New York Times* has 500,000 circulation [*sic*] while the *Daily News* has 2 million. That, I suppose, is roughly the ratio of appeal of tabloid journalism to the more serious form. But what has happened over the years in newspapers, and what I hope would happen with television, is that eventually the tabloid form can also be serious. In other words, you can be bright, you can be brief, you can appeal to a mass audience, and at the same time gradually begin to uphold some principles."

What Is Happening to Blacks in Broadcasting?

EDITH EFRON

TV Guide, vol. 20, 34 (August 19, 1972). Reprinted with permission from TV GUIDE® Magazine. Copyright © 1972 by Triangle Publications, Inc., Radnor, Pennsylvania. Edith Efron is a contributing editor for *TV Guide*. She has published several books on broadcasting, gaining particular attention for *The News Twisters*. This article is one of a series published in *TV Guide*.

"The mass media, institutions that remind us continually that they are opposed to evil, corruption, deception and wrong-doing of every shade,

151

have consistently failed to point out the hypocrisies of their own existence in dealing with blacks. . . . These experts at exposing the wrong-doers of our society use the same rhetorical skill to hide their own failures."

This indictment of the media was made [early in 1972] by black Rep. William L. Clay. It represents a view that is both long-enduring and deeply felt in the black community—the view that the media, while preaching civil rights to everyone else, are guilty of entrenched racism.

This charge acquired a new potency [in March, 1972] when a group of Democratic representatives known as the Black Caucus gave a platform to angry black journalists. One portion of the Black Caucus—Reps. Louis Stokes (Ohio), its chairman; Augustus Hawkins (Cal.), vice chairman; Charles Rangel (N.Y.); John Conyers (Mich.); Ron Dellums (Cal.); and Clay (Mo.)—held two-day hearings into the problems of blacks in the mass media. The intensity and gravity of the denunciations may be judged by some of the Black Caucus's final charges:

> That the "black community, the black media worker and the black movement are grossly excluded, distorted, mishandled and exploited by the white-controlled news media. . . ."

> That the "mass media have failed miserably in reporting honestly the day-to-day news emanating from black communities."

> That "black people are systematically excluded from employment at most levels in newspapers, radio and television stations, though token numbers are to be found."

> That "the mass media are directly responsible for the inability of black and other disadvantaged people to improve their standards of living, enjoy full protection of the law, and develop their full potential as individuals."

All this can be reduced, in essence, to two broad charges; that the hiring-promotion-and-firing process is racist; and that news coverage is racist.

These charges have been leveled equally at both the print and the electronic press. The Associated Press has come under heavy fire from Austin Scott, for 11 years its star black reporter—precisely because he was its star. Scott resigned from the AP because he had, he said, received "exceptional" treatment accorded none other of the AP's crew of 18 black reporters. And the *Washington Post,* one of the most important newspapers in America, is now being sued for racist practices by its entire black staff, acting in a body.

But the harshest and most systematic attack has been leveled at broadcasting. In this series, we will examine both the charge of racism in hiring, and the charge of racism in coverage.

To begin with hiring: What are the facts as they pertain to broadcasting? The chart [see "Blacks in Broadcasting"] will give you the figures on the network-owned stations alone, which are among the richest and presumably the most progressive stations in the country.

On the surface these figures suggest that little has been done to break the virtually lily-white stranglehold by the unions on technical jobs.

These figures also suggest, next, that in the "professional" area, hiring is moving toward a uniform but unavowed 10 per cent quota system—a tacit cut-off line which is approximately the abstract national black population percentage. They also tell us that black managers are as rare as hen's teeth. The total picture—leaving causes aside for the moment—reveals tight control by whites over the media's intellectual, political and technological operations, with a limited number of blacks being filtered into staff jobs. (However, the facts behind the figures, if they were available, might suggest other interpretations. A recent court decision on Washington's WMAL-TV made it plain that discrimination cannot be determined by numbers alone.)

And what of the firing patterns? Here no facts of any worth can be given, although gossip abounds. At the Black Caucus hearings, a string of cases of clashes and of firings, or forced resignations, were described by Samuel Yette, professor of communications at Howard University, who himself had been fired from *Newsweek*. Professor Yette, a black functioning as self-appointed spokesman for the group, cited the cases of Gene Simpson at CBS; of Bill Matney, who left NBC for ABC; of Wallace Terry at *Time;* of Don Alexander who left WTTG-TV in Washington, D.C., for CBS—plus other reports of acute conflicts of black newsmen and white editors. The point of view expressed, as distilled by Professor Yette, was always, of course, a charge of racist discrimination and suppression of views; employees' and colleagues' opinions were not cited.

We checked into two outright firing stories in detail, and can only report this: that in these particular cases, not only the employers but black colleagues declared that the firings were merited. "In fact," one black reporter told us, "if X hadn't been black, he'd have been canned long before this. He was incompetent and he was nasty. The real racism lay in hiring him, not firing him. They wanted a token, and they grabbed a black face without regard for competence. I think it's a sign of *diminishing* racism that they're getting up the nerve to fire an incompetent black."

The criticism by a black reporter suggests, reasonably, that all black firees are not automatically to be seen as racial martyrs.

In most cases it is impossible to get all the facts about firings and failures to win promotions. These situations are complex, and fraught with subjectivity. It is wiser to try to interpret the hiring figures which have —or appear to have—greater objectivity.

How, then, are we to interpret them? Do they, in fact, reveal network racism?

The most optimistic construction of the hiring figures comes, of course, from the heads of network-owned stations, who present a picture of earnest, steady efforts by the stations to incorporate black employees. Kenneth H. MacQueen, vice president and general manager of WABC-TV, declares: "There has been significant improvement in the hiring of minority personnel over the last three years. The number of minorities employed at the station has increased by more than 85 per cent."

Arthur Watson, executive vice president and general manager of WNBC-TV, says: "Currently, the minority work force at WNBC-TV comprises some 20 per cent of the total employee roster; and minority workers fill some key positions at the station."

Watson adds that his station has "an active program of internship in the areas of news and sales," and has a tuition-loan program to enable employees to improve their skills. "Currently," he says, "10 students, all minority members, are enrolled at Columbia University School of Journalism under a scholarship program sponsored by NBC.* Fifty graduates of this program are now working as writers or reporters for television stations in New York and elsewhere."

Finally, Robert L. Hosking, vice president and general manager of WCBS-TV, pointing out that blacks constitute 16 per cent of total employees at the station, says: "We've been steadily increasing our black staff, and I'm very proud of what they've done. Chris Borgen won

*The scholarship program actually is jointly underwritten by NBC, the CBS Foundation and the Ford Foundation.—Ed. [The programs have since been reduced.]

Blacks in broadcasting

Here are the employment figures filed with FCC in May 1972, for the TV stations owned and operated by the networks. They do not include clerks and the unskilled.

Station	Officials and Managers		"Professional" Staff*		Technical Staff**	
	Total	*Blacks*	*Total*	*Blacks*	*Total*	*Blacks*
⌠ WABC-TV, New York	26	1	51	4	32	2
KABC-TV, Los Angeles	29	1	79	8	25	3
WLS-TV, Chicago	45	4	68	8	92	4
WXYZ-TV, Detroit	38	2	40	5	94	5
⌞ KGO-TV, San Francisco	26	0	74	10	70	5
⌠ WCBS-TV, New York	37	3	72	10	52	5
WCAU-TV, Philadelphia	37	1	52	3	88	5
WBBM-TV, Chicago	35	1	58	5	94	6
KMOX-TV, St. Louis	22	1	26	2	53	1
⌞ KNXT-TV, Los Angeles	39	2	83	3	105	8
⌠ WNBC-TV, New York	42	3	52	9	80	4
WRC-TV, Washington	38	1	40	14	83	11
WKYC-TV, Cleveland	32	4	42	3	71	6
WMAQ-TV, Chicago	41	2	79	10	106	9
⌞ KNBC-TV, Burbank	36	1	51	6	70	5

*This category includes trainees, production staff, researchers, writers, reporters *plus entertainment staffers.*

**This category includes cameramen, sound men, and all technological workers.

Source: FCC reports in 1971 and 1973.

an Emmy last spring. Lucille Rich is on virtually every night. Vic Miles is the anchor man on both the 7 and 11 o'clock news on Saturday nights. I answer the charge of tokenism by cases. It depends on how you use black staff. Our people are used well."

Hosking, too, reports that his station has various training programs for "entry-level" jobs—in particular one based at City College of New York.

He explains why there is no reporter-training program: "To train people in these complex jobs is difficult. Here, we hire blacks who have already received training—usually from out-of-town stations." He concedes that blacks on the managerial level are a rarity, but reports that progress is being made: "That's the area where most stations are thinnest. Most stations get their management people through sales. We're beefing up our staff in this regard. We've hired a black with a graduate degree in business, and we hope he works out well. Also, we've just promoted a black woman to the job of assistant head of continuity."

For those who see the black problem in the media as one of lack of educational and professional training, these progress reports can be seen as a record of good faith and genuine effort on the part of the stations. For that matter, the performance of the network-owned stations is brilliant compared to that of newspapers and magazines. Recent research done by the American Society of Newspaper Editors reveals that out of 40,000 people in the professional newspaper force, only 253 come from minority groups—a speck over half of 1 per cent, and minority executives number, in total, 8. The foundation of the American Newspaper Publishers Association has awarded 52 scholarships to black journalism students for a total of $23,700—or $456 per head. As for magazines, an important sampling of liberal and left magazines of opinion* reveals no black editors at all, almost no black contributing editors, and very few black writers.

Nonetheless, there are other noncongratulatory interpretations of the broadcast situation. A harsh interpretation comes again from Professor Yette: "What currently appears as progressive moves toward black employment in the white media is largely . . . pacification, not unlike other pacification measures aimed at blacks during the last decade." This "pacification," he says, seeks to "increase the oppressor's credibility with (and control over) the oppressed; hiring black reporters—visibly—does this." According to Yette, the black reporter who assists the media in this "pacification" process is welcome; the reporter who sees through it and protests is fired.

One white editor commented on hearing Yette's analysis: "Do you realize what he's saying? He's saying we're racists if we *don't* hire blacks—and that we're racists if we *do* hire blacks. You're damned if you do and you're damned if you don't."

The Yette type of analysis also irritates many whites on the grounds [that] it also implies a conscious, coherent conspiracy among them. It is interesting, therefore, to report on three other interpretations of the black hiring pattern given by white media chiefs whose editorial policy has strongly endorsed civil rights—one speaking on the record, two off.

On the record, Ben Bagdikian of the *Washington Post,* faced with a

*Atlantic Monthly, Harpers, Nation, New Republic, New York Review, Ramparts, Saturday Review, Washington Monthly—surveyed by Washington Monthly, June, 1972.

black staff revolt, confessed that he "in 20 months as an editor . . . was just as guilty as anyone else in failure to hire blacks." And he said: "Most metropolitan newspapers, wire services and television stations didn't take hiring of black professionals seriously until the ghetto riots of the mid-'60s when black faces were the only ones that could get to where the news was. . . . When ghettoes stopped burning, the brave promises of massive change were forgotten." And Bagdikian qualified the usual excuse given—that there is a shortage of trained blacks. "Chances," he said, "were constantly taken with untrained young whites, on the basis of editors' 'hunches.' Such 'hunches' about young blacks rarely occurred to white editors," he said, "because of cultural 'unknowns.' "

Off the record, a top decision-maker of an important New York TV station said:

"Listen, you're in there to protect that station license. That's your prime consideration. So you weigh and measure this against that. How many blacks can you put on the tube before the public starts calling you 'the black station'? How many inexperienced blacks can you carry in a news department before the work begins to sink? How many blacks can you put on your sales force before those people in the ad agencies take their business elsewhere How many blacks without real managerial experience can you put in decision-making jobs before they bankrupt you? What you do is, you look for the most brilliant ones you can find, screen out the troublemakers, and keep the number down to a minimum. Of course, I grant you, this is a double standard. Our staff is loaded with white mediocrities. *Every* staff is loaded with white mediocrities. But we're *used* to white mediocrity. When it's a black mediocrity, it feels as if somebody forced him down your craw. I grant you, it's racism.

And finally another editor in the trade press that covers broadcasting says: "Listen, I want *excellence*. I've been looking for competent blacks for years and can't find one. I've tried, and discovered myself running a journalism school. Where *are* the blacks who can write? Who are they? Give me some names! The whole thing is ridiculous."

When you put these analyses together, you see that all are really saying the same thing. Professor Yette's analysis, couched in master-slave language, is seeing the situation from the "outside." The white bosses are explaining it from the "inside." But all are telling us that it is "the system," and it's rigged against blacks—and that whites are aware of it.

What, then, does it all add up to? It seems to add up to this: that black unpreparedness, due to historical racism, is a reality . . . that contemporary network efforts to improve the black position are a reality . . . and that contemporary racism is also a reality. One can only argue about which of these three elements is dominant in the black hiring picture.

The argument is futile, however, since the role played by these three elements will vary considerably from case to case. One can say this: that when one looks at the over-all pattern of blacks on media staffs, it is obvious that racism, past *and* present, has left its brand.

The Majority Sex

BARBARA RIEGLE

Published from original manuscript with permission of author Barbara Riegle. Barbara Riegle is Orange County (California) correspondent for KFWB, Group W in Los Angeles.

Morning, noon and night, millions of people push buttons and switch dials to absorb news, opinion and commentary from "the men who know." In cities large and small, the population hears, sees and reads "keep informed, our NEWSMEN do." But do you recall ever picking up a newspaper and finding a female face under a television adline such as "Get the News from a WOMAN Who Cares"? Have you ever seen a billboard or a magazine ad featuring a feminine voice of authority on network television? On local television? On radio, either?[1] Where is there any indication that women are part of the electronic news gathering segment which observes, writes, reports, edits and broadcasts news?

True, once in awhile, here and there, the faces and voices of a few women do appear on network television. But in network TV's twenty years, only one has reached the stature enjoyed by many top newsmen: NBC's Barbara Walters of the *Today* show.

Pauline Frederick's name was almost synonymous with the United Nations to NBC viewers. But she was the lone woman broadcaster there

—and few people know *how many men* tried to push her into second place when the United Nations became a popular news item for broadcasting, after Ms. Fredericks had been buried there for years doing a job no male reporter previously wanted.

Marlene Sanders appeared briefly in the ABC News anchor spot in the spring of 1971, but the viewer had to stay up very late on weekends to see her. She has surfaced on documentaries, too, turning in a job which should have convinced those who control the fate of newscasters that she only needs exposure to take a place out in front in news reporting. Where is she now? Out of sight until another major assignment?

NBC gave us Liz Trotta in Vietnam, but not often enough to build her image. NBC also produced Aline Saarinan, who moved from coverage of the art world on the *Today* show to head the Paris bureau. She died shortly after the move.

In the 1960's the name Nancy Dickerson was a household word, but an entire generation of new voters went to the polls in 1972 without political comment from this astute woman. Ms. Dickerson is one of a long list of women who have gone up the stairs of broadcasting success only to find the door at the top leads not to the executive, or corporate, network offices. Up the stairs and out the door.

Esther van Wagoner Tufty is another woman whose voice and intellect should be available to American viewers and listeners. "The Duchess" brought news broadcasts to the public in the 1950's, along with Arlene Francis on *The Home Show*. She is still dominant on the Washington, D.C., scene but not for the nation.

"TRADITION"

Why are women excluded from status positions in news departments of the electronic media? General executive consensus is that they are not *excluded,* they are simply *not included.* The reason given most often is *tradition*—"it's just the way things are." Men are the reporters, editors, writers, broadcasters, cameramen, etc., and the metamorphosis is complete at the top with anchorMAN.[2]

During my years of news gathering I have been able to compile, through diligent research, a list of some 500 women who can professionally claim the title "broadcaster." Before you say "that's more than I would have thought" or "that's pretty good," bear in mind that this is a total figure for the entire United States. Of this total, about one-fifth are school teachers, employed by local school boards to teach on educational television. A second sizable group is employed to "teach" on a children's program with scripts provided by a national toy company which also provides the training for the teachers. About 200 women broadcasters have their own regular programs which run a half-hour to an hour daily—Monday through Friday. And the balance of the 500 are working as reporters/commentators/broadcasters in areas of hard news/documentaries. This balance teeters at about the level of 100 women.

The numbers are growing, very slowly, but still growing—not so much because more women are becoming broadcasters as because those already on the air are finding ways of communicating with each other, making themselves known outside the local areas. The *listing* of women broadcasters has doubled in a year; the actual increase is probably less than 10 percent in five years.[3] This expanding list is important, especially because it can be used to refute a *second reason* network executives give for the lack of women broadcasters. After *tradition* they add "there are no qualified women."

Producer David Susskind, who may pay more attention to the idea of women broadcasters than any other TV executive, asked me "Do you really think there is any marvelous woman who ought to be on TV who isn't? Nonsense, nonsense!" Susskind has been closely involved with women in broadcasting. He backed his wife, Joyce, and socialite Barbara Howar with *For Adults Only*. He says he makes it a point to look at women broadcasting on local stations and mostly he finds them "boring and pretty rotten." He agrees, however, that lots of male broadcasters are equally boring and rotten, but adds, "there are some good ones just from sheer force of numbers." Why, then, can't audiences have the privilege of watching women in sheer force of numbers so the *good ones* can be seen?

In Salt Lake City, Jackie Nokes has been broadcasting *Midday* for 12 years on KSL-TV. She gets over half the viewing audience at noon, leaving the other half to the other two stations. One-fourth of her audience is male.

Great Falls's Norma Ashby (KTVR) has produced and broadcast *Today in Montana* since 1962, winning the Greater Montana Foundation award six times for the best television show in the state. Two years ago she went statewide (and adopted two small children at the same time).

The Georgia Association of Broadcasters gave its 1970 award of Outstanding Broadcaster to Rozell Fabiani, whose morning women's program long ago expanded from cooking and sewing to exploration of social problems, notably the American Indian.

But even with these woman calling attention to excellence on the distaff side, few women in broadcasting have been able to move into executive positions—despite the titles which give outsiders the impression they are in decision-opinion jobs. Where did they come from, the women who are on the air today? The majority gained broadcast positions by taking jobs well below their qualifications and then by being in the right place at the right time. Secretaries, traffic girls, weather girls and copy writers—they were *there* when management began to look for something to put between cartoons and old movies, and suddenly they found themselves ad-libbing through a totally new environment with one eye on the little red camera light which signals "you're on!" This was true when television was an infant, and it is true today. In Los Angeles, Westinghouse Broadcasting's Joy Nuell and KABC-TV's Morgan Williams each graduated from "secretary" to "broadcaster" within the past year.[4]

What is it like for those who have breached the male bastion? Statistically, the average woman broadcaster works fourteen hours a day, six days a week, and earns the average pay of less than $5,000 a year. True, reporters such as Connie Chung (CBS, Washington, D.C.) are moving from one professional job to another and counting take-home pay of over $20,000 annually. Equally true, a qualified reporter in Indiana says her fantasy goal is to take home $100 a week. After ten years of local broadcasting, she earns less than $75.

But, no matter where you slice the money pie—high or low, east or west—it always comes out smaller when the word "woman" precedes "broadcaster." Dorese Bell, with Mutual Broadcasting Company as its token woman covering the political scene for ten years, estimates her paycheck was probably $5,000 a year less than those of the ten men who worked the Washington newsbeat with her.[5] This discrepancy is not unusual even where base pay is set by union regulation because of on-air "fees" and the exclusion of women from anchoring newscasts. (Published reports following the retirement of Hugh Downs as host of *Today*, put his income at $450,000 a year.)

Latest statistics show that the *average* pay scale for women is increasing because more young women are being accepted in news and documentary jobs where big money is paid. It doesn't take many earning five-figure checks to upgrade the numbers for those at the lower pay of $50 a week. The average woman broadcaster today has been on the air for about fourteen years. There is a very large group which falls between ten and twenty-two years, a scattering between five and ten years and a newcomer trend crowding the "under two" category.

What is it like in our industry for women broadcasters? Are conditions any different for the young newcomer in comparison to those which existed, and still exist, for the long-time broadcast personality? Apparently not. Regardless of time and age, the story they tell is the same. Women say they lack status, get no advertising exposure, and must battle harder than men for special ideas—even for "just another camera for the show." They report being left out of executive and sales meetings, even when decisions are being made about what women call "my show." This one really hurts them.

In a business where "putting down" is a way of life, women say they are given a double dose. "Putting down" women in broadcasting has more than one benefit for management. It keeps the lid on importance and thus effectively depresses salaries. It also keeps alive the trap of dual responsibility: because of the "putdown," television—and radio, too—gets more than double its money's worth from a woman on the payroll. The Women's Editor, or Director of Women's Activities, or Public Affairs Coordinator does more than fill air time. She is the volunteer representative of her station or network at civic affairs, teas, fund raisers, and usually is called on to judge the local beauty pageant, too. She often makes speeches in place of her boss when he finds he must be in two places at once. She is watched with proprietary interest by management and the audience. Since she is usually the *one* woman broadcaster; there is nobody else to try a buckpassing routine on, even when exhaustion becomes routine for her.

Women television broadcasters write their own letters, cook half the night for homemaking shows, get up at dawn to load the car, drive to work and unload before setting up the broadcast—which seems like an anticlimax at this point. After the cheery "see you tomorrow," they clean up the oven and sink while the crew devours the dish of the day. Then supplies must be checked, lists made for tomorrow, and finally, the woman broadcaster can head out to sell commercial time on her show or to service clients. At the same time she can do the shopping for the next program, which is probably titled "How to Give a Relaxing Party for a Tired

Executive Husband." The local female TV star also organizes special events, from getting viewers to sew hundreds of stuffed dolls to delivering food baskets on Christmas Eve.

Once a year vacation time rolls around and the woman broadcaster does double duty, putting everything on tape in advance, ever mindful of the line of women just waiting for her job. She is kept aware of this fact by the men with and for whom she works. Even after preparation (for job protection), she can't help but worry about what will happen if someone erases her tapes, leaving her air time unattended. This fear arises from the "we have one" syndrome. Perhaps it will disappear when hiring *more* than one woman broadcaster is the rule rather than the exception. Keep in mind, also, that many women broadcasters—in order to be on the air—have regular staff jobs. They often head the copy department, promotion department, or that ghastly chamber of statistical horrors, the traffic department, where daily logs of books and sales are coordinated. Some women say they handle both traffic and sales and write copy, too. One broadcaster is head bookkeeper. Almost all are hyphenates, sometimes middle management, sometimes clerk. On occasion women broadcasters work under a minimum wage law and some under union contract. Most often they are assigned a devised title which belongs to no other employee in the organization and carries with it a nebulous schedule of responsibilities and a salary to match.

There are even a few women broadcasters who are completely "volunteer" and work without salary. Just recently a woman wrote to tell me that her station, after six years, has finally agreed to pay her a flat talent fee of $25 per program. However, she is now limited to a show once a week, where before—unpaid—she could do one a day. She questions, "Did I win or lose?"

What is the summary? These statistics show that women broadcasters work for less, do twice the labor and have little chance to become executives. They are seldom thanked publicly or privately and are often decried as they struggle to live happily on a lower standard than that afforded the male broadcaster. Added to this, the longtime woman broadcaster now has the additional secret worry that the kind of show she is doing has become passé. She sees other women retire not to be replaced. She knows of women forced out by the youth kick, only to be replaced later by a man in his middle years.

Younger women are switching from cook-and-sew to what Claire Klees Lyon *(The Claire Show,* Washington, D.C.) calls the "shock show." This is where ladies sip tea and discuss homosexuality with neither raised eyebrows nor lowered pinkies.

Virginia Graham *(Girl Talk* and *The Virginia Graham Show,* syndicated) kept her format out of the stove although it was often in the fire. After twenty years with a talk-show-shock-conversation-double-entendre format, she still had to live with "syndication" rather than outright network involvement.

Betty Groebli, who traveled from Santa Barbara radio to the nation's capital, takes the position that women's programs are "archaic" and a woman's world section in newspapers is "barbaric." Although her broadcast program titles indicated "for women only," the content of her shows is as varied as a high-class zoological garden. She says her mail indicates more men than women listen to her daily radio program, and other women broadcasters agree with her. Despite ratings and demographics to the contrary, my own mail and telephone calls during several years on CBS in Hollywood indicated a large audience of male listeners—particularly men at the executive level.

Still, women broadcasters are being eased out of the few "hostess" or "anchor" spots they hold and the "woman's" show is being replaced by "morning news," or a news-talk show. The female hostess is moved over to make room for a male host. This format switch followed the successful lead of the *Today* show where every effort at equality for Barbara Walters left the viewer watching her as an adjunct. However, it must be noted that Ms. Walters, slowly but surely, has become the "host" of the *Today* show and is definitely in control now. *Not for Men Only,* which has been on the air in New York for many years, even before Barbara Walters took it over, went network in 1974.

NBC has long taken the lead in putting women in good broadcast jobs. Not top jobs, but good ones. And not in terms of numbers, but in terms of "we have one" here and there. Spokesman Russ Tornabene (NBC, New York) alleges there is a short supply of women available, even though he admits there is a "less aggressive program" working to find women than there is to search out men. Tornabene also admits to having no women newscasters on NBC radio, but blames this on the network's 230 affiliates. He claims "they tell us audiences do not accept women as news authorities." At the same time he agrees that the practice of putting women in television news and excluding them from radio is "illogical." "That's prejudice," he says, "but it's *old* prejudice, nothing new."

Which brings us to the question, "What do women broadcasters think of themselves?" How do those who are *there* already view any attempt to open up the industry? The majority of them don't like it, some don't care and few will move over to help another girl get a job. The woman (especially local) likes being the "one token" female staff member—it's nice. It's nice to have the president call you by name and members of Congress know who you are without explanation. It's an ego trip to have the governor's wife include you in her little dinner parties. Because of this liking for special consideration, many longtime women broadcast personalities are jittery over the thought of losing "pedestal status" in return for equality. During a recent convention of women broadcasters in Washington, D.C., one woman called a special meeting in her hotel room to warn other women broadcasters against my efforts to expand our job situation. She insisted "it would just mess things up for those who have already made it."

It was during that same convention (American Women in Radio and Television, 1971) that Vincent Waslewski of the National Association of Broadcasters drew down the wrath of 600 women by claiming he did not believe there is any discrimination against women in the industry. He pointed out he had a wife, some daughters and a legal assistant in his office and they were all women. Waslewski's position is similar to that taken by CBS executive Sam Digges in New York. To quote Digges from a taped interview on the subject of women, opinion, attitudes and broadcasting: "All they have to do is pick up the phone and call in any of the talk shows and they [women] can express any opinion, anytime."

After considering the position of women in advertising, the question must be asked and answered, "What difference does it make?" What difference would there be if the doors suddenly opened and 50 percent of the opinion-decision making broadcasting posts were filled by women? One can only conjecture. For instance, elected female officials might find their speeches getting better coverage, with expanded numbers of newscast quotes which, in turn, might lead to an equal sharing of hard-news coverage in local papers rather than minimal exposure in women's pages. Feminists recently shrugged off an almost total lack of coverage by the media at a national convention of NOW (National Organization for Women) in Los Angeles. They weren't pushing for press coverage then, because male editors expect male reporters to come up with a "cutesy" piece of tape or film to be used in the "kicker slot" to close a newscast on a light note. Perhaps women editors and newscasters would concentrate on the mental rather than the physical status of females.[6]

Women political candidates might find themselves treated as intelligent people rather than "some freak who ought to be home in the kitchen," and thus might be elected in greater numbers. *More elected women could mean more appointed women.* In the long run, it might even change the entire legislative and judicial systems, from police departments and city councils to the United States Supreme Court. Certainly there would be an end to headlines such as "Will Grandma Reed Change Things After Appointment to Federal Communications Commission?" What has Congresswoman Charlotte Reed's capacity to breed have to do with her ability as a commissioner, unless one considers the sexual capacity of Dean Burch in the same thought process?

Think about it. If you see few women on your television screen and hear little about women in authority—what they are doing or saying—is it because women are passive and silent? Or is it because they are systematically excluded? And if you see "one" and hear "one," isn't it possible the product of broadcasting is out of balance? Something *is* missing in broadcasting—the majority sex of the United States population.

NOTES

1. Recently KNBC (Los Angeles) has been including pictures of women in their ads and Channel Five (Los Angeles) under Clete Roberts has promoted a female coterie of reporters. When KFWB (Los Angeles) ran its full-page ad "Now You Can See the Voices," it included the three women broadcasters on the air at that time. There may have been a few others, but tokenism is still the watchword.

2. This is changing. There are enough women reporters now so they no longer stick out as "unusual." I have noted in recent months that an occasional network newscast will have the top two-three-four reports from women reporters. But the "anchorman" remains pretty stationary, and if you really want to see a man choke try out the word "anchorperson" on him.

3. A recent check finds the numbers about the same although the jobs are changing—you might honestly add 100 to the total. Please bear in mind that this article is written solely about the people the audience sees, not those who are behind the scenes. Those numbers are indeed increasing but *not* in the positions of decision and authority, and that's a whole other story.

4. Mal Johnson of Cox Broadcasting in Washington, D.C., says that's a good way to go, take anything you can get. On the other hand, an NBC vice-president advises "Never, never." When my first boss in radio-television heard I was taking a course in

shorthand he told me to throw away the book and never tell any man I worked for I could "take a letter."

5. This figure is certainly higher now because many women have moved into the reporting slots at the network level, even though working at owned-and-operated stations. But some ladies still are "volunteering" (unsalaried).

6. This male syndrome is still prominent. Recently there was a convention of prostitutes in San Francisco and a convention of the American Medical Association in the East. One local L.A. radio station headlined the "hookers" with salacious glee. Every 15 minutes for three days running from 5 A.M. to 10 A.M., I personally called the station and questioned the imbalance (there was no reporting about the AMA); I was told by the editor on duty that he was personally axing the hookers' story daily when he came to work, but others did not agree with him. Some of the morning newscasters could be heard salivating every time they repeated the story. The same situation holds with every rape story, and to this day, the listener gets a constant barrage of 36-26-36 with every beauty contest.

Broadcast News: A Trade in Need of Professionalizing?

HARRY J. SKORNIA

Reprinted from *Educational Broadcasting Review*, vol. 7, 3 (June, 1973) with permission of publisher. *Public Telecommunications Review* is successor to *EBR*. Harry J. Skornia is professor of radio and television at the University of Illinois at Chicago Circle, Chicago.

There seems to be general agreement that electronic journalism is in crisis.

The condition is not necessarily peculiar to the United States. Dr. Kaarle Nordenstreng, of the Finnish Broadcasting Service, in the introduction to a paper presented in September 1970, at the Conference of the International Association for Mass Communications Research held in Konstanz, West Germany, declared: "The starting point of this report is the recognition of the fact that news diffusion through mass communication is in a world-wide state of crisis."[1]

Skornia

167

There are a number of problems, beyond those seen by broadcasters, which critics, educational and church organizations, congressional committees, and various professional groups have been raising regarding news trends and practices in the U.S. Let us consider a few of the more disturbing ones before looking at possible solutions.

SOME DISTURBING PRACTICES
Value System
The value system that seems to prevail in U.S. network, corporation-controlled television has been the source of concern to many Americans in recent years.

Robert A. Gessert of the Research Analysis Corporation, speaking at a conference in Washington, D.C., January 30, 1970, sponsored by the Council on Religion and International Affairs, speaking of the military-industrial complex, listed characteristics of normality, or status quo, as accepted by news media generally as:

1. "The economy of death," i.e., acceptance of warfare as a normal, natural, probably inevitable, condition.
2. "The ethos of enmity," a state in which "the military-industrial complexes of Russia and the United States feed on each other in a ceaseless escalation of suspicion, justifying huge military budgets."
3. "The self-fulfilling ideology," by which each dire prediction comes true, and each violent act is followed by imitations of still greater violence.
4. "The self-consuming technology," in which increased production and consumption are accepted as essential, in both military and civilian sectors, despite depleted resources and mounting pollution and disposal problems.

Others have expressed concern that we as a nation do not challenge the introduction of all innovations, whatever they may do to human labor or values, if they make possible greater corporate profits; and that there seems to be little mass media concern over the war-related Pentagon contracts of many of the same firms that operate many of our media. Are these the conditions we should consider normal rather than "news"? Is a national news service based on acceptance of this as normal reality the best of all sources of the information available to democracy's citizenry?

Is an information system in which the most admired and quoted symbols of success (measured in money and popularity) are show business stars, sports figures, and wealthy broadcast personalities, likely to provide the best models toward which the nation should aspire in its value system?

News Definitions

The representatives of U.S. broadcasting maintain Americans are the best informed people in the world. Visitors to our shores often ask if we aren't perhaps best informed about trivia, commercial products, and violence? To meet the definition of news, an event must be either accidental, illegal, violent, or immoral; or be about a show business celebrity, sports figure or politician; or represent a confrontation of some sort.

Students each year at the Chicago Circle campus of the University of Illinois monitor newscasts, short-wave and domestic, in order to compare what is considered to be "news" by the U.S. media, including the Voice of America, with radio (and when possible television) news on or from Canadian, British, German, Japanese, and other foreign systems. For the first time students discover that many newscasts talk about scientific, medical, agricultural, educational, historical, cultural, and economic developments that rarely find their way into U.S. broadcasts. The latter contain the least news about other nations and the most news of violence, military developments, commercial products, confrontations, scandals, crime and sports. America is an ugly place as seen in U.S. newscasts.

Less expected were the results of interviews conducted by and with students on campus, on what they rated as the principal "news" developments of a day. On March 2, 1973, for example, the return of prisoners of war was in first place. In second place was the news that Richie Allen had signed his baseball contract for $675,000.00.[2] In later studies two of the stories identified as "principal news" dealt with the wife swap of Yankee players Peterson and Kekich, and, two weeks later, the testimony in hearings of Burt Reynolds and Sarah Miles concerning the death of Miss Miles' business manager, David Whiting. Gradually, entertainment owned and operated broadcast news and morality seem to be training America in what is *really* important!

To what extent does the coverage by the media of the life styles of its popular heroes legitimize such behavior? What research have news organizations done to indicate that we need not worry about such things?

Dr. Herbert Otto of the Stone Foundation in Chicago, speaking to a New York symposium in October of 1968, declared:

> It is crystal clear that the overwhelming emphasis on "bad news" greatly contributes to the climate of violence which characterizes this country today. It is my point that we desperately need to balance the bad news with the good news in order to create a healthier climate for our citizens. The widely prevalent concept of what constitutes news is a narrow, destructive concept—a sick concept, destructive to society as a whole. The news format in all our media is, in general, inimical or opposed to the development of human potential.[3]

In "A Policy of News Transmission," Dr. Kaarle Nordenstreng[4] suggests that our definitions of news are all wrong. Significance, not what is most entertaining, should govern news selection. He divides news into two kinds: raw news, which is "information about events and matters existing in the real world . . . an extension of our senses . . . without explanation or background," and "background commentary," which is absolutely essential if news is to have any significance. Commentary is intended, without slanting or favoring any particular world view, "to mobilize the individual's thinking," to be a switch that "turns on" mental activity.

Fires, accidents, sports, weather, etc., belong in broadcasts of service information. "News of an event which affects the life of only a few individuals" is not truly "news." For example, publicizing the names of the people who died when a private house burned down is not appropriate, unless they happened to be especially prominent individuals. The same would be true of crimes, accidents, confrontations, etc., unless they influence the lives of many people. However, "the news of negotiations between the ministers of industry of the four largest copper-producing countries in Peru *is* of considerable value. . . . Copper is of strategic importance."

The selection of significant items would not be left to a single editor or newsman. For this an editorial board is necessary. "Many different ways of thinking should be represented on the editorial board to guarantee balance."

By Nordenstreng's criteria—and many nations are adopting them—the great majority of items on U.S. television newscasts would be classified as either trivia or local service information. These, like obituary columns in newspapers, should have their own programs, so that news programs might concentrate on items of significance and relevance to the lives of citizens.

Should U.S. broadcast news concentrate on America's faults? Should doom, confusion, and distrust be the effects of broadcast news, however intended? Can we truly believe we can have a world in which peaceful solutions and relations dominate, when present practices so predominantly show violent solutions to problems? If only superficial (activity, motion, noise, vulgarity) symbols fill the screen, how can viewers be expected to find the deeper significance lying beneath the surface? Are new definitions of news not overdue in the United States?

Quantity, Diversity and Presentation of News

Industry leaders from the National Association of Broadcasters, Television Information Office (TIO), and elsewhere quote Roper surveys indicating that television is the primary source of news for more people than any other new medium. Press organizations contest this claim. Leo Bogart, among others, has reported that his research proves that "newspapers are still the dominant source for news despite contrary assertions of the broadcast media." In fact, he has declared, "television also creates news because things happen on television that have to be reported in the paper. But it's simply not true that television is the public's main news source."[5]

Whatever the merits of the claims and counterclaims, many people do get most of their news from television. This being true, the results of monitoring by Chicago Circle students of both radio and television news outputs of Chicago stations in early 1973 are very disturbing. These students found that the CBS owned and operated "all-news" station repeated essentially the same "stories" hour after hour, the number of "news" items reaching barely forty for a sort of "top forty" on many days. As the three principal television critics of the principal newspapers in Chicago noted, whole hour-long blocks in successive hours were sometimes repeated in toto, with no additions or deletions. The "electric newspaper," on close inspection, proved to feature only reruns of a very limited number of news items daily and reruns of commercials on an unlimited basis running sometimes to hundreds of times. How such operation could have a principally informational rather than anesthetizing or deadening effect was a baffling question to most of the students.

Equally baffled were the students who monitored the television newscasts of the NBC-TV station, modestly admitting to be the finest news operation in Chicago. After noting that all the principal television stations seemed to "attend" the same press conferences, speeches, fires, accidents, etc., as if they traveled by the same bus, one of the students who decided to get "all the news" in depth by monitoring all the newscasts of the NBC-TV stations from the *Today* program on through the 10 P.M. newscast concluded: "My main observation about our news service is that the same news is broadcast four or five times throughout the day. The exact same stories, the exact same films, and the exact same order."

Though different anchor men and one woman host the different newscasts on this fine NBC-owned news outlet, on February 12, 1973, to take an example, "The Carole Simpson report on the Kerner trial—the same identical report—was given on the noon news, the evening news and the nightly news. Even the length was identical in each case. . . . Throughout all three newscasts the following other stories also appeared, always in this order: (1) Laos cease-fire; (2) Cambodia with more fighting; (3) U.S. dollar crisis; (4) fire kills mother and three children; (5) film of fire chief at the scene; (6) the Kerner story."[6]

Are these the vaunted CBS and NBC radio and television news services, which purport to keep Americans the best informed people in the world? "Top forty"? Perhaps "top ten" or "top fifteen" would be a better description of the coverage of the news. "Is this what special legislation is needed to protect?" students asked.

As aspiring professionals, how much abuse and misrepresentation will newsmen stand aside and see administered to their loyal viewers who are seeking only to be informed? Are these the characteristics of a great tradition of service, one that becomes a profession?

Autonomy: Resistance to Outside Pressure

During the period of blacklisting in the forties, probably no medium provided a lesser example of courage than did broadcasting under pressures to fire employees without hearings or grievance procedures.

A master's thesis a few years ago found that sixty per cent of the news directors at stations in a midwest state admitted to yielding to management and sales department pressure to either withhold stories they would ordinarily have used or insert stories that they considered undeserving of coverage, on the orders of superiors, or in the hope of ingratiating themselves with management.[7]

The American Association of University Professors (AAUP) has sought to professionalize higher education. For example, the national organization may put on the "censure" list an institution which violates academic freedom, tenure agreements, and professional standards. Newsmen as a group seem to have taken the opposite course. How many cases are on record in which newsmen have "gone to the mat" as a group with management, over their rights to be judged by their peers and their rights to full hearings in case of threatened dismissal?

In his "Statement on Newsmen's Privileges," Willard E. Walbridge, on behalf of the National Association of Broadcasters (NAB) declared: "Gentlemen, we agree that our record of responsibility as journalists has been good." After this self-congratulation, Walbridge revealed how broadcasters have kept the record good—by an "off with their heads" approach, which brooks no nonsense: "What if a newsman is lying, someone asked. That would presumably include staging and other tricks and distortions. . . . I say if you catch a newsman lying . . . fire him. That simple—and note that this puts the responsibility right where it belongs—with the broadcaster at the source. . . ."[8]

Suppose hospital administrators were to talk like this about surgeons, who are professionalized? Would there not be national challenge? Or, suppose doctors or lawyers were to be told how much time they have for surgery or some other professional service—as newsmen are told how many minutes, sandwiched in amongst how many commercials, they may have for news, however urgent, day after day? What kind of a true professional would work in such conditions?

The steady retreat of newsmen and the NAB codes before the pressures of commercialism would seem to indicate the need for a genuine revolution in thinking before anything like a proud profession can emerge. Such status rarely comes without a struggle, and so far most newsmen's protests seem to have been on behalf of their superiors rather than their own kind. Surely the efforts up to now of television and radio newsmen to achieve such status is hardly comparable to the struggle for professionalism or independence of labor, education, medicine, or other professions. Let us hope for that status. But let us recognize how far from that status broadcast journalism now is, conspicuously in its relations with and surrender to management.

A Crisis in Credibility and Identity

In recent years the John and Mary R. Markle Foundation has concentrated great resources and interests in communications. The results of research are beginning to come in from the Aspen Institute for

Humanistic Studies, the Stanford Program on Communications and Society, and other foundation financed research into the effects, particularly, of television on society.

In the Markle Foundation's 1971–72 *Annual Report* President Lloyd N. Morrisett traces the increased freedoms won by the press through the years. "Thus, over the years, the press has won the freedom to make honest mistakes, in good faith . . . a situation in which the press often stands as sole judge of its own accuracy." Now the public has a right to inquire about "the right of the press to inaccuracy and error without penalty." On the basis of the record, people are beginning to have less faith than they used to in broadcast and print media credibility. "The paradox is that as freedom has been won, credibility has diminished."[9]

Some of the recent loss of newsmen's credibility would seem related to their willingness, or eagerness, to "moonlight" by doing commercials. Members of the public who have bought, and found to be faulty, products which a newsman enthusiastically praised or misrepresented (often speaking in the first person) should be forgiven for wondering if there is any more truth to what he reads as news than what he reads as commercials.

Will some "newsmen" say *anything* for money? Does that mean, increasingly, that if citizens or groups don't have money to buy exposure or sponsorship, their side (labor, poverty, teachers) will not get fair exposure?

In their study of "Professionalization among Newsmen," McLeod and Hawley[10] quote a study indicating that the public accords newspaper reporters prestige equal to that of "undertaker," below physicians, lawyers, and professors but above store managers, insurance agents, and automobile dealers. Would broadcast newsmen's prestige be higher or lower than that today?

If there is a sharp decline in credibility for broadcast newsmen, it would seem to be traceable more to the newsman's own greed for commercialism, and lack of exclusive loyalty to what should be his profession, than to any restrictions by government, or harassment by critics or intellectuals. Is this a clue regarding the way new freedoms won under shield laws would be used?

The "identity crisis" mentioned by mental health specialists would also seem related to station practices. Broadcasting assures viewers and listeners that it is serving them, the public. "We" is the relationship. Government, the ogre, is "they"—although this is the only part of the system in which we have a legal vote. Newsmen say their loyalty is to the public. How come, then, that "we" the newsmen, say "we" with regard to the sponsor, when urging *you* to come in? Was the old rule about no endorsement of products by station staffs—certainly station newsmen—not perhaps a good practice, after all? With which "we" can the public identify? Is it any wonder that society is confused?

Scoops and Retractions

In their haste to "scoop" the competition, broadcast newsmen have established a long record of scoops that later turned out to be false reporting. From the CBS broadcast by mistake of a pre-recorded tape August 23, 1944, stating that Paris had been liberated, on through the alleged arrival of Dag Hammerskjöld in Africa in 1961, when his plane had really crashed and he was dead, and scores more, the record is not good[11].

It would be less serious if newsmen were to establish regular and prompt procedures for corrections and retractions. Their "allergy" to admissions of human failure is costing them dearly.

In its discussion of the Rosenbloom case, in which Metromedia Station WIP was sued for libel for defamatory broadcasts, but damages were denied, the Freedom of Information Center *Report* on "Rosenbloom and Libel" notes: "It is the rare case where the denial overtakes the charge. Denials, retractions and corrections are not hot news, and rarely receive the prominence of the original story."[12]

Markle Foundation President Lloyd Morrisett also declares that few newspapers have adequate provision for retractions:

> Exceptions are the *Louisville Courier Journal* and the *Louisville Times,* (which) have utilized prominent correction boxes for the past few years. . . . On television the use of correction techniques is far rarer. . . . Seldom is an error even admitted on a television program. In fact there are no standard methods for doing so.[13]

If professional status, including credibility and constitutional protection, is to be earned, the broadcast media would seem to have some little distance to go.

Skornia

175

Anti-Intellectualism

In a recent anthology, David J. LeRoy has written: "The profound anti-intellectualism of the American press flows from its assembly line bureaucracy considering the 'news product' as if it were an automobile."[14] In the cases of television and radio it also probably is traceable to the tendency of newsmen to embrace the value systems and biases of their superiors, in management and sales.

TIO Director Roy Danish illustrated both the defense of the "freedoms" of the newsmen (but not against management), and expected anti-intellectualism, when he declared, in denying the charges of news bias in television:

> . . . broadcast newsmen, like all journalists, are united in the conviction that their job, their duty to the public, is the reporting of truth, so far as they can discover it and communicate it accurately. It is that belief alone which raises the practice of journalism to a profession, for degrees are not necessary for success as a reporter. Professionalism is measured by one's reputation as a competent and honorable journalist. This quality cannot be calibrated by professors. Even less can it be regulated by a commission of government-appointed bureaucrats.[15]

If the newsmen of the nation dispute Mr. Danish's right to speak in their name, they have done so quietly, and that is a shame. For to some, the establishment of educational standards of journalists seem desirable. Would Mr. Danish be satisfied with doctors, the teachers of his children, architects, or engineers with no more specific standards than he here lists?

To some it appears that the greatest limits to their freedom have been imposed by management, sales, and sponsors. By holding government and intellectuals at bay they may be depriving themselves of allies they could well use if their freedom from dictation of news policy by merchants, salesmen, and managers is ever to be realized. Do newsmen really have so little pride in their status as newsmen, in their product, and in their freedoms, that they would like to be left alone to do as the boss orders, stay in line, and give up any further pretense of practicing those qualities which characterize professionalism? If so, the public and the once-proud practice of journalism—not merely government and intellectuals—are the losers. And it has taken the media of television and radio to bring about this deterioration.

SOME ALTERNATIVE SOLUTIONS

There is no question that both the media and various segments of the public consider the freedom of information, and the adequacy of our nation's news services, to be in serious trouble. What remedies are there?

Gradualism

The situation can be left as it is, leaving hope for change to the power of the First Amendment, under which, in fact, considerably expanded freedoms, rights, and immunities have been won by the press in recent years. Support for this solution is difficult to find among either the press or worried critics.

Piecemeal Reforms

The public and Congress could press for piecemeal reforms: more adequate news definition, selection, and services; better fairness and retraction-correction procedures, guaranteeing access and the right of reply, etc. The outlook for these is not sanguine, even if it were deemed wise to continue only to tinker with the problem.

Press Councils

The establishment of a national press and/or separate radio-television council, somewhat on the model of those in Britain and Sweden, or the state of Minnesota, is supported by writers like John Dart, who feels that, "if the media are truly a fourth branch of government, then media merit the expert news coverage given the other three branches."[16] This function might have been expected to be created by the press itself, but since the press has set up no such mechanism for self-criticism, surveillance, or discipline for malpractices, who is to take care of policing the press while the press is watchdogging government?

Harold M. Evans, editor of the *Sunday Times* of London has suggested that "What is needed in my view are academic centers for the dispassionate analysis of press performance."[17] He hopes journalists would cooperate with such centers, and calls for an international digest to publish accounts of the status of press accomplishment and the work of such centers. Such councils might also study the desirability of (possibly non-government) licensing of journalists, to forestall government licensing of journalists comparable to that of doctors, teachers, and lawyers as suggested by Dr. Walter Menninger and others.[18]

Since there is a considerable body of writing regarding the press council concept, no further attention will be given it here; except to note that probably more than one of the proposed solutions listed in this article will be necessary, since not all are mutually exclusive.

Alternative Outlets

Public or other non-advertising-supported media outlets have also been proposed, if necessary, based on public subsidies.

A real step in this direction is likely with the advent of cable television. With broadband communication, for example, it might be desirable to have dedicated channels to telecast exclusively courtroom cases, hearings, city council meetings, and other such proceedings. The objections to television in the courtroom, which have been based on the inability of a primarily entertainment (commercial) medium to have either the time periods, the legally trained personnel, or the capacity for balanced coverage that is necessary, would all be met by such a differently conceived and differently based channel or medium.

Other such dedicated or specialized channels might provide only news: more adequate news than can be secured from the present headline service approach of television and radio.

Shield Legislation

Another solution being advanced by the media is greater freedom for reporters, particularly as conceived in proposed "shield laws," on a federal level. State shield laws are already in effect in some twenty states. Before proceeding to our final alternative proposal: professionalization, let us take a closer look at this proposal, since the aspects of the problem available to the public from the press, which is itself biased by being the principal interested party, seem somewhat one-sided.

For example *Broadcasting* magazine and the daily press and broadcasting networks have widely reported the testimony of NBC news president Richard Wahl and ABC news president Elmer Lower[19], both insisting on nothing less than "an absolute privilege bill" and the support of a wide range of congressmen and other leaders for such a bill. Little coverage of the position of the Supreme Court or other opponents seems to have been presented, particularly with reference to the aspects of the problem illustrated by the following circumstance: A reporter refuses to violate the confidentiality of his source (for a report he published) except to say it was an attorney in the case; whereupon, all the attorneys in the case are questioned and deny being the source. Is jailing a reporter in such a case an effort to get him to violate the confidentiality of his source, as we generally hear, or only an effort by the court to ascertain whether such evidence, in effect, exists, and if so, whether it meets the standard of truth? After all, it was no less prestigious an individual than a U.S. Senator, Joseph McCarthy, who used to wave a handful of "evidence of communist affiliations" of individuals, which later proved to be only blank sheets of paper. Is the record of the press through the years so good for accuracy that the courts need not make sure?

William Loeb, president and publisher of New Hampshire's largest Sunday newspapers, the *Manchester Union Leader* and the *New Hampshire Sunday News*, not granted extensive exposure for his minority views in the national media, wrote in a letter distributed to members and subscribers by the Forum for Contemporary History:

> I am nauseated intellectually at the hysteria emanating from re- porters, editors, and publishers to the effect that the freedom of the press is in danger and that they should be given special privileges not granted any other segment of our society. This is one of the most ridiculous outcries ever raised in this country, and alas, it is symp- tomatic of an even deeper sickness. . . . To assert that somehow a reporter's profession is superior to the needs and requirements of society as a whole . . . is an absurdity. . . .
>
> Politicians eager to see their names in print and to curry favor with sources of publicity are rushing into the state legislatures and into Congress in Washington with bills. . . . A more illogical . . . anti- democratic and . . . unnecessary procedure is hard to imagine. . . .
>
> The special privilege laws demanded by the press are an open invitation to mendacity. . . . It is a small indication of . . . arrogance, self-satisfaction and smugness.
>
> They (newspapers and other press media) are no longer the watchdogs of the Republic. They are rather its lap dogs. (These prac- tices) may lead in the end to their destruction. They will have bored their readers into extinction and hurried themselves into oblivion.[20]

Of even more concern, however, to the writer of this paper is the spread of the demand for the right to secrecy. How ironic that the very reporters and editors who protest "shield" protection when exercised by the President, under the title of executive privilege, or when called "executive session" or "closed hearings" by congressional committees, school boards, city councils, etc., should themselves now seek such immunity and yet wonder why their credibility as watchdogs of democracy is reduced. Are they already the "lap dogs" of the corporation in the lack of protest they have raised regarding the "legitimate secrecy of the corporation," their network or group station, when disclosure of profits or other "internal" matters are involved? Does an informed public not need this information as well? Can we tolerate this much dog-in-the-manger freedom and secrecy for press and the business corporations which control its largest units: print and electronic? If so, who is to be America's watchdog, in an age of increasing secrecy?

STEPS TOWARD PROFESSIONALIZING BROADCAST NEWS

In closing, we come to the solution believed by this writer to be essential, regardless of which of the other alternatives are adopted. That is professionalization.

In their research into the characteristics of an occupation that aspires to be a profession, U. S. journalism scholars Jack N. McLeod and Searle E. Hawley list the following (here paraphrased slightly).

A profession must (1) perform a unique and essential service; (2) emphasize intellectual techniques; (3) have a long period of training involving a substantial body of knowledge, based on research; (4) be given a broad range of autonomy; (5) require its practitioners to accept broad personal responsibility for judgments and actions; (6) place greater emphasis on service than on private economic gain; (7) develop a comprehensive self-governing organization; and (8) have a code of ethics clarified and interpreted by concrete cases.[21]

David J. LeRoy lists five belief "clusters" that constitute attitude structures characteristic of any professional person. Reduced to key words, and slightly paraphrased, these are: (1) allegiance to the field (his group) as his principal reference group; (2) altruism: belief in public service above private; (3) a deep commitment, a "calling," to the field; (4) autonomy—freedom to make his own decisions; (5) belief in self-regulation, recognizing only his peers as having the right and competency to judge his performance.[22]

In *Television and the News* this author has discussed at some length the history of professionalism and reviewed the codes, oaths, standards, and self-discipline provisions of several such professions as medicine, law, education, engineering, accounting, and the clergy.[23]

With full recognition of the protests it may arouse, the following amended list of suggested steps is offered as one of several efforts needed if the media are to provide an information service democracy needs, and if news personnel are to regain and maintain the respect, credibility, and pride in their work that characterize a true profession. Discussion, amendment, and improvement of this list are welcomed from whatever source. It is humbly offered as a starting point for a needed effort.

1. The professional has and shows respect for human dignity and the rights and sacredness of the individual. Each individual needs the respect of others if his sense of human dignity is to be preserved. This refers to all peoples, regardless of color, race, nationality, or station in life.

The professional does not ridicule or belittle the good name of others, except for the protection of the public good.

His respect extends to the institutions of the home, the family, the church, and the school, in whatever form they exist.

The professional recognizes also the rights of all men to privacy, especially in times of grief, tragedy, crisis, or joy. The invasions of that privacy and the publicizing of alleged flaws, misdeeds, and intimacies shall be tolerated only when essential to the overall public good.

2. In accord with the adherence of this nation to the United Nations' principles of peace and understanding, positive and peaceful values shall be promoted whenever possible as opposed to negative, violent, or warlike ones.

In the selection and presentation of news, peace shall be featured over violence, and love over hate and intolerance, in order to advance the humane aspirations of civilization and mankind.

3. The professional journalist is not a judge. Guilt is left to the courts to decide. He shall seek the truth wherever it lies. Intellectual honesty must prevent concealment or favoritism. Editorial comment shall be kept separate from factual reporting, shall be clearly identified, and shall be balanced by access for other interpretations.

4. Since freedom of information is essential in a democracy, freedom of speech shall be promoted with care and courage. The professional recognizes that he should exercise his freedom of press and speech *as an agent of society*, not for any special rights, privileges and needs of his own, or as a member of the press.

5. It is not the function of the press to serve as a police blotter or chronicle of the crimes, offenses, failures, accidents, and catastrophes of a society.

Over-concentration on deviations from the daily life of a nation, or on its flaws, blemishes, or scandals, is a disservice to a nation. Events of relevance and significance should be the story of a nation's day.

A professional constantly reviews with responsible advisors his definition and selection of news, realizing the dangers of suggestibility and imitation of the value systems and behavior patterns demonstrated by their very presentation.

6. Being dedicated to revealing truth and opposing its concealment, the professional shall provide an example of his belief by the full disclosure of the internal events of his profession and of organizations with which he is affiliated, with the exception of confidential personnel files.

Secrecy, except as it shall serve broad public rather than private organizational ends, must be avoided at all costs.

7. In order to deserve the confidence of his clientele, the professional uses only fair and ethical means to secure his information. He dissociates himself from the vigilante, the howling mob, the blackmailer, and the character assassin. A professional does not deal in stolen or illegal goods. He exercises daily care to resist pressures for the imposition of the values of materialism, commercialism, or others, in order to maintain his first loyalty to human and rational values. As a professional, he is his own man, jealous of his autonomy, the slave of no group or organization.

8. The true professional takes the utmost care not to broadcast or publish material without careful checking. He does not get caught up in a rush for firstness.

When material is released in error, there shall be used regular procedures for correction and retraction, designed in advance.

9. The professional looks to no outside organization for establishing principles of fairness. The practice established by the professional should exceed legal requirements to be truthful, fair, and open.

This doctrine shall include ample provision for access and the right of reply.

10. A professional's loyalty is to his field, the public, and the service he provides, not to any single corporation or group. When a service can better be performed by other organizations or groups than his own, he presses for such service, avoiding the temptation to damage public good

for private gain. The service is more important than the preservation of the monopoly of any one type of service or medium.

His loyalty is to truth rather than to the prerogatives or monopoly of any one employer or group.

11. The models a professional features in his coverage, thereby holding them up to the nation, shall be worthy ones—not those of superficial popularity, notoriety, scandal, wealth, crime, sports, or other surface values. The model of a professional is excellence, not "popularity."

The picture of reality and excellence which reaches the public through the media will shape their lives, attitudes, decisions, and values. It is unworthy of a professional to subvert the nobility of human values, aspirations, and goals to trivial or immoral or wasteful ends.

12. A journalistic professional is clear about the crucial and indispensable nature of his function to the democratic process; though he does not confuse his role with that of the gods, he recognizes the sacredness of his function to society. By his respect for his colleagues, he promotes respect for his profession.

13. Recognizing the importance of his role, the journalist recognizes the importance of training for it just as the surgeon or architect must, if wasteful and dangerous "amateurism" is to be prevented.

To this end the professionals shall press for the establishment of educational standards for their profession through their organizations. The life-blood information flow of the nation deserves to be entrusted only to professionals trained in the effects of their function and resolved to exclude from the profession any who would abuse it for private gain.

14. Having established and met specific character and educational standards, news professionals shall govern their private lives and behavior with a realization of the models they are to the nation.

They shall not promote cheapness, or take part in commercial activities that will reduce their credibility. Nor shall they accept gratuities which might limit their standing as professionals.

15. As respecters and promoters of the national culture, professionals shall avoid practices which, by exaggeration, vulgarity, violence, or linguistic misuse, may reduce the precision of communication.

16. In the enforcement of its high standards as professionals, newsmen shall discipline their own members, and shall as a group refuse to accept the interference of management, sales, government, or pressure groups on their performance or role.

To this end they shall design systems of penalties for malpractice by their own peers, and censure procedures for employers who expect or request them to violate professional standards in the selection or handling of news and comment, including its placement, and the time periods required for its presentation.

17. Professional newsmen, recognizing that the old order must change, and that life is dynamic, must see themselves as agents for the facilitation of peaceful change.

To this end they must become exponents of peaceful conflict resolution, and informed proponents of alternatives to confrontation and violence.

18. Since television by its nature and presence risks changing the course of events, sometimes inciting to violent, vulgar, or otherwise undesirable behavior, the utmost care must be taken to keep such coverage responsible, inconspicuous, and respectful of the rights of others.

19. As a great profession, broadcast news personnel will sponsor, promote, and conduct extensive and continuing research into the effects of television—both in its fictional and news-public-affairs offerings.

There should be particular research into the effects of techniques with which newsmen are associated: how the repetition of news items and commercials affects the human attention factor; and the effects of violence, noise, confusion, and other ingredients used to compose a newscast.

Such research will seek to measure the frustration levels of viewers in response to commercial or news reruns, the effects of newsmen doing commercials, and other data essential to newsmen's understanding of the conditions they must insist on if the nation is to be maximally informed and served.

Such a program of continuing research into its product and techniques is an essential characteristic of every profession worthy of the name, and must be of high priority to the news profession.

20. These provisions shall be reviewed and revised annually at a conference in which responsible advisors from the principal professions and disciplines shall participate.

CONCLUSION

These then, are the few modest suggestions for professionalizing television and radio news at which all the rest of this piece has been aimed.

As stated earlier, these suggestions are not offered as final. They are offered with the invitation, indeed the appeal, for newsmen and others to help add to them, revise them, or otherwise make them workable without again "selling out" to management. Only by devising, enforcing, and honoring some such set of standards, sooner or later, will newsmen again enjoy the credibility, respect, and influence they must have in America if democracy is to work.

REFERENCES

1. Nordenstreng, Kaarle. Original (mimeographed) paper. Published in slightly edited form as "A Policy of News Transmission." *Educational Broadcasting Review* 5 (October 1971): 20–30.
2. St. John, Alexandra. "The News, as Interpreted by Three Different Sources, for the Five-Day Period 2/26/73 to 3/2/73." Unpublished manuscript.
3. Otto, Herbert. Quoted in ANPA (American Newspaper Publishers Association) *Newsletter*, November 27, 1968: 3.
4. Nordenstreng, Kaarle. *Op. cit.* (see 1).
5. Bogart, Leo. Quoted in ANPA (American Newspaper Publishers Association) *Newsletter*, February 28, 1973: 3.
6. Stengle, Gary. "Newscasts of WMAQ–TV, Channel 5, Chicago, February 12, 1973," Student monitor report.
7. Liptak, Gregory James. "Influences on News Broadcasting in the State of Illinois." December 9, 1963. Mimeographed. Later published as a master's thesis, 1964, as "An Investigation and Analysis of Pressures and Influences on News Broadcasters at 100 Radio and Television Stations in the State of Illinois and Adjacent States." (Available at the Urbana Campus Library of the University of Illinois.)
8. Walbridge, Willard E. "Newsmen's Privileges," Statement on behalf of the NAB Ad Hoc Committee, NAB Board Meeting, Palm Springs, California, January 12, 1973. Mimeographed, p. 3.
9. Morrisett, Lloyd N. "The President's Essay." In *The John and Mary R. Markle Foundation Annual Report, 1971–72*, p. 12.
10. McLeod, Jack M. and Hawley, Searle E., Jr. "Professionalization Among Newsmen." *Journalism Quarterly*, 41 (1964): 538.
11. Skornia, Harry J. *Television and the News.* Palo Alto: Pacific Books, 1968.
12. Geldmacher, John L. and Lumpp, James A. "Rosenblum and Libel." *Freedom of Information Center Report* 297 (January 1973): 3.
13. Morrisett, Lloyd N. *Op. cit.* (see 9).
14. LeRoy, David L. "Journalism as a Profession." In *Mass News*, eds. David J. LeRoy and Christopher H. Sterling. New York: Prentice-Hall, 1973.
15. Danish, Roy. Television Information Office press release, February 23, 1973, p. 4.
16. Fields, James E. "Press Access Rationale and Response." *Freedom of Information Center Report*, 296 (January 1973): 3.

17. Fields, James E. *Op. cit.* (see 16): 6.

18. Graham, Fred P. "Background Paper." In *Press Freedom under Pressure.* New York: Twentieth Century Fund, 1972, p. 79.

19. "What's at the End of the Tunnel on News Privilege?" *Broadcasting* (March 5, 1973): 34–36.

20. Loeb, William. *Letter*, March 9, 1973. Santa Barbara, California: Forum for Contemporary History, pp. 1–4.

21. McLeod, Jack M. and Hawley, Searle E. *Op. cit.* (see 10): 530.

22. LeRoy, David. J. *Op. cit.* (see 14), p. 253.

23. Skornia, Harry J. *Op. cit.* (see 11), pp 193–217.

ADVERTISING

Entertainment programming is the basis for our commercial system of broadcasting because it attracts the largest mass audiences possible on a regular basis, which in turn attract advertisers who want to reach the most people for the least cost. Not only has television developed into an effective medium for reaching a large audience, but its visual qualities also make it a persuasive selling medium.

In the past few years the development of the consumer movement has brought various pressures on television and radio advertising. Some groups have had a direct impact upon television and advertising—Action for Children's Television (ACT) and the Council for Children, Media and Merchandising, among other groups and individuals, have forced broadcasters to employ self-regulatory measures regarding advertising aimed directly at children. One continuing concern is the advertising agency methods used to determine what successful techniques can be used in children's commercials to create a desire for the product. Marilyn Elias describes some of these techniques.

Often, the number of interruptions during programs irritates the viewer. In recent years the increasing use of 30-second announcements rather than 60-second commercials has increased the number of commercials but not the amount of time devoted to advertising. Between programs, commercials of various lengths—60 seconds, 30 seconds and 10 seconds —may expose us to four or five different products. While some stations limit the amount of time given to commercials within and between programs to abide by the code of the National Association of Broadcasters, many stations do not subscribe to the code and therefore are free to set their own commercial time standards. Even when time standards are adhered to, the code does not specify how many individual commercials may be run. The article by Richard K. Doan elaborates on this problem of clutter and Stefan Kanfer takes a humorous approach to the enigma of commercials in "Is There Intelligent Life on Commercials?"

A serious subject to any station manager is the position his station holds in the ratings among other stations in his community. If a station ranks low when compared with its competitors, it is much harder for the manager to sell his advertising time and he cannot receive as high a price for his time because the low rating reflects the small size of his audience. A serious problem is described in "Station Rankings to Shift in Ethnic-Rating Storm." Here we find that black and Spanish-language stations are complaining that the samples of homes used by rating services do not reflect the true ethnic mix, and their stations are suffering lower rankings unjustly.

The content of advertising has been and will continue to be an issue for the future. False and misleading advertising is watched over by the Federal Trade Commission, but stations and networks must screen commercials to determine if they meet the standards of accuracy and good taste. Another area related to the content of commercials is tied in with the FCC rule known as the Fairness Doctrine, which states that if a station airs a program or message about one side of a controversial issue, it must provide an opportunity for those holding other views on the topic to express them on the air. In the last half of the sixties, cigarette advertising was being attacked because of the product's link with cancer and lung disease. This issue was, in the opinion of the FCC, a controversial issue and, therefore, deserved to be treated under the Fairness Doctrine. The connection was this: cigarette commercials advocated smoking and because smoking had been linked by medical research to serious illness and death, a controversial issue existed. The outcome was that the FCC ruled that radio and television stations broadcasting cigarette commercials were required to carry the opposing view—this was the birth of countercommercials. This type of commercial was also used to counteract gasoline and automobile commercials in the New York City area because such products create pollution and that was considered a controversial issue. In July, 1974 the FCC changed its rule about countercommercials; now they cannot be used to respond to *product* advertising. They may be required against a commercial only if that commercial is addressed specifically to a controversial issue and without attempting to sell a product. At press time no article of note has appeared on this topic that could be included here but this decision may have future ramifications.

BIBLIOGRAPHICAL ESSAY

The relationship between advertising and broadcasting has always been a close one. Broadcasting has offered the persuasive art of advertising a very persuasive medium, whether it is radio or television. And advertising has reciprocated by supporting broadcasting in the way to which it has become accustomed. Two excellent survey articles on the effects of radio and television on the advertising world will be found in the special edition of *Advertising Age* (November 21, 1973) entitled "The New World of Advertising."

In the process of performing its self-serving economic role as purveyor of advertising, the television industry has permitted some questionable practices to grow up. One of those practices concerns advertising to children on television. Our selection, an overview of methods for reaching children through television commercials, is prepared by Marilyn Elias, assistant editor of *Human Behavior*. An article by Robert Berkvist, "Can TV Keep Giving Kids the Business?" *The New York Times* (May 12, 1972), sec. 2, 1+, brings the same viewpoint to the subject. A more thorough treatment, with documentation, is William Melody, *Children's Television: The Economics of Exploitation*, Yale University Press, New Haven, 1973, which includes an extensive bibliography plus the NAB principles for children's programs. A scholarly look at the entire issue is Shel Feldman and Abraham Wolf, "What's Wrong With Children's Commercials?" *Journal of Advertising Research* (February, 1974), 39–43. The authors categorize the charges against children's commercials and review the research in these areas as well as indicate needs for further research. An especially useful publication is Charles Winick, *et al., Children's Television Commercials: A Content Analysis,* Praeger, New York, 1973.

Richard K. Doan has amply illustrated the problem most viewers of television express at one time or another—the clutter of advertising messages. Articles and comments frequently appear in the trade press, especially advertising magazines, because of the potential effect too many messages have upon a particular commercial. An interesting essay on a related area, "Creative Clutter," is given by Arthur Bellaire, *Advertising Age* (January 14, 1974), in which he argues that many advertisers "clutter up" their commercial by including extraneous scenes or information. To most people, however, the word "clutter" will continue to express concern about the large number of commercials and announcements that crowd into programs today. Stefan Kanfer's interesting little essay reprinted here presents a rather common though debatable view about the quality of television commercials.

Television/Radio Age's survey of the current controversy over ratings and their exclusion of certain ethnic groups should be supplemented by other readings dealing with the rating systems themselves. An excellent survey of ratings, their uses and problems, is given in an in-house report prepared for the FCC by Commissioner Robert E. Lee. The report was first reprinted in *Television/Radio Age* (February 19, 1973), 26–27+. The American Research Bureau (ARB), New York, and A. C. Nielsen Co., Chicago, the two top television audience research firms in the nation, have produced large numbers of pamphlets and brochures to promote their services. These publications usually contain excellent information of interest to students in the field. ARB has two booklets which include maps for each market: *Radio Market Survey Area Guide* and *Television Market Survey Area Guide.* Each is revised annually. ARB also publishes *Television USA,* a booklet which statistically denotes the types of sets in use in America. Nielsen produces *Television,* an annually updated brochure that includes data on set ownership, cable television, and ratings of the top shows. *NSI Reference Supplement* provides information about Nielsen's sample methods and interpretations while *NIT in Action* provides information on gathering and using ratings.

An important issue not covered in our readings is the current trend toward comparative advertising, particularly on television. Tom Bradshaw, "Comparative Ads: What's Their Status Now?" *Television/Radio Age* (April 29, 1974), 29–32+, gives an excellent overview of the problem, citing specific cases and detailing those broadcast review agencies that have the responsibility for evaluating commercials and their fairness. The 10-point AAAA Comparative Ad Guidelines also are given in summary form. To keep abreast of this issue, consult *Advertising Age* regularly.

We have indicated in the introductions to this section that the FCC has acted to reduce some areas of counteradvertising while affirming the goal for other areas. Perhaps the best, single attack on the rationale for counteradvertising is "The Politics of Advertising," by Lee Loevinger, former FCC Commissioner, which was an address before The International Radio and Television Society, January , 1973. Loevinger is against counteradvertising and is a spokesman, in part, for the industry's views in this case. The Television Information Office, New York, has published Loevinger's extended remarks on the issue.

STUDY QUESTIONS

1. Do you object to the use of motivational research techniques to determine the effectiveness of television commercials directed toward children? Explain.
2. What action, if any, should be taken to make changes in television advertising directed toward children? Should the broadcasting and advertising industries be given the responsibility for self-regulation or is government regulation required? Discuss.
3. What are the ramifications of reducing the time devoted to nonprogram material (clutter) in television programs?
4. Explain how ethnic radio and TV stations might be affected if, as they allege, rating services fail to include sufficient minority representation in their population samples.
5. What steps can be taken to solve the problem of ethnic representation in rating-service population samples?

How to Win Friends and Influence Kids on Television

MARILYN ELIAS

Human Behavior, vol. 3, 4 (April, 1974). Copyright © 1974 *Human Behavior* Magazine. Reprinted by permission. Marilyn Elias is an assistant editor of *Human Behavior*.

A group of 10 preschoolers is clustered together on the floor in a cozy, shag-carpeted living room. The room is one of numerous homey "labs" set up inside the test facility of a major motivation-research house. As an adult enters, the tots are enthusiastically playing with toys, coloring with crayons in fat books and chatting with one another. They're part of a group of 150 who will be tested today for their reactions to a commercial pushing a new type of toy, and all have just seen this commercial in an auditorium, sandwiched between cartoons and other familiar ads. Now they're isolated in small groups, says a company official, "to overcome shyness and verbal limitations so that they can show the analyst how they really think and feel."

The "analyst" is a child psychologist, and he begins to interview the kids one by one. The shiest ones will tell their reactions to the commercials via a Smiley Scale. This is a cardboard tool, shaped like a ruler, that starts at the far left with a scowling kid's face and works its way to the right getting more and more happy. The joyful grin that breaks out at the far right is what the sponsor is trying to get. The gray-haired psychologist is prodding a four-year-old boy, a little towhead with bangs and freckles, to point to the face that tells how he felt about the commercial. The kid is kind of shy and reluctant but after a few minutes he complies.

During the next hour, these children also are asked to draw their "feelings" about each part of the commercial. These drawings are collected and later will be carefully analyzed by specialists who link the content of the drawing with how a youngster feels about the commercial, and, ultimately, how much money can be made off his emotions and vulnerabilities.

Some of the analysts have had special training in Stanislavski dramatic techniques. They organize the kids into improvisational teams, and the tiny guinea pigs then act out how their parents are likely to react to their request for this product, what "pitches" they themselves would use on adults and how playmates would feel about the product.

The entire process is enormously revealing, for it draws out just what the profit seeker is doing right in his pitch to the young and precisely where he needs to make changes in order to attain maximum exploitation of the child market.

Added to this battery of psychological tools are physical ones, sophisticated equipment used like mental pliers to pull out even more about how commercial appeals can be designed so that they capture the young television viewer.

Children like these are now targets for the most intricate instruments of manipulation in the hands of behavioral scientists. A multibillion-dollar commercial profit is the payoff in this unequal contest between young people and the flourishing motivation-research business, a trade that emphasizes penetration of natural defense and exploitation of vulnerable soft spots in the psyche. This sport has quietly grown by leaps and bounds during recent years.

The American corporate tab for children's television advertising approached $400 million in 1973, but it all started in a small way. For the endeavor of pitching to kids has grown up along with television, as Marshall McLuhan's "global village" brought together a captive young market for selling in addition to an entertainment audience.

After the 1954 debut of "Disneyland," the first successful kids' TV program, sponsors of children's products began to milk a generous new source of revenue. This Disney experience had shown that the children's market could provide an enormous potential for profit. During the next several years, programs for youngsters were scattered around the adult programming schedule, but by the mid-60s a definite "children's ghetto" had begun to develop. The ghetto was dominated by cartoons, including poor-quality reruns that crackled with violence, from 7 a.m. to 2 p.m. on weekends.

"By 1967, the three networks were engaged in increasingly intense competition for the attention of the weekend-television-viewing child, which had developed into a multimillion-dollar market in network television alone," notes Prof. William Melody of University of Pennsylvania in his new book, *Children's TV—The Economics of Exploitation.* Advertisers found they could reach large numbers of a demographically "pure" market for lower relative costs if they stuck to repetitive, 30-second spots in the children's ghetto. This programming served to concentrate the market of young minds they were making a strong effort to influence.

Toy, cereal, candy and snack-food commercial spots now crowd into the children's ghetto, and since many more U.S. homes have TV than indoor plumbing, the commercial sweep offered by the medium is truly vast. The moderate child viewer sees more than 25,000 commercials per year, spending more time in front of the tube than in his elementary school classroom on the average.

But quantity of exposure represents only a superficial part of the children's advertising world. The phenomenal amount of money expended for ads is worth it to the profit makers because the ads themselves are meticulously constructed to burrow beneath the surface to a gut level at which many children simply do not possess the perceptual resources to resist. "Selling to children on TV is like shooting fish in a barrel. It is grotesquely unfair," declares Joan Ganz Cooney, president of the Children's Television Workshop, at a Yale University symposium on children and TV. Fair or not, the winning over of small minds shows how vanguard social science techniques can be harnessed to the head of a profit-seeking machine and lead the way.

A visit to one motivation firm located in a West Coast suburb brought to light some of these techniques. Company officials asked not to be identified. "Frankly, we'd rather not have the publicity; we try to operate quietly. The competition is very, very fierce in children's package goods," says one co-owner. "In fact, if there's a backup tape of the kids that the client doesn't carry out with him, we burn the tape."

The work is done in a large unobtrusive facility on the second floor of an older office building. Cozy wall-to-wall aqua carpeting and tasteful furniture lend quite a homey feeling to the place. The children's "lab" is actually a colorful play haven, astutely designed to ply the young and to pry out what may be hidden in their reactions to products and commercials. A round, kid-high captain's table sports appealing decals and is ringed with 12 tiny chairs. Framed drawings of animals and other juvenile favorites decorate the walls. A variety of toys are scattered around—a miniature princess phone here, across the room a dwarf of a refrigerator.

Then there's the mirror, a rectangular mirror like the kind often put above buffets in dining rooms. It makes the place seem so homelike, but the mirror is there for a far more important reason. Behind the dazzling glass is a room that the children inside this "lab" do not know about. People will be seeing and hearing their reactions. Cameras behind the one-way mirror capture every gesture, and recorders pick up the inflection and content of everything said, for nearly-hidden microphones are screwed into the ceiling.

Who sits behind the mirror, and what will he get that is worth all this effort? A closed door leads to the "client's room," a narrow cubicle dominated by one raised pedestal that has a leather couch on it. The client sits there. When you sink into the leather couch you can see the entire children's room, but a faint cast of grey makes it look like you are wearing tinted glasses. None of the children, of course, can see you. Inside the lab, as tots are exposed to commercials and products, they are sometimes filmed with special cameras to measure the amount of their eye pupil dilation, a reaction that has been linked to involvement and pleasure. Psychologists and marketing specialists will probe their reactions via play and discussion techniques.

The children may be equipped with finger sensors, which allow monitoring of the degree of resistance to the passage of minute electrical currents. This automatic measure relates to the degree of subconscious involvement with the product. When the co-owner was asked if this firm provided clients with the finger sensors, she replied, "We don't have them, but when the client wants that kind of measurement, they bring the equipment in and we use it here." Later, the other co-owner, who was much more reluctant than her colleague to discuss what the company did, was asked about the sensors. She quickly said, "Oh, no, we don't do that type of work." Neither partner would reveal the firm's annual receipts or the number of children they work with in an average year.

Another type of motivational probing goes on at Hollywood's Audience Studies, Inc. (ASI), which has a 150-seat theater for testing commercials and pilot programs. They work mostly with adults, but a substantial amount of children's testing is done. The youngsters are located through forms filled out by parents who have been tested or through telephone recruiting, like most motivation houses. ASI keeps an extensive bank of names on file. Kids register their reactions to commercials on an "interest machine," a hand dial that offers five degrees of pleasure and involvement. This provides a second-to-second graph of feelings about ads that can be broken down by age, sex and other factors. "It's very important to grab kids in the first few seconds of commercials," explains ASI Executive Vice-President Roger Seltzer, so the graphs are vital. Questionnaires asking for product preferences are filled out before and after the commercial spots. Then small group discussions are held. ASI has used a machine that records eye movements and how long a child's eye lingers, but this machine is no longer used, Seltzer claims. The firm declined to show their facilities, but permitted an interview with Seltzer. "It's a security-type thing," explained Sharon Pollack, Seltzer's executive secretary. "You wouldn't see much unless you went into the machine room and saw all our machines, and I don't think they'd ever let you do that."

ASI tests between 3,000 and 4,000 youngsters each year, starting with people as young as three, according to Seltzer. The motivation house's clients include major cereal companies, toy manufacturers, soft drink

Elias

195

companies and makers of food snacks for children, but Seltzer would not reveal the names of any clients.

The closely guarded secrecy of the children's motivation business has spurred recent criticism from a variety of quarters—Congress, the Federal Trade and Federal Communications commissioners, physicians and psychiatrists, and burgeoning consumer groups. The two most prominent consumer groups in the children's advertising field are Boston-based Action for Children's Television (ACT) and the Council on Children, Media and Merchandising in Washington.

Robert Choate, a 48-year-old civil engineer and the father of three, started the Washington organization four years ago after he got a client's-eye view of what the motivation houses offer. "I was trying to market a nutritional supermarket game that I got together, a toy that would be constructive for kids," says Choate. "I went to a number of ad agencies and they couldn't tell me much. I found out that they would go to the motivational research houses to get all the marketing information, so I decided to go directly to the houses myself."

He queried 25 firms (the trade publication *Mediascope* lists at least 15 such agencies specializing in children in New York City alone) and was motivated to use what he learned for the sake of exposing the booming business.

Choate maintains that the real mission of the research firms is to "perfect the type of 30- or 60-second message which will penetrate the child's natural defenses and alter his behavior so as to serve industry within the home." The child's parents often see the effectiveness of the sales pitch on their offspring but do not understand why it works so well.

"The problem is serious, and the more I see the more convinced I am that something needs to be done about the use of media to influence children, to guide them in an unknown way to feel a certain need," says Sen. Frank Moss (D-Utah). Moss is sponsoring a bill that would create a new motivation-research unit supervised by the National Science Foundation (NSF). The goal is to develop a body of information on how advertising affects people, including children. This pool of new data would be made public, providing consumers for the first time with the proprietary type of secrets that industry now keeps hidden in its tight grasp.

Even without the proposed NSF team, some facts are starting to trickle out. But the most significant work in children's advertising has only been done since 1970. Advertising executives Melvin Helitzer and Carl Heyel report in their book, *The Youth Market*, that a survey of mothers has revealed that because children demand specific products and brands, they spend an average of $1.66 more per household in the supermarket each week. Thus Junior's zealous consumerism adds $1.5 *billion* annually to grocery retail sales alone. Yet television's role as the dominant advertising medium to children is just starting to be explored. The surgeon general's 1972 report on television and social behavior included a bibliography with 550 separate citations of research on children and television. Not a single one dealt specifically with the impact of advertising on children.

The issue prompts two questions: whether young people are influenced to become "salesmen within the home" and thus agents for moving products; and, apart from the sales message, whether there are piggyback-style damaging values that American children absorb by osmosis from the 350,000 TV commercials they have seen by the age of 18.

"All television is educational television. The only question is, what is it teaching?" observes former FCC Commissioner Nicholas Johnson. One of the lessons kids learn from ever-present TV ads is early cynicism, disbelief in adults who had been trusted earlier, according to the work of Dr. Scott Ward, a professor at Harvard Graduate School of Business. Ward found that young tykes tune in more ardently on commercial messages; they're true believers. But as children get closer to the teen years, they're more likely to discount ad claims and to tell investigators that TV commercials are not truthful. Even this cynicism may harm young people, for psychiatric testimony given during FTC hearings revealed that a child's body pays with nervous exhaustion when he's forced to "tune out" what he believes to be lies.

The potent pull ads have on young consumers is shown in a 1973 project supervised by Dr. Charles Atkin, a communication professor at Michigan State University. After surveying 538 Lansing area students in grades one to five, Atkin reports that 75 percent said they asked their mothers to purchase the cereals they had seen on TV. Two-thirds of the mothers confirmed such requests. More than four-fifths of youngsters recalled asking for toys after seeing commercials for them, and 75 percent of the mothers' group said this had happened. "These findings suggest that television commercials do stimulate desire for toys and cereals and similar products among young viewers," concludes Atkin. But considering the refined techniques used on kids in motivation-research houses, the striking effectiveness of commercials should come as no surprise.

More facts were revealed in a still-unpublished pilot study by Columbia Graduate School of Business professors John Howard, James Hulbert and Donald Lehmann. They did 96 interviews with children two to six years old and also queried their mothers. Two-thirds of the interviewing was done in rural New Hampshire, another third in urban New Jersey. The children said they remembered ads about cereal and toys more frequently than any other. And mothers of these youngsters said toys and cereals happened to be the two items most frequently asked for. Eighty percent of the mothers expressed the conviction that television pitches did cause their children to ask for products. When the kids were asked if Mother buys the cereal they pick out, 45 percent said "always" or "most of the time," another 51 percent said "sometimes," only three of 78 youngsters responding in the survey said "seldom" and none said "never."

Confirming some of Ward's findings, 90 percent of mothers responding reported that their young children considered TV commercials "real" and only 10 percent said they were "make-believe." This childlike confusion of reality with fantasy apparently is exploited by ad makers. Charles Winick, a sociology professor at City University of New York, recently analyzed 236 typical non–toy commercials aimed at children. He found that in 61 percent of the spots the product was jazzed up with fantasy actions or magical settings that could never exist in the real world.

Psychology professor Freda Rebelsky capsuled the problem succinctly in a speech delivered to the Advertising Club in Boston: "Children will not see, hear, interpret and feel as we do. They are likely to say, 'It goes so fast,' not 'It looks like it goes so fast.' 'He is happy because he's smiling,' not 'He is paid to smile and is just acting.' "

Kids' commercials are essentially 30-second-long TV shows, frequently repeated on the screen. And there is a clear body of evidence that television shows can shape children's action. In fact, the very techniques that have proven *most* effective for stimulating imitation behaviors in youngsters through entertainment television are being used in many TV ads, maintains Dr. Robert Liebert, professor of psychology at State University of New York, Stony Brook.

Liebert has been hired by the United Methodist Church as a consultant in the production of three 30-second spots similar to commercials, hopefully for airing on TV stations all over the nation starting this spring. But these spots, using some of the most effective techniques of television ads, will be "selling" pro–social messages, such as how children can resolve personal conflicts and express anger in constructive ways.

Research has demonstrated that certain types of TV shows are most apt to trigger imitation behavior in child viewers. Absolute clarity of meaning must exist for the child. A degree of conflict and tension, plus characters he can identify with, help to provoke the desired behavior. And actual portrayal of somebody doing the act you want imitated is another important way to stimulate imitation. "Perhaps nothing is more important than the reward aspect," Liebert stresses. "You need to dramatize as much as possible the positive outcomes that come from this behavior you want imitated." These are some of the techniques that have been shown to work best in influencing kids.

After listening to what studies and experts had to say, kids' ads began to take on the déjà vu quality of reruns for me. There were the potato chips that turned into "a bag full of fun," a great reward for the kid on the tube (and his peer sitting at home can take it from there). The huge box of cereal set in front of a tiny child in the background certainly showed that cameras could lie. But even this small tot gets the reward of miraculous playing energy after eating one quick bowlful. The fellow in the space suit just happens to tumble down into the kiddie drive-in. Marvelous elf-like characters turn up in cereals and a talking zebra pops out of a package of sugary gum. Because children can confuse the fantastic with the real, sales messages seem to grab them hard and stick with them.

But psychologists and consumer groups are now starting to look beneath this obvious effect of TV commercials to the values that are blanketing young minds day after day via ever-present commercials.

What do children learn from TV ads? "The most important things about you are what you look like and what you own," declares Liebert. The tendency to define personal success as acquisition, to view material devouring as an effective way to solve problems, probably are sad by-products absorbed by children. Some ads submitted to the FTC by ACT, a consumer group that is trying to get children's commercials banned, show how kids are told that they need never be unhappy or bored as long as an appealing product waits nearby.

"Many children's commercials I've seen emphasize the importance of physical force," adds Liebert. "They show in a variety of ways that force can be used and make a person successful. Force can be used in a comic and acceptable context, which we know from research into entertainment television leads to violent behavior." He singled out as an example the Hawaiian Punch television commercial in which one character asks another, "How would you like a Hawaiian Punch?" and then gives him a quick smash. "It puts that kind of action into an aceptable funny context, teasing and tormenting other people so as to get a laugh out of it," says Liebert.

ACT's 1973 petition to the FTC includes an illustration of how current commercials exploit a variety of basic human values. Racial brotherhood and ecology, for example, have been twisted into sales messages directed at small children. Political power, common sense and fame all have been linked with the purchases of specific products in ads aimed at the young.

"The images your children are growing up with are not those of Washington, Jefferson and Lincoln—they're images of commercials saying father is a jerk; mother is stupid and a gossip; all kids should make out; and elderly people sit around arthritic and constipated." The statement sounds like an angry tome from a consumer advocate who detests the ad game. But this assessment of some values that hit kids over the head was made by Jerry Goodis, an ad agency executive, to an audience at the University of Missouri.

Some people who believe that American children sustain harmful effects from omnipresent TV commercials, and who recognize that motivation research is getting more refined all the time, still place the blame wholly upon parents for allowing their youngsters to be exposed to the ads in the first place. And no doubt some of it belongs there. Lewis Engman, chairman of the FTC, spoke realistically about this problem in a 1973 speech: "Parents are not monitoring every commercial message weekday afternoons and Saturday and Sunday mornings, and, in many cases, working parents are simply not able to exercise the necessary control over their children for extensive periods of time." Cutting down a child's television-viewing hours may not even prove that effective in stemming sales influence. Harvard researcher Scott Ward found that when restrictions were placed on a child's TV hours, this did not lead to a lower frequency of purchase influence attempts.

Some parents do care a great deal about this issue. When ACT first petitioned the FCC to end advertising on children's television hours, the FCC's Notice of Proposed Rulemarking drew more than 100,000 letters and supporting petitions from private citizens and citizen groups, the largest public response in the *history* of broadcast regulation. The overwhelming majority favored the ACT proposal.

Commercial saturation may be particularly strong among children of the poor, for American studies have shown that low-income children watch more TV than the offspring of the middle class. The tube may serve these families as a baby-sitter, especially in one-parent homes when the one parent must be away working for long hours and cannot afford a human baby-sitter. Ad industry spokespeople do a lot of verbal wristslapping of parents, but their words cannot rub out the reality of how poor people live. A pilot study carried out by Daniel Yankelovich, Inc., found that "Lower income mothers particularly resent the stresses and strains imposed by the demands suggested by television commercials. Either they end up by spending money they can't afford—or their children feel left out and 'different' than other children."

If significant change does come in children's TV advertising, and the motivation-research industry that buttresses it, the change is apt to be by federal fiat and over howling protests from the major children's interest firms, ad agencies, motivational research houses, the National Association of Broadcasters (NAB) and TV networks. That's a lot of protest from powerful people, so pessimists on the issue have plenty of basis for their views. The explosion of kids' ads on the home screen, in particular their clustering inside the "children's ghetto," has unearthed a gold mine for too many adults who are not about to abandon the cache voluntarily.

We're so mythically sentimental about kids that looking into childhood as a major profit center to be exploited does not inspire comfortable feelings. But Professor Melody did it anyway in his new book, *Children's TV—The Economics of Exploitation*. Melody explores the economic forces that have shaped the children's TV ghetto into its current form, and he offers some signposts to the future.

> Forecasts of the potential market for specialized child-audience advertising all tend to indicate that exploitation of this market for its full profit potential by advertisers and broadcasters will not occur for some time to come. . . . In this regard, marketing in children's television is just nearing the end of its stage of embryonic growth and getting ready for substantial additional growth, as more sophisticated techniques of market segmentation, cultivation and advertising are brought to bear on it.

As the potential profit of the children's market becomes greater and greater, it also becomes more and more economical to bring more sophisticated techniques for market analysis and more managerial time and effort to pinpointing the precise characteristics of the children's markets and submarkets so that advertisers can exploit them to their full potential.

Who can control this trend as it races into the future? The NAB is the group that is supposed to uphold a "code" for children's advertising and claims to enforce fair business practices. Code regulations have tightened in recent years—on paper. For example, starting April 1, [1974], advertisers are not supposed to recommend the immoderate use of snacks, candy, soft drinks or gum. Also, breakfast products ads, which stimulate kids to gobble up a vast array of artificially sweetened cereals of little nutritional value, must include audio and video depictions of the product's role in a balanced diet.

Like other NAB regulations for selling to children, these new ones sound good. The problem has been that the NAB Code Authority operates via voluntary compliance, with no workable enforcement mechanism. Violations of the NAB's current ethical standards for children's ads occur frequently. So why should consumers assume that tightening these paper regulations will make any difference in actual commercials?

Also, 43 percent of the nation's licensed commercial TV stations do not even belong to the NAB, so the Code Authority has no jurisdiction over these outlets.

ACT and Choate's Council on Children, Media and Merchandising are hopeful for constructive change through the FTC, whose new chairman, Lewis Engman, has evinced strong concern about children's advertising, and through Sen. Moss's bill as an outside possibility. Hearings were first held in February 1973 on Moss's proposal to create a market-research agency under the NSF. An important aim is to provide consumers with some of the "proprietary" general research on motivation now used against them and their children. Moss expressed cautious optimism that the bill would make it through Congress in 1974. "So far, everything has been somewhat slow, but it's also quite a new idea, it's a pioneering thing that has to have time to gain some legislative acceptance," Moss said in an interview. "It's a little startling when people first hear about it, that we would attempt to invade the advertising field that way."

Since the '73 hearings, the Consumer Subcommittee of the Committee on Commerce has circulated questionnaires about the bill to a number of behavioral scientists, add agency people and their clients in the children's market. "People in the advertising business have been quite receptive; it's their clients who have been resistant. The food and toy manufacturers just don't feel comfortable about it," Moss said. That's understandable. For what such a research team might find out, and make public, about how children's minds are influenced could arouse a lot more consumer uproar, ultimately puncturing these firms' bloated profits along with the motivation houses that helped build them up.

Meantime, FTC Chairman Engman has tried to get some voluntary action going, while warning that the commission may crack down if improvements are not made voluntarily. After delivering a major speech on children's television commercials last August, Engman called together representatives from advertising, child-oriented companies and consumer organizations. He wanted the three diverse interest groups to hold a series of meetings that would hopefully produce a mutually acceptable, voluntary code. "FTC set up the meetings, and then those meetings quickly ran out of gas," says Choate. "Almost in desperation, the FTC allowed to some of us in the consumer field that they'd be appreciative if we'd submit to them some of our best ideas for a code and its enforcement."

Choate believes the issue has been accorded serious attention by Thomas Rosch, the 34-year-old former San Francisco antitrust attorney who took over last September as director of Consumer Protection for the FTC. Rosch has put an aide, Gerald Thain, full time on the subject of children's advertising. When asked if the trade commission might impose new rulings that would not be voluntary, Rosch replied, "Absolutely. If satisfactory enforcement can't be worked out in a voluntary way, we may well take action." Rosch said the input from consumer groups would be carefully evaluated by his staff.

While emphasizing that he prefers voluntary action, Rosch pointed out that a June 1973 Appeals Court decision upheld the FTC's powers to make rules on a general problem. "So far we've handled the children and advertising issue by bits and pieces, a case here, a case there," noted Rosch. "But now we realize we can make rules to cover problem situations and so do all the various parties involved." Meanwhile, Rosch is negotiating with the NSF in an effort to stimulate more research into the impact of commercials on children.

Dr. Seymour Banks, vice-president for media and program analysis at Leo Burnett Advertising Agency in Chicago, and a veteran industry spokesman, said in an interview that he hoped the FTC would not take rule-making action because "under trade regulation rules, the innocent suffer for the guilty." He pointed out that last June's court decision is on appeal and "we won't know until the Supreme Court decides."

But he sees stiffer regulations as quite likely if the FTC ultimately can set general rules. "The power is too tempting and too beneficial for somebody who believes in regulations not to do it," says Banks.

"The FTC is manned by lawyers, and we're getting the law's rules for whether something is deceptive or not. Their model as to whether something is deceptive or not is the reactions of a wayfaring fool," snapped Banks. "Traditionally, they don't give the children any credit just as they don't give the adults any credit. They practice 'Murphy's Law,' anything that can mislead will mislead."

Banks points out, "This is a crucial area, because whatever is done in this area may be taken as precedential for adult advertising." Many shows viewed by youngsters are outside the weekend ghetto slot intended exclusively for them, so a crackdown on children's TV commercials could lead to tougher scrutiny of ads that are aired on adult TV.

Existence of the children's ghetto as a major profit center in television makes ACT's proposal to end all pitching to kids a highly unrealistic expectation for the immediate future. Even an FTC regulation ordering drastic changes may not be in the immediate offing.

But a clear *mood* of change exists now in the agency and it could have long-term implications. FTC Chairman Engman's speech last August [1973] contained his own forecast on the issue:

> I believe that the time has come for action on children's television advertising. . . . The FTC will stand ready to take enforcement action if necessary. But I do not believe that matters must come to such a pass. There is still time for voluntary, concerted action. . . . However, as I said a moment ago, the time has come for action. And, whether it is voluntary action, or action by the Congress, or by the Federal Communications Commission, or by the Federal Trade Commission, or by any other branch or agency of government, is up to the interested parties. But I am confident, and I assure you, that there will be action.

We Pause Briefly . . .
for Seven or Eight Commercials

RICHARD K. DOAN

TV Guide, May 12, 1973. Reprinted with permission from TV GUIDE® Magazine. Copyright © 1973 by Triangle Publications, Inc., Radnor, Pennsylvania. Richard K. Doan is with the New York bureau of *TV Guide* and prepares a regular column, "The Doan Report," for the magazine.

"I'd watch TV more," a fairly common plaint goes these days, "but I just *can't* stomach all those commercials. They ruin my enjoyment of the shows. Sometime they just drive me up the wall!"

For whatever consolation it may be to such viewers, the people who spend millions of dollars yearly for those TV commercials aren't oblivious to this beef. Some of them are openly worrying about it. Recently, for example, a top adman, Ogilvy & Mather chairman Jock Elliott, warned that TV is being overcommercialized. "We are fouling our own nest," he admonished.

Even some broadcasters are alarmed. The president of a five-station group, Corinthian Broadcasting's James C. Richdale Jr., predicted that "if we don't clean up our business and reduce the clutter, we're dead."

And a network president, ABC's Elton Rule, fretted that if advertisers persisted in "splitting" commercial time into smaller pieces, the industry could experience "a backlash of protest" from viewers.

So far, though, viewers are suffering in silence—unless the networks and stations are receiving a lot of squawks they don't own up to publicly. There's no evidence of viewer defection. Indeed, TV watching in the average household is at an all-time high.

Aside from a few like Richdale, most TV executives appear to feel the clutter problem has been largely met by a new restriction in the National Association of Broadcasters' voluntary code governing commercials. It forbids multiple-product announcements in a unit of time that is less than 60 seconds in length, unless the products are related and the sales pitches are "integrated so as to appear to the viewer as a single announcement."

This is seen as putting a stop to further fractionalization of spots, thus halting the growing illusion (and actual fact) that the *number* of commercials is growing, even if the amount of time they occupy isn't.

Doan

205

As for cutting back on the over-all commercial time, perish the thought!

On Madison Avenue there's more lip service than action. The Association of National Advertisers has inveighed for years against clutter, magnanimously contending that broadcasters ought to increase the amount of entertainment in programs. That, of course, would give commercials more splendid isolation, presumably at no added cost to the sponsor.

The TV industry's response to anticlutter pressures has been mainly to whittle back a few seconds here, a few there, on such *non*commercial elements as production credits, stay-tuned blurbs, "the following program is in living color" announcements and the like. The viewer can scarcely tell the difference.

Any curious TV watcher could, of course, sit down with pad and pencil and stop watch and soon document what his eyes and ears tell him—that he's subjected to a relentless barrage of nonprogram stuff in the course of a typical hour's viewing.

TV Guide, also wondering how typical station-break patterns look in cold type, asked one of the industry's most widely used monitoring services, Broadcast Advertisers Reports, Inc., to take a sampling of the nonprogramming on a random list of stations—large and small, network-affiliated and independent—across the country.

BAR's findings were both expectable and impressive. They boil down to this: If 30 or so commercials per hour is clutter, then clutter is epidemic. BAR's log of commercial larding in non-prime time represents the pattern in almost any city, on any station.

The pattern will vary with the type of program and the time of day—the Code permits fewer commercials during prime-time hours than at other times. It also varies with the state of business. If the commercial time is not all sold, it will be padded out with announcements in behalf of the American National Red Cross and the American Cancer Society or with program blurbs, called "promos."

Take what Tulsa, Okla., viewers saw on KTEW-TV, the NBC outlet in their city, the morning of last Dec. 21:

The network's *Jeopardy* game show came on at 11 A.M. and was interrupted as follows: at 11:03 for two 30-second spots, at 11:12 for four 30s, at 11:18 for a one-minute network promo, at 11:23 for a 30-second network promo and a 30 for CARE, at 11:26 for two 30s and at 11:28 for a close-out with nearly a minute more of network blurbs and two 30s and a 10-second spot.

That brought everybody down to 11:30 and the *Who, What or Where* game, which stood by for the following breaks: at 11:31 for a 30 followed by a half-minute promo, at 11:38 for a 60-second promo, at 11:46 for a 30-second promo and a commercial 30, at 11:49 for a minute of network plugs, at 11:51 for two 30s, at 11:54 for a 10-second network promo and at 11:55 for a one-minute commercial, a 10-second and a station-identification.

Score for the two shows: more than 15 minutes of plugola, commercial and otherwise, interrupting the two game shows a total of 11 times.

The pattern is not strikingly different from one locality to another or between big-city and small-city stations.

It's commonly believed that non-network "independents" have a tendency to load up on commercials more than network affiliates do. Some may, but in general they do not appear to be more heavy-handed: In all truth, the situation cannot be laid at the door of the independent stations alone. Furthermore, the NAB Code restrictions are generally met.

For example, in the matter of network versus independent stations, take a dinnertime rerun of *The Wild Wild West* on Los Angeles's independent KHJ-TV last Dec. 22. Three minutes into the 6 P.M. show the station broke for two minutes and 10 seconds of sales pitches, with similar batches at 6:15, 6:22, 6:41, 6:52 and 6:58. The 6:22 break reeled off five 30s, a one-minute, an ID and a promo—all back-to-back. Altogether the hour had only about 45 minutes of *The Wild Wild West*. A *Sherlock Holmes Theatre* at 11 that night was similarly stocked with commercial distractions.

For comparison, look at a late-afternoon movie on CBS's Seattle affiliate, KIRO-TV, on Dec. 19. In two hours viewers saw pitches for:

Crest tooth paste, Hills Bros. coffee, Sears, Roebuck items, a local florist, Safeway foods, General Electric Toast-R-Ovens, Clear Eyes drops, a Miracle brush, Remington shavers, *TV Guide*, a shopping center, Imperial margarine, an appliance store, Schick, another shopping center, Household Finance Corp., Melody Radio & TV, Sunbeam appliances, Bufferin, the Washington potato, a Pres-Kwik cigarette case, One-A-Day vitamins, yet another shopping center, Household Finance again, Certs mints, Melody TV again, a Kel-Tel record selector, an Optigan Music Maker, Golden Griddle syrup, Waring blenders, Philco color TV, a fourth shopping center, MJB coffee, Listerine, Comet cleanser, Lady Schick

Doan

207

curl spray, a fifth shopping center, General Electric skillets, an Arnold power shovel, and, as a do-good suggestion, donating to the Salvation Army. For good measure, there also were a couple of invitations to tune in a UHF channel, a promo for *Hee Haw*, and the usual IDs.

Here it may well be pointed out again that, as far as can be determined, most stations do obey the NAB Code, which was revised early this year to forbid, among other practices, splitting 30-second commercials into two 15-second spots back-to-back. This could have led, some feared, to further fragmenting the time into 7½-second spots and maybe even to split-second subliminal commercials.

Well, the Code has spared us that at least, and perhaps we should be happy with the clutter we've got.

A typical daytime hour

It's coming up 5 P.M. on Dec. 4 in Chicago. NBC affiliate WMAQ-TV is about to air the local news. But first . . .

One minute for a *Dennison Buttoneer* device, another for *Hav-A-Maid mops*, 30 seconds for *National Car Rentals*, 30 for *Heinz steak sauce*, then 10 for *Worth Parfums*. A *station identification* and, at last, the news.

Six minutes later, the pitches resume: half-a-minute each for *Osco Drug Store, Farah jeans, Fleischmann's margarine*, and *Selchow & Righter games*.

As the news hour progresses, the commercial breaks come with clutterful regularity.

5:11—*Norelco products* (30 seconds), *Tuborg Beer* (30), *Seiko Watches* (30), *Max Pax coffee* (30).

5:21—*Bahamas resorts* (1 min.), *True Value Stores* (10 sec.), *Wieboldt department store* (30). *American Greeting Cards* (30).

5:29—*Admiral color TV* (30), *Birds Eye Foods* (30), *Karoll's Men's Wear* (30), *Optigan Music Maker* (30).

5:35—*Stouffer frozen foods* (30), *Joy liquid detergent* (30), *Sears, Roebuck* (30), *Washington Park Jockey Club race track* (30).

5:45—*Oster cooker* (1 min.), *National Food Stores* (10 sec.), *Sunbeam iron* (30), *Shake 'n Bake* (30).

5:53—*Kodak cameras* (30), *Bayer aspirin* (30), *Martini & Rossi wines* (30), *Albolene face cream* (30).

5:58—*Nirvana bath massage* (1 min.), *Sears, Roebuck* (10 sec.), and a *station ID.*

Altogether, 30 different commercials, occupying 15-and-a-half minutes—not counting the two minutes and 10 seconds of plugs leading *into* the newscast.

And somewhere in there was the news.

Is There Intelligent Life on Commercials?

STEFAN KANFER

Reprinted by permission from *Time*, The Weekly Newsmagazine; Copyright Time Inc. Stefan Kanfer is an associate editor of *Time*.

TO: ZB*33 + X

FROM: 45 = K29-¼

RE: EXPLORATION OF MINOR PLANET

We had intended to observe this little ball "RTH" for a longer period. But we developed engine trouble over Omega, and by the time we entered orbit, we were only getting six light-years to the gallon. In our brief visit, however, we discovered what generates those high-frequency signals that have been jamming our radio telescopes. It is a small box called TEEVEE, present in nearly every dwelling in the YEWESS, a small land area between two oceans.

TEEVEE is the display window of the national store. Its merchandise, like all valuable goods, is displayed against a plush but vapid background. This background is called PROGRAMMING and is of no importance. The key elements of the broadcast day (and night) are called SPOTZ. These SPOTZ are 30 seconds to 60 seconds long and cost their manufacturers about $500 per second. Programs, by contrast, cost $50 per second.

From observing SPOTZ we are able to report the following conclusions:

The YEWESS is a vastly troubled land, emerging from a complex, ambiguous struggle against an implacable foe. The name of this enemy is WETNESS. New scientific weapons, however, go on like a powder and give unprecedented protection. Thus, for the first time in this soul-searing conflict, there is the fragile promise of peace.

To amuse themselves YEWESSERS also sing and dance. To this end, the SPOTZ, which are also called commercials, sell them an entertainment called NOSTALJYA. According to the announcements, the top numbers for 1973 include *The Hut-Sut Song, Moonlight Serenade* and *The Woodpecker Song*. The year's most highly regarded

Kanfer

209

artists are the Andrews Sisters and Snooky Lanson, singers; Sammy Kaye and Glenn Miller, bandleaders; and Woody Woodpecker, a bird.

These ingenious people are bothered by many plagues. When the distress appears, the person moves in ten quick, jerky motions and booms: "No headache is going to make me yell at my son [or daughter]." Thereupon the victim takes a miraculous white tablet, which dissolves in the stomach faster than another tablet. Just 3.1 seconds later, this incredible pill enables the victim to change his outlook and handle the most difficult household chores with ease. Other tablets simultaneously drain all eight sinus cavities, rearrange the background music and style the hair in 3.2 seconds.

If pain persists or recurs, YEWESSERS always see a physician.

YEWESSERS are of various hues, but mix freely with no trouble whatsoever. In every SPOT involving the young, there is a ratio of 1.5 black children to 4.9 white ones. Their smiles are constant and blinding. At adult cocktail parties, the commercial ratio is 2.2 black couples to 6.8 white. They smile with equal candlepower.

Some YEWESSERS dwell in apartments, where they live on either side of a flimsy medicine cabinet. All others live in white split-level houses. The males are cranky in the morning and astonished when the coffee is not bitter or the breakfast is palatable. Then they beam and demand to know the name of the product, which they repeat nine times. The wives then proceed to their day, which consists of eight hours of unmitigated jealousy and fear. The jealousy is exhibited at wash time. During this period they stare enviously at their neighbor's laundry, which is always whiter—and the colored things brighter—than their own. With wide eyes, they then proceed to learn a series of mysterious monosyllables, among them Biz, Fab, Cheer, Dash, All and Bold. They do not exhibit fear until nightfall, or on weekend afternoons. At these points the MOTHER-IN-LAW arrives for a white-glove inspection of the home. This includes a revealing scrutiny of the kitchen (with its telltale odors), the male's collar (with its inevitable ring) and the salad (too vinegary). On the next visit, 3.8 seconds later, all is perfection, thanks to the intervention of a remarkable product that scents the air, sanitizes the collar, emulsifies the dressing, rearranges the background music and restyles everyone's hair.

Children are encouraged to visit their father's place of business. There they interrupt proceedings with a ritual cry: "Only one cavity!" Children may also be seen in the early morning, when they ingest the seven essential vitamins every child needs for perfect health. Toward evening they grow pale and cough until a powerful potion brings speedy relief.

YEWESSERS each chew 180 lbs. of gum a year. This was deduced from the size of the gum package (roughly 3 ft. in length).

All YEWESS pets are fussy but highly literate eaters who meticuously examine the labels of their canned food before dining.

YEWESSERS sing while eating and drinking. The song is usually an apostrophe to hamburger or a dithyramb dedicated to cola, un-cola or the beverage the citizens are forbidden to quaff on-camera: beer.

After the singing and eating, the YEWESSERS are remorseful and repair to salons, where they shed unsightly pounds and inches with the aid of wonder-working machines.

An elaborate etiquette prevails at supermarkets. Consumers are encouraged to squeeze the white bread and forbidden to squeeze toilet tissue. They are also urged to look for chickens by name, beef by price and coffee by reputation.

All waitresses, dishwashers and plumbers supplement their incomes by peddling products to customers. These products range from paper towels to soaps, and are invariably superior to the leading brand.

The YEWESS is really two nations. Citizens of one prefer the Pink Pad; citizens of the other buy the Blue one.

The automobile is the greatest friend nature ever had. Cars are affectionately named for animals (cougar, mustang, falcon, impala); gasolines keep engines clean; and there are seldom more than three vehicles on the road at any time.

At this point in the time-space continuum, we found it necessary to re-enter the intergalactic void for our millennial tune-up. As for your query: Is there intelligent life on RTH? Having peered at length at the little windows, our answer must be negative. How about a visit to Jupiter? The only SPOTZ there are the ones caused by meteors.

Station Rankings to Shift in Ethnic-Rating Storm?

TELEVISION/RADIO AGE STAFF WRITERS

Reprinted from *Television/Radio Age*, vol. 20, 14 (February 19, 1973) with permission of publisher. Copyright 1973.

Pressures that are being brought to bear on the rating services by minority group broadcast interests may well affect the way television and radio stations are ranked in the future.

The latest hot rivet to be tossed at the American Research Bureau and A. C. Nielsen comes from black and Spanish stations and groups over what they say is inadequate reporting of ethnic audiences in the rating books. Though the battle has been going on quietly for years, the minority broadcasters are just now beginning to break through the defenses.

Take for example a recent court case brought against ARB by WDAS, a black-oriented radio outlet in Philadelphia. Charging that ARB's under-representation of black listeners had cost it sales revenue, the station sued the researcher for $2 million. Though it didn't get the money or prove that ARB acted in bad faith, WDAS did win a big concession— ARB has agreed to change its radio rating methodology to more adequately reflect black audiences in Philadelphia. And though the case didn't come to a decision—it was settled during the course of the trial so other stations can't sweep in on precedential coattails—ARB has stated that the same revised methodology will soon swing into other cities. The market list or timetable has not been worked out yet, however.

For television, a similar upheaval is underway, though, of course, it can't be as severe as in radio since there are no black tv stations. But there are Spanish channels and these outlets have been after ARB and Nielsen for years to change their sampling routines to bring more Spanish-speaking households into the books. After being frustrated in this endeavor since 1966, Rene Anselmo, president of the Spanish International Network [SIN], finally brought his case to the attention of the Federal Communications Commission. Though it's doubtful right now that the FCC will take any direct action on the matter . . . , the waves that have been churned up are already beginning to rock the boat under both ARB and Nielsen.

What it means is that the rating services are under intense heat to change their ways. Nielsen and ARB have been labeled "racist" by ethnic broadcasters on the grounds that the services' incomes and prestige rest largely on their relations with affluent VHF majority-oriented stations, mass market advertisers and "lily white" agencies. Say the ethnic broadcasters: ARB and Nielsen were created at a time when no advertiser really cared about the minority, the poor or the non-English speaking population and the services deliberately failed to bring these groups into focus. Now, with pressure on from these segments in all facets of American life, it's time for the ratings services to get their share of heat.

What's going to make the combat even more intense is that as ethnic audiences become increasingly reflected in ratings, somebody's share must fall. After all, there are only so many viewers and listeners in the total audience and if one station goes up another must come down. For radio stations, that means that white-oriented sounds like middle-of-the-road and album music will probably suffer, while more rhythmic sounds will benefit.

In television, the see-saw may rock a little differently. The small amount of research that's been done into viewing preferences by race . . ., indicates that blacks have certain station and program preferences, but they tend to be highly subjective and not easily explained.

Of course, in the case of Spanish language tv stations it isn't hard to predict what will happen. In those markets where there's a sizable Spanish population and a Spanish-language station, it's more than conjecture that its audiences will grow to the detriment of English-language outlet shares in the market.

The other side of the coin, of course, is the effect any changes in rating methodology will have on "white" stations. If a market-leader fears his ratings will shrink, will he pay for the added samples that will be needed to boost his competitor's ratings?

And what about ethnic samples themselves? Even if Nielsen and ARB wanted to, could they get more cooperation out of black and Spanish households? If not, will their estimates of what these people *may* be watching be accurate or speculative? If the latter, will the services be able to withstand another withering assault from their clients, like the blast ARB took two years ago when its change in methodology caused viewing levels to drop and stations around the country threatened a revolt? And what will agencies say about any new methodology that's temporarily shoved into a leaking dyke?

Insiders say one reason that the issue has been so explosive of late—though simmering for years—is that it marks a change in the way ethnic stations have been presenting themselves to agencies. Up to about five years ago black and Spanish broadcasters were content to take portions of advertising budgets "earmarked" for ethnic stations. A normal chunk might be 20 per cent of a total market budget set aside for all ethnic media.

In more recent years, however, ethnic stations aren't content with that kind of segregation. They want the same considerations that are handed to any station in the market—including the chance to pitch for a budget on the same basis as their competitors. This may have to do with the self-image that minorities are now projecting, or it may be due entirely to economics.

So now ratings are suddenly extremely important to them. For an ethnic outlet to get its equitable share of a budget its ratings have to be competitive, and its cost-per-1,000 in line with other stations. Hence, the sudden interest in reliably reporting ethnic audiences and giving these stations numbers to sell.

Aside from the publicity it's gotten, SIN's campaign against the rating services has borne some tangible fruit so far. J. Walter Thompson, a Nielsen shop, has agreed to use ARB books in Miami and in other markets with heavy Spanish concentration and a Spanish tv station.

At a few other agencies, says Anselmo, "We're getting attention from people who would have said 'go away' a year ago. The climate is improving."

But what are the ratings services going to do to get the minorities off their backs?

ARB is going to change its weighting policies for radio, and will do essentially what Pulse has been doing for some time, projecting ethnic samples to conform to ethnic population estimates in a market. This means adjusting ethnic listening preferences to their ratio of the total audience, as is done with age and sex breaks.

There's also a chance that ARB's Expanded Sample Frame—intended to bring more non-listed and non-telephone homes into the sampling—may work better for radio than for tv canvassing. ARB will try to apply its experience from the tv ESF during the April-May radio rating period.

For television, ARB has pretty well decided that minority viewing patterns don't differ enough to warrant the added expense of permanently implementing ESF.

What it will probably do is continue its amended procedures for getting more Spanish and black people into tv samples—personal delivery and pickup of diaries, incentives for urban minorities, oversampling, etc.

Rupert R. Ridgeway, ARB's research vice president, says the results of experiments so far with ESF in tv have "provided no surprises."

Ridgeway says the service didn't expect to find marked differences in viewing preferences among telephone and non-telephone homes, and none appeared. He adds that he doubts the results of the test in tv will warrant the higher costs of applying it to tv on a regular basis, though it may be a different story with radio.

Ridgeway also notes that the ESF didn't add as many minority respondents as hoped. He says that about 18 per cent of the total population fits under the ethnic minority heading, and a larger proportion than that was contacted for the ESF. But only about 12 per cent of the final total were minority people, Ridgeway explains.

Nielsen's attempts to pacify the restless minorities have resulted in slightly modified procedures for including more Spanish homes and a number of experiments to build up sampling.

Late last summer Nielsen instituted two additional research projects with minority implications, then added a third project in December. Henry Rahmel, executive vice president, media research, says he can't disclose what the three experiments are, only that two involve diaries and one involves field interviewing.

Nielsen's Spanish-oriented improvement is Spanish instructions with its English diary, and a tabulating procedure to weight special cells in heavily Spanish or black neighborhoods.

Rahmel denies that Nielsen has been lax in its endeavors to report on minorities. "We've been at this for years," he says, "and have done a great deal of research and expended a great deal of activity on this subject. Our work is in good order."

Rahmel says Nielsen has been using special methods for five or six years to improve minority reporting "and we continue to be involved."

The Nielsen executive adds that the research effort extends beyond Spanish and black minorities and includes others, such as whites at the low end of the economic scale.

At ARB, the WDAS case could lead to some additional reports for Philadelphia, though ARB isn't saying at the moment if it's planning any. William T. McClenaghan, vice president and general manager of ARB's radio division, will only say that "We have no definite plans to turn out a black report for Philadelphia, but it can be done." The new race control which ARB will soon be using to report ethnic audiences in Philadelphia and other markets could be used to produce special reports, McClenaghan says.

ARB's television division, says McClenaghan, "has been spending an inordinate amount of money trying to find out how to get a better black response. That information may be applicable to radio. When the tv data is thoroughly assimilated, we'll decide three things: (1) how samples from minorities can be expanded; (2) the cost; (3) the effect it will have on audience estimates."

McClenaghan says points one and two are applicable to radio. To learn more about point three, experiments will have to be conducted for radio, and they'll take place during the March/April radio report period.

He also points out that ARB had been working on methods of improving its black survey techniques for over a year and was ready to institute them this year and would have done so even if the WDAS case hadn't come up. In fact, adds ARB's radio chief, the researcher didn't expect the WDAS case to be called for two or three more years, by which time the new methodology would have been well entrenched.

However, the case came up earlier than expected—McClenaghan hints at some judicial partiality—so the settlement only acts as a catalyst to implement the new weighting procedures.

Looking at comparative rankings of WDAS in ARB and Pulse it's not hard to see why the station claimed foul. In a special Negro tab of Philadelphia, Pulse estimated that fully a third of the city's blacks tuned to WDAS; in its July–September, 1972, report, Pulse ranked the station as fifth in the market, 6 a.m. to midnight, Monday to Sunday, with an 8 percent of audience. In the most comparable ARB report, October–November, 1972, that service had the station's share at 2.2 per cent, 10th in the market. Most ARB books fixed WDAS's position at number 9 or 10, while Pulse consistently ranked the station around 5th.

One way ARB has been attempting to give better ethnic balance to its tv reports is a zip code weighting procedure which it's been using in nine markets with heavy black and Spanish concentration. (In other markets stations may request the controls at additional cost.)

Counties with high ethnic density are examined and defined as an ethnic area of a group of zip codes. An ethnic zip code is a county zip code with an ethnic population of at least 35 per cent.

ARB then sets up control and non-control counties based on a complex formula of ethnic population. The total households in the control area are applied to the total tv household estimates for the entire county to determine the number of tv households that are in the ethnic control area and the non-control area. Each is then treated as though it was an independent sampling unit with the diaries from these areas representing only their respective households.

Anselmo charges that even this procedure is stacked against minorities because the diaries from ethnic respondents are applied only to the control area, they don't influence the entire market ratings proportionately.

Worse, says Anselmo, is a Nielsen device for disregarding minorities entirely. This is a 10 per cent rating minimum cutoff which Nielsen claims is essential to maintain rating accuracy.

In New York, says Anselmo, his WXTV doesn't even make the rating books because it doesn't get 10 per cent of the total viewing audience.

Anselmo argues that if every Spanish-speaking tv household in the New York area were tuned to the station at the same time it *still* wouldn't get into the Nielsen report because they don't represent 10 per cent of the total audience. But they *do* represent some 2 million people who are not reported.

Nielsen says without the rating cutoff any station drawing less than 10 per cent of the total audience runs the risk of a 50 per cent statistical error factor in its measurement.

Asked whether his complaint against the cutoff was academic, since even if reported WXTV's ratings would be minuscule, Anselmo retorts, "I'd settle for 2-300,000 people and so would the other Spanish station in the market."

But the problem goes even deeper, Anselmo contends.

"They look upon Spanish and black as not part of the market," says the irate SIN president. "When they first set up their systems they didn't notice that blacks and Spanish were there. And it's still that way."

The question of cost is often put up as a defense of the rating services' failure to probe deeper into the tastes of minorities.

Anselmo doesn't buy that excuse. "Is it honest research?" he asks. "Is it based on what clients are paying for, or what the truth is?" Anselmo has taken his case before the Broadcast Rating Council, the industry research watchdog, to ask that ARB and Nielsen lose their accreditation because they're not sampling total audiences. The BRC would say only that Anselmo's case had some merits, but ARB and Nielsen had some problems. Reaching the boiling point, the president of SIN implies that the BRC is a stooge of the networks and the big broadcast interests.

"When the rating services talked about their problems I used to have sympathy for them," says the president of the Spanish tv group, who sounds like a man at the end of his tether. "Now I'm no longer tolerant. Other factions ask for special procedures and ARB and Nielsen run right out and measure them. Like cable operators. But would they do the same for minorities?

"Advertisers don't care. You've got a lot of bigots in this business. Spanish and blacks don't have money, so why bother to measure them?

"The diary system doesn't work. A few years ago I recommended a phone coincidental. Nielsen turned it down—you need demographic information and you can't get it in a phone coincidental. They said you can't mix phones and diaries. A few years later they had no trouble mixing diaries and meters in New York when other stations wanted it."

Rahmel says that Nielsen has "spent a lot of money exploring the subject" of minority reporting and Nielsen "isn't ignoring it." In fact, he recalls back in 1966 he agreed to install meters in San Antonio to improve measurement of Spanish audiences, but SIN then declined the offer.

Asked to explain this contradiction, Anselmo digs back through his letter file and refreshes his memory. Nielsen did indeed agree to install meters in San Antonio—at a cost of $96,000, which SIN would have had to pay by itself because the other stations in the market refused to contribute. Nielsen wanted the payment over four years, Anselmo wanted seven years to pay off. He also asked that Nielsen give him sole proprietary rights to the reports so that he could sell them to the other broadcasters to amortize his expenses. The deal fell through, no one remembers exactly why.

Today, Rahmel observes: "What we're doing represents a substantial improvement over what we were doing 10 years ago. It's hard to find the money from our clients at large that are willing to do a better job for the few stations that would benefit."

Anselmo doesn't argue this point. "Whether conscious or subconscious," he says, "they've taken a racist approach to the problem. They claim there are all kinds of problems in measuring blacks and Spanish, but we say there are no more problems than in measuring anybody else. The difficulty is with the methodology in measuring them.

"Spanish and blacks are measured in other parts of the world, why should it be any different here?"

So far, Anselmo hasn't gained much ground with the BRC or the FCC, nor does it appear he'll induce the Bureau of Weights and Measures to establish standards for measuring television markets as he's proposed.

However, in a letter to Commissioner Lee commenting on Anselmo's charges, Hugh M. Beville, Jr., executive director of the BRC, did admit that Anselmo's arguments "may have some validity."

However, he contended that "A completely satisfactory solution to all of these problems by an on-going rating service with the responsibility for measuring the total market has thus far defied solution—not only by the rating services, but by various industry committees which have wrestled with it. . . ."

Beville denied that the BRC has ignored the problem. "I can safely say that this subject has had as much, if not more, attention in Council activities than any other single problem," he wrote Lee.

SIN's president, reviewing the Beville response for Lee, said he didn't sympathize with the rating services problems, nor did he have much faith in the BRC's position on the problems of sampling minorities.

"The 'problem' exists because both rating services, for reasons that best suit their own purposes and the interests of their clients, employ methods of measuring markets which practically assure the under-representation and non-cooperation of the Spanish-speaking and black population. . . . We are despaired of being told that measuring Spanish and blacks require special techniques. The theory of random probability does not, to my knowledge, rest upon the color of a person's skin, or the language one speaks."

Anselmo then listed 10 ways that the rating services could make their market surveys reflect the total market. Included were a proportionate sample of black and Spanish households in densely-populated minority markets; meters to be placed in homes in the same proportion;

acknowledgement that the diary system is a "poor method" for measuring these minorities; supplementation of diaries with telephone coincidentals; over-sampling of black and Spanish homes; personal placement and retrieval of diaries in some markets; employment of black and Spanish interviewers; and yearly updating of Spanish and black population figures just as the rating services have them done for the 'total market.'

"What ARB, Nielsen and the BRC really need is not solutions but a great big kick in the ass from Washington," he concluded his letter to Lee.

Anselmo's wrath is becoming typical of the feelings being generated by this issue. Some admen describe it as "sensitive," but it's more than that. It personifies many of the black-white, Anglo-Spanish conflicts that have gripped this country in the last 10 years.

One reason that the rating services give for the poor showing of ethnic stations is that minorities are notoriously uncooperative with interviewers. Many poor people fear they're being sold something; many don't understand what ratings are; some don't put any trust in them, and many have something to hide.

Research consultant Mel Goldberg of the firm that bears his name, puts it this way: "It isn't that the rating services don't want to include minorities; it's that it's a very difficult thing to do. The census people went through this in the 1970 survey, they've had to revise their original minority estimates because they couldn't get the cooperation rate they needed. They underestimated the minorities, who are skeptical of their intentions, and they couldn't get the responses."

Goldberg figures it could cost three or even four times the amount of money to sample a minority group as it would cost to sample other groups. "You need minority interviewers, and many of them, because others fear going into so-called 'bad' neighborhoods. And, they better not be in uniform.

"What's needed is an all-out community-industry effort in public relations," continues Goldberg. "An effort that will show minority people that there are long-run benefits to answering questions. But part of that is it's essential that the courts reaffirm the confidentiality of the responses. People are fearful of answering questions if they suspect that their answers may be used for purposes other than those of the immediate survey."

The public relations effort sounds like a good idea to some, but even that poses problems. Suppose broadcasters and research people did drum up a big campaign and ghetto people opened their doors. What's to prevent thieves and muggers from riding in on their coattails and posing as interviewers to prey on those who want to cooperate? If this happened, the rating services would again be suspected of "taking" the minorities and the cooperation rate would plummet to zero.

It's prospects like this that complicate an already thorny problem.

The rating service which has so far been able to cope with the problems of the ghettos is Pulse.

Bob Galen, research vice president for Blair Radio and co-head of the GOALS Pulse task force of the Radio Advertising Bureau, who's supposed to suggest ways to improve Pulse's procedures, makes this observation:

"Pulse is doing a reasonably good job in sampling minorities. The problem is being able to identify them and delineate them in your sample. Pulse's interviewers are able to do this better than ARB or Nielsen because the Pulse interviewer knows who he's interviewing and they can weight their responses accordingly."

Larry Roslow, associate director of Pulse, explains that the market's ethnic population is known from the 1970 census, then minority interviews are weighted to bring them up to meet that ratio, and this is reflected in the preface to each Pulse book that is affected by heavy ethnic concentration.

Roslow implies that Pulse has also taken a more progressive attitude toward minorities than the other rating services, though he stops short of criticizing ARB and Nielsen.

"My feeling," he says, "is if you don't get the proper percentage of minorities in your sample you're not getting an accurate representation of the market. You've got to go out of your way and make an effort to get the proper representation. If you don't you're really not giving an advertiser an accurate picture of that market."

Roslow makes no bones about the added cost of sampling minorities. In order to get interviewers to go into ghetto areas, Pulse has instituted an "escort" service, two interviewers per interview, with commensurate increases in costs. Still, says Roslow, it's worth it because "it's gotten us into places where you have to go to get a representative sample."

Another advantage of the Pulse personal interview technique is that it leaves no doubt about the racial affiliation of the person interviewed, and it doesn't bring up any potential invasion of civil rights safeguards that may have impeded ARB's or Nielsen's phone, diary or meter techniques. It also doesn't run into the telephone/non-telephone snag that has bedevilled the other services and brought charges that large chunks of the population—rich and poor—are excluded from samples because they can't be reached by phone.

ARB has been trying to get around this problem two ways—with ESF and with the personal drop-off technique in Spanish neighborhoods. In the first method, names are culled not from phone books, but from resident lists; but it's expensive and, as mentioned earlier, the results may not be worth the cost, especially for tv measurement. The second method could be an improvement, since after the Spanish diary is personally left with the cooperating family, the interviewer then tries to enlist neighbors in the sample, and asks them if they want an English or Spanish diary. However, this method has been used only in certain markets.

Another problem has been in actually identifying Spanish respondents. Even the Census Bureau has made a game of musical chairs out of this one, and at various times and in various censuses "Spanish" has been defined as those with Spanish surnames, those who speak Spanish primarily at home, or those to whom Spanish is the mother tongue. At present, the latter description seems to be the prevailing one.

The question of the diary is one that many ethnic-oriented station men raise repeatedly. They say the diary is a "white" measuring yardstick that other races don't relate to.

Mark Olds, general manager of black-oriented radio station WWRL Woodside, New York, puts it this way:

"By and large, there is a lower level of literacy and writing consciousness among black people. It's unfair, like some tests are unfair. Ask a kid who's never seen a cow to describe a cow. Because he can't he flunks the test, right, and he's stupid. There are some people in this business who think you shouldn't count in certain people."

Just the same, Olds contends, there are 2.5 million black people among Greater New York's 19 million, and they comprise up to 20 per cent of the population density, depending where you look. "Omitting them penalizes them if you do live diaries," he argues, "and I think the diary method is the wrong one."

With methodology like ARB's, says Olds, "the affluent, literate audience will always come out ahead. Our numbers have suffered in ARB. In Pulse, overall, we're two to five in the market. We never go below number five. With ARB, you've got to use a microscope to find us. We wind up owing them points."

What makes Olds sure that Pulse is closer to the truth than ARB is the amount of retail advertising on his station. He thinks this is one of the best gauges of listenership because when a retailer advertises on radio he gets immediate, measurable results. And since WWRL is one of the leading retail stations in the city, observes Olds, he's convinced that his audience is not as minuscule as ARB reports it is.

Also, Olds charges, up to a few months ago ARB had been using out-dated and prejudicial census figures for placing its diaries. These were 1960 census breakdowns by zip codes, which put blacks in the wrong places in the wrong proportions.

ARB's McClenaghan explains that the 1960 figures were the only ones available at the time, and as soon as all the 1970 zip code lists were out, which was last month, they went into use.

What's the solution to the many-sided, highly complex and extremely explosive question of measuring ethnic minorities? Like many other people in the business, Mark Olds hasn't got the answer. "You need the best research brains in the business to puzzle this one out."

Most insiders, on both sides of the ethnic fence, would have to agree.

GOVERNMENT AND BROADCASTING

No mass medium in America is regulated to the extent that broadcasting is regulated. It is true that all mass media are circumscribed by certain laws, but only broadcasters must receive approval of a special government agency, the FCC, before they can begin "publishing," so to speak. It is this singular fact that conditions much of the concern among broadcasters about FCC policies and federal court decisions. For background reading on how this regulatory relationship has developed, review the Schramm article in the Introduction.

Growing out of this unique government-broadcasting relationship are a host of issues—issues that reflect broadcaster, citizen, and government concerns. We have selected four issues for discussion here: (1) the Fairness Doctrine and its relationship to broadcast performance and the First Amendment; (2) access, the desire and efforts primarily of minority groups to receive access to the airwaves either to express their opinions or to operate the stations themselves; (3) cross-ownership, the quest for diversity of voices in certain communities where broadcast and print media may be owned by one individual or a single corporation; and (4) the presidency and broadcasting—the relationship between the executive branch of government and the broadcast media in a time of crisis.

The Fairness Doctrine, a continually evolving concept in Commission thinking, has created such a climate in broadcasting today that many people both in and out of the industry, including severe critics of the medium, have called for its repeal. Sig Mickelson's article traces the development and expansion of the doctrine's effect upon other Commission policies such as license challenges, access, and counteradvertising is permitted. Even this move is a giant step beyond thorough restudy of the Fairness Doctrine, completed in 1974. The FCC accepted as policy the conclusions of that study. The new policy has wiped out some of the expansive features that had crept into this doctrine through ad hoc decisions by the Commission and by judicial decision. Briefly stated, the Commission reaffirmed its faith in the Fairness Doctrine by concluding that the public's interest in free expression through broadcasting "will best be served and promoted through continued reliance on the Fairness Doctrine, which leaves questions of access and the specific handling of public issues to the licensee's journalistic discretion." A major shift in the doctrine's emphasis was the Commission's specific removal of the "cigarette ruling" from its precedent-setting position. See Mickelson's article for a discussion of this ruling, which created an entire set of counteradvertising principles and practices in broadcasting. The Commission specifically *excluded* ordinary product advertising from Fairness Doctrine application (ordinary commercials do not create a "controversial issue of public importance"), but it also specifically *included* other types of commercials such as those that take a stand on a controversial issue of public importance and those institutional commercials that bear an "obvious relationship" to an ongoing public debate. So, even while taking ordinary product advertising out of the Fairness Doctrine's realm (whether the courts will agree must yet be determined), the Commission has carefully indicated that some commercials still may create a situation where counteradvertising is permitted. Even this move is a giant step beyond what the Commission had imagined back in 1949 when the doctrine first was expressed and directed at issues outside of advertising. The point is, today certain commercials on television may be subject to Fairness Doctrine interpretation and, therefore, may require counteradvertising. (See the chapter on advertising for further information.)

This entire area of Commission reregulation has been pursued by several proponents. One of them was Clay Whitehead, who was head of

President Nixon's Office of Telecommunications Policy, for several years before his resignation in 1974. The article by Tracy A. Westen responds to several of Whitehead's suggestions, and because Westen repeats Whitehead's ideas in the body of his article, it is sufficient to reprint only the Westen article. It is Westen's viewpoint concerning the need for regulation of broadcasters, particularly so far as the Fairness Doctrine is concerned, that bears repeating. His method of exposition is to attack Whitehead's proposals; his reasons for disagreeing with those proposals constitute a strong position in support of broadcast regulation. Finally, our reprint of a speech by Commissioner Richard A. Wiley, now chairman of the FCC, gives insight into the chairman's philosophy regarding broadcast licensing procedures. The issue of license challenges because of program practices (lack of ascertainment, inadequate programming for minority groups in the community, etc.) and employment practices (too few minority members on the staff or in positions of influence) has been a real issue in the broadcast field for several years—since the WLBT-TV Jackson, Mississippi, case in 1966, which established the right of citizens to participate in a station's license-renewal proceedings. This rule has been expanded and restricted in several particulars by court and Commission action. Nevertheless, the issue of access, particularly through the means of license challenges, is an issue that will continue to be discussed and cussed throughout the seventies.

Another issue which the Commission has broadcast at one time or another for over thirty years is the problem of cross-media ownership. Basically, the issue centers around what the Commission feels is the desirable goal of representing the diversity of voices in a community. It is argued, therefore, that when a newspaper publisher owns the only newspaper(s) in town plus a television and/or radio station, the number of "voices" has been reduced; the chances of getting a diversity of views in these media are not very great. Whether this is indeed so is debatable. However, the issue of cross-media ownership and of FCC inaction in the face of Justice Department pressures is clearly explained in our selection from *Congressional Quarterly*.

These, then, are some of the crucial issues in the contemporary government-broadcasting relationship. While our readings deal only with these, there is another related concern that can be explored here. In the bibliography that follows, suggested articles are given that will amplify this additional issue, which grew out of Section 315 of the Communications Act, requiring licensees to "afford equal opportunities to all" candidates for a particular office *if* the broadcaster has permitted a "legally qualified candidate for any public office to use" his station.

Unless the candidate appears on a regular news program without a change of format, his opponent or opponents (they may be legion) can demand and get an equal opportunity to appear on the station. All too frequently the FCC has considered "equal opportunity" to mean "equal time," although the law does not use that term. The issue is whether the public good is served by this law. Those in favor of the law argue that all candidates for a public office should receive like treatment (or nearly like treatment) on the air; that is, opponents should have the same opportunity to get their message across to the audience as did the "favored" candidate who first appeared on the air. Opposed to this view are those who suggest that not all candidates for a particular office are necessarily serious candidates and, therefore, do not deserve "free" exposure to the public. Perhaps the more serious criticism, however, is that the current law cuts down on public exposure to leading candidates because broadcast stations refuse to expose themselves to the equal opportunity provisions of Section 315. They do so by keeping all candidates off the air, except for regularly scheduled news programs and paid commercials.

BIBLIOGRAPHICAL ESSAY

The relationship of the First Amendment to broadcasting has attracted attention since the development of the FCC as a regulatory agency. Sig Mickelson's article admirably summarizes the development of our present concern about this relationship. The growing chorus of voices asking for the application of the principles of the First Amendment to broadcast news is indicated in just a few of the following citations. Harry S. Ashmore has brought together views on this issue in *Fear in the Air: Broadcasting and the First Amendment—The Anatomy of a Constitutional Crisis,* Norton, New York, 1973. This also should be read in conjunction with our articles on the presidency and the press. Much of the same material can be found in a special edition of *The Center Magazine* (May/June, 1973), which is published by the Center for the Study of Democratic Institutions, Santa Barbara, Calif. The application of the Fairness Doctrine to broadcasting, particularly in editorial comment and documentaries, has long been a point of discussion among media practitioners and lawyers. Tracy Weston's viewpoint is in favor of this application. A current legal discussion of the issue can be found in "Radio and Television—Fairness Doctrine—Evaluation of Basis For and Effect of Broadcasting's Fairness Doctrine," in *Rutgers Camden Law Journal* (Fall, 1973). For a useful look at the issue from a network

Government and Broadcasting

standpoint, see " 'Fairness' Today (Censorship Tomorrow?)" by Julian Goodman, a speech given before the "Great Issues Forum" at USC in October 1972, when he was president of NBC, and published by NBC, New York.

Commissioner Wiley's exposition of his views on "license challenges" can be elaborated on from a wide variety of sources. Two recent books on television regulation, although complicated, should be consulted for an overview of the relationship between the FCC and broadcasting. They are Roger G. Noll, *et al., Economic Aspects of Television Regulation,* Brookings Institution, Washington, D.C., 1973, and Erwin Krasnow and Lawrence Longley, *The Politics of Broadcast Regulation,* St. Martin's Press, New York, 1972. See also, in conjunction with these books, Nicholas Johnson and John Jay Distel, "A Day in the Life: The Federal Communications Commission," *The Yale Law Journal* (July, 1973), 1575–1634. Richard W. Jencks, then president of CBS/Broadcast Group, gave a scathing speech about license renewal challenges in 1971. His speech, "Broadcast Regulation by Contract," has been reprinted in Michael C. Emery and Ted Curtis Smythe, Eds., *Readings in Mass Communications,* 2nd ed., Wm. C. Brown, Dubuque, Iowa, 1974.

Cross-media ownership is another issue that long has been debated in the United States. Our report from *Congressional Quarterly* may be supplemented by the excellent "Merger, Monopoly and a Free Press," *The Nation* (Jan. 15, 1973), 76–86. This article, by Stephen Barnett, outlines some of the problems created by the broadcast industry's argument that the case-by-case approach to cross-ownership problems is better than an industry-wide ruling requiring divestiture. In the summer of 1974 the FCC held final hearings on the issue, with the likelihood being, according to *Broadcasting* magazine, that divestiture of existing ownerships will be by "voluntary sales, individual antitrust suits or, perhaps, some kind of FCC rule that makes action possible in cases of clear and undesirable monopoly." For a scholarly study of media performance under a cross-media monopoly, consult Guido H. Stempel III, "Effects on Performance of a Cross-Media Monopoly," *Journalism Monographs,* No. 29 (June, 1973). A similar study James A. Anderson, "The Alliance of Broadcast Stations and Newspapers: The Problem of Information Control," *Journal of Broadcasting* (Winter, 1971–72), 51–64, arrives at a different conclusion.

An important issue not covered by readings in our text is that of the use of television by the president during campaigns and while in office. The books in this field are extensive and students can readily find material to cover the issue. Taking them in chronological order, students can consult books by Gene Wyckoff, *The Image Candidates: American Politics in the Age of Television,* Macmillan, New York, 1968; Joe McGinniss, *The Selling of the President,* 1968, Trident Press, New York, 1969; Kurt Lang and Gladys Engel Lang, *Politics and Television,* Quadrangle, New York, 1968; Edward W. Chester, *Radio, Television and American Politics,* Sheed & Ward, New York, 1969; Harold Mendelsohn and Irving Crespi, *Polls, TV and the New Politics,* Chandler, Corte Madera, Calif., 1970; Sig Mickelson, *The Electric Mirror: Politics in the Age of Television,* Dodd, Mead, New York, 1972; Robert E. Gilbert, *Television and Presidential Politics,* Christopher Publishing, North Quincy, Mass., 1972, and Newton N. Minow, John Bartlow Martin, and Lee M. Mitchell, *Presidential Television,* Basic Books, New York, 1973.

STUDY QUESTIONS

1. Professor Mickelson believes that there is nothing wrong in principle with a "Fairness Doctrine," but he expresses concern that the doctrine has changed in recent years. Discuss his views.

2. What was the evolution of the Fairness Doctrine?

3. Should the Fairness Doctrine, as it is now interpreted, be repealed and replaced with proposals similar to those proposed by Dr. Clay Whitehead, former director of the White House Office of Telecommunications Policy?

4. Do you see any significant agreement or conflict among the ideas expressed by Dr. Mickelson, those attributed to Dr. Whitehead, and those expressed by FCC Commissioner Wiley?

5. Do you believe it is a function of the court to restructure the system of broadcasting in the United States? Why or why not?

6. What are the advantages and disadvantages of cross-media ownership? Should future cross-media ownerships be prohibited? Should newspapers be forced to sell local broadcast stations?

THE FIRST AMENDMENT, FAIRNESS AND LICENSE CHALLENGES

The First Amendment and Broadcast Journalism

SIG MICKELSON

Reprinted with permission from the Final Report of the Annual Chief Justice Earl Warren Conference sponsored by the Roscoe Pound-American Trial Lawyers Foundation. Professor Mickelson was the first president of CBS News. He is now professor of journalism at the Medill School of Journalism, Northwestern University.

Broadcasting is such a volatile business and memories are so short that it is probable that few persons now remember a cause célèbre of the 1950's.

It was an event in which broadcasting's relationship to the First Amendment received a solid buffeting; an event in which a major setback could have been suffered. No specific conclusions were reached as a result of the curious storm that raged for several weeks. No landmark precedents were established but, in a sense it was a watershed since it cleared the air and at least negatively established that broadcast journalism couldn't be throttled at the whim of an irritated government.

The event was a special "Face the Nation" program produced by CBS News and featuring Nikita Krushchev, the First Secretary of the Russian Communist Party, as the guest.

The program was filmed at the Kremlin in Moscow. Ground rules agreed on with the Soviet leadership were relatively open. The format was essentially the same that the show still follows except for the fact that an interpreter intervened between guest and panel. The First Secretary was vigorous, ebullient and responsive to questions. It was in this program that he uttered what has now become a famous phrase, "We will bury you."

Government and Broadcasting

230

The program was broadcast on a late Sunday afternoon of May 1957, at a time when television as a force in news and public affairs coverage was still in its experimental infancy. There were no warnings at the time of an impending storm. The next morning the Krushchev interview was the headline story over the entire country: *The New York Times*, the *New York Herald-Tribune*, and the *Washington Post* ran the full text. It was clearly the most newsworthy effort performed thus far by television.

By Monday afternoon proof was at hand. It was unmistakably evident that the Secretary of State, John Foster Dulles, was outraged by the network's effrontery in furnishing an outlet for a national appearance by the leader of the country's principal enemy. The President was said to be upset. Critics on the right who had not fully recovered from the McCarthy period started cannonading CBS by telegram, letter, telephone calls and messages to their congressmen.

CBS absorbed the early shock with confidence but then it began to waiver. On the Tuesday morning after the Sunday program, I was summoned to the twentieth floor CBS Board Room at 485 Madison Avenue immediately on arrival at my office. The meeting, which began almost at once, carried on throughout that entire day and well into the next day. The participants included CBS News' Public Affairs Director, Irving Gitlin, and Director of News, John Day. From the corporate executive staff there were Frank Stanton and Richard Salant, who later succeeded me as President of the News Division. News Division personnel couldn't see any problem arising out of the special Krushchev "Face the Nation" program; only clear advantages to CBS. Corporate management saw it differently. They anticipated a genuine threat to CBS' freedom to cover the news and, what is worse, believed that the interview might have given impetus or might in the future give impetus to the passage of restrictive legislation in Congress. Of course, there always was that overriding fear that something might be done to the licenses of the five CBS-owned television stations, which constituted a principal source of net revenue to the corporation.

It took the arrival of an outside public relations counsel to resolve the dilemma. He encouraged the adoption of an affirmative position rather than a negative one. He urged CBS to take the offensive; show pride in "Face the Nation" rather than embarrassment; brag to the country about having made a major contribution to better world understanding rather than apologize for having given the Russian leader an opportunity to speak directly to the American people.

Even more significantly the CBS response—reflected in full page ads in the New York and Washington newspapers on the next morning—became the springboard for a campaign on behalf of broadcasters' freedom of the press that was to last for several months. The campaign demanded first amendment protection for broadcasting.

Whether anything specific was gained as a result of this campaign, at least nothing was lost. More importantly, broadcasters were set on a course that would lead to increasing claims on the first amendment protection, as complete as that claimed by the printed press.

Since that occasion, the Frst Amendment has become a rallying point for defenses by broadcasters against all manner of criticism. First amendment defenses have been triggered by causes ranging from the closing off of news sources, the issuing of subpoenas to reporters for appearances and subpoenas to editors for outtakes, to more general material with less obvious immediate results including various applications of the "Fairness Doctrine."

In fact, there is some reason to think that the "First Amendment" phrase may have been worked so hard that it begun to lose its meaning. Some broadcasters tend to use the words "First Amendment" much as the Israelites used trumpets at the Battle of Jericho. Recite the words "First Amendment" seven times, and the barriers to full protection will collapse, permitting broadcasters to walk unchallenged into the inner sanctum so long occupied by the printed press.

The matter is not nearly so uncomplicated. It is true that the Federal Communications Act of 1934 seems to promise a "hands-off" attitude on the part of government toward broadcast program content. Included in the Act is the paragraph which reads:

> Nothing in this Act shall be understood or construed to give the Commission the power of censorship over radio communication or signals transmitted by any radio station and no regulation or condition shall be promulgated or fixed by the Commission which shall interfere with the right of free speech.

There is only one exception to this affirmation that broadcasters shall have the right of free speech and that is found in the Federal Criminal Code which specifies that fines up to $10,000 can be assessed for use of "obscene, indecent or profane language." The Criminal Code also forbids broadcasts of information about "any lottery, gift enterprise or similar scheme." This would seem to give broadcasters reasonably clear sailing insofar as their news policies are concerned. But the actual record of performance of government in its relationship with broadcasting suggests that other considerations frequently take precedence over this apparently clear and incontrovertible statement.

There are two facets of the Federal Communications Commission's (FCC) regulation of broadcasting which permit, at least by indirection, an abridgement of the freedoms which seem to be so clearly guaranteed. The first of these arises out of the licensing procedures and the second is from the "Fairness Clause" in Section 315, which did not become a part of the Communications Act until 1959.

The licensing procedure itself is sufficiently complicated and, therefore, vulnerable to a variety of abuses. Since there is no way of designing a foolproof scale on which to judge competing applications, the commissioners must rely on fallible and subjective human judgments.

The procedure becomes vastly more complicated when taken in context with the great variety of new elements added by the application and growth of the "Fairness Doctrine." The "Fairness Doctrine" itself added a sufficiently complex new element but, when it was not only affirmed but somewhat convoluted by the *Red Lion* decision in 1969,[1] the opportunity for utilization of the licensing procedure for the imposition of a philosophy became vastly strengthened.

It's a curious fact in the development of broadcasting in the United States that what passes for progress has frequently been nothing more than a series of trade-offs. When broadcasters were given the right to editorialize in 1949, they were obligated to follow a "Fairness" rule. They were quite willing to live with "Fairness" as it applied to editorials but found that it tended to be inhibiting when applied to straight news broadcasts and documentaries, which exhibited any genuine courage in attacking community problems.

In 1959 broadcasters succeeded in softening the "Equal Time" clause of Section 315. They were granted the right to cover candidate appearances in regularly scheduled news broadcasts, news interviews and news documentaries without being forced to yield equal time. Here, too, there was a trade-off. For this privilege they gave up any claim they might have had to the elimination or weakening of the "Fairness" clause. It was written into the law and was no longer a simple statement of FCC policy. And the increasing complexity of interpretations, growing like barnacles on a ship's hull, added new and complex dimensions.

The *Banzhaf* cigarette case in 1966 extended the application of the "Fairness Doctrine" to commercials.[2] This move was reinforced by the *Friends of the Earth* case.[3] In the midst of the gradual extension of the application of the "Fairness Doctrine" came the *Red Lion* decision, handed down by the Supreme Court in 1969.

It's odd how an innocuous little sentence, which simply specified that broadcasters have the obligation to "afford reasonable opportunities for the discussion of conflicting views on issues of public importance," could be stretched to the point where it could be applied to almost any part of the broadcasting schedule. The *Red Lion* case really didn't add any new elements; it only shifted the focus. No longer could a broadcaster assume that following the good journalist's rule of objectivity would insure compliance. The Court shifted the emphasis from the rights of the media to the rights of the listener-viewer to hear and see a diversity of voices, attitudes and ideas. Thus was born the controversy over "public access," a controversy which has been raging since the Red Lion case and shows no promise of abating.

The problem with the application of the "Fairness Doctrine" is that, once you expand the list of criteria and apply a set of standards no matter how vague they may be, it is necessary for human judgment to be applied to determine whether performance measures up to standards. The standards themselves must necessarily have been set as a matter of human judgment.

"Ascertainment" is a logical by-product of the strict application of the "Fairness Doctrine" as it relates to measurement of station performance. A station manager is under obligation to ascertain the needs, interests and desires of his community and to build a program schedule which caters to those needs, interests and desires. If his license comes under challenge he must prove that his "ascertainment" procedures were thorough and sound and that his program schedule recognizes all the factors discovered in his ascertainment exercise.

All of this sounds very logical and quite innocuous. Obviously the trustee of a public award of a frequency to communicate should perform in the "public interest, convenience and necessity." But unfortunately, there are no hard and fixed guidelines on which to judge his performance;

no scientific units of measurement that can be applied; no objective devices available for judging.

It is the subjective nature of this process that frightens broadcasters when a Vice President on a speaking platform in Des Moines, Iowa, or the Director of the Office of Telecommunications Policy in Indianapolis, Indiana, lays down criticism of "elitist gossip" and "ideological plugola." If his locally generated news programming or that obtained from the network is to be judged on the basis of political prejudice couched in scare words, he has a just reason to fear that his position is insecure.

If intemperate criticism comes from officials holding high office, the fears can be intensified. The gradual erosion of the defenses implied in the censorship phrase in the 1934 Act is small comfort. No wonder he worries whether his license may be at stake if he broadcasts any matter which might be regarded as critical of those in power.

The Chairman of the Federal Communications Commission, Dean Burch, conceded at a hearing of the Subcommittee on Communications of the Senate Commerce Committee in February that there are dangerous elements in the "Fairness Doctrine." Senator Pastore asked him the question: "We're getting into the area of censorship here, aren't we?" Burch's answer: "I'm afraid that the 'Fairness Doctrine' by definition comes a little close into the area of censorship in the sense that we require certain things to be put on the air."

The trouble with "Fairness" is that it has broad parameters. If "Fairness" were simply construed as a requirement to maintain the news tradition for objectivity and balance, enforcement would be a relatively simple matter. Most broadcasters are dedicated to objectivity anyway and the extremists who have no interest in maintaining it could be quickly identified.

When "Fairness" is projected into national political affairs or the elections, it becomes more complicated. A network has an almost impossible position in trying to keep some reasonable balance between the party in power and the out-party. The American system does not lend itself to the easy identification of the logical spokesman for the loyal opposition. The "Equal Time" provision takes care of the appearances of candidates during election campaigns but "Fairness" is a much more subtle thing and subject to a vast range of interpretations.

CBS' ill-fated attempt to set up a mechanism for giving an opportunity to the loyal opposition, to be heard in a program entitled "The Loyal Opposition" in the spring of 1970, illustrates the difficulty involved in trying to work out an institutionalized system for performing the role. CBS furnished the Democratic National Committee a half hour of time to respond to a number of presidential speeches. Party Chairman Lawrence O'Brien, rather than answer precisely the points made by the President in his preceding half hour message, ranged broadly over a number of issues in which he flayed the Republican Party vigorously. The Republicans asked for time to answer. The Federal Communications Commission decided that they were, under the terms of the "Fairness Doctrine," entitled to such time. CBS did the only thing it could do: It put the program in mothballs and hasn't been heard from since.

I walked headlong into a very carefully constructed trap eight days before the 1958 election. On a Sunday afternoon I received a call asking whether I was interested in giving live coverage to a meeting of President Eisenhower's Cabinet, scheduled to take place the next day. I replied in the affirmative, provided it would be a genuine Cabinet meeting with all members present. My theory was that the public had never seen the inside of the Cabinet Room, had never seen the Cabinet members assembled with the President and that they had no idea as to the procedures followed in regular Cabinet meetings. This seemed to be an eminently useful first in the television business and so I took the next step which was to call Jim Hagerty, President Eisenhower's press secretary at the White House, to discuss the offer more fully with him.

Hagerty told me that he could schedule the Cabinet meeting at our convenience on the next day, a Monday. We decided on a one-hour period between 7:00 and 8:00 P.M. Affiliated stations were quickly informed of the decision, a mobile unit and crews were assigned to start setting up first thing next morning and the special events director in Washington was given the responsibility of handling all the logistical details.

Hagerty was as good as his word. Secretary of State Dulles failed to appear because he was on one of his many trips, but the other members of the Cabinet were all on the scene. The President called on them, one by one, to make reports. The cameras were placed in advantageous positions to get both the members of the Cabinet delivering their reports and the reaction of the President. Response to the program suggested that the public was interested and grateful for the opportunity to see an American institution, about which they had read many times, in action.

It was equally obvious, however, that this Cabinet meeting was staged.

236 The purpose was not to conduct the normal business of the United States;

it was not to discuss serious issues and arrive at honest conclusions. The purpose was to display the President and the Cabinet of the United States, Republicans all, to voters of both parties, just eight days before a national election. I had unwittingly given the Republican Party one hour of free time on the CBS radio and television networks in the guise of its being an event of public importance.

For this error CBS could surely have been charged with violation of the "Fairness Doctrine," unless it were to make amends by furnishing the Democratic Party with a similar hour at some reasonable time before the election. The Democrats complained about the so-called "Cabinet Meeting." They described it as a trick, which it surely was, but they did not demand time to answer. The Democrats became the winners of the election and apparently no damage was done, except to my own standards. Since those days "Fairness," however, has become a much more complicated commodity.

Turning to the *Banzhaf* cigarette case, Mr. Banzhaf was able to convince the Federal Communications Commission that cigarette smoking—which is potentially injurious to the health—was a matter of public interest and concern. He further argued that the "Fairness Doctrine" demanded that messages calling attention to the possible damaging effects were urgently required. The Commission agreed and a new interpretation of "Fairness" has been written into the history of the Communications Act. Under this new interpretation not only news and public affairs programs were subject to "Fairness" interpretations, but also commercial advertising.

Many broadcasters had long followed a policy of refusing to sell time for the discussion of controversial issues, but sometimes the policy had been breached. CBS television for a number of years had permitted the electric light and power companies to broadcast commercials in connection with the "You Are There" television programs, which were obviously designed to sell the virtues of private utility systems. Network and corporate officials eventually, however, discovered the error and insisted that the commercials sell products and not ideas. The advertising was duly changed to conform.

David Wolper, the Hollywood producer of documentaries and feature films came into my office one day in 1958 with a one-hour documentary program relating to man's effort to conquer space. The program was entitled "The Race for Space." I screened it with Wolper, found it thoroughly researched, skillfully produced and about as entertaining as a documentary could be, but I turned it down. The basis for the decision was that the protagonist in the program which placed heavy emphasis on the efforts of the U.S. Army to develop a space program, was General Medaris, the head of the Army space program. It so happened that at this point in history the Army, the Navy and the Air Force was engaged in a vigorous battle to see which of the three services would gain command of the country's entire space program. As it turned out none of the three did. The responsibility was ultimately given to the National Aeronautics and Space Administration (NASA). But carrying that program at that particular time with its strong Army bias and its glorification of General Medaris would certainly have been unfair to the other two services and, in a sense, to the Administration as well, since it was undoubtedly preparing even at that early stage to award the plum to NASA.

Our decision, later supported by both ABC and NBC, turned out to be an unalloyed boon for Mr. Wolper. He took his program to the Music Corporation of America, built an independent network for it, engendered a groundswell of favorable response and was off to a highly successful career in film production. CBS was undamaged. It retained its self-respect and pride and, as a matter of fact, produced a vastly better show in the "CBS Reports" series. However, the "Fairness Doctrine" was begining to close in. We were criticized in the most vigorous way for keeping the network to ourselves, for not permitting divergent voices to be heard, for not permitting the development of new talents, for closing off the channels of access for persons outside the narrowly limited sphere of broadcasting.

Public access has surely become the battleground for more criticism of the present structure of broadcasting than any single issue. In the 1940's the center of controversy was the "Blue Book," an FCC report recommending certain principles with respect to radio programming; in the 1950's among other things the Quiz Scandals commanded the major share of attention; the 1960's brought Civil Rights and the coverage of dissident elements in our society. Now, in the 1970's, the dominant theme is "Public Access."

"Access" has become almost as overworked a word in the language as "relevant" was in the late '60's and "meaningful" before that. Not only is it overworked, it is so loosely used as to obscure its real meaning and its method of application to the broadcast scene.

What kind of access are we speaking of? Obviously we must include diverse opinions, ideas, attitudes. Obviously, opportunity must be granted to a diversity of groups, who now have little opportunity to be seen or heard, or to have their opinions seen or heard, on the established broadcast communications facilities.

However, providing such "public access" invites a great number of knotty problems.

Should the broadcast facility become a speakers' corner where all dissident or dispossessed groups have the opportunity to ascend the soap box and speak to the fulfillment of their utmost desires?

Should the role of the gatekeeper be transformed so that the gatekeeper becomes more a traffic policeman, regulating the flow of diverse persons, groups and ideas, than the executive charged with responsiblity for policy formulation? Which serves the public interest better: A system in which management, responsive to a diversity of public interest, needs and desires, consciously establishes a policy and a mechanism to implement it, where the ultimate responsibility for the selection of the diverse ideas, attitudes, and opinions rest with him, or one in which the initiatives lie with groups seeking to utilize his facility for "public access" purposes?

Should groups with adequate financial resources be permitted to purchase blocks of time to carry their views to the public? Or, should broadcasters be permitted to impose "flat bans" against the sale of time for the discussion of controversial issues?

Should access be achieved on the basis of direct contact between individual and station management, or should it be indirect access achieved through participation in advisory councils?

Could access requirements be solved through more careful attention to a diversity of voices and views in regular news and documentary programs, or must they be achieved through new and special efforts?

Will attention to a diversity of voices lead to fragmentation and chaos, or to a sounder approach to national problems since more ideas have been aired, more alternatives explored, more dissident voices brought into the formulation of policy?

Should more efforts to open access to communications media be supported in the interest of catharsis, or so that the nation will be better able to formulate sound policy by broadening the inputs?

More importantly, does the "right to speak" serve as a sufficient guarantee of first amendment rights, or should there be some concomitant "right to be heard" in order to carry out fully the mandate of the *Red Lion* case? Groups or individuals using "public access" are likely to be shocked by the paucity of viewers or listeners to their performances unless they are integrated into existing programming.

The cumulative effect of the *Banzhaf, Friends of the Earth,* and *Red Lion* decisions seem to have established, as a matter of public policy, an obligation on the part of broadcasters to furnish "public access." The *Business Executives Move for Peace-Democratic National Committee* case is still to be heard from but the decision most likely will relate only to part of the problem—the question of "paid access" as opposed to "free access."

The matter of furnishing such access is a complicated one. Carried to its ultimate end we would be creating a new "Tower of Babel," in which the cacaphony produced by a multitude of voices would leave nothing but chaos, confusion and frustration. At the same time a legitimate question can be asked as to whether freedom to use the air waves serves a more real purpose than simply giving the speaker an opportunity to blow off steam. If so, is it worthwhile devoting a segment of an enormously valuable public franchise for the purpose? We run the real risk, unless public access questions are settled judiciously and with restraint, of creating so many opportunities, giving them to so many varied petitioners representing so many diverse sources that we will be guilty of an "idea and opinion overkill." As a matter of fact, some think that we are being subjected now to an excessive volume of diversity.

Broadcast licensees are already committed to furnishing the type of diversity that is described in the *Red Lion* case and in the "Fairness Doctrine." Questions regarding how it should be carried out, however, are worthy of careful consideration.

It is self-evident that a license holder should be more than a traffic policeman. He obviously must know his community. "Ascertainment," even though the word has the tinge of government jargon, is a necessary requirement for understanding the problems and people of a community. The crucial question is whether the broadcast licensee can meet the requirements of "diversity" through his normal broadcast schedule and on a voluntary basis, or whether he must yield some control to outside, non-professional, special pleaders.

This country has had reasonable success in the past by entrusting the control of its media to a corps of professionals. For the most part these professionals have acted with wisdom and sensitivity to the public's welfare.

A voluntary commitment to fairness, balance and objectivity has provided a bench mark to guide their decision-making.

On the other hand, there are distinct dangers involved both in too rigid an application of requirements for "public access" and in too broad an extension of the "Fairness Doctrine."

One danger arises from the fact that the broadcasting station could become an oriental bazaar, dedicated to the hawking of strange and exotic ideas, scheduled with no editorial judgment, no selectivity and no guaranteed relevance to current problems.

It is entirely likely that an uncontrolled or lightly controlled public access system could be monopolized by the more aggressive and articulate elements in society, which are neither the needy ones nor those with the most to contribute. The microphones and cameras could go to those with the greatest resources, the loudest voices, the most demanding attitudes and, in some cases, possibly the most frightening threats.

Counteradvertising, a linear descendant of the "Fairness Doctrine" and the *Red Lion* case, sounds like a completely reasonable theory. If detergents foul up sewer systems, why shouldn't ecology-minded groups have the opportunity to present messages countering advertising for the detergents? If gasolines pollute the air and contribute toward the onset of disease and eventual choking of cities, why shouldn't opponents have an opportunity to express a contrary point of view? If the construction of the Alaskan pipeline will damage the ecological development of the territory through which it passes, why shouldn't attention be called to this fact?

There are a number of distinct fallacies in this type of reasoning. In the first place, in the cases cited above, counteradvertising wasn't necessary to stimulate an intensive discussion of the issues. A national debate was generated without the aid of counteradvertising. However, more importantly, while little that is affirmative can be accomplished (note that cigarette consumption is higher now than it was when radio and television stations carried cigarette commercials), serious damage can be wrought to the economy of the broadcasting business. There is no point in arguing here whether economic strength is desirable. The fact is that our economy is governed by a profit motive. Until there is a better method of operating our communications media, it seems reasonable that we should do what we can to keep it economically viable. We can always switch to a public broadcasting system although the recent controversies over the Corporation for Public Broadcasting suggest that we haven't done too well yet in that area.

A greater concern stems from the fact that, as we broaden the application of the Federal Communications Act of 1934 by rulings, policy statements, amendments, court decisions and interpretations, we increase the number of entry points for government interference or intimidation and move further away from the theoretical protections of the broadcaster once thought offered by the First Amendment. It is true that broadcasters have been far too timid in the past. They have been much too inclined to tremble in terror at governmental criticism. They have been much too quick to fly the white flag for fear of government penalties. We should understand that there is a vast array of opportunities open to the government official for exacting punishment of one kind or another. Anticipation of punishment is frequently a sufficient threat to force a licensee to invest many hours of manpower and many thousands of dollars in building defenses. Encouragement of a competing application for his license, or hints of impending legislation serve as subtle constraints on his freedom to operate. Many of these fears are doubtlessly exaggerated, but a government license offers little defense if a government is determined to exact penalties or force compliance with a specific point of view, even though the First Amendment exists as a theoretical bulwark against government encroachment.

In short, there is nothing wrong with the principle of a "Fairness Doctrine" provided it is fairly imposed and is not used as a vehicle for broadening government controls over all phases of broadcasting. The definitions, so far furnished by the courts, superficially appear reasonable.

There are three principal interpretations: (1) A broadcaster must give adequate coverage to public issues. (2) Coverage must be fair in that it accurately reflects opposing views. (3) Coverage must be afforded at the broadcaster's own expense, if sponsorship is unavailable. Any of these three interpretations could lead to excesses, but, if adopted as general statements of principle, no broadcaster could take exception.

A general requirement for operating in the "public interest, convenience and necessity" assumes that the broadcaster will give adequate coverage to public issues.

A voluntary "Fairness Doctrine," which assumes that fairness is largely related to maintaining objectivity and balance, has previously ensured the broadcasting of a wide diversity of views, attitudes and opinions. And, with the addition of some creativity and ingenuity on the part of management, it could also succeed in presenting a diversity of faces.

The Cullman principle, the third of the interpretations listed above, is not unreasonable if it is employed only in significant cases. Where the controversy is of such demonstrated public concern that response is required as a matter of public policy and not of government whim, a non-paid response is probably in order.

The main dangers involving the "Fairness Doctrine" arise from the tendency of the Doctrine to encourage timidity on the part of broadcasters, the bracketing of "fairness" with "public access," and the decision in the *Red Lion* case.

The newly refurbished "Fairness Doctrine" is thus more than a negative constraint disguised to maintain balance. It is becoming a positive force demanding that broadcasters take the initiative in seeking out voices, opinions and ideas which do not otherwise make themselves heard. If this is accomplished by voluntary "ascertainment" procedures, the broadcaster can't really object. It is to his advantage to know his community well for business as well as program reasons.

The danger is that he can be penalized for having missed some obscure element, and that his responsibility to follow up "ascertainment" can be judged on a set of standards that are subjectively established.

Maintaining objectivity is not a wholly mechanical procedure. Human judgment is required to measure the degree of objectivity or conversely of imbalance. But the human factor plays a greatly enlarged role in assessing the sins of omission as opposed to the sins of commission.

An FCC commissioner would require the vision of a clairvoyant and the wisdom of a Solomon to determine who deserves to be heard and who to be overlooked. Additionally, his decision must be made without the benefit of living and working in the community in which the case arises.

It is no wonder that the application of the First Amendment to broadcasting becomes baffling. The First Amendment protects the right of free speech but the government functionary decides how the broadcaster exercises it and who else in the community may have access to his facilities to use the privilege.

The Federal Communications Act prevents the Commission from exercising any power of censorship, but it can decide what is fair or unfair, and who has a right to use the facility to reply to management.

The Federal Communications Act specifies that "no regulation or condition shall be promulgated or fixed by the Commission which shall interfere with the right of free speech." Yet it can revoke a license if the broadcaster doesn't furnish diverse members of his community with the right to respond to his "free speech." Can speech really be free if it may result in license revocation? Of what value is the constitutional assurance if a single individual or a group of commissioners or the whole apparatus of government is in a position to make a subjective decision as to what is fair and unfair?

It is the response to this question that caused broadcasters to react so vigorously to criticism from the Vice President, the Director of the Office of Telecommunications Policy and other Administration officials in the period since the Vice President's Des Moines speech of November, 1969.

The vulnerability of broadcasting is predicated on the fact that it is difficult to separate content from other aspects of regulation. A drift from an assigned frequency can be judged objectively by mathematical calculations. Performance of service in the community furnishes no such mathematical scale.

Critics insist that broadcasting must be treated differently from the printed press because it uses a valuable and scarce commodity, the limited radio frequencies. It is true that the spectrum available for broadcast use is too limited to permit any applicant who wishes one to obtain a license but this doesn't necessarily furnish decisive proof that broadcasting is a dangerous monopoly. There are approximately 1,700 daily newspapers in the United States but there are 8,253 broadcasting stations. Of this total 922 are television stations, the remainder radio. Of the television licensees 701 are commercial.

The City of New York has three mass circulation daily newspapers. There are six commercial VHF television stations and one non-commercial.

Chicago has more mass circulation dailies than any other city in the country—four. But there are four commercial VHF television stations, three commercial UHF stations, one non-commercial VHF and one non-commercial UHF. In addition, there are more than 60 radio stations in Chicago and Cook County.

The limited spectrum is a serious constraint against obtaining a license to broadcast, but the investment costs required to go into newspaper publishing are equally onerous and serve as a very real obstacle, if not quite so obvious as that faced by broadcasting.

The scarcity of new metropolitan dailies starting up in the last three decades is testimony to the fact that the day of the pamphleteer with the mimeograph has long since gone.

It is true that there are only three national networks but there are likewise only three national weekly news magazines, two national wire services and two principal news syndication services. The networks may be a monopoly, but not quite as virulent a one as critics argue. Not enough for the imposition of restrictions that would chip away at the underlying philosophy of the American tradition for free dissemination of news and information.

Admittedly, there is a vital need for channels for the expression of a greater number of ideas and opinions. There is a danger that our communications media might become so tradition bound and inwardly oriented that they would not be responsive to new thought or novel suggestion. There is the possibility that broadcast frequencies would be used, if all constraints were removed, for the maintenance of the status quo.

But we must weigh the advantages of free expression against a tightly controlled system of public access, which could conceivably require more restriction and more interpretation in an evolving process of growing complexity in order to be workable.

At a recent conference at Ditchley Park in Oxfordshire, England, devoted to considering the relationship of broadcasting to media in eight countries with free election systems, there was widespread agreement that broadcasters should abide by a general self-imposed standard of fairness. There was concern, however, that fairness should not be so encrusted with detailed definitions, interpretations and requirements as to make it an objective in itself, rather it should be a broad-gauge guide to service to the listener-viewer. And the British delegate was particularly firm in pointing out that British broadcasting is fair without government rules.

Not all our broadcast deficiencies can be cured by a hands-off policy, nor can broadcasters rely wholly on the First Amendment to ward off criticism but our broadcast policies would be best served by giving the broadcaster freedom from the constraints imposed by Section 315, the ascertainment procedure and such other rules and policy statements as may open the door for influence of content. Perhaps in the future public access on the widespread scale, for which some broadcast critics now yearn, can be accomplished through cable. A broadband communications system with 20 or 40 or even 60 to 80 channels will, in all probability, furnish ample opportunity to all who wish to use it, without conflicting with the interests of others. If we can wait until cable is ready to create an environment in which all voices can be heard and all ideas expressed before imposing restrictions which interfere with the basic rights of freedom of speech, we can maintain reasonable respect for the First Amendment.

In the interim, it is time for a thorough new look at the Federal Communications Act of 1934 and its instrument for the execution of government policy—the Federal Communications Commission. The Communications Act has been patched up, amended and expanded to cover new communications media and a myriad of new and unanticipated problems since its inception. Television was only a dream in 1934, radio in a primitive stage, and broadband communications unheard of by lay persons. Communications satellites were something only for science fiction writers.

Radio news in 1934 was barely out of the prehistoric stage. Lowell Thomas, Boake Carter, and H. V. Kaltenborn were broadcasting news from network headquarters but the Associated Press was suing KSOO in Sioux Falls, South Dakota and KVOS in Bellingham, Washington for piracy of the news. A short-lived CBS News Service was organized in 1933 but was soon allowed to die quietly. Edward R. Murrow was in Europe hunting up speakers for the CBS "Talks" programs. Associated Press and United Press service to radio stations came later, as did the organization of network news departments.

In 1974, forty years will have passed since the Communications Act became law and the FCC organized, forty years of the most rapid changes in world history. The Communications Act like the Constitution may have been written for the ages but it is more likely to have been designed to meet a specific set of needs which existed in 1934.

The future is not likely to furnish breathing spells when we can pause to have a look at the whole communications regulatory structure. We shall have to do it on the fly. Therefore, it is appropriate to appoint a commission at an early date to examine the past 40 years of service, foresee the needs of the future, determine *not* where the Communications Act should be patched up but *whether* it should be retained, or a new structure established. Perhaps the impetus should come from a disinterested citizens group funded by non-profit agencies, rather than by an administration or congressional agency.

Broadcast communications have become so essential to the functioning of late Twentieth Century society that they deserve the best efforts of the most thoughtful people to make it possible for them to operate most effectively in the public interest. Special attention should be found toward developing mechanisms to keep them as free of government constraint as they can possibly be, consistent with the necessity of maintaining some type of licensing system. And regulations affecting content should be consigned to whatever final resting place accommodates all those old government laws, rules and agencies that have been found wanting.

EDITORS' NOTES

1. *Red Lion Broadcasting Co. vs. FCC*, 395 U.S. 367, 89 S.Ct. 1794 (1969). Red Lion Broadcasting refused Fred J. Cook free time to respond to a personal attack on him by Billy James Hargis, a program moderator on radio station WGCB.
2. 8 FCC 2d 381, June 2, 1967. In 1967 John F. Banzhaf, III, complained to the FCC that television station WCBS-TV in New York was violating the Fairness Doctrine. He claimed that since smoking had been cited as a hazard to health, the Fairness Doctrine required that stations carrying cigarette advertising were obliged to afford free time for responsible spokesmen to offer anti-smoking messages. The FCC concurred with the Banzhaf complaint.
3. *Friends of the Earth vs. FCC*, 449 F. 2d 1164 (D.C. Cir.) Aug. 16, 1971. The national environmentalist organization known as Friends of the Earth complained in 1970 to the FCC that WNBC-TV, New York, should be required to give free time under the Fairness Doctrine in response to commercials advocating purchase of automobiles and gasoline. These products, the group claimed, were damaging to the environment and to health. The FCC did not agree with this petition and appealed to the court. The Friends of the Earth won this appeal and countercommercials subsequently were placed on WNBC-TV.

Fair Play on the Air ...

TRACY A. WESTEN

Reprinted from (MORE), vol. 2, 1 (January, 1972). Copyright (MORE), 750 Third Avenue, New York, N.Y. 10017. Reprinted by permission. Tracy A. Westen is professor of law, UCLA law school, specializing in communications.

In calling for the abolition of the "Fairness Doctrine" not long ago, Dr. Clay Whitehead warned that "Kafka sits on the Court of Appeals

247

and Orwell works in the FCC's Office of Opinions and Review . . . 'Big Brother' himself could not have conceived a more disarming 'newspeak' name for a system of governmental program control than the Fairness Doctrine." Refreshing as such attempts at erudition are these days in Washington, one wonders whether it's not the Administration itself that harbors the big brotherly ambitions.* After all, Dr. Whitehead presides over something called the White House Office of Telecommunications Policy, a newly created Presidential agency that seeks to supervise the electronic media and in recent months has pushed hard for legislation that would line the pockets of the broadcast industry while stripping the nation's poor, disenfranchised and voiceless of their already limited access to radio and television.

Dr. Whitehead, a 32-year-old economics Ph.D. out of the Massachusetts Institute of Technology and the Rand Corporation, labels the Fairness Doctrine a "quagmire" of governmental regulation "masquerading as an expansion of the public's right of free expression." But he offers broadcasters a good bit more than rhetoric. In laying down "The Whitehead Doctrine" before a luncheon of radio and television executives at the Waldorf-Astoria last fall, he proposed, first, that the government, on an experimental basis in a few markets, should hand over radio licenses to their present owners, somewhat like gifts, to be operated in perpetuity without periodic "public interest" review by the Federal Communications Commission. Second, he suggested that competing businessmen and public interest groups should not be allowed to file "competing applications" for incumbent station licenses, even though they promised to give the public "superior" programming service. Finally, Whitehead promised to give Congress legislation for his proposals if he received broadcast industry support. Under the circumstances, it was like promising lions raw meat if only they roared.

Whitehead's proposals were perfectly in phase with earlier Administration actions—the Agnew broadside, the attorney general's

---

*Actually, Whitehead's metaphors are more than somewhat misplaced. The "Kafkaesque" architect of many important U.S. Court of Appeals decisions involving the First Amendment, the "fairness" and "access" doctrines, and the right to monopolize a broadcast license, was Judge Skelly Wright, respected by many lawyers as one of the nation's most scholarly and imaginative advocates of individual First Amendment freedoms. As for the "Orwellian" Office of Opinions and Review, it had *no* drafting or supervisory responsibility for *any* of the Fairness Doctrine opinions under Whitehead's attack.

subpoenas, and the Pentagon's anti-CBS ("The Selling of the Pentagon") campaign. Frank Shakespeare, former "television advisor" to Nixon and now head of the United States Information Agency, laid out the strategy bluntly during the 1968 campaign.

> I thought I'd go to Walter Scott, the NBC board chairman . . . and say, 'Here are the instances . . . where we feel you've been guilty of bias in your coverage of Nixon. We are going to monitor every minute of your broadcast news, and if this kind of bias continues, and if we are elected, then you just might find yourself in Washington next year answering a few questions. And you just might find yourself having a little trouble getting some of your licenses renewed.'

The "trade-off" was implicit. If the broadcast industry failed to provide favorable media coverage of White House spokesmen and policies, then the White House would take reprisals against their economic interests. If the industry complied, then the Administration would protect profits. *Variety* reported:

> The industry's decision to accept censorship in exchange for security has been apparent at practically every management event . . . (T)he ordinary broadcaster . . . is willing to surrender still more of his first amendment freedom for the promise of a perpetual license to do business.

The Administration has kept its part of this bargain. While the Vice President criticized the media for concentrating its decision-making power in too few "Eastern liberal" hands, the White House overruled its own Justice Department antitrust experts and supported the newspaper industry's monopoly authorization bill (the "Failing Newspaper Act"). And when Sen. Thomas J. McIntyre (D., N.H.) proposed a bill to diversify ownership of newspapers and broadcast stations, Herb Klein, Nixon's Director of Communications, publicly opposed it. The White House has also consistently appointed business-oriented commissioners to the FCC. When Nixon named Dean Burch as chairman of the FCC, his appointment was "hailed by broadcasters who were seeking a chairman to protect their interest as businessmen," according to the *Washington Sunday Star*. Another Nixon appointee, Commissioner Robert Wells, a life-long station owner, announced his own biases: "My views on broadcasting naturally are formed by the business I was in. I just don't know that you can separate the interests of the citizens and the interests of the broadcasters."

Unwilling to rely solely on FCC appointments, Nixon created the Office of Telecommunications Policy and named Dr. Whitehead its first director. With a staff of 55, he soon became a potent Administration spokesman. Whitehead first influenced the FCC to abandon its Comsat-controlled communications satellite experiment, and permit any private corporation to acquire domestic satellite facilities "for its own needs." He proposed that federal funds be channeled directly to individual educational television affiliates, thereby diminishing the power of the liberal network programmers. And he helped negotiate, without consulting the public, a "compromise" on cable television policy between the competing industries, which will diminish potential future service to the public.

But the Administration had not yet stacked the U.S. Court of Appeals, and despite the FCC's pro-industry bias, the Court continued to issue expansive First Amendment and Fairness Doctrine rulings. Three cases, in particular, really hurt. The first involved an extraordinary attempt by FCC Chairman Burch to pass a "policy statement" to protect station licenses against challenges at renewal time. Nixon spokesmen were clearly implicated in this move and kept in frequent contact with Burch. "Basically it was [Burch's] idea," reported Whitehead, "but it was a policy we supported. "In *Citizens v.* FCC, however, the Court of Appeals quickly struck down the policy statement as illegal, and again left broadcasters open to challenge at renewal time. The second decision, *Friends of the Earth*, held that advertisements for high-powered automobiles and high-octane gasolines raised controversial environmental issues of public importance, and that licensees had a Fairness Doctrine obligation to present contrasting views. The third, *Business Executives for Vietnam Peace*, held that licensees could not refuse to sell available "commercial" time to individuals wishing to speak out against the Vietnam War merely because the broadcaster had a "policy" against selling time for "controversial" views, or feared he would have to provide free rebuttal time for opposing views. In all these cases, broadcasters felt their profits under attack. What made matters worse, citizens groups, led by the Rev. Everett Parker of the United Church of Christ and Al Kramer and Bob Stein at the Citizens Communications Center in Washington, had begun to challenge individual broadcasters at renewal time, asking the FCC to revoke their licenses for failure to serve community interests.

The court decisions and the license challenges were more than the industry could bear. The National Association of Broadcasters pushed its lobbyists into high gear. Communications attorneys began to draft legislation to protect licensees' profits. Letters soliciting support and pledges of money were sent to every broadcaster in the country. Then, at the peak of the alarm, Dr. Whitehead stepped forward with his proposals. He suggested three revisions to the Communications Act. The first two were for television only—"eliminate the Fairness Doctrine and replace it with a statutory right of access" and prohibit competing applications at license renewal time. His third revision was for radio only—immunize ("deregulate") it from all FCC or "public interest" supervision. The three proposals were oddly interrelated. The Fairness Doctrine was designed to prevent a monopolist from suppressing dissenting opinions. Obviously this danger would be greater—and the need for a Fairness Doctrine greater—where only a few licensees owned all the broadcast stations in a market. One would naturally expect that anyone proposing to eliminate the Fairness Doctrine would also want to diversify media ownership, hoping that multiple owners would replenish the marketplace of ideas. Whitehead, however, not only proposed to abolish the Fairness Doctrine, but proposed to *prohibit* competing license challenges as well–at least until the incumbent lost his license or gave it up of his own accord. Whitehead's proposal was like preventing a candidate from running for public office until the incumbent had first been impeached. Whitehead's radio proposals were even more extreme. As with television, Whitehead would abolish the Fairness Doctrine. Unlike television, he would not permit individuals to purchase spot-announcement time for controversial issues, and would prevent any review of program performance at renewal time. Whitehead, in other words, would make irrevocable gifts of radio licenses to their current owners—to sell off or exploit as they might desire.

Whitehead assumes that radio in large markets will specialize its programming for particular audiences—all news, talk, classical, rock, etc.—and that there is no need for FCC regulation to compel diversity of service. Even in large markets, however, most stations still compete for mass audiences and bypass minorities which are small in number, or too impoverished to purchase the sponsor's products. In smaller markets, Whitehead's proposal would result in disaster. Many small-town stations are run by businessmen who care or understand little about programming, and import hours of tapes a day from fundamentalist preachers and right-wing propagandists. Only the Fairness and Public Service Doctrines require these stations to devote even minimal service to the diverse needs of their listener minorities. The Whitehead Doctrine would create a stifling uniformity of programming in these smaller communities.

Though "competing renewals" and "radio de-regulation" are certainly bad policies, the most destructive consequences would flow from loss of the Fairness Doctrine. Whitehead would substitute for it an individual right to purchase as many spot announcements as one could afford in open competition with commercial advertisers. This right of speech-for-purchase, however, would benefit only those with money to pay going prices. Under the FCC's 1967 cigarette ruling, the American Cancer Society and others were given free time to oppose cigarette commercials. Their public service announcements had a remarkable impact. Cigarette consumption in the United States dropped from 549.2 billion cigarettes in 1967, to 528.9 billion in 1969. As these spots left the air, cigarette consumption again rose—536.4 billion cigarettes in 1970, a projected 546.0 billion in 1971. The Whitehead Doctrine would have made this impossible. In 1970 the cigarette industry spent $195,215,200 on television advertising. No public interest group has $200 million to spend on anti-cigarette commercials. Whitehead's proposed elimination of the Fairness Doctrine would hopelessly skew this country's "marketplace of ideas" in favor of business and commerce.

Under the commission's "personal attack" doctrine, an analogue of the Fairness Doctrine, persons are entitled to a right of free reply whenever their honesty, character, or integrity has been attacked. The original *Red Lion* decision, for example, enabled a journalist to deny that he was dishonest or worked for a "Communist-affiliated publication." Presumably under the Whitehead Doctrine he would have no right of reply—unless, of course, he could afford to purchase the time. Defamation would become the privilege of the rich. Current FCC rules also give a political candidate a right of reply whenever a station editorializes against him or in favor of his opponent. This provision is designed to prevent broadcasters from dominating political debates in campaigns with poor or minority candidates. Again, Whitehead would toss this important right of self-defense out with the Fairness Doctrine.

Whitehead proposes a right to purchase commercial time. He is notably silent on the right to purchase *programming time*—half-hour or full-hour segments for comedies, dramas, satires, documentaries, or public debates. Under his plan, for example, the Democratic National Committee would not be allowed to purchase a half-hour of television time to oppose President Nixon's war policies. Nor would licensees be obliged to "balance" their political programming. In 1970, for example, the FCC ruled that five speeches by Nixon on the Vietnam War entitled Democratic spokesmen to one hour of free rebuttal time. Under Whitehead's proposal, this limited right of rebuttal would disappear.

Whitehead also proposed that the FCC should not be allowed to resolve specific case-by-case programming complaints. Rather, the FCC would be limited to judging at renewal time "whether the broadcaster has, over the term of his license, made a *good faith* effort to ascertain local needs and interests and to meet them in his programming." This proposal has two serious drawbacks. First, imbalances in programming, unanswered personal attacks, and other forms of program "censorship" by licensees would go unredressed for up to five years. (Whitehead proposes extending the license period from three to five years.) By then the subject of the programming imbalance—an election or a timely political issue—will have long passed. Second, by eliminating case-by-case remedies for Fairness Doctrine violations and substituting only license revocation as a penalty, Whitehead would effectively eliminate all relief from programming distortions. By analogy, if a parks commissioner refused to let anti-war groups demonstrate because he didn't like their views, Whitehead's remedy would only enable the protesters to ask five years later that the parks commissioner lose his job. And because the FCC will never "fire" a licensee for anything short of the grossest misbehavior, broadcasters will acquire permanent licenses secure from all fairness regulation. In a system where "capital punishment" is the only remedy for all crimes, minor offenders inevitably go free.

Finally, Whitehead argues that complaints involving the right to purchase commercial time should be enforced through the courts, not the FCC. At present, citizens wishing to file Fairness Doctrine complaints with the commission can do so informally, without hiring a lawyer and without incurring the many costs (depositions, witness fees) of court proceedings. Whitehead's proposal would eliminate this easy access to the FCC. The added complications, expenses and delays might easily deter many individuals from pursuing even legitimate rights.

Whitehead would eliminate the Fairness Doctrine, yet he leaves untouched the fundamental profit maximizing motive that drives broadcasters toward conformity and middle-of-the-road programming. Indeed, Whitehead aggravates this condition by decreasing competition

The Fairness Doctrine

The Fairness Doctrine requires broadcast licensees to present all major viewpoints on "controversial issues of public importance" in a fair, balanced and evenhanded manner. The doctrine has evolved out of FCC decisions over a 40-year period:

1929 Great Lakes decision: Fearful that radio station owners might operate their "public" frequencies for "private" or selfish motives, censoring some views off the air, the commission announced: "Broadcasting stations are licensed to serve the public and not for the purpose of furthering the private or selfish interest of individuals or groups of individuals. . . . Insofar as a program consists of discussion of public questions, public interest requires ample play for the free and fair competition of opposing views."

1934 Communications Act: Congress gave the FCC full regulatory power over broadcast stations, requiring them to operate in the "public interest, convenience, and necessity." The "public interest" standard incorporated the Great Lakes standard into statutory law.

1949 Editorializing Report: The commission authorized stations to editorialize, but cautioned that the "broadcast licensees have an affirmative duty generally to encourage and implement the broadcast of all sides of controversial public issues over their facilities, over and beyond their obligation to make available on demand opportunities for the expression of opposing views."

1959 Law: Congress codified the commission's Fairness Doctrine into law, amending the 1934 Communications Act to acknowledge broadcast licensees' "obligation . . . to afford reasonable opportunity for the discussion of conflicting views on issues of public importance."

1967 Cigarette Ruling: The commission applied the Fairness Doctrine to cigarette advertisements. Because cigarette commercials portrayed the joys and rewards of smoking, they presented one side of an issue of "controversy and public importance." Broadcasters must warn their audiences of smoking-caused lung cancer, emphysema and slow death. Anti-smoking commercials must be broadcast free if no one tries to pay for time.

1969 Red Lion Decision: The U.S. Supreme Court upheld the FCC's Fairness Doctrine as constitutional. The broadcast industry had argued that the Fairness Doctrine violated its First Amendment right to withhold from the public whatever view and information it wished. The Supreme Court disagreed, stating: "a licensee has no constitutional right . . . to monopolize a radio frequency of its fellow citizens." Indeed, the Court hinted that the Fairness Doctrine might be a required part of the First Amendment itself: "It is the purpose of the First Amendment to preserve an uninhibited marketplace of ideas in which truth will ultimately prevail, rather than to countenance monopolization of that market . . . [by] a private licensee."

between persons wishing to operate a station, thereby excluding those new entrants who might provide newer and more creative programming. Before the Fairness Doctrine's safety valve can be eliminated, the broadcast system must be diversified in ownership, entry for competing applications must be eased, program time must be available for purchase, and the right of access to *free* spot announcement *and* programming time must be increased. Finally, a system of case-by-case complaint enforcement must be developed to provide speedy and inexpensive remedies to persons who have been deprived of media "access." Until Whitehead is willing to deal with the *causes* of media mediocrity, his proposals to eliminate the Fairness Doctrine can only generate greater blandness and tedium over the airwaves.

License Challenges

RICHARD E. WILEY

Reprinted with permission of Richard E. Wiley, Chairman, Federal Communications Commission, from a speech he delivered to the Florida Association of Broadcasters, July 10, 1972, in Orlando, Florida.

The issue which I find uppermost in the minds of station operators throughout the country is, quite naturally, license renewal. Broadcasters know better than anyone that challenges to renewal have swelled from a solitary incident in 1967 [Ed. note: The WLBT, Jackson, Miss., case] to a raging tide of protest in [this decade]. Petitions to deny have been filed in some fifteen states and the number grows with each new renewal period . . . this is hardly an academic issue.

Objections to the renewal of a broadcast license have come in several forms. And, depending on the nature of the challenge, the rules of the game and the arena in which it is played are markedly different. As one who must play, albeit unwillingly, this form of regulatory Russian roulette, it behooves you to know those rules, to play well, and—when the

Wiley

255

seven "Great Scorers" come to mark against your name—to be deserving of victory. For in this contest, as you would doubtless agree, it matters very much whether you win or lose. Since we at the [Federal Communications] Commission are also interested in how you play the game, perhaps we can profitably take a look today at the Commission's rules governing both comparative renewals and petitions to deny and how those rules have been interpreted by the ultimate umpire—the Courts.

As in all "federal cases," the most recent news on this last count is both good and bad. First, from your standpoint, the bad news—comparative renewals.

In the *Citizens Communications Center* case, you will recall that the U.S. Court of Appeals for the District of Columbia Circuit held that the FCC's 1970 Renewal Policy Statement was unlawful because it denied to competing applicants a full comparative evidentiary hearing. The Court specifically rejected the Commission's finding that "substantial service" by the licensee would confer on him a preference over the newcomer warranting a grant of broadcaster's renewal application. The Court suggested, instead, its own standard which would provide the incumbent licensee with a plus of major significance at renewal time— "superior performance." The Court also supplied specific criteria to be used in determining whether an incumbent had performed in a "superior" manner including (1) elimination of loud and excessive commercials, (2) delivery of quality programs, (3) independence from governmental influence in promoting First Amendment objectives, (4) diversification of mass media ownership, and (5) the extent to which the licensee has reinvested the profit from his license to the service of the viewing and listening public. Lest anyone believe that these suggestions were in the nature of off-the-cuff judicial observations, the Court, in a recent opinion (May 4, 1972), once again reiterated its five "suggested" standards.

As a member of the administrative body specifically set up by Congress to regulate the broadcasting industry, far be it from me to suggest that the Court might be extending its judicial reach beyond both its jurisdiction and its expertise. However, I will have at least the audacity to comment on the Court's five criteria.

With the first two, the elimination of loud and excessive commercials and the delivery of quality programming, I have absolutely no problem— although I hasten to add that I am not among the school who believes that one commercial is one too many. Commercials, after all, are what makes the delivery of quality programs possible in the first place. As to the third criterion, let me make one thing perfectly clear (to coin a phrase): you *should* be free of governmental influence. Indeed, the Commission's record in this regard is, I believe, above reproach. We have consistently eschewed the censor's role and will, I am confident, continue to do so.

The Court's final two suggested norms, however, seem to me to raise more questions than answers. For example, diversification of mass media may well be a legitimate goal, but I personally do not believe that the renewal process is the appropriate vehicle for restructuring the industry. If we are to restructure, if every multiple owner is thus to be in jeopardy, I believe that such "regulatory engineering" should be accomplished through appropriate rule making with a reasonable opportunity to all parties to comment fully. Moreover, if restructuring rules are subsequently adopted (and I would suggest that there are some very serious public interest considerations here which must be carefully examined), they should allow reasonable periods for divestiture or other appropriate arrangements, rather than a summary forfeiture of some very valuable property which, in many instances, has taken years and years of hard work and high financial risk to develop—all to the benefit, in my opinion, of the American public.

The fifth criterion, reinvestment of profit, is perhaps the most difficult to understand. If it means that broadcasters, as public trustees, must continue to devote financial resources to local programming needs, I couldn't agree more. If, on the other hand, the reinvestment of profit criterion means that the government should regulate profits not only in the operation of stations but also as to their assignment or transfer, then it seems that the broadcast industry is being subtly transformed from a free enterprise operation to a public or eleemosynary system. In my opinion, that is contrary to the express language and legislative history of the Communications Act, to myriad judicial precedents, and, most importantly, to what is in the public interest.

Frankly, perhaps it is time that we openly recognize certain salient and I believe unassailable facts about broadcasting: that it takes a huge financial investment to successfully operate a broadcast facility within the public interest; that no businessman in his right mind would make such an investment if he thought he stood a good chance of losing it all in three years to a newcomer who might *promise* more for the future than he, the incumbent, might have reasonably performed in the past; that without such investment, the public (and in reality primarily the public) will be the ultimate loser; that, in any case, the degree of profitability of any particular station, in and of itself, may have little or no relationship to the level of public service afforded by the broadcaster involved; and finally, that this is a nation which was built on the concept of profit incentive—of delivering a quality product which the American people need or want in return for reasonable financial remuneration. And even in an industry which is, *and must be*, public-interest oriented, profit— at least in my vocabulary—is simply not a dirty word.

Needless to say, the issues raised in the Citizens Communications Center case are yet to be resolved. But, whatever our view of the Court's definition of "superior performance," it is important not to forget the essence of that decision—that when a renewal application is challenged by a competing applicant, a full comparative hearing is necessary. When, however, the challenge comes in the form of a petition to deny, Section 309(d) of the Communications Act requires a hearing only if the petitioner meets his burden of showing that a grant of the renewal application would be *prima facie* inconsistent with the public interest. Unlike the challenge brought by a competing applicant, the petitioner to deny must earn his right to a hearing by alleging facts with sufficient specificity to raise substantial and material questions that can only be resolved in the crucible of a full hearing. In the absence of such a showing, the petitioner is not entitled to a hearing.

And, now, after laying the Citizens Communications case on you once again, if you're still above water, here's the good news: ten days ago, the same U.S. Court of Appeals for the District of Columbia handed down an extremely important decision affirming the Commission's renewal of the license of Washington's WMAL-TV, a renewal which had been severely challenged by a petition to deny. In light of the interest and impact of the WMAL case, I would like to take this opportunity to discuss with you the extent and import of the Court's ruling as I visualize it.

The history of the WMAL proceedings is not unlike that of a number of broadcast stations throughout the country. The Evening Star Broadcasting Company was first granted a license to operate a television station on Channel 7 in Washington, D.C. in 1946. On July 1, 1969 the licensee filed its application for renewal of WMAL-TV. And, within two months of that date, a group of individuals filed a petition to deny requesting that the Commission designate the application for hearing and thereafter deny the renewal of WMAL because the licensee failed to operate in the public interest.

The petitioners, identified as sixteen Washington, D.C. black community leaders, made the following principal allegations:

1. The licensee failed to adequately *ascertain* the needs of the Washington, D.C. black community
2. The licensee's *programming* failed to serve the needs of the black community
3. The licensee's *employment* practices were discriminatory against blacks

After evaluating the pleadings and the renewal application, the Commission concluded that no substantial and material questions of fact were raised and that the public interest would be served by renewal of WMAL's license. Specifically, the Commission found that the petitioners had failed to meet their Section 309 burden of establishing a *prima facie* case that the licensee was unresponsive to the needs of the black community or that it had engaged in discriminatory employment practices.

With respect to the ascertainment issue, the Commission's policy over the years has been consistently to emphasize the broadcaster's obligation to make a positive, diligent, and continuing good faith effort to determine the tastes, needs, and desires of his community. When a petition to deny is filed that challenges the validity of a community survey, as in the WMAL case, the broadcaster must demonstrate to the Commission that honest and conscientious efforts were made to consult with representative cross-sections of both majority and minority members of the public and community leaders.

The thrust of the complaint in WMAL was that the licensee's *primary* obligation was to ascertain and program to meet the needs of its community of license, Washington, D.C., and that the needs of suburban areas within WMAL's Grade A contour were of *secondary* importance. Of course, the practical significance of petitioners argument was that while blacks represent only 30 percent of the surrounding suburban Washington area, they represent 70 percent of the District of Columbia population and, therefore, were inadequately represented in the licensee's ascertainment and programming efforts.

The Commission's position with respect to this matter has long been made clear. Stations located in a particular city are licensed to serve not only the needs of the population of that city but also the needs of persons residing within the station's *entire service area*. Service area, in other words, must be defined in terms of coverage and not in terms of artificial political boundaries. That was the Commission's response to WMAL, and it was supported by the Court. In any event, the WMAL survey recognized the racial composition of its city of license and doubled the number of community leaders interviewed in Washington. Consequently, petitioners failed to demonstrate that the licensee's ascertainment efforts were unrepresentative of its community of service.

With respect to programming, the Commission has similarly refused to play a numbers game by requiring a licensee to devote fixed percentages of its programming to correspond to the ethnic or racial composition of its viewing public. While emphasizing that the problems of cities are particularly complex and pressing, and that the problems of minority groups should be covered in a meaningful manner, the Commission has not considered it necessary to require broadcasters to devise programs specifically for those groups. Minority interests may be adequately covered in programming which has a wider range of appeal.

As we said in the WMAL proceedings, many types of programming cannot be broken down into that appropriate for black people and that suitable for others. Since at least 1965 the Commission has held that there is no requirement that a licensee divide his programming so that each minority group is afforded a specific portion of time proportionate to the group's percentage of a given community's population. Such a pattern of operation would be "broadcast segregation," based upon the false premise that programming of general interest does not serve the needs and interests of blacks or some other minority group.

The Court in WMAL agreed, holding that how a licensee responds to the competing needs and interests of regional or minority groups is largely a matter of licensee discretion. While a licensee may not flatly ignore a strongly expressed need, the Court emphasized that "There is no requirement that a station devote 20 per cent of its broadcast time to meet the need expressed by 20 per cent of its viewing public." And the scope of FCC review in such matters should be limited to a determination of whether the licensee has reasonably exercised its discretion.

With respect to the allegations of employment discrimination, the Court endorsed a policy of not requiring minority employment proportional to their number in the community. The Court thus supported the

Commission's long-standing policy, articulated most recently in its 1970 Report and Order adopting the requirement that every broadcast licensee must have an affirmative equal employment opportunity program—an initiative, incidentally, which I fully support. As the Commission noted in the 1970 *WTAR* case, in language specifically quoted with approval by the court in *WMAL*: "Simply indicating the number of Blacks employed by the licensee, without citing instances of discrimination or describing a conscious policy of exclusion, is not sufficient to require an evidentiary exploration."

The Court's decision in WMAL was a reaffirmation of the Commission's belief that responsible and diligent licensee effort is the industry's best safeguard at renewal time. The Commission repeatedly has emphasized—and I personally concur—that service in the public interest means nothing if it does not include assiduous attention to the needs and interests of minority groups. On the other hand, it seems to me that we are, in effect, looking through the wrong end of a telescope if we direct broadcasters to isolate their audience and program accordingly. Broadcasting's all-important role in the fulfillment of the American dream can never be obtained by treating its viewers and listeners as individuals rather than as a community. The problems of each of us should concern all of us, and the unique characteristic of "broadcasting" (as opposed to "narrowcasting") is that this almost universal medium of communication may hopefully make brothers of us all.

In my opinion, the broadcast industry has generally accepted the challenge of full public service as a part of its credo to make the dissemination of information, the advancement of our national interest, and the betterment of us all its life's work. Were it not so, we would not have the nationwide reliance on broadcast news rather than printed news or the popular appreciation and preference of the public for broadcast entertainment to the theater or film. But despite the fact that broadcasting has made great contributions to the public interest, I think it is fair to say that the great challenge facing your industry in today's turbulent world is how much more needs to be accomplished. Perhaps an anecdote concerning Britain's late and great Prime Minister, Winston Churchill, most vividly describes the point I am trying to make. Sir Winston had many talents, not the least of which was his capacity to absorb alcoholic beverages. And on one such occasion, when he was demonstrating his ability in this regard, a proper English lady who never allowed alcohol to touch her lips reprimanded the statesman by holding her hand halfway to the ceiling and observing, "You have drunk enough liquor to fill this room up to here." Sir Winston, never one to fail to realize the significance of his conduct, gazed upward and somberly replied, "So little time, so much to do."

Notwithstanding the *WMAL* decision, broadcasters still have much to do and perhaps little time in which to do it. And the picture is, I think, crystal clear—the more you do to meet the public interest, the less we in the regulatory arena will be required to do to guarantee that it is met.

Very candidly, I hope and personally believe that within an appropriate regulatory climate you will indeed meet the great challenge of public service which your role as public trustees devolves upon you. In determining what that climate should be, I think it is worthwhile to remember that, in both the print and electronic media, it has been private enterprise—and *not* governmentally controlled communications —which has contributed to making this the best informed, and indeed best entertained, country on earth. And thus, as a government regulator, I have always believed that electronic journalism will best serve the public interest when provided with a large dose of discretion, and that applies both to license renewal policy and day-to-day regulation.

To the extent that the WMAL decision seems to lend credence to this abiding principle, it is indeed a favorable precedent for each of you. And, to my way of thinking, to the extent that this opinion contributes to the restoration of some reasonable stability within the broadcast industry, it is also a beneficial decision for the American public. For it seems to me self-evident that an industry which is subjected to constant attack and continual instability will inevitably lose the resources, both human and financial, needed to provide the quality of broadcast service to which citizens of this great country are so clearly entitled. And in the final analysis, ladies and gentlemen, it is, after all, concepts like licensee discretion and reasonable stability—rather than Government fiat and incessant and irrational change—which are the ultimate guarantors of a free, healthy, and independent press serving a free, healthy, and independent people.

CROSS-MEDIA OWNERSHIP

Congress, FCC Consider
Newspaper Control of Local TV

CONGRESSIONAL QUARTERLY STAFF WRITERS

Congressional Quarterly, March 16, 1974. Copyright 1974 Congressional Quarterly Inc.
Reprinted with permission.

After more than 30 years of sporadic debate, the Federal Communications
Commission (FCC) is under strong pressure to decide whether a
newspaper should be allowed to own a television or radio station in its
main circulation area.

The question has been a hot one since it was first considered by the
FCC in 1941. All three branches of government—Congress, the federal
courts and the White House—have all been drawn into the controversy.

The FCC staff in [early 1974] began the preliminary work necessary for
a ruling on cross-ownership of newspapers and broadcast stations as a
direct result of prodding by the Justice Department.

In 1968, the department proposed that the FCC adopt a rule
prohibiting newspaper-broadcasting combinations in the same city and
requiring that existing combinations be broken up within five years. With
no rule forthcoming from the commission, the Justice Department took
action itself on Jan. 2, 1974. The department filed two petitions with the
FCC opposing renewal of broadcasting licenses for three major publishers:
Pulitzer Publishing Co. and Newhouse Broadcasting Corp. in St. Louis,
Mo., and Cowles Communications Inc. in Des Moines, Iowa.

On March 1, the Justice Department underscored its determination to
pressure the FCC for a cross-ownership rule by filing a third petition, this

Congressional Quarterly Staff

263

one to deny broadcast license renewals to Midwest Radio-Television Inc., which operates WCCO AM and FM radio and television stations in Minneapolis-St. Paul, Minn. The petition said the Minneapolis Star and Tribune Co., publisher of the only general circulation daily papers in Minneapolis, owns 47 per cent of the Midwest Radio and Television. Northwest Publications Inc., publisher of the only dailies of general circulation in St. Paul (the *Pioneer-Press* and the *Dispatch*), owns 26.5 per cent of the Midwest. The petition said the firms controlling Midwest take in about 85 per cent of the ad revenue received by local media.

"The Justice Department's action has made rulemaking (on cross-ownership) a top priority of the commission," said an FCC staff assistant. And Commissioner Robert E. Lee told Congressional Quarterly, "Right at the moment, this is one of the biggest issues we face, precisely because of the Justice Department's petitions."

IMPACT ON MEDIA

Whether it is the FCC, Congress or the Justice Department which plays the dominant role in the debate, a lot rides on the answer to the cross-ownership question. According to an estimate made in 1972 by law professor Stephen R. Barnett of the University of California, there were

93 newspaper-television station combinations in 85 cities. The American Newspaper Publishers Association in 1970 reported that 99 television and 300 radio stations worth almost $2 billion, were owned by companies operating newspapers in the same area.

BROADCAST LAWS

Congress, in the 1927 Radio Act, provided for the control of the public airwaves by licensing them for profit. Seven years later, Congress passed the Federal Communications Act of 1934 setting up the FCC to regulate broadcasting. Under the 1934 Act, television and radio broadcast licenses were to be granted, and renewed every three years, on the condition that "public convenience, interest or necessity will be served thereby. . . ."

Television-newspaper cross-ownership in the top 10 broadcast markets

Newspaper	TV Station	Owner
New York Daily News	WPIX-TV	News Syndicate Co. (Wholly owned by the Tribune Publishing Co.)
Chicago Tribune	WGN-TV	Continental Broadcasting Co. (100 percent subsidiary of the Tribune Publishing Co.)
Detroit News	WWJ-TV	Evening News Assoc.
Cleveland Press	WEWS-TV	Scripps Howard Broadcasting Co.
San Francisco Chronicle	KRON-TV	Chronicle Publishing Co.
Washington Post	WTOP-TV	Washington Post Co.
Washington Star-News	WMAL-TV	Washington Star Communications Inc.

Source: FCC reports in 1971 and 1973

Over the years, the FCC, the Justice Department and Congress have taken different positions on applying the public interest standard to newspapers which own broadcast stations in their circulation areas.

FCC POSITION

Initially, the FCC not only permitted newspapers to own and operate television stations, but encouraged newspaper owners to pioneer the new

Should newspapers be forced to sell local TV stations?

The FCC in February 1974 began to review what action to take on a pending rule to prohibit newspapers from operating broadcast stations in their main circulation areas. At issue was whether newspapers should be forced to sell their hometown broadcast stations. Participants in the debate raised the following arguments:

Pro: sell the stations

Among the most influential groups pressuring for adoption of a rule against newspaper-broadcast cross-ownership have been local citizens and minority organizations opposed to broadcasting policies in their own communities.

These groups have argued that concentration of media ownership allows one company to exert too much control over the views communicated in one community. Groups in New York City; Columbus, Ohio; Boston, and Washington, D.C., have challenged local broadcasters in license renewal hearings before the FCC based on charges of media concentration.

In some cases, citizens groups have charged media conglomerates with failing to represent all the views of various community groups, and with excluding certain minority groups from expressing their views.

Proponents of the rule also have argued that in a city where the local newspaper, radio and television stations were all owned by the same company, management had little incentive to respond to local pressure groups.

Both the National Council of Churches and the United Church of Christ have been longtime advocates of adopting the newspaper rule. Rev. Everett C. Parker, director of the United Church of Christ's communications office, has argued that maintaining concentration of control over the media at renewal time would "exclude new faces and new ideas from most of the major markets."

Albert H. Kramer of the National Citizens Committee for Broadcasting said the basic argument was the "presumption that the more diversity of voices in the media, the more likely you are to get robust debate and critical scrutiny of the media itself."

Con: keep them

Arguing against stripping newspapers of their hometown broadcasting stations were the National Association of Broadcasters and the American Newspaper Publishers Association.

Publishers argued that the FCC encouraged newspapers to take out broadcast licenses in the early 1940s when television broadcasting was just beginning. It would be unfair to punish those companies which developed broadcasting facilities in their communities just because they own newspapers.

Broadcasters also argued that while media concentration might be a fair issue to consider when a li-ing the situation at renewal time would threaten the stability of the industry and discourage broadcast-ers from making large-scale invest-ments in facilities they might lose later.

Moreover, some newspapers rely on revenues earned by their broad-cast stations to stay in business, broadcasters have said. Divesting all newspapers of their local broad-casting stations would force more newspapers to close down. New newspaper monopolies would be created in cities which were unable to support more than one or two daily papers.

Opponents of the rule also have argued that newspaper owners pro-vided superior broadcast service because they lived in the commu-nity, were familiar with local needs and issues, and generally devoted more broadcast time to reporting local news.

Clay T. Whitehead, director of the White House Office of Tele-communications Policy, argued that "the only thing that ought to be considered at (license) renewal time is whether the station is put-ting out the kind of programming the public wants."

and promising field. Television was slow in developing immediately after World War II. Between 1941 and 1945, 10 television stations had been licensed, but in January 1946, only six of the 10 actually were on the air.

The FCC took the position that it could not deny licenses to newspapers. In 1937, testifying before Senate Interstate Commerce Commission, FCC General Counsel Hapson Gray said the commission had no authority to deny a newspaper application because of common ownership "in the absence of an expression of public policy on the subject by Congress."

In 1941, the FCC decided to hold hearings on the question of cross-ownership. The hearings, known as the "newspaper investigation," ended in 1944 and the commission decided in that year against adopting any rule prohibiting newspapers from owning broadcast stations in their circulation areas. Instead, the FCC agreed to deal with the issue on a case-by-case basis.

As a result, many of the first television stations were owned and operated by local newspapers. According to a 1971 study for the American Newspaper Publishers' Association, the *Detroit News* established the first television station in that city in 1947; the *San Francisco Chronicle* began

KRON-TV in 1949; the *Buffalo Evening News* started WBEN-TV in 1948, and the *Greensboro* (N.C.) *Daily News* began WFMY-TV in 1949.

The study listed other cities in which newspapers started the first television station. These included: Fresno, Calif.; Atlanta, Ga.; St. Louis, Mo.; Fargo, N.D.; Cleveland, Ohio; Dayton, Ohio; Portland, Ore.; Dallas-Fort Worth, Texas; Norfolk, Va., and Milwaukee, Wis.

In all these cases, the FCC granted licenses to newspapers which already controlled major chunks of media advertising and readership in a single community.

In addition, the FCC also approved transfers of local television stations to newspapers which published major daily editions in the same area. For example, the FCC in 1950 approved the transfer of a Houston station, KPRC-TV, to the Houston Post Company, publisher of one of the city's two daily newspapers.

But by the late 1950s, the Justice Department had begun court actions challenging cross-ownership, claiming in some cases antitrust laws had been violated by media concentration. In 1958, the department took the *Kansas City Star* to court and forced it to sell WDAF-AM-TV Kansas City, on the grounds of concentration of media ownership.

During the late 1960s, groups competing for licenses and some citizens' organizations increased pressure for a FCC rule banning cross-ownership.

In 1968, the Justice Department called attention to "the existing concentration of media ownership in many . . . cities," and asked the FCC to consider a rule banning cross-ownership. The FCC took no action on the proposed rule. But in 1969 the commission sent a shock through the broadcasting industry with an unprecedented decision stripping a Boston newspaper of its local television station.

The FCC refused to renew the license of WHDH-TV, held since 1957 by the *Boston Herald-Traveler,* at the time one of Boston's three daily newspapers. (The *Herald-Traveler* ceased publishing June 18, 1972, when it was purchased by the Hearst chain and merged with the *Record American* to form the *Boston Herald American.*) In reaching its decision, the FCC said it had considered the "criteria of diversification of communications media control" as one factor in revoking the license.

Finally, in April 1970, the commission agreed to consider the Justice Department's recommendation for a ban of cross-ownership. The FCC received comments on the proposed rule and ended its proceedings in August 1971. Again no action was taken. Then the Justice Department forcefully revived the issue in January 1974 with its petition involving Pulitzer, Newhouse and Cowles.

JUSTICE DEPARTMENT

Since the 1950s, the main advocate for a cross-ownership rule has been the Justice Department. The department has taken the position that cross-ownership violates antitrust policy.

"Other people may have all sorts of reasons for adopting a rule," Bruce B. Wilson, deputy assistant attorney general for the antitrust division, told *Congressional Quarterly.* "But we look at the economics. It doesn't make any difference to us if it's a good TV station or a crummy one, if it's liberal or conservative. We can't make judgments like that.

"Congress has already made the value judgment that competition is a basic value in terms of our economic policy," Wilson said. "I like to think . . . we are simply serving our mandate to preserve a competitive market."

Using the antitrust argument, the Justice Department in 1967 blocked an attempt by the International Telephone and Telegraph Corp. (ITT) to buy the American Broadcasting Co. (ABC). The case was appealed, but never was decided. Because of the Justice Department's opposition, ITT withdrew its petition with the FCC to buy ABC.

In the late 1960s the Justice Department began taking a new course of action—filing petitions to deny licenses with the FCC; then the commission, using its hearing process, tried the case. For example, in 1968, the department blocked the sale of KFDM-TV, one of three regular television stations in the city of Beaumont, Texas, to the city's only daily newspaper, the *Beaumont Enterprise and Journal.* The newspaper withdrew its application when the department filed a memorandum opposing the transfer.

The Justice Department, in November 1973, began escalating pressure for an FCC rule against cross-ownership. In a letter to the FCC, the department asked the commission to deny renewal of a license held by the Milwaukee Journal Co. (owner of the morning *Sentinel* and evening *Journal*) for WTMJ radio and television stations.

Although the department had missed the deadline for filing a formal petition, it charged that the company occupied a near monopoly position in local advertising and newsgathering. The impact on the large urban area

Media concentration rulings

The FCC has long used rulemaking to prohibit individual broadcasting companies from controlling large chunks of the radio and television markets—both nationwide and in a single area. Key rules adopted to promote diversity in the broadcasting industry included:

Duopoly Rules. An operator of an FM radio station was not allowed to buy another FM station in the same broadcasting market (adopted, 1940); an operator of a television station was not allowed to buy another television station in the same market (adopted, 1941); and an operator of an AM radio station was not allowed to buy another AM station in the same market (adopted, 1943).

7-7-7 Rule. A single company was allowed to operate no more than seven AM, seven FM and seven television stations throughout the United States. Of the seven television stations, only five VHF (very high frequency) stations were allowed per owner. The rule further stated that no company was allowed to exert excess concentration of control over the media (adopted, 1953; modified, 1954).

Fixed Contour Rules. To clarify the cross-ownership regulations established by the duopoly rules, the commission adopted fixed engineering standards to measure and limit the degree of overlap between any two broadcast stations in adjacent areas owned by the same company (adopted, 1964).

One-to-a-Customer. Any one company operating either a radio or television station was prohibited from buying another broadcasting station (AM, FM or TV) in the same area. The rule, however, did not affect existing AM-FM-TV combinations. Instead it prohibited purchases or transfers of broadcast combinations in the future (adopted, 1970).

UHF Exception. The commission decided not to adopt a rule to govern cross-ownership of UHF (ultra high frequency) stations. Instead the commission said it would consider media concentration issues for UHF station operators on an individual basis (adopted, 1971).

FM Exception. The one-to-a-customer rule was further amended to allow AM-FM combinations in the same area to be operated by a common owner, and brought or transferred as a block (adopted, 1971).

Cable Television. A television station broadcasting over a certain medium frequency range (the line marking the end of a predicted signal strength, generally about 55–60 miles, although the exact range varied from station to station) was prohibited from operating a cable television system in the same area (adopted, 1970; modified, 1973).

"must necessarily have a dominant influence on local opinion formation," the department asserted.

In its letter, the Justice Department said pointedly the FCC "could not have contemplated eliminating concentration as a public interest factor for nearly two full renewal periods" following the original 1968 department proposal for a rule banning cross-ownership.

Assistant Attorney General Wilson told *Congressional Quarterly* that the department, in effect, was telling the FCC that "we've urged rulemaking and then two and a half years go by, but we're not going to sit around forever."

Since 1969, when the FCC revoked the WHDH-TV license held by the *Boston Herald-Traveler,* communications subcommittees in both the House and Senate have been struggling to report out bills limiting the commission's power to deny a broadcaster's license at renewal time. But the subcommittees have had difficulties resolving differences between broadcasters on one hand and dissatisfied citizens groups, minority organizations and license competitors on the other.

In the wake of broadcast industry reaction to the WHDH-TV case, Sen. John O. Pastore (D R.I.), chairman of the Senate Commerce Communications Subcommittee, introduced a bill (S 2004) to restructure broadcast licensing procedures. The Pastore bill would have prohibited the FCC from considering a competing application for a radio or television license, except in cases where the commission already had decided to revoke the license because the broadcaster had failed to serve the public interest.

Pastore's bill was introduced in 1969 with 18 co-sponsors, including Majority Leader Mike Mansfield (D Mont.), Commerce Committee Chairman Warren G. Magnuson (D Wash.), and then Minority Whip Hugh Scott (R Pa.). Six of 10 subcommittee members sponsored the bill. But strong opposition from citizens and minority groups blocked subcommittee action. Testifying before the subcommittee, Rev. Everett C. Parker, director of the communications office of the United Church of Christ, claimed the bill would "exclude new faces" in broadcasting. "Negro broadcasters at present own almost no stations," he said.

Support for the Pastore bill came from broadcasters and newspaper publishers who said that the uncertainty created by the WHDH-TV case would inhibit broadcast owners from making long-term investments. Nine days of hearings ended Dec. 5, 1969. No action was taken on the proposal.

New Legislation

Both the House and Senate subcommittees received a barrage of new bills during 1973. By March 1973, 201 representatives and senators had introduced broadcast license renewal proposals.

The Communications and Power Subcommittee of the House Interstate and Foreign Commerce Committee focused its attention on two key bills —HR 3852, backed by the National Broadcasters Association, and a Nixon administration bill, HR 5546. Both bills would severely limit the power of the FCC to revoke broadcast licenses at renewal time.

The White House bill, written by the Office of Telecommunications Policy, went further than most 1973 measures. It prohibited the FCC from considering a broadcaster's holdings in other media outlets at renewal time.

On Feb. 27, the House subcommittee sent to the full committee a clean bill (HR 12993) which, according to Subcommittee Chairman Torbert H. Macdonald (D Mass.), would prohibit the FCC from revoking a license at renewal time because of media cross-ownership even if the the commission adopted a rule prohibiting newspapers from acquiring local broadcasting stations in the future.

On March 6, the House Interstate and Foreign Commerce Committee by voice vote agreed to report the subcommittee bill.

The committee's bill specifically stated that the FCC could not consider an applicant's "other ownership interests or official connections . . . in other stations or communications media . . . unless the commission has adopted rules prohibiting such ownership or business activities. . . ." The committee gave the FCC six months from the day the bill was enacted to adopt any new rules.

There was strong sentiment among subcommittee members against the Justice Department proposal that existing newspaper-broadcast combinations be broken up within five years. "I don't think the FCC would adopt such a rule," Rep. Macdonald told *CQ*.

Macdonald added that "the bill that has come out of the subcommittee has indicated the performance by a licensee would be the criteria by which renewal would be granted or rejected. What the FCC and Congress should be properly interested in is the service the licensee provides."

Subcommittee member Fred B. Rooney (D Pa.) agreed. "I don't see the justification for automatically putting a broadcaster out of business because he owns a newspaper," Rooney said in an interview with *Congressional*

Even John E. Moss (D Calif.), a strong antitrust proponent, concurred. "In my opinion and, I think, over the years in the opinion of Congress, cross-ownership should not be a test nor the basis for limitation," he said. "The important question is whether there is meaningful competition in both media."

ADMINISTRATION VIEWS

In stark contrast to the Justice Department position, the administration has opposed FCC consideration of cross-ownership at renewal time. Clay T. Whitehead, director of the Office of Telecommunications Policy, said the FCC should focus instead on the matter of local programming.

"The key question here is whether the federal regulatory agency is going to have total discretion over a licensee," Whitehead told *Congressional Quarterly*. He said the FCC's licensing authority should not be used to prosecute criminal abuses such as antitrust violations, equal opportunity disputes and taxation problems. According to Whitehead, such issues should be settled by government agencies set up to prosecute the violations, such as the federal courts, the Equal Employment Opportunity Commission and the Internal Revenue Service.

"If Justice thinks a station is violating antitrust laws, it should take its case to federal court," Whitehead said. "Just because the FCC has great power over a particular business doesn't mean that power should be brought to bear just because it's easier than going through the courts."

Whitehead said the FCC's license renewal process has become too broad. "We think the only thing that ought to be considered at renewal time is whether the station is putting out the kind of programming the public wants," he stated.

Some members of Congress and broadcast industry officials have expressed concern about Whitehead's proposals for FCC review of programming, however.

Media observers thought they saw an attempt by Whitehead to drive a wedge between local broadcasters and the television networks. In a controversial speech before the Sigma Delta Chi professional journalism fraternity in Indianapolis, Ind., Dec. 18, 1972, Whitehead said broadcasters should take "responsibility for all programming, including the programs that come from the 'network.'" He added that "station managers and network officials who fail to act to correct imbalance or consistent bias in the networks—or who acquiesce by silence—can only be considered willing participants, to be held fully accountable by the broadcaster's community at license renewal time."

OUTLOOK

[Early in 1974 the FCC began to "rethink the question of adopting a rule on cross-ownership and divestiture." During that summer oral arguments were held on any possible rules changes with a decision to be made at a later time. According to *Congressional Quarterly,* the commission had several courses it could follow:

Adopt a rule banning cross-ownership and requiring divestiture.

Adopt a rule banning any new cross-ownership, but allowing newspapers that held broadcast licenses in their main circulation areas to renew them.

Reject any rule on cross-ownership.

Delay the rulemaking proceedings.

As this book went to press, the FCC adopted rules banning future media cross-ownerships in the same community. The rules did not affect the majority of the existing combinations; however, sixteen small- and middle-sized cities that lacked competition were affected. They included seven newspaper-television ownerships and nine newspaper-radio ownerships. *Broadcasting* (Feb. 3, 1975) lists the broadcast properties that were affected. For a list of both broadcast stations and newspapers, see *Editor & Publisher* (Feb. 1, 1975). Cross-ownership will be a continuing issue during this decade; the serious student will need to consult relevant publications to keep abreast of the latest developments.]

CABLE
TELEVISION

We have separated the issues in cable television into three parts: the nature and status of the medium, pay television, and access. As a medium, cable television was conceived originally as a technological device for extending the television signals of local stations into areas where reception was bad or impossible because of mountainous terrain. Over the years new technical developments have permitted many "blue sky" services (such as satellite network and two-way communication facilities) to be promoted as potential services of cable systems. These systems have grown in number throughout the United States during the Sixties and Seventies and they now are serving millions of subscribers. Predictions made a few years ago that the nation would soon be wired for cable television appear to be falling short for a number of reasons. One reason is that the new medium is not expanding fast enough into the major metropolitan markets where television reception is usually very good. Subscribers in these multiple-channel markets want more for their monthly fee than better reception, for they already have good reception So far, cable systems have not been able to offer a product that can lure mass subscriptions in these markets. Other reasons for the slow development grow out of the uncertainty of the regulatory and economic **275** climate of the mid-seventies. David L. Jaffe's article clearly explains the regulatory and technical development of the cable system from its start as CATV to its promise as "cable communications." Jerrold Oppenheim, on the other hand, offers several reasons why the "promise" of cable is not being met.

Cable system owners appear to be basing their hopes on one major service to attract widespread buyers of the cable connection in highly populated areas, and that service is pay TV. Once a large number of homes are linked into the system, individuals can select movies, dramas, and sports events for which they pay an additional per-program or monthly fee. Broadcasters, especially the networks, are concerned that this pay service will severely cut into commercial television, to the detriment of the viewer. These pro and con views on pay TV are presented by James MacGregor and Arthur Taylor.

One of the most exciting promises offered by the technology of cable television is its multi-channel capability. On-the-air television stations find it impossible to serve all of the tastes and provide time for all of the views of the audience in the time available. With a multichannel system, specialized programming and citizens' views can be broadcast. The FCC foresaw this important value in cable when it ruled that three channels must be reserved in each community within the top one hundred population centers for public access, education access, and government access. Public access has received the most active reception because it provides a way for individuals and groups to create inexpensive programs, which range over an almost unlimited spectrum of topics, and to present them over the local cable outlet. Most of the programming of this type is produced voluntarily by ordinary citizens interested either in presenting a particular subject or expressing a particular view. One recent complication of this access programming is that union leaders are questioning the fairness of nonunion members engaging in the technical production of programs without pay. This problem is explored by Ralph Lee Smith.

Programming is one aspect of access and Charles Tate describes other aspects—the need for ownership and operation of cable systems by minority groups. He views cable as one of the last communications frontiers open to minority ownership.

BIBLIOGRAPHICAL ESSAY

Cable television became a recurring topic in America's popular professional and scholarly press toward the end of the sixties. It was seen as a new medium, technologically, with great potential, particularly when it moved into urban areas. Our readings are built around the potential of the medium, the desire for public access to it, and the role that pay television may play in making this medium successful. The citations that follow will deal with these issues in the same order; there also will be an extensive bibliographical paragraph citing articles and books that will deal with issues not included in our readings.

An excellent survey of the field, its potential and its development, is by Ralph Lee Smith, *The Wired Nation: The Electronic Communications Highway,* Harper & Row, New York, 1972. Students using the bibliography in Smith's book and the one by Don R. LeDuc, "A Selective Bibliography on the Evolution of CATV 1950–1970," *Journal of Broadcasting* (Spring, 1971), 195–234, should be able to find important articles and books published before 1972. The citations given in this essay will deal with publications from 1972 on.

Our article by David L. Jaffee, on the regulatory and technical development of cable television, deals tangentially with the "promise" of the medium. It should be supplemented by William Bresnan's, "The Cable Television Revolution: 'Blue Sky Services,' " *Vital Speeches of the Day* (May 1, 1973), 446–448, and Edward Lamb's "Tomorrow's Communications: Cable TV Can Serve All of Mankind," *The Churchman* (August/September, 1972), 10–12, which illustrate the "promise" of cable. Both of these articles emphasize the potential of the medium; Bresnan's deals largely with his organization, TelePrompter. Two books that concern marketing problems and their solutions grew out of workshops held by the National Cable Television Association. They are *The Selling of Cable Television* and *The Complete Guide to Cable Marketing,* 1972 and 1973 respectively, NCTA, Washington, D.C. The books are especially valuable for the treatment given practical problems of selling cable television, particularly in the cities, and also deal realistically with the many problems confronting cable companies. A well-written article that clearly outlines some of the problems and "failures" of cable in New York City is David M. Rubin's, "Short Circuit in the Wired Nation," *(More)* (September, 1973), 16–18. These last three sources offer excellent material to supplement Oppenheim's article on the failed promise of cable.

One of the expectations of cable television is that it will permit individual access to the media in a way never possible before. An interesting report on this issue is David Othmer, *The Wired Island, the First Two Years of Public Access in Cable Television in Manhattan,* Fund for the City of New York, New York, (September, 1973). This typescript report details the accomplishments and the problems of access. It should be supplemented by "The Cable Fable," a special issue of *Yale Review of Law and Social Action* (Spring, 1972). See especially the article by Thomas Freebairn, "Public Access in New York City: An Interview with Theadora Sklover," 227–237. Michael Shamberg, *Guerrilla Television,* Raindance Corp., New York, 1971, offers help on how to get into television, commercial and cable, and how to produce programs with light and inexpensive videotape equipment. Two recent works are Videofreex, *The Spaghetti City Video Manual,* and Chuck Anderson, *The Electronic Journalist,* both from Praeger, New York, 1974.

Charles Tate's concern for access and control of cable television systems by local groups, particularly minorities, is covered in an extended treatment in Charles Tate, Ed., *Cable Television in the Cities: Community Control, Public Access and Minority Ownership,* The Urban Institute, Washington, D.C., 1971. Students also should consult the work from which our article is reprinted: Ithiel de Sola Pool, Ed., *Talking Back: Citizen Feedback and Cable Technology,* MIT Press, Cambridge, Mass., 1973. See Also Walter S. Baer, *Cable Television: A Handbook for Decision-Making,* Crane-Russak, New York, 1973, a how-to-do it and what-to-watch-out for manual on establishing a cable system in your community. This is one of a very valuable series of reports on cable television prepared for the National Science Foundation.

Two excellent books related to the regulation of cable television are Martin H. Seiden's *Cable Television U.S.A.: An Analysis of Government Policy,* Praeger, New York, 1972, and Don R. LeDuc, *Cable Television and the FCC: A Crisis in Media Control,* Temple University Press, Philadelphia, 1973. Both are excellent studies of the regulatory morass in which the FCC finds itself (and to which it has contributed); both have useful appendices. While similar in many ways, the serious student will want to read both books, especially for the different case studies included in each.

Pay television, as James MacGregor indicates, may be the salvation for cable television in urban areas. The best book on the subject is Richard Adler and Walter S. Baer, *The Electronic Box Office: Humanities and Arts on the Cable,* Praeger, New York, 1974. The subtitle indicates a part of the focus of the book, but several chapters, particularly "Pay Television at the Crossroads," illuminate the methods by which pay television currently is brought into homes. That particular chapter has several diagrams clearly explaining the different methods. The book should be supplemented by the two cable marketing books published by NCTA, mentioned earlier. Arthur Taylor's article is a rebuttal from an important industry figure to the proposed expansion of pay television over-the-air or via cable.

An area of concern not covered in our readings but important, nevertheless, is the role of cable television in education. There are many specialized reports available on this subject. Two general, up-to-date and readable books are *Cable Television & Education: A Report From the Field,* National Cable Television Association, Washington, D.C., 1973, and Richard Adler and Walter S. Baer, *Aspen Notebook: Cable and Continuing Education,* Praeger, New York, 1973. Both books contain case studies of cable television-supported educational programs; the *Aspen Notebook* is more detailed and, therefore, more useful. Both have excellent bibliographies.

STUDY QUESTIONS

1. Do you agree with the FCC that cable stations of a certain size (in number of subscribers) should be required to originate programs? Why or why not? What are some of the possible effects local origination might have on local newspapers and television stations? Why?

2. What do you see as possible effects upon the local stations and the national networks if the union between cable and communications satellite becomes a viable operation?

3. It is said that the rules governing cable television have been the result of lobbying by various groups. On which side would you lobby and for what purposes and goals?

4. What services should cable provide to its subscribers?

5. Why is "pay TV" a major service consideration of the cable TV operators? In what ways might it affect the present television system? What are the strongest arguments for and against pay TV?

6. In what ways can ownership and control of cable television outlets help the black community and other minority groups?

7. Should the union movement forbid the use of volunteers for the production of television programs on cable TV? Why? Why not?

THE REVOLUTIONARY MEDIUM

Cable Communications: Up from CATV

DAVID L. JAFFE

Reprinted from *Educational Broadcasting* (July/August, 1974), "CATV: History and Law," with permission of publisher and author. Copyright 1974 by Acolyte Publications Corp. David L. Jaffe is associate professor of speech communication, University of Oklahoma, Norman.

Despite its nearly quarter-century history, CATV is a virgin industry. At its birth CATV did not possess the capacity to originate TV programming; it did not even have the capability to retransmit broadcast TV signals. CATV was merely a long twin-lead wire between a TV receiver and an antenna. In fact the twin-lead wire was not unlike the dual wire currently connecting millions of TV receivers with rooftop antennas. In the communities in which CATV was born, however, rooftop antennas were not adequate for TV reception due to the nature of radio wave propagation.

Radio wave propagation—"the radiation of waves through space"[1]—is limited to three paths: a ground wave path, which follows the curvature of the earth; a sky wave path, which bounces off the ionosphere back toward earth; and a direct wave path, which behaves much like light waves, *i.e.,* the waves follow a straight line and can be completely or partially blocked by solid objects or the atmosphere.[2]

Because of the straight-line characteristics of direct waves, ground and sky waves tend to bridge greater usable distances over the surface of the earth. Unlike AM radio signals, which are radiated as ground waves or sky waves permitting long-distance transmissions, TV signals are radiated as direct waves, thereby decreasing usable signal transmission distance due to the curvature of the earth. More specifically, the propagation of TV signals is directly affected by natural terrain and man-made structures. For example, the average useful TV signal of approximately "50 miles over fairly level terrain"[3] is significantly reduced by mountainous terrain or tall buildings.[4] It was the problem of mountainous terrain that led directly to the birth of CATV. A second factor which contributed to the development of CATV was a Federal Communications Commission freeze on the issuance of construction permits and new licenses for TV stations between September 30, 1948, and July 1, 1952.[5,6]

Communities in two states—Pennsylvania and Oregon—were the first to be served by CATV. In 1948 John Walson, an employee of the Pennsylvania Power and Light Co. and part owner of an appliance store which marketed TV receivers, erected an antenna atop a mountain near Mahanoy City, Pa. Walson strung twin-lead cable from the mountaintop antenna to his Mahanoy City store. He was then able to receive TV signals from the three Philadelphia TV stations over 60 miles away. Walson is reported to have connected 725 subscribers—a substantial portion of the community—to the master antenna by the summer of 1948.[7]

During the same year, L. E. Parsons, an Astoria, Ore., radio station operator, installed a CATV reception system similar to the one devised by John Walson. Parsons mounted a master antenna atop an eight-story hotel.[8] He used a combination of receiving/sending units and coaxial cable to retransmit the TV signals to other subscribers in the community. The subscribers did not pay a monthly fee. "Rather, the lines and reception equipment were considered the cooperative property of all participants in the project."[9] New subscribers paid approximately $100 to be wired into the system.[10]

The Parsons TV reception system was, in short, a community system. Each subscriber in the community was wired into a system of cables connected to a master antenna for TV reception. Accordingly, an FCC attorney, E. Stratford Smith, coined the acronym CATV—"community antenna television."[11]

CATV continued to grow during the four-year TV licensing freeze. Although the freeze limited the number of stations to 108, the number of receivers in use continued to rise from approximately 250,000 in 1948 to over 15 million in 1952.[12] A portion of the TV sales can be attributed to the increased demand for receivers due to new and expanding CATV systems.[13]

Surprisingly, the end of the freeze did not result in a decrease or even a substantial slowdown in the development of CATV.

> Within about a year and a half [after the end of the freeze] it became apparent that the cost of constructing and operating a television station was such that, in order to be economically viable, stations could only be built in the larger metropolitan areas. This meant that . . . small communities throughout the United States would not have television stations. There would be a continuing need for cable television.[14]

The history of CATV development and regulation can be divided roughly into three periods: 1948 to the mid-1960s, the mid-1960s to 1972, and 1972 to the present. Each period highlights new functions served by cable systems.

THE EXPERIMENT

During the period 1958 to the mid-1960s, CATV systems operated as common carriers by transmitting broadcast TV signals over coaxial cable. A common carrier communications system distributes messages prepared by others for a fee or some other form of consideration. For example, the telephone companies provide common carrier services; for a monthly fee they provide equipment and service for transmission, distribution and reception of messages prepared and encoded by users of the telephone system. A pure CATV system operates in much the same way. The CATV system receives broadcast signals off-the-air and distributes these signals to the subscribers' TV receivers for a monthly fee. No new or nonbroadcast messages are introduced and distributed by the CATV system.[15]

THE BIRTH

From 1948 to the mid-1960s, the vast majority of CATV systems limited their services to retransmission of broadcast signals. But a few systems did experiment with program origination, *i.e.,* transmitting original, nonbroadcast programming on the cable system. One such system, operated by Martin F. Malarkey in Pottsville, Pa., "televised over the cable by closed circuit one local origination before the winter of 1951."[16]

Program origination, however, did not really begin in earnest for another 15 years.

By the mid-1960's, most cable systems, even the smallest CATV systems, conventionally used an otherwise unused channel or two by permitting an open, untended camera to transmit news directly off a [news wire] ticker or weather off the faces on an instrument panel. A few systems transmitted low-cost local programming, usually prepared and performed by amateurs or high school groups; a few had even gone so far as to transmit local amateur athletic events.[17]

One of the first CATV systems to originate regularly scheduled programming was Berks Cable Co. in Reading, Pa. After originating, occasional programming during the spring of 1967, the CATV system inaugurated regular daily programming, including early evening newscasts. The originating channel was programmed in cooperation with a local radio station, WRFY-FM. Accordingly, the cable channel was identified as "WRFY Cable Channel 5."[18]

During this period, the FCC kept a watchful eye on CATV systems' program origination channels. In a series of significant rulings beginning in 1968, the FCC assumed the role of advocate of program origination. In June 1968, the FCC authorized unrestricted local affairs program origination over the San Diego, Calif., CATV system.[19] One year later, in October 1969, the FCC *required* CATV systems with 3500 or more subscribers to originate programming.[20]

Thus the role of CATV in the U.S. was in a state of transition. CATV, a retransmission system designed to provide acceptable TV pictures in communities with poor or marginal reception, was becoming *cable television*—a system which provided both traditional CATV transmission and TV program origination services.

The result was that CATV systems were being established not only in pockets of poor and marginal TV reception, but also in cities with more than adequate reception—cities which lacked the financial resources to sustain the costs of a broadcast TV station. The role served by CATV systems was changing. The master community antenna developed a rival— the cable transmitter. The cable transmitter or "modulator," is to the cable subscriber what a broadcast TV transmitter is to an off-the-air televiewer. Simply stated, a modulator transmits a TV signal over the cable distribution system. With the increased emphasis on TV program origination and the changing role of CATV, the term community antenna television was used less frequently; it was replaced by the term cable television.

THE PRESENT

The most comprehensive body of basic CATV rules promulgated by the FCC was issued on February 12, 1972.[21] These rules, which went into effect on March 31, 1972, documented what many had suspected since 1968: the FCC was firmly committed to CATV program origination. From the outset the FCC rules clearly showed that CATV was destined to be more than a retransmission system. What is more, the rules hinted at the development of something more sophisticated than the traditional CATV system; they appear to provide legal guidelines for a comprehensive cable communications system encompassing broadcast retransmission services and extensive program origination services. Interestingly, certain types of program origination can also be classified as common carrier service, e.g., transmission of messages prepared by persons other than the cable system operator especially for distribution on the cable system; again a fee or some other form of consideration is involved.

The FCC identified four separate classes of cable channels which are detailed in Table 1.

Table 1
The four classes of cable channels identified by the FCC.

Class I channel—a signaling path provided by a cable television system to relay to subcriber terminals television broadcast programs that are received off-the-air or are obtained by microwave or by direct connection to a television broadcast station (*i.e.,* a retransmission channel).

Class II channel—a signaling path provided by a cable television system to deliver to subscriber terminals television signals that are intended for reception by a television broadcast receiver without the use of an auxiliary decoding device and which signals are not involved in a broadcast transmission path (*i.e.,* a program origination channel).

Class III channel—a signaling path provided by a cable television system to deliver to subscriber terminals signals that are intended for reception by equipment other than a television broadcast receiver or by a television broadcast receiver only when used with auxiliary equipment (*i.e.,* controlled receiver access program origination channel which can accommodate private or "point-to-point"[22] transmissions as well as public or "point-to-mass"[23] transmissions).

Class IV channels—a signaling path provided by a cable television system to transmit signals of any type from a subscriber terminal to another point in the cable television system. (This channel is similar to a Class III channel, but the transmission originates at the subscribers' cable outlet.)[24]

To summarize, Class I channels retransmit over-the-air broadcasts. Class II channels distribute programming, originated on the system, which is available to all subscribers. Class III channels distribute programming and other data transmissions originated on the system cable TV receivers fitted with auxiliary equipment, e.g., filters or decoding devices for pay-cablecasting, etc. Class IV channels distribute subscriber-originated signals.

These four classes of cable channels identified by the FCC are capable of providing a broad spectrum of cable communications services. Not surprisingly, the 1972 FCC rules clearly state that certain cable communications services are required, others are recommended and still others are open for experimentation. In fact the FCC in its "Reconsideration of Report and Order" on cable communications specifically stated that "we are entering into a period of experiment."[25]

We can obtain a better understanding of present and future cable communications services by examining these federally-required and recommended services. In general, cable communications services can be divided into two broad categories: retransmission services and program origination services. As noted previously, the latter category includes, but is not limited to, common carrier services.

Retransmission services

On the whole, the FCC requires cable systems to carry all signals of broadcast stations within 35 miles of the cable system as well as all off-the-air signals significantly viewed in the community.[26] Additionally, other broadcast stations can be imported and carried by the cable system.

The FCC has established a concept of "adequate" service. Adequacy varies . . . according to market size, and on it hinges the determination of what additional service may be imported from other markets. . . .After carriage of required local signals, *i.e.*, stations within 35 miles, those from the same market, and those meeting the viewing test, the following are the complements of signals up to which additional service may be achieved if not thereby available:
1. In television markets 1-50 . . .[27]
   a) Three full network stations and
   b) Three independent stations [*i.e.,* stations not affiliated with ABC, NBC or CBS]
2. In television markets 50-100 . . .
   a) Three full network stations and
   b) Two independent stations

3. In smaller television markets . . .
   a) Three full network stations and
   b) One independent station[28]
4. In communities outside of all major and smaller television markets, "any additional television signals may be carried."[29]

The FCC also addressed itself to two specific classes of broadcasting stations: educational and foreign language stations.

In general, the FCC has required "all cable systems to carry, on request, all educational stations within 35 miles and those placing a Grade B signal on all or part of the community of the cable system."[30,31] The FCC also permits virtually unlimited importation of educational stations. "For major and smaller markets the rules permit carriage of any noncommercial educational stations operated by the state in which the cable system is located, and also by any other educational station."[32] The FCC recognized that importation of educational stations may reduce local viewing of the local educational station, possibly resulting in an erosion of financial support. Accordingly, the FCC permits importation of ETV broadcast stations "in the absence of objection . . . by any local noncommercial educational station or State or local educational television authority.[33]

With foreign language stations there is no prohibition on the carriage of non-English language programming. Broadcast stations programming predominantly in a language other than English can be imported and carried on cable systems without limitations of any type.[34]

Program origination services

That the FCC is fully committed to program origination services is made crystal clear in the following FCC statement:

> We emphasize that the cable operator cannot accept the broadcast signals that will be made available without also accepting the obligation to provide the nonbroadcast bandwidth and . . . access services [*i.e.,* program origination service]. The two are integrally linked in the public interest judgment we have made.[35]

Accordingly, the FCC has required each major market cable system to make available one channel for program origination (*i.e.,* Class II or Class III channels) for each broadcast channel carried.[36]

Additionally, all cable systems in major markets must provide the following program origination capability:

Cable Television

Minimum channel capacity—Each such [cable] system shall have . . . (the equivalent of 20 TV broadcast channels) available for immediate or potential use for the totality of cable services offered. . . .

Two-way communications—Each such [cable] system shall maintain a plant having technical capacity for nonvoice return communications [from the subscriber's television receiver].

Public access channel—Each such [cable] system shall maintain at least one specifically designated, noncommercial public access channel available on a first-come, nondiscriminatory basis. The system shall maintain and have available for public use at least the minimal equipment and facilities necessary for the production of programming for such a channel. . . .

Educational access channel—Each such [cable] system shall maintain at least one specifically designated channel for use by local educational authorities.

Local government access channel—Each such [cable] system shall maintain at least one specially designated channel for local government uses.

Leased access channels—Having satisfied the origination cablecasting requirements [above] . . . for specially designated access channels, such [cable] system shall offer other portions of its nonbroadcast bandwidth, including unused portions of the specially designated channels, for leased [*i.e.,* common carrier] access services. However, these leased channel operations shall be undertaken with the express understanding that they are subject to displacement if there is a demand to use the channels for their specially designated purposes. On at least one of the leased channels, priority shall be given part-time users.

Expansion of access channel capacity—Whenever all of the [public, education, local government and leased access] channels . . . are in use during 80% of the weekdays (Monday-Friday) for 80% of the time during any consecutive three-hour period for six consecutive weeks, such [cable] system shall have six months in which to make a new channel available for any or all of the above-described purposes.

Program content control—Each such [cable] system shall exercise no control over program content on any of the [public, education, local government and leased access] channels; . . . however, this limitation shall not prevent it from taking appropriate steps to insure compliance with [other] operating rules. . . .

Assessment of costs—. . . From the commencement of cable television service in the community of such [cable] system until five (5) years after completion of the system's basic trunk line, the [education and local government access] channels . . . shall be made available without charge.[37]

One additional program origination requirement is included in the 1972 FCC rules and regulations. The FCC incorporated the rule originally promulgated in 1969, and subsequently "upheld by the Supreme Court (by a 5-to-4 vote) in *U.S. v. Midwest Video Corp.*,"[38] requiring cable systems with 3500 or more subscribers to operate "to a significant extent as a local outlet by origination cablecasting and . . . [have] available facilities for local production and presentation of programs other than automated services."[39]

Thus cable communications has come a long way in a short quarter of a century. It has progressed from an infant industry with a few subscribers on a handful of CATV systems to a major cable communications industry with over seven million subscribers in over 5400 communities.[40] In Oklahoma alone there are nearly 100,000 subscribers in over 70 communities.[41]

The role of cable systems has shifted slowly but consistently from providing broadcast retransmission services to program origination services, a metamorphosis from a parasitic industry dependent on broadcast signals, to an independent program-generating industry also offering a broad range of common carrier services. The shift to program origination services is likely to continue.

The Report of the Sloan Commission on Cable Communications has described cable as "the television of abundance." In a discussion of the promise of CATV, the report boldly speculates on the reality of cable communications.

> If one has any faith at all in the value of communications, the promise of cable television is awesome. The power of the existing system is immense; it dwarfs anything that has preceded it. Never in history have so many people spent so much time linked to an organized system of communications.
>
> But where it has dominated communications in power, it has been almost trivial in scope. It has dealt primarily with entertainment at a low level of sophistication and quality, and with news and public affairs at their broadest and their most general. It has been obliged

to think of the mass audience almost to the exclusion of any other, and in doing so has robbed what it provides of any of the highly desirable elements of particularity.

Cable television is no threat to the power of the total television system. Whatever radiated television can do, cable television can do quite well. But those characteristics of radiated television that flow from spectrum scarcity need no longer characterize television as a total system, for the television of abundance can offer television the scope it requires to be a complete communications service. The communciations system of unrivaled power becomes then a system of unrivaled scope as well, not doing quite the same things as the printing press, doing many things better and a few things worse, but wholly commensurate with the press.[42]

REFERENCES

1. Sydney W. Head, *Broadcasting in America: A Survey of Television and Radio*, 2nd ed., Boston, Houghton Mifflin Co., 1972, p. 35.
2. *Ibid.*, p. 37.
3. Mary Alice Mayer Phillips, *CATV: A History of Community Antenna Television*, Evanston, Ill., Northwestern University Press, 1972, p. 12.
4. Wave propagation depends also on power, antenna height and frequency. Head, p. 76.
5. Phillips, p. 3.
6. Frank J. Kahn, ed., *Documents of American Broadcasting*, rev. ed., New York: Appleton-Century-Crofts, 1972, p. 551.
7. Phillips, pp. 7–8.
8. *Ibid.*, p. 13.
9. *Ibid.*, pp. 13–14.
10. *Ibid.*, p. 14.
11. *Ibid.*, p. 19.
12. Head, p. 194.
13. Don R. LeDuc, *Cable Television and the FCC: A Crisis in Media Control*, Philadelphia: Temple University Press, 1973, p. 68.
14. Phillips, p. 42.
15. James Davis, "Isn't It About Time . . . Again?", Little Rock, Ark., 1973, p. 2.
16. Phillips, p. 43.
17. *On the Cable: The Television of Abundance*, Report of the Sloan Commission on Cable Communications, New York, McGraw-Hill Book Co., 1971, p. 27.
18. Recollections of David Jaffe, News Director, WRFY Cable Channel 5, May 1967, to September 1967.
19. Phillips, p. 111.
20. *Ibid.*, p. 124.

21. Federal Communications Commission, "Cable Television Service, Cable Television Relay Service," *Federal Register*, Vol. 37, No. 30, Part II, 1972, pp. 3252–3341.
22. A point-to-point transmission is analogous to a common telephone transmission. A message is transmitted from one point (the person dialing the telephone) to another point (the person answering the telephone). No one else is involved in the transmission. Point-to-point transmissions are also referred to as limited access, *i.e.*, access to the transmission can be controlled.
23. A point-to-mass transmission is analogous to a typical TV station transmission. The signal is sent from one point (the transmitter) to many points (the various TV receivers tuned to the transmitter's frequency).
24. *Ibid.*, Section 76.5 (2), (aa), (bb), (cc), p. 3279.
25. Federal Communications Commission, "Cable Television Service Reconsideration of Report and Order," *Federal Register*, Vol. 38, No. 136, Part II, 1972, p. 13859.
26. More accurately, signals of stations within 35 miles of the cable system must be carried at the request of the broadcasting stations and may be carried in the absence of such requests. Federal Communications Commission, "Cable Television Service; Cable Television Relay Service," paragraphs 81 and 83, p. 3263.
27. Norman, Okla., is within the Oklahoma City market. The FCC has listed the Oklahoma City market as number 39. For a complete listing of the top 100 markets, see *Ibid.* Section 76.51, p. 3281.
28. *Ibid.*, Section 76.5 (i), p. 3278.
29. Steven R. Rivkin, "Cable Television: A Guide to Federal Regulations," a report prepared for the National Science Foundation, Rand, Santa Monica, Calif., March 1973, p. 22.
30. *Ibid.*, p. 24.
31. For a definition of "grade B signal," see: Section 73.683(a).
32. Rifkin, p. 25.
33. Federal Communications Commission, *Cable Television Service; Cable Television Relay Service*, Section 76.59(c), p. 3284; Section 76.61(d), p. 3285.
34. *Ibid.*, Section 76.59(d), p. 3284.
35. *Ibid.*, paragraph 120, p. 3269.
36. *Ibid.*, 76.251(a)(2), p. 3289.
37. Federal Communications Commission, *Cable Television Service; Cable Television Relay Service*, Station 76.251(a)(1), (3), (4), (5), (6), (7), (8), (9), (10), p. 3289.
38. Rifkin, p. 36.
39. Federal Communications System, *Cable Television Service; Cable Television Relay Service*, Section 76.201(a), p. 3287.
40: "Countdown on Cable Television," *Cable Television Sourcebook 1974*, Washington, D.C., Broadcasting Publications Inc., 1973, p. 5.
41. *Ibid.*
42 *On the Cable . . .* , pp. 167–168.

The Unfulfilled Promise of Cable TV

JERROLD N. OPPENHEIM

Reprinted from *The Progressive*, vol. 38, 2 (February, 1974), with permission of publisher. Copyright 1974 by The Progressive. Jerrold N. Oppenheim is editor of *Cable Report*, a Chicago-based publication. He has testified as an expert witness on cable television before state and federal commissions.

If the cable television industry were as responsive to social needs and desires as it is to balance sheets, the technology it exploits could help transform America.

The present television networks could well follow *Life* and *Look* into picture heaven, as viewers with the choice of sixty or eighty channels become discontented with more Lucy. Ethnic singing and dancing might appear on television regularly from some of the many diverse cultures that never really melted into the pot. Community group leaders could mount their soapboxes during prime time. Religious leaders could reach their flocks during the week, instead of Sunday morning when their potential audience is at services.

Cable television could replace crowded Main Street stores with giant distant warehouses, connected to our living rooms by a wire over which we could both see and buy—an electronic Sears catalogue. Opera could be available to everyone for a couple of dollars—at home.

More important, cable could be the means for opening up lines of communication that have never existed before. Political leaders could appeal to large groups of people over one of the ubiquitous cable television channels. Hot disputes could be negotiated by the preparation of reasoned positions for transmission by the cooler medium of television.

Public participation in political events and meetings might even be increased by their direct cablecast. Others could watch excerpts prepared for viewing at a more convenient hour.

A lot of these developments might provoke some people to flee to the countryside to avoid the newfangled gadgets, but they would probably find that cable television has been there even longer than in the city. Cable might make living on a farm the cultural equivalent of a condominium on the edge of downtown—complete with the latest

Oppenheim

291

movies, current theater, imported television, and even the city crime news.

However, little of what I have just described is a reality today, although isolated experiments have been conducted of just about all of these examples (and many, many more). The hardware is available, the technology is designed, the engineering is done. But it all sounds like a fairy tale.

The one dream about cable television that has come to pass is the corporate profits it is capable of producing. A report sponsored by some movie producers (who hope to reduce cable profits by the amount of their copyright fees) estimates that urban cable systems will return a profit on investment of as much as 23.4 percent *a year*. One investment proposal circulating three years ago projected sixty-five percent a year.

Yet little public policy has been developed to harness some of those profits to serve the people who pay them. The potentials of cable television—sometimes called broadband cable communications—are well known to many government officials. But no agent of national public policy has gone on record about which of these developments should be encouraged and which should be discouraged. Or how the technology that brings us the ability to order books and speeches over the tube at home ought to be controlled to prevent cabletappers from keeping track of which books and speeches have been ordered at each home.

Those social decisions have been left to the free market place—the cable industry. And what has it come up with? What has it, in its profit-seeking wisdom, decided the most important first function should be of the most important technological advance in communications since the telephone?

Movies. Not-quite-first-run feature films on a premium payment basis. The industry is virtually united: the only way cable will sell in big cities is if it offers a new service. Robert J. Lewis, president of Cablecom-General, Inc., describes the rest of this social theory: "The solution is much closer cooperation between the movie producers and other program sources with the various pay television entrepreneurs and cable television companies willing to take some risks." Sell us your pictures, moviemen, and we will all profit by hitching pay-TV boxes to home television sets.

In theory, of course, cable television is a regulated industry, and the instrument of regulation is the Federal Communications Commission (FCC). The present set of FCC cable television rules went into effect on March 31, 1972, but the FCC's own advisory committee has criticized their laxness. The committee declared in a report last August that "after eighteen months of experience, it appears that the FCC's non-directive posture is promoting a regulatory free-for-all. . . ." The group reaching that conclusion was appointed by the FCC, mostly from the ranks of the cable industry.

In assessing the committee's conclusion, it is important to consider more than the rules themselves. What really counts is how seriously the Commission takes its own rules, how it enforces them, how it interprets them, and even how it waives them (sometimes into oblivion).

Some of the major rules from 1972 that remain more or less intact require cable operators in the 100 most populous areas to provide at least twenty channels. Of these, one must be made available free to the public (together with some equipment and a studio) on a first-come, first-served basis. Another channel goes to the municipality and a third to educators. All local broadcast stations must be carried, and additional signals can be brought in from out of town. The cable operator can put his own programming on a channel if he likes (often this amounts to no more than a camera scanning three weather instruments and a bunch of ads) and any channels left must be made available for lease.

To understand FCC "policy" on cable television (or anything else), you must understand that the Commission does not sit down and make rational plans or decisions based on what would be best for the inarticulate public it is commissioned to protect. Rather, like any other agency of government, the FCC is a political body and it responds to whatever political pressures are applied to it. Since its job is to regulate the highly profitable communications industries, it tends to hear most often from members of those industries with a great deal of money riding on Commission decisions; the amount of pressure applied is in direct proportion to the amount of that money.

In the case of cable television, the broadcast industry sees its entire existence at stake. That represents a lot of money—many big city broadcast operations make forty to sixty percent profit on sales before taxes—so broadcasters exert a lot of pressure. Thus, most FCC decision-making is most intelligently viewed as a reflection of immense broadcast industry pressures.

Of course, there are other pressures, which is the reason the cable television industry has not been totally wiped out. The cable industry itself can exert a little pressure of its own. Equipment manufacturers, looking for new markets, have something to say. Program producers, especially movie-makers, do too.

Sometimes the public interest even gets considered in the battle, especially if there is someone around to advocate it. But it is never more than one of the interests to be compromised against all the others. Thus, the public interest is always compromised.

When cable television was first invented in the late 1940s, broadcasters and television set manufacturers viewed the new industry as a boon to coverage and sales, respectively. At that time, all cable did was to bring broadcast signals into areas that had previously been unable to receive television at all. Nobody wanted the FCC to do anything and the FCC left the industry to develop on its own.

Perceptions began to change around the late 1950s, though, as the cable industry itself entered a new phase. By this time, most of the outlying areas without prior television service from over-the-air stations had been cabled if it was economically feasible to do so. So cable systems sprang up in places where television reception was already present, if often marginal. In these places, cable offered not only better reception but brought in additional television signals from more distant points.

This importation of distant channels was of marginal significance to the operators of the stations being imported; the additions to their audiences were small and, in any event, not reported by the ratings services. From the manufacturers' point of view, there was also little to get excited about. Cable was now entering markets where television sets were already present in virtually every home, so cable did not create many new sales.

But the broadcasters in the cities where the new cable systems were being built felt that their territory had been invaded. They did not object to the better reception, especially on color sets, that the cable brought to their audience. What they objected to were the new television signals the cable brought to compete with their own. In Utica, for example, the five network-affiliated stations were suddenly facing competition from a CBS affiliate in Albany, 100 miles away, and three non-network stations in New York City. A city that had been served with clear pictures by three outlets and marginally by two others was suddenly well-served by nine stations.

Up until that time, only a few of the nation's largest cities had been thought by broadcasters to be capable economically of supporting so many stations. Chicago, for example, is served by seven commercial stations.

The Chicago area has 2.6 million television homes, compared to metropolitan Utica's 91,000.

Utica broadcasters, and all other broadcasters in similar positions, were scared. If their audiences were attracted away by the new stations that cable made available, their ratings could plummet and advertising would become difficult to sell. Eventually, they could even face extinction.

The networks were also somewhat shaken by that possibility. Each had spent the past twenty years or so building its stable of local affiliates to carry network programs to some ninety percent of America. This attractive advertising package would now be threatened if viewers in large numbers started to watch cable-fed out-of-town non-network stations. Even more threatening to the networks was the perceived possibility that cable television would come into the largest areas, where the networks themselves own profitable stations, and attract audiences—and thus advertisers—away.

The pressure that the frightened broadcast industry put on the Commission resulted in the so-called freeze of 1968. The Commission did not actually outlaw the importation of distant signals into the 100 largest metropolitan areas, but it made the procedure so tortuous as to rule it out effectively.

So the cable industry continued to grow slowly in the outlying areas of America. It also became somewhat more sophisticated about political infighting at the FCC and developed an imaginative rhetoric about the marvelous technological possibilities that cable television represented—especially, of course, in the largest cities, where one might expect a demand for services like banking-by-cable, automated meter reading, and school-by-television.

The industry also cultivated community groups on the basis of the increased access to the television studio that could be possible if there were a large number of cable television channels in every city. This potential pressure valve for forum-seeking dissidents was also of some appeal to city administrations beleaguered by organized groups of unhappy constituents, many of whom could be quieted with the opportunity to speak.

Now the FCC was in the middle of a real battle: the networks and network affiliates versus the cable industry and its new coalition, with citizens inadequately represented as an uneasy and demanding part of the latter.

The most active compromise-maker turned out to be the White House, in the person of Clay T. Whitehead, director of the White House Office of Telecommunications Policy (OTP). In August 1971, the FCC had proposed a set of rules in an unorthodox "letter of intent" (to issue cable rules) submitted to Congress. Congress did not react, largely because it adjourned for the summer the next day. But Whitehead responded with a series of closed-door sessions with the various industry interests: the National Cable Television Association, the National Association of Broadcasters, and the Motion Picture Producers Association. The organized public was not formally represented at any of these meetings. The consequence was pressure on the FCC to change its proposal.

The result, as befits a political process, was a compromise more or less representing the relative political strengths of the parties. It was codified, albeit with a sweeping waiver provision, by rules issued in February 1972, to take effect on the last day of the following month. The policy had been shaped mostly by the FCC, the broadcast industry, the cable industry, movie producers, Congress (by silent ratification), and the White House. The courts also played a part by upholding the FCC's broad jurisdiction over cable television. The FCC's role in the development of the cable television industry has thus been highly political, with little citizen participation, and often without clearly defined rules. This is not atypical of the way policy is developed at the FCC.

If any private interest got the short end of the stick in the compromise, it was the network affiliates, especially those in smaller cities that are unused to much competition. Cable can now bring one or two distant signals in to compete, plus whatever nonbroadcast competition it can find, such as pay-television movies. In the long run, it is possible that the networks will find the affiliates superfluous. The networks will be able to get blanket coverage of the nation by leasing channels on a full-time basis on each cable system instead of affiliating with local entrepreneurs who do not always broadcast every show the network offers.

The big winners, on the other hand, appear to be the large-city stations that are not affiliated with any network and therefore produce or buy their own programming. The new rules permit distant-signal importation and these are the stations that the cable systems will want to import, since they carry the only non-network programming (largely movies and sports). In effect, these stations are slowly becoming regional networks. For example, most cable systems in the upper Midwest import the popular

WGN-TV from Chicago. It is not quite so certain that non-network UHF stations will benefit so handsomely. It depends on what these stations have to offer; Chicago White Sox baseball encouraged at least seventy-seven cable systems in five states to import WSNS-TV from Chicago.

Roger Rice, vice president of Cox Broadcasting and chairman of the Association of Independent Television Stations, happily cites the "profound effect" cable carriage is having on independent station circulation. The station he manages, KTVU-TV in Oakland, is carried by cable into more than 610,000 homes in at least thirty-six California counties. The station's audience is also spreading into Colorado and Utah. Rice concludes that "cable is going to make regional stations out of independents."

The results for the other participants are not as clear. The networks are probably still threatened, especially by new kinds of special-interest networks that will soon be inexpensively created by satellite.

Because of the lower cost of networking by satellite, Teleprompter's director of satellite development, Robert Button, predicts "a network bigger than anything we've ever seen." Costs will be low enough to permit several more networks to operate at once and when they run out of over-the-air broadcast television stations with which to affiliate, as they will quickly, they can turn to the plethora of unused cable television channels.

As regionalization and specialization spread, audiences for the present three networks may well diminish, Currently, the networks pull at least sixty-nine percent of the audience in New York; in most of the country, they do considerably better than that. But the Media Research Division of the Needham, Harper, and Steers advertising agency predicts that by 1985 the national networks will together attract less than fifty percent of the audience. Paul Klein, once NBC-TV's program director and now pay-cable executive, predicts the demise of the networks in their present form at such low (for them) audience levels. Mass advertisers will no longer support them.

The outlook, then, is for a lot more television networks—but this is my prediction, not the FCC's design.

The new rules also promise citizens local access to cable television studios and a local public process in the award of cable franchises. But the FCC offered little enforcement, if any, and only one ambiguous line about the protection of privacy.

Motion picture producers would seem to come out ahead since the cable industry has been given enough growing room to become a substantial customer. Movie theaters, on the other hand, were not protected at all and they presumably face competition from movies-by-cable, whether on pay-cable channels or free channels imported from out of town.

Perhaps the most inconclusive results were those obtained by the cable industry itself. There is little question that it will flourish in small and middle-sized cities (in television markets smaller than the fifty largest), where one or two distant signals are permitted with few significant restrictions.

What is not clear is what will happen in the fifty largest metropolitan areas. The reason for the confusion over whether the new rules help cable television in the big cities is that no one really knows what the economic base of cable in the cities will be. If it is to be the importation of distant signals (movies from Milwaukee, for instance), then the Commission has wounded cable by making distant signal importation difficult in the top fifty cities—perhaps insuperably difficult.

Essentially, the FCC has said that a local broadcaster in the biggest cities may buy up broadcast-and-cable rights to a program and thereby prevent, forever, that program from being carried on the cable via a distant signal. A movie purchased by WGN-TV in Chicago cannot be carried into Chicago by cable when it is played on a Milwaukee outlet, even if WGN never puts it on the air.

In this way, cable operators in these areas are prevented from purchasing many popular programs. At the same time, the copyright-holders can sell their movies to broadcasters on the basis that the purchase is necessary to keep it permanently out of the hands of local cable operators. The price of a movie becomes the price of survival in the broadcasters' eyes, potentially a handsome sum indeed in the moviemakers' pockets.

If, as many think, the economic basis of cable in the big cities has more to do with new services—banking, shopping, neighborhood channels, public access, specialized programs—than with distant signals, then the FCC's elaborate attempt to protect big city broadcasters will not make much difference to cable operators.

Whichever prediction you favor, it is worth considering whether the FCC properly discharged its obligation to serve "the public convenience and necessity." It is clear that the Commission went to great lengths to determine what would be convenient, if not necessary, for the various economic interests involved. If any public benefit spun off the Commission's deliberations, it was purely fortuitous.

Public Access and Union Fears

RALPH LEE SMITH

Reprinted from *The Nation*, vol. 218, 14 (April 6, 1974), with permission of the publisher. Copyright 1974 by The Nation. Ralph Lee Smith, a regular contributor to *The Nation*, is the author of *The Wired Nation*.

A few years ago in New York City, William vandenHeuvel, at that time chairman of the city's Department of Corrections, held hearings on prison conditions. On the first morning crews from two commercial TV stations were on hand with their equipment. Another group also showed up—a team from the Alternate Media Center (AMC), a foundation-funded, nonprofit videotape group based at New York University.

The commercial crews were there to record a few segments of the hearings, which would then be edited down for a presentation of perhaps a minute on that evening's news roundup. AMC's group planned to tape the entire proceedings, for showing during prime evening time on the public access channels of Manhattan's two cable systems, so that interested persons could see the hearings in full. In addition, the center keeps a permanent file of such tapes, and makes them available to cable systems, and to civic and community groups throughout the country.

Smith

299

But at the hearings, the commercial crews took one look at the AMC group opening up its portable equipment and phoned their union shop stewards. The cameramen then told vandenHeuvel that if the AMC group were allowed to tape, the commercial cameras would be shut off. Faced with the choice of a possible minute on commercial TV, or full coverage on the city's cable access channels, vandenHeuvel did not hesitate. The AMC group was ordered not to videotape the hearings until the commercial crews had filmed everything they wanted and left the premises.

VandenHeuvel's decision speaks volumes about the relationship of public officials to mass market television. It also highlights an important item on the nation's agenda—the relationship between labor and emerging forms of communications.

The community videotape movement came into being when a new generation of relatively inexpensive portable videotape equipment reached the market in the late 1960s. The first in the field was SONY, with the Porta-Pak; more recently, comparable equipment has been marketed by Panasonic. So far, no American manufacturers have entered the field. The SONY and Panasonic equipment, which takes half-inch tape, costs about $1,600. A broadcast TV camera, using 2-inch tape, costs about $80,000. The low cost of the half-inch cameras is matched by their ease of operation. Workshops conducted by video groups throughout the United States have shown that almost anyone can begin making videotapes after about fifteen minutes of instruction and "hands-on" experience.

The growth of the community videotape movement coincided with the rise of local origination and public access channels on cable systems. The camera groups were quick to see that cable offered a means of local distribution for the tapes that they were making. Many cable system operators, for their part, welcomed the community tapes, since they provided a ready source of program material. Increasingly, tapes made by video groups began to appear on local systems, with community residents doing the work, and the cable operator supplying channel space without charge. Here and there, conflicts began to occur with unionized TV cameramen.

For a number of reasons, few community videotapers are members of unions. First, community videogroups, loosely organized and without commercial intention, are not union shops. Second, the videotapes are made either on a minuscule budget or on no budget at all. If the camera operators had to charge community groups union scale for their time and observe union work rules, most of their output would cease, since no one in sight at this time is prepared to pay such money for these activities. Third, union membership is at best irrelevant and at worst incompatible with one of the purposes of the movement, which is to break the monopoly in the creation of television that has hitherto been enjoyed by a small group of professionals. Videotape groups put their equipment directly into the hands of individuals in communities—teenagers, old persons, minorities, the disadvantaged, the handicapped—show them how to use it, and encourage them to make tapes reflecting their interests, their concerns, their friends and their world. "The videotape movement," says one of its leaders, "is simply people making television."

On February 6 to 8 of this year, a little noticed milestone was reached in the relationship of unions to the new forms of community television. The AFL-CIO Labor Studies Center in Washington, D.C. held a first of its kind three-day seminar for union officials on the subject of "Union Strategies for Cable TV." The Labor Studies Center was established five years ago as a nonprofit educational institution; its board of directors is composed of both labor leaders and public members. Its programs include professional training for labor leaders, special conferences and seminars, and broader programs on public issues, social sciences and the humanities. Beginning this year, the center, in conjunction with Antioch College, is offering a full four-year external degree program leading to a B.A. in labor studies, for union staff and full-time elected union officials.

Twenty-eight union officials from all over the country signed up for the center's cable seminar. They included officials from a number of unions in the field of communications and the performing arts—the International Brotherhood of Electrical Workers, whose membership includes many TV cameramen; the Utility Workers Union, the Communications Workers of America, the National Association of Broadcast Employees, the American Federation of Television and Radio Artists, and Actors Equity. Unions in other fields also sent representatives. Many of those attending knew relatively little about cable, and the seminar was designed to provide an intensive introduction that could serve as a background for discussion and debate.

Wednesday morning, February 6, was devoted to presentations by staff members of the Ford Foundation–funded Cable Television Information Center. In the afternoon the group visited the cable system in Reston, Va., being briefed on the technology and watching some local programming go out on the system. On Thursday morning the seminar heard Earl Haydt, manager of the Reading, Pa., cable system, and Robert Fina, director of TV services at Kutztown State College, describe extensive program origination activities in which the Reading system has been involved, and saw excerpts from some community-made tapes that have been shown on the Reading cable.

At the end of the morning the group saw and heard something even more experimental—application of community videotape techniques to union work. Leslie Orear, assistant for publications of the Amalgamated Meat Cutters and Butcher Workmen and a panelist at the seminar, has been one of the first union officials to acquaint himself with the new communications technologies; he is convinced of their importance for the labor movement. On a recent trip to Alabama, he interviewed union and non-union workers in the poultry industry, making no suggestions about what they should say, but simply letting them tell about their working experiences. The result, seen in excerpts from the tapes that Orear showed at the seminar, was a far more immediate and persuasive document than could ever have been turned out by the mimeograph machines in a union publicity office. And it was created at almost no cost by a union official on the job who had no training in TV camera work or production.

Showing videotapes on portable equipment is as simple as making them, and Orear's plan had been to put a shortened version of his Alabama tapes into the hands of union field workers and local organizers, for showing at workers' meetings. So far, however, he has found it hard to overcome the lack of familiarity with the new techniques, and the human tendency to continue doing things the way they have been done in the past. Lack of familiarity with the technologies was one of the problems that the seminar was designed to attack. On Thursday afternoon the group learned to use portable video equipment in a workshop period. Individual participants then made tapes that same afternoon, and these were shown after supper.

Controversy erupted on Friday morning, during a round-table discussion of programming at which Red Burns, executive director of the Alternate Media Center, was the featured speaker. Burns, a slim, attractive woman with a warm, electric personality, is one of the evangelists of community video. As she and others spoke, two Antioch students videotaped the proceedings.

In her opening remarks, Burns said: "The idea that nonprofessional media people could suddenly have access to media is a kind of mind-blowing thing. What can we do with it?" By contrast with present broadcasting, she said, the emphasis in community television should be on teaching nonprofessional people how to use the new technologies of half-inch videotape and cable. People and communities should make programs according to their needs, and interaction should be the central concept. "We must find a way to plug the people back into the nation's media," she said. "We must get this equipment into the hands of the people. We must let *them* make tapes. . . . We are not the experts. It's the people who are the experts."

The union officials, some of whom had devoted their working lives to making certain that only persons certified as professionals or experts laid their hands on the operating equipment of television technology, pondered her words. Leslie Orear approached the hydra-headed issue cautiously. "About that programming on the Reading, Pa. system that was shown here yesterday," he said, "we saw a lot of stuff that looked pretty dull to us. We find it difficult to believe that a great cable system was built on such material."

"It *should* be dull to you," Red Burns replied. "There are lots of small audiences, even within a city the size of Reading, and that programming was designed for specific interests of small audiences and groups. It's programming made *by* the local people, and programming in which people in local communities within the city of Reading can see themselves, their communities and their problems, on television."

"Are you urging," he asked, "that we use cable not just for promoting labor's point of view, but that we should take the broad point of view of using labor programming to present, sponsor, and help to create a public forum for the community to use in expressing itself"

"You are part of a community," Burns replied, "and we are interested, not just in union problems but in the community. . . . What you're going to be doing is developing a consciousness and an awareness in your community that can only help your movement."

John Carr, an international representative of the International Brotherhood of Electrical Workers, reached for the throat of the problem as his union saw it:

My interest in cable TV is organizing it and serving it. I have a great fear that we are getting back to child labor again, by letting high school students run tapes all over the community. My interest is to organize the fellow who runs the camera, and get him a week's pay, and not to have volunteer help.

Now I noticed, with regard to the operation in Reading, that they are, in my opinion, making a profit on volunteer help. They started out with 850 subscribers, went dynamically into local programming and public access, and now have some 30,000 subscribers. An awful lot of the reason why that subscribership increased is public access. I think that this is where the union has a stake in this. . . . My experience has been that it's best to organize a field where there are three or four companies in it, not when there are 30,000 or 40,000. Someday this industry is going to be bigger than the telephone company. . . .

Local origination is the most important part to organize. How long do you tell the community to go ahead and use it for nothing, use it themselves, and when do you say, "Stop, now we're going to use it, and we're going to get paid for using it . . ."?

We want local origination organized and we want the people paid. Local origination is an advertisement for a profit-making venture. . . . I know one thing—you have a world of greedy, miserly owners out there.

The theme was pursued by Gordon Spielman, editor of *The Union Advocate*, the newspaper of the St. Paul, Minn. Trades and Labor Assembly. "We in the labor movement can't afford the amateurs," he said. "I take a jaundiced view of the guy who will replace me, and who will be doing just what I am doing, but will be doing it for nothing. Whoever is going to be hired to do this, we're going to insist that he be a member of a trade union, getting union pay. . . . The issue is whether we're going to develop a new scab medium." The problem, Spielman added, is as important to the economic future of today's young videotapers, as it is to those now making a living in the field.

Jay Barney, counselor for Actors Equity, suggested that those who appear on videotapes, as well as those who run them, should be professionals. "Amateur supper theatre, as a rule, is poor," he stated. "The program origination that we saw on the Reston system was amateurish. People will demand professionals both behind and in front of the cameras."

Responding to these and similar statements, Red Burns held firmly to her view that unions are part of the community and cannot pursue a separate path. Unionization of local access and community programming at this time, she said, would seriously harm or destroy them, and it is in the mutual interest of unions and the community that this not occur. Union policy toward community video, she maintained, should be to avoid or postpone organization of the field and "let it grow." At one point she waved her hand at the pair of students who were videotaping the meeting. "The power is not mine," she said, "it is not yours. It is theirs."

A communications professor from a local university agreed with her about the adverse effect of unionization on community television, but Albert Zack, director of the AFL-CIO public relations department, and Gordon Spielman sharply disagreed. "This is the excuse that is used anytime we organize anywhere," Spielman said. "They say we are raising the cost, therefore we are raising the price to the consumer, therefore organized labor is inflationary, organized labor ought to be suppressed, it is a conspiracy, and everything else."

John Taylor, an officer of Local 279 of the Houston, Tex. Moving Pictures Machine Operators, tossed a couple of ideas into the pot. He suggested, first, that union funds be made available for subsidizing the cost of running public access channels on cable systems. Second, he suggested that the franchise fee which cities collect from cable companies be devoted to paying union scale to persons involved in access programming.

The discussion shifted to ways in which unions might themselves use the public access channels. "The labor movement just doesn't know what to do with cable—doesn't know how to use it," said Zack. "Channels are available, but who will use them, and how? And where will the funds come from, for programming?" Spielman agreed. "We could get a labor channel in St. Paul, all for ourselves, just by asking for it," he said. "But what in the world would we do with it?

"You could use it as part of a community information system," Burns replied, returning to her theme. "You must develop the concept of feedback." The subject fascinated Beverly Shulman, public representative of the International Ladies' Garment Workers' Union. On a union channel, or on a public access channel, she asked, who would speak for the union? The officers? The shop ladies? "The shop ladies, of course, go on public access, and say anything they want," Zack replied, "but the shop ladies don't represent the position of the union."

Whoever may or may not speak for unions on access channels, the group was told that at least one union group is doing more about cable than just thinking or worrying. The AFL-CIO Labor Council in Chicago, they were told, is considering bidding for a cable franchise. Throughout the morning, the various subjects—unionization, professionalism versus amateurs, labor use of cable—were revisited, and debate was lively. It was hard to shut off the discussion at lunchtime.

Some days after the Washington seminar, a reporter called Art Korff, an organizer for the International Brotherhood of Electrical Workers, who had been involved in organizing the workers at Sterling Manhattan Cable TV in New York City. Korff had attended the seminar and was eager to discuss the issues; in particular, he was anxious that one aspect of his union's position be understood.

"I'm sure you know," he said, "that the unions do not wish to destroy public access. Our view is exactly the opposite. We want public access to thrive and grow, if for no other reason than that public access is strongly in our interest. We plan to use it."

For all parties involved, however, dialogue and decision have barely begun, and a hard road lies ahead. Here are a few of the issues:

Unity of the community television experience. Many, probably most people in the community television movement, believe that television, the most powerful medium in modern society, must be demystified and put in the hands of the public. Individuals must have the experience of creating television. They must, however, have the full experience, not just part of it. At the seminar Red Burns gave memorable expression to the movement's credo: "The manner in which one acquires his stock of knowledge is part of that knowledge."

How is this to be reconciled with the union's equally strong belief that the welfare of many workers requires that part of the process be retained in professional hands?

An immediate area of conflict is the use of videotape cameras, and the operation of the equipment for showing videotapes in the studios of cable systems whose workers have been unionized. In a current situation that could easily become typical, community video groups are still able to make tapes outside the studio of a cable system that has been unionized, but cannot tape programs in the studio, and are required to turn over to union personnel any tapes that they wish to have shown on the system. The group has in effect lost its home, and its spirit has been notably affected. "As a result," said one bitter videotaper, "the community hates the union." While this is undoubtedly overstated, it would be unwise of unions to ignore the potential of this issue for alienating the labor movement from legions of natural grass-roots allies, as community video comes to the cities and towns of the United States.

A potential solution to this problem, not yet explored, lies in noting and acting on the distinction between two different types of community channel on the cable: the local origination channel and the public access channel. Local origination is the name usually given to a channel controlled by the cable operator. The cable operator programs the channel, and retains the final say on what is or is not transmitted. He can, and often does, accept advertising on this channel and, in short, acts essentially as a broadcaster. The public access channel, as the name indicates, is the true soapbox. The cable operator does *not* choose the material to be shown on these channels. Anyone who wishes to appear or to show tapes, need only show up at the studio. The Federal Communications Commission's cable rules, adopted in March 1972, require that any cable system constructed after that date in the nation's top 100 markets—which comprise 90 per cent of the U.S. population—have at least one channel dedicated to public access.

The question that naturally arises is, why not restrict the operation of cameras and transmission facilities on local origination channels to union personnel, but permit local video groups to become involved in all phases of the creation and transmission of the material shown on public access channels?

Labor's relationship to government and education channels. In its cable rules the FCC, in addition to mandating public access channels on top-100-market cable systems, also requires that such systems provide, without charge, one channel for governmental use and one channel for educational use. The commission made clear that the requirement for all three types of free channel was for an experimental five-year period, at which time their usage and value would be analyzed to determine future policy.

Labor's interest in strong development of education channels is self-evident. With regard to government channels, these can be used to transmit information on jobs available through state employment offices, on unemployment and welfare procedures, and many other types of government information on matters of direct interest to workers.

Creation of union-sponsored programming. One of labor's long-standing grievances has been its belief that America's system of commercial TV does not provide sufficient coverage of problems relating to labor. Unions share this grievance with many other interest groups in society. The coming of cable has, in effect, put them all in the position of having to put up or shut up. Channel space for labor programming will become available as the wired nation comes into being; in some places it is already here. But labor does not yet have policies and programs for developing its great opportunities.

To those who say that cable is not yet sufficiently developed for labor to advocate policies on programming, one must reply that, if it is sufficiently developed to be a candidate for unionization of workers, it is sufficiently developed for labor to create policies for its use.

Labor's relationship to alternate plans for cable development. So far, cable has developed as a commercially owned medium, with the operator retaining control over the use of many of his channels, and having the right to program some of them himself. Labor has only begun to come to grips with the question of what its policies should be with regard to this model of cable communications, and has not come to grips at all with the question of whether this model is the best both for labor and for the country.

One alternate model for cable development, usually called "common carrier," suggests that cable system ownership be completely divorced from cable programming—that the owner would merely lease channel space to others. The common carrier, suggested by me in "The Wired Nation" (*The Nation*, May 18, 1970), and by the President's Cabinet Committee on Cable Communications in its report released in January 1974, could transform labor's relation to the programming and transmission aspects of the medium, since the operator would do no programming and might not be the employer of cameramen and programming technicians.

Other models are also being proposed to overcome the problems of financing and construction cost that cable is encountering in urban centers. Cable's traditional services—more channels of over-the-air TV and a better picture—which have made it commercially successful in rural areas and in smaller towns and cities, may not be sufficiently attractive in metropolitan centers that enjoy better over-the-air TV service. Private capital for building the systems may therefore not be forthcoming, and other sources of funding may have to be sought.

Various plans now being proposed usually involve some type of public or governmental participation in building the systems, with civic boards and/or public authorities involved in certain aspects of their operations. If labor does not develop positions on such proposals now, it will have no complaint if the plans, when inaugurated, turn out to be ill-advised or insufficiently responsive to labor's needs.

Involvement of labor leadership in communications policy making. Labor has a great stake in the new media of communications, and the way in which they evolve. Yet several participants in the Labor Studies Center seminar said that one of their problems was the lack of interest in the issues on the part of labor's top leadership. "This group here isn't a 'power group,' " one union organizer said. "The problem is, how do we reach the real power people in the unions? Too many of them have the attitude, 'Let's keep on doing things the way we are doing them now.' "

The agenda is twofold. First, labor must develop specific policies with regard to the role of workers in these new fields, and with regard to using the new technologies by labor for its own goals. Second, in the national dialogue that has been swirling around these technologies, and out of which America's new communications policies will emerge, the voice of labor has been notably absent. In many of the FCC's Notices of Inquiry regarding new rule-making proceedings in these areas, one can find thoughtful responses filed by nearly every segment of the community— business, trade associations, community groups, churches, colleges and universities, civil rights organizations, political action groups—but one looks in vain for filings by unions or by the combined labor movement, on behalf of their members or in the interest of the nation at large.

This failure of labor to participate in one of the most important dialogues of our time should be speedily repaired. Union members have a right to be represented in the policy-making proceedings that will govern the coming of the new communications to America. And the nation, for its part, cannot create intelligent policy without the participation of labor.

Community Control
of Cable Television Systems

CHARLES TATE

COMMUNICATION TECHNOLOGY AND COMMUNITY CONTROL: CONFRONTATION AND CHALLENGE

Black self-development and self-determination efforts have consistently emphasized the necessity for control of those public and private institutions that operate within their communities. Pan-Africanists, integrationists, separatists, and black nationalists advocate community control of community institutions. DuBois, Booker T. Washington, Marcus Garvey, Malcolm X, Stokely Carmichael, Elijah Muhammad, and Huey Newton are in agreement on this issue. Furthermore, the increased urbanization and concentration of the black population in the central cities has given additional impetus to this historic movement for community control.

Because of the sophisticated and complex structure of racism and decision making in urban governments, community control has become the dominant theme in the struggle of urban minorities for social justice. Community control challenges white control of those institutions that operate in and serve predominantly black communities. Through these institutions, whites exercise control over the resources needed for local development.

The public school system, poverty programs, unions, police departments, welfare agencies, United Appeal, and every form of urban-based institution and organization controlled by whites are now being challenged. The urban oppressed are demanding jobs and economic benefits as well as a controlling voice in the policy-making functions of those institutions, agencies, and programs operating in their communities. The results thus far are small, but important changes are taking place in the degree and quality of minority participation and control of local institutions, organizations, and programs.

Community leaders and organizations are now faced with a new challenge in their efforts to achieve community control. Cable television, a futuristic communications system ideally suited for community control and local programming, is on the verge of broadscale expansion into the cities and ghetto communities. This development could provide the leverage needed by local communities to achieve a much greater degree of independence and self-determination, or it could seriously weaken the movement. Cable television will have a decided impact one way or the other. Its importance and its potential as a social, cultural, economic, and political force cannot be ignored.

Cable television may be the last communications frontier for the oppressed. Yet, most community leaders and organizations know nothing about this revolutionary communications technology and the plans underway to install sophisticated video systems in homes, schools, hospitals, health centers, courtrooms, police stations, banks, fire stations, supermarkets, and department stores.

A major power struggle is underway among broadcasters, cable operators, the FCC, Congress, the Administration, newspapers, publishers, motion picture producers and allied media interests, and a variety of professional groups and associations. All are jockeying to influence the development, expansion, use, and control of cable systems in the cities. The stakes are high.

Because there is great power and profit potential in the ownership and control of this medium, the oft-repeated "rip-off" by big business interests for private gain at the expense of the public interest is taking place once more. If it succeeds, it will stifle the diversified, highly specialized, local programming potential of CATV and prevent local control and community development. Diversified public and private ownership offers the best assurance that social benefits rather than social disaster will be the end product of this new medium. Concerted action by minority groups can bring positive results.

Among those public groups engaged in the policy debates, most advocate a regulatory arrangement that would guarantee minority groups and individuals public access to one or more channels on a free or minimum-charge basis. A regulatory scheme requiring uniform toll rates similar to the rate system used for long-distance telephone operations has been suggested.

Access is extremely important to minority communities, but it does not go far enough. Access alone will not provide the measure of control required over capital, labor, and technology to stimulate and sustain economic and social development of ghetto areas. Ownership and control must be achieved to meet this objective. A sizable portion of the income and profits from CATV in the major cities will come from minority subscribers, particularly blacks. Unless these systems are controlled by the communities served, the resources urgently needed for development will be lost.

If this proposed "access" policy were applied across the board, there would only be white-owned businesses in every sector: a conclusion not only at odds with the goals of self-determination, but one certain to render blacks and other minorities even *more* powerless and dependent. If it is adopted as the public policy for minorities in the field of cable communication, it is certain to increase the power of the white business community, utilizing minority revenues as a subsidy. In other words, ghetto communities will be placed in the position of "paying" for their powerlessness and economic dependency.

Access and community ownership and control are not mutually exclusive or antagonistic. Regulated public access and community ownership and control are equally desirable objectives. In fact, ownership and control may provide the only safe guarantee that access will be accorded to minorities on a nondiscriminatory basis.

The continuing oppression and exploitation of blacks and other racial minorities is directly related to their lack of control over indigenous institutions and resources. For example, it is estimated that the annual disposable income of blacks alone is about $40 billion. On the other hand, a current survey of minority businesses by the Bureau of the Census revealed that receipts of *all* minority businesses in 1969 were less than *one percent* of total U.S. business receipts—a meager $10.6 billion. Minorities own less than five percent of the total businesses in the country, and most are small retail and service operations with fewer then five employees.

Minority ownership and control of cable television systems could dramatically alter this situation over the next five to eight years. There are approximately twenty-five cities with black populations in excess of

100,000; eight of these have populations in excess of 200,000; five have populations over 500,000; and two have populations over 1 million. After five years a cable system with 10,000 subscribers would generate revenue of approximately $500,000 annually and a system with 20,000 subscribers would generate up to $1,000,000 in revenue annually. Obviously, many of these communities could support several cable systems. Six cable districts have been proposed in Washington, D.C., where the black population is over 500,000.

THE NEW FRONTIER

From a few isolated cable systems in small communities and rural areas of the United States, this new industry has aroused nearly every power bloc and organized interest group in the country. Their excitement centers around three aspects of CATV: (1) profits, (2) the vast signal transmission capacity of cable, and (3) the imminent expansion of cable television into the cities and major metropolitan centers.

Cable systems seem to offer unlimited opportunities for making money. First of all, cable operators have avoided programming costs by retransmitting programs produced by broadcast television. This air piracy was upheld by the U.S. Supreme Court. Accelerated depreciation schedules enable operators to gain the benefits of a tax loss while increasing the book value of their investment. The practice has been to depreciate systems over a five- to eight-year period even though equipment life is actually twenty years. The results—a guaranteed paper loss during the first three to five years of operation. This loss is allocated on a pro rata basis to investors who then claim the loss on their individual tax returns. Meanwhile, the cash deductions made for depreciation before taxes are available for use to expand the system or purchase new ones. Hence, the assets of the system and the book value of the stock are increased. When the system is totally depreciated, it may be sold and the entire process can be started all over again.

The vast signal transmission capacity of cable television is further cause for excitement among power blocs and organized interest groups. The "economics of scarcity" common to over-the-air broadcasting can be eliminated by the enormous channel capacity of cable. Early systems provided up to twelve interference-free channels, and those now under development will offer from 24 to 60 channels. This abundance means the general public can now afford video programming for a wide range of purposes; for example, education, community meetings, and information programming concerning health, jobs, and legal matters, to mention a few. Private access, similar to the telephone system, is possible using rate schedules like those for long-distance calls.

Cable technology has a potential, however, that goes far beyond increased channel capacity. Two-way communications, home computer terminals, home banking and shopping services, transmission of mail, fire and burglar alarm systems, piped-in music for each home, and other 1984–style communication services can be provided over the same cable that transmits the video signal. "Cable television" is a misleading term; "cable communications" more accurately defines the technological parameters of this new medium.

With the highly probable interconnection of systems between cities by domestic satellite within this decade, the communications prospects of cable technology are genuinely "mind-blowing."

Another, and perhaps the most crucial, factor generating the growing interest and controversy over this medium is the introduction of cable systems into the major central cities and metropolitan areas.

If the present trends continue, minority communities will be excluded and disenfranchised. White capitalists who own and control the major print and electronic media systems in America will own and control the cable communications industry, including the systems that serve black communities. Fifty percent of the cable industry is already controlled by other media owners. Broadcasters own 36%, newspapers 8%, and telephone companies, advertising agencies, and motion picture companies, 6%. Further, there is a rapidly developing concentration of ownership within these groups. Ten companies now control 52% of the industry. The top ten, in order of rank are: Teleprompter, Cox Cable, American Television and Communications, Tele-Communications, Cypress Communications, Viacom, Cablecom-General, Time-Life Broadcasting, Television Communications, and National Transvideo.

The white middle class that manages and operates major educational, social, and cultural institutions (that is, schools, colleges, universities, foundations, theaters, museums, and churches) is actively vying to dictate public programming policies for cable systems, including those serving black communities.

These two groups—white capitalists and the white middle-class intellectuals, managers and technocrats who have worked so effectively together in controlling and operating everything from the Pentagon to the poverty programs (at a handsome return to each group)—are now moving toward an accommodation of interests in this new communications field. If this act is consummated, the promise and the potential of CATV as an instrument for empowerment and development of underdeveloped ghetto communities will be seriously diminished, subverted, and perhaps entirely lost.

WHAT YOU SEE IS WHAT YOU GET

The requisite conditions for commodity control of resources and development are mass mobilization and unified action.

For example, urban renewal programs provided a significant opportunity for unified action by varied interest groups within urban black communities. Many ghetto communities united to stop these projects because of the insensitive treatment of residents by urban renewal agencies and the disruption of the community for the benefit of white profiteers. Serious attacks were made against the traditional system of planning and decision making from the local to the national level. Blacks demanded and secured important concessions affecting policy making, jobs, and other aspects of the urban renewal process.

Cable television is a better vehicle for achieving sizable gains in community organization, unification, control, and development. Several factors support this statement. First, cable television systems are not presently installed in black communities and central cities. Therefore, no entrenched interest group or power bloc can claim public protection for its investments. Second, franchises are issued by local, municipal governments, and the FCC has recommended the continuation of this process. Third, installation requires the actual stringing of cable on poles or the laying of cable underground along the streets of the ghetto. Individual hookups must be made from these trunk lines to homes and apartments, and outlets must be installed within these living units. Fourth, black communities are a substantial segment of the urban subscriber market. Fifth, the great potential of cable in technology, economics, and the power of mass influence is ultimately tied to cablecasting or local programming origination.

Sixth, cable will be used in a wide variety of applications, apart from entertainment programming. Education, health, welfare, safety, crime prevention, and police operations are a few of the likely uses.

Viewed together, these factors reveal significant opportunities for community participation and the imperative need for community control. Each of the listed factors will require a series of crucial political decisions at the local level. How will CATV be regulated? How many franchises will be awarded? Will a single franchise cover both system management and system programming? What are the qualifications for franchise applicants? How will franchise fees collected from CATV enterprises by the local government be used? Who will own and operate the systems? Who will determine the program content? Who will install the systems? Who will decide on the areas to be served? These are political issues that will be decided with or without community participation, but the options for black communities are still open. How long they remain open will depend on the initiative, ingenuity, and determination of community leaders and organizations.

Whether or not a franchise has been awarded, broad-scale community participation is possible. Early involvement in the franchise process is crucial. Local franchising involves several steps. The commission or city council usually adopts an ordinance giving the political body the legal powers to regulate CATV within the community—including procedures for awarding franchises. The ordinance may stipulate that public hearings must be held prior to franchise awards and that public notice must be given regarding the period established for filing franchise applications by interested parties. The ordinance may further state that multiple franchise awards will be made for various geographical areas within the city or county.

Community organizations should view the entire franchising process as an area of vital interest to their constituencies. Ideally, disenfranchised black communities should be consulted by the local government and included in the discussion and development of the ordinance and all other regulatory aspects of CATV systems for their communities. Needless to say, that is not happening. Local politicians, who are not well informed about CATV, have been selling the "communications birthright" of minority communities to the highest bidder.

Community participation should begin with a systematic, factual determination of the status of the franchising process within the local

316

government. The city attorney or council should be contacted for this information. If no ordinance has been adopted or franchise awarded, action should be taken to establish procedures for community inclusion in the policy-making process.

If an ordinance has been adopted and/or a franchise awarded, a detailed review and evaluation should be made to determine the provisions made for community participation in the monitoring, control, programming, and ownership of the system that serves them.

Most CATV franchises are nonexclusive agreements between the city and the cable operator. Thus, community groups may organized their own company and apply for a franchise covering the same territory as previously awarded.

As a last resort, it may be necessary for the community to exercise its veto power over those CATV projects that disenfranchise blacks. Legal and other forms of protest actions may be required to achieve community participation in the policy-making discussions and the achievement of community control and development objectives.

OPPORTUNITIES FOR COMMUNITY DEVELOPMENT

Cable television provides a substantial opportunity for urban minority communities to develop and control the most powerful cultural and social instrument in their communities. It can also provide a viable economic base and political leverage for power-deficient communities.

A partial listing of the wide variety of program uses will give some idea of the development possibilities:

Educational Uses

Video correspondence courses

Special education programs for unskilled workers, housewives, senior citizens, and handicapped persons

Home instruction for students who are temporarily confined

Adult education programs

Exchange of videotaped educational programs with other schools, for example, science, travel, and cultural programs

Interconnection of school systems to facilitate administration, teacher conferences, and seminars

Greater use of computerized testing and grading—thus giving teachers more time for individual instruction.

Health Uses

Interconnection of medical facilities (private offices, clinics, hospitals) to provide a wider range of consultation services to patients on an emergency or nonemergency basis—especially those without means of transportation

Wide dissemination of preventive medical and dental information to the community

Information programs concerning sanitation, sewage, rat control, garbage control, and similar problems

Legal and Consumer Uses

Listing of substandard and abandoned housing

Review of leases, agreements, and installment contracts

Discussion of labeling, marketing, pricing of food, drug, clothing, automobile, and other consumer products

Establishment of a "hotline" in legal aid and consumer protection agencies to provide immediate notice of fraudulent and exploitative practices

Use of videotaped records and depositions in nonjury cases.

Safety Uses

Installation of fire emergency and burglar systems in every home (these systems can operate over the same cable that brings in video signals)

Automatic gas, water, and electric meter readings

Rumor control

Disaster and emergency warning systems.

Cultural and Entertainment Uses

Minority-owned cable systems in the top 50 television markets alone would provide a major market as well as a distribution system for professionally produced films, plays, concerts, sports events, talk shows, and every other form of artistic, creative, and intellectual expression. There is no shortage of professional talent in the community—only the lack of a mass-based communications and distribution system could have promoted the Ali/Frazier fight. The white promoter of the fight, Jack Kent Cooke, is a major CATV owner.

Production of a black history series from the voluminous materials written by DuBois, Hughes, Malcolm X, Cullen, Woodson, Bennett, and thousands of minority historians, politicians, writers, poets, and leaders who have prepared records of their people's struggle. Such a series could now include an oral history of the important historical events by elders of the community.

IS THERE GOLD IN THE GHETTO?

The economic potential of CATV for minority communities should not be minimized or overlooked.

The urban ghettos in America comprise a compact, differentiated, and lucrative market for cable television—a conclusion that is supported by the phenomenal economic success of soul radio stations. This fact has not escaped the attention of Teleprompter, Time-Life, and other white entrepreneurs who are scrambling for ownership and control of cable systems in every large city.

Cable is uniquely suited to serve as a vehicle for economic development, because it is a subscriber-supported system. If an adequate number of households in the community purchases the service, sufficient income can be derived to maintain the system and to produce a profit.

Most community-based enterprises that depend on black customers (with the exception of white-controlled, high-risk illegal operations like the numbers and narcotics rackets) are small, marginal operations. Cable television is inherently a monopolistic enterprise. Although it is possible, it is highly unlikely that there will ever be more than one cable system serving a given community. Therefore, a black-owned system serving the entire inner city or just the black community would have a captive market—just as a white-owned system serving a ghetto community would have a captive market. (Soul television is not a remote possibility.) The point is that a community-owned system would not have to compete with white-owned systems downtown or in the suburbs as minority-owned grocery stores, restaurants, hotels, motels, clothing stores, drug stores, and so on, must.

SUBSCRIBERS—THE KEY TO CONTROL

As stated earlier, CATV has grown and developed in rural areas and small towns where no television was available or in areas where signal reception was poor.

The major incentives to residents of these rural and out-of-the-way communities to purchase cable services have been (1) better reception and (2) more signals or channels. Similar incentives exist in New York City and a few other major cities where tall buildings and atmospheric conditions cause poor signal quality. However, these conditions are not duplicated in the majority of black population centers. In most central cities there is fair to good signal quality and five to seven broadcast television channels are now available.

Ghetto residents are not likely to subscribe for cable services just to get better signal quality or more channels. Other reasons must be found. The emphasis on community control and development can provide some of the necessary incentives. The few soul radio stations owned by blacks and the total exclusion of blacks from ownership of television stations provide additional motives for local communities to prevent the continuation of these patterns in the cable communications industry. Blacks own none of the more than eight hundred licensed commercial television stations and only about twelve of the three hundred and fifty soul radio stations. Most black communities do not have a local newspaper or magazine produced by and for them.

The strongest incentive for local residents to subscribe to a community-owned and -controlled cable system may well be the opportunity to combat the insensitive programming of the existing media, the exploitative practices of soul radio stations, and the discriminatory hiring practices of the radio, television, and print media enterprises.

The National Advisory Commission on Civil Disorders reported that ". . . television and newspapers offered black Americans an almost totally white world; and far too often, acted and talked about blacks as if they neither read newspapers nor watched television."

As lawyer Donald K. Hill pointed out, however, ". . . The Commission's Report only touched upon the tremendous impact which the white culturally oriented media has on the black community. Although black Americans have the opportunity to fully observe the white world, communication flows in only one direction; blacks never see themselves as they perceive themselves, nor does communication flow from blacks to blacks. . . ."

The opportunity for ownership, control, management, and programming of CATV systems in the cities can be a powerful incentive to powerless minorities. If they are aware of the economic and social potential of this medium for their neighborhood, ghetto residents can be persuaded to subscribe to a community-owned system as a matter of enlightened self-interest. *Five dollars per month is probably the lowest price they can pay to secure a share in the wealth and power of the country.*

Collective ownership and control of systems will undoubtedly enhance the incentive to local residents to subscribe. Shares in the enterprise should be offered to local residents, just as AT&T offers its stock to its employees on a payroll deduction basis. CATV systems could apply a portion of the monthly service charge to the purchase of common stock by the subscribers.

Selling cable to urban residents who already have good reception and multiple channels will not be an easy proposition for whites or blacks. It should not be any more difficult, however, for minority entrepreneurs than for whites. In fact, it may be easier if the strong desire for community control is recognized and if entrepreneurs are willing to include the residents in the ownership.

STRATEGIES FOR DEVELOPING COMMUNITY SYSTEMS

Communications experts estimate the cost of wiring each of the major cities will range from $2 million to $20 million. Where will community-based corporations get the financing to build and operate CATV systems? Financing will not be simple or easy. On the other hand, it's not impossible. Joint ventures with white or nonresident minority investors are one possibility. Such investors are one possibility. Such investors might be banks, national and local church groups, wealthy individuals, insurance companies, savings and loan associations, high-income blacks (such as athletes and entertainers), and local or national industrial concerns.

Available resources within the black community should not be overlooked. In fact, that's where the initial organizing efforts should start. Many black professionals (doctors, dentists, ministers, lawyers, teachers, and businessmen) have relatively high incomes and accumulated savings that can be tapped. The professional class can also provide collateral assets in securing outside financing because of stable employment and high incomes. Black churches and insurance firms are also potential sources of equity capital.

Community development corporations and model cities programs deserve special attention and consideration because of their uniqueness. These groups, operating with both public and private funds, have been established to plan, design, and implement community redevelopment and development projects in the inner-city ghettos. One or the other of these entities, and sometimes both, are presently operating in most of the major cities. These groups usually have a working knowledge of city hall politics, the local financial community, the federal funding structure, and the national philanthropic community. They also have the staff and technical expertise to package a community proposal.

In short, both the community development corporation and the model cities programs are in a position to act as effective brokers for the community in planning, designing, and implementing a program for community control of CATV systems.

There are several approaches that could substantially reduce the financing burden on local communities. One approach that is practical for large cities like Washington, D.C., is to divide the city into four to six cable districts. If a franchise were awarded for each cable district, four to six cable companies with roughly 30 to 40,000 households could be established. Fifty-five percent market saturation in each district would result in a 15 to 20,000 subscriber system. Under this arrangement, each company would have to raise only $1 to $2 million in financing in lieu of one company attempting to raise $10 to $20 million to build a city-wide system.

Tom Atkins of Boston, one of the most knowledgeable public officials in the country on CATV, suggests that municipal governments should "wire up" the entire city and then take bids for system management and operation. This approach would eliminate the big cost of system construction and place community groups in a highly competitive position for franchise awards. This is an attractive proposition where multiple cable districts are established and the minority community is not fragmented into several predominantly white districts. Blacks, in particular, have been disenfranchised by such gerrymandering in the past.

A common practice in the CATV industry is the "turnkey" system of construction. Hardware manufacturers have financed, designed and built systems, turning the completed system over to the owner. Some hardware manufacturers prefer to enter into joint ventures for turnkey systems, providing from 30 to 50 percent of the financing. Care must be exercised, however, to assure that community-owned equity in the system is the controlling interest. The community corporation should also secure an option to buy out joint venture partners on a first-sale-offer basis.

PAY TELEVISION

Pay-TV May Hold Key to Cable-TV's Future

JAMES MacGREGOR

The Wall Street Journal, May 17, 1973. Reprinted with the permission of the Wall Street Journal, © Dow Jones & Company, Inc., 1973. James MacGregor is a staff reporter of *The Wall Street Journal*, specializing in mass media topics.

SAN DIEGO   Marguerite Dallin thinks pay-television is just great. There's no fuss and bother, and it saves a lot of money," she says. But down the street, Rose Lindner isn't so sure. "You know, the way we live, I'm not sure how much we'd use a service like that."

In this area, a lot more people seem to agree with Mrs. Dallin than with Mrs. Lindner. Or so says Jeffrey Nathanson, president of Optical Systems Inc., which offers a pay-TV package of movies and other events over the local cable-TV system. For every five demonstrations his salesmen give in homes here, he says, four salesmen walk out the door with checks for $32.50 in hand.

This is, quite possibly, the best news the cable-television industry has had in years. For most of those years, the industry has tirelessly promoted a future in which it would make the lowly TV set into everyman's movie theater, sports arena, shopping center, classroom, town hall and protection service, among other things.

And this is the year the cable-TV industry begins trying to make that future come true. A Federal Communications Commission freeze on cable construction in the nation's 100 largest cities has been lifted, opening the door for $3 billion to $4 billion in cable-TV capital spending over the next

MacGregor

decade. To many cablecasters, pay-television—and millions of enthusiasts like Mrs. Dallin—are needed to make the investment pay off.

"REASON FOR OUR VERY EXISTENCE"

"In these cities, it is absolutely essential to have additional services (beyond the improvement of normal TV signals that all cable-TV offers). Pay TV has to be the most important of these services in the near future," says Alfred M. Stern, president of Warner Cable Corp., a unit of Warner Communications Inc. Monroe Rifkin, president of American Television & Communications Corp., another major cablecaster, says "pay-TV may be the reason for our very existence in the large cities."

Pay-TV's success or failure is also of considerable interest to the motion-picture industry, which, even after its recent financial retrenching, sorely needs the extension of its box office that pay-TV could offer. The success is similarly of interest to professional sports teams, which need much the same things, and to television networks and local stations, which increasingly find it profitable to fill larger chunks of their time with movies and sports, the basic fare of pay-TV.

Thus, a lot of eyes are focused on the baker's dozen cities, from San Diego and Vancouver to Reston, Va., and Wilkes-Barre, Pa., where pay-TV operations are under way or planned for this year. In a year or so, it's generally agreed, what has happened in these cities should give a good idea of both the magnitude of pay-TV's future and its particular direction.

So far, the results of these pay-TV programs have been reasonably promising for cablecasters. Mr. Nathanson of Optical Systems says it will be at least August before his company can judge the success of its San Diego operation, and he declines to give interim figures on "penetration" or the percentage of potential subscribers actually enrolled. But Warner Cable's Mr. Stern says penetration is currently "about a third" in the first small cities where Warner's Gridtronics pay-cable system is being tested. (Three other cities were recently added.)

THE NUMBERS

Home Box Office Inc., a subsidiary of Time Inc. and Sterling Communications Inc., began offering a sports-and-movies package in

Wilkes-Barre in November with free installation and a month's free service. Predictably, "our phenomenal initial penetration rate was followed by a phenomenal disconnection rate" as the free months ran out, a spokesman says. He says the "penetration rate has leveled off for the moment at about 30%" of those who've been offered the service.

That 30% figure has considerable economic significance. Cable-television is simply a means of transmitting TV signals through wires rather than through the air, as conventional broadcasters do. It grew up in mostly rural areas, where terrain, weather and the like made over-the-air signals either weak or nonexistent. Paul Kagan, whose firm, Paul Kagan Associates, studies the cable-TV industry, says that, as a rule, a rural cable-TV system that enrolls 30% of the homes passed by its cables "can service its debt and pay its own way."

But when that penetration rises to 55% or 60%, as it does in many of the older, rural systems, TelePrompTer Corp. president William J. Bresnan says it's reasonable to expect a system to return 50% of its revenues in income before interest, depreciation and taxes, or 15% to 25% in net earnings. A report by Arthur D. Little, Inc., the research firm, estimates these cable-TV systems provide a 20% to 30% annual return on investment.

Most of the current 6.5 million cable-TV subscribers live in problem-reception areas of this sort. But the equation changes considerably when you consider the large urban areas opened by the lifting of the FCC freeze. (Of course, construction began in some of the largest cities, such as Manhattan and San Diego, before the freeze went into effect.)

For one thing, building costs rise faster than population density in many of these cities, so it costs a cablecaster more to wire up to a potential subscriber (cable franchises normally require that all homes in an area be passed by the cable). Warner Cable's Mr. Stern says saturation of 35–45% is required to make money in larger cities.

It's also tougher to persuade city folk to subscribe to cable-TV. The report of the Sloan Commission on Cable Communications in 1972 estimated only 15% of potential subscribers in large cities could be persuaded to subscribe just to improve reception, which is a major selling point in rural areas. That percentage is obviously higher in cities like San Diego, where reception is, in many neighborhoods, just plain awful.

One attraction cablecasters can offer is the so-called "distant signal," which is the programming of a TV station outside the viewer's normal reception area. A recent FCC ruling allows cable-TV systems in many of the larger markets to import one to three distant signals, depending on how many stations already operate locally.

Mr. Kagan says that in 55 of the top 100 markets, only three commercial-TV stations exist, allowing considerable latitude for distant signal importation. He feels "many of the top markets can be sold in the traditional way (signal improvement plus distant-signal importation)," leaving a relatively small number of populous markets that will require something extra to sell cable-TV.

MOVIES AND SPORTS

Others aren't so optimistic about the value of distant-signal importation in big cities. As almost all major markets have three network-affiliated stations, distant signals must come from independent stations. In New York and Los Angeles, which have a dozen independent stations between them, these stations split up a quarter or less of the TV audience, leading critics to suggest that their schedules, which run old off-network reruns and still older movies, won't draw many new subscribers to cable.

If cablecasters are unlikely to reach an economic penetration with material they can pluck off the air, they'll have to turn to things they cannot pluck off the air. They pay for such programming, and normally charge their subscribers for it (though the Manhattan franchises run by Sterling Communications and TelePrompTer offer subscribers free movies and pro basketball and hockey games). Normally, a subscriber pays $20 to $25 for a converter that sits atop his TV set and activates the program he pays for. He'll usually pay $5 to $7 for a monthly subscription, or $1 to $3 for individual events, or some combination of the two—in addition to the $6 or so he is already paying just to have cable in his house.

Optical Systems in San Diego will offer both live entertainment events (anything from rock concerts to Shakespearean plays) and self-improvement courses (learning Spanish, speed-reading or guitar-picking) this fall. But for the most part, pay-TV's menu will consist of the two staples: movies and sports events. "Existing software will be the principal vehicle," says Warner Cable's Mr. Stern, "because quite justifiably, nobody is willing to take the risk of creating new things for the small number of urban homes you can reach today." "Software" is jargon for programming.

WILL THE FORMULA WORK?

Warner Cable's parent, Warner Communications, also owns the Warner Bros. movie studio, while Paramount Pictures parent, Gulf & Western Industries Inc., also has a large interest in a smaller cablecaster, Athena Communications. Other movie studios are also interested in pay-cable as a new step in their distribution process: first the movie theaters, then cable-TV, then the TV networks, and finally syndicated sales to networks or individual stations.

Arnold Rimberg, a securities analyst at Mitchell, Hutchins Inc., is among those who believe the formula will work. He cites the greater disposable income of people, "the need for greater selectivity of entertainment" than what is offered by the TV networks, and the attractiveness of cable to people who "don't care for the time and money it takes to get a babysitter, get dressed up, drive to a theater, pay to park and get into the theater."

Similarly, professional sports clubs view pay-TV as a logical extension of their box office to people who, for whatever reason, won't come out to the game. The most marketable sports event available for cable, National Football League home games, are "blacked out" in their local areas by current NFL rules. The NFL has made it clear that rights to such games won't be sold to cable-TV until cablecasters can more than make good the loss of audience for other games shown on regular TV at that time, and resultant loss of revenue.

There are, however, some noticeable clouds on this horizon. One is that pay-cable's market opening, at least for movies, is being squeezed a little at both ends. At one end, Mr. Nathanson of Optical Systems says, "We are getting virtually all the major movies, after they finish their theater runs. But with a real smash, obviously they (the movie studios) will milk all they can out of it before releasing it to us."

At the other end, the lag between theater runs and TV-network premier for major movies has shrunk in recent years from about four or five years to as little as 18 months after theatrical release, as the TV networks bid higher and higher for top attractions. Viewing the trend, a few analysts

MacGregor

327

fear cable-TV may wind up in a bidding war with either the theater owners or the TV networks for the best attractions.

CONCERN AT NBC

In a speech earlier this month to National Broadcasting Co. affiliates, NBC president Julian Goodman staked out the ground the TV networks would occupy, presumably before Congress, if such a confrontation came to pass: "Our concern is that cablevision may be pushed in a direction that is contrary to the public interest, simply to counterbalance television. That push can come if cable is allowed to siphon off the television staples it is reaching for—sports and feature films." Current FCC rules preclude "siphoning" of movies and sports events now on over-the-air TV, but it's expected those rules will give way to eventual legislation of an as yet unknown form.

Cablecasters concede there's one significant gap in the pay-cable evidence to date. Pay-TV pilot operations so far have been instituted in systems with very high percentages of homes already hooked up on the cable, in part because the cost of failure in a relatively unsaturated system would be huge. Selling pay-TV in a market where most homes have cable already is quite different from selling cable and pay-TV together in a completely new market. So no one can say for sure that pay-TV would push any given new cable system from the red into the black or beyond.

Frank Biondi, a TelePrompTer business analyst, argues that the profitability of any given cable-TV service must be viewed in the context of the high cost of running a cable past and into a viewer's home; once the basic cable-TV "black box" is inside the home, innumerable services, including pay-TV, can be sold to the viewers. So even though one of the services appears unprofitable by itself, it may still be desirable if it helps recoup the cost of wiring the home and makes possible the sale of later services at relatively little cost.

TWO BASIC QUESTIONS

Meanwhile, within the cable-TV industry, there's considerable concern over two basic questions. What role should the cablecaster play in pay-TV? And in what form should pay-TV be sold to the viewer? The latter has more interest to the viewer, the former to the investor.

At one end of the pay-TV ownership spectrum is Warner Cable's approach through its Gridtronics subsidiary; Warner simply does everything itself. At the other end is the "leased-channel" approach of Optical Systems in San Diego. Optical Systems provides the hardware, the marketing and the programming; Cox Cable takes 10% of Optical Systems' gross revenues in return for making the channels available in cities where it has the franchise. For Cox and other cablecasters, this type of arrangement minimizes both their capital commitment and their risk if the pay-TV venture falls on its face. It also minimizes their profit if the pay-TV venture is a financial success.

Somewhere between is the "supplier" arrangement of Time's Home Box Office subsidiary in Wilkes-Barre. There, the cablecaster, Service Electric Corp., provides the hardware and (with Home Box Office aid) does the marketing. Home Box Office provides the programming and takes up to 58% of the gross revenues, with the balance going to the cablecaster.

On the viewer front, the big question is whether to have people pay by the month for a whole flock of events, or by the individual event. The per-event theory finds champions at Viacom, where executive vice president James Leahy says it "would make us a newer and more efficient version of the movie theater." Here, the viewer would pay only for what he actually watched; the sports team or movie studio would rise or fall on how many people its product would draw to the TV set, just as it does now in stadiums and movie theaters; the cablecaster would take his percentage of the gross.

If Mr. Leahy wants to be a better movie theater, Mr. Stern of Warner Cable wants to be a better TV network. He believes offering viewers a full package of TV attractions conforms with their present TV viewing habits, especially the "impulse-viewing" instinct.

If, as often happens, the eventual outcome is somewhere between the extremes, the Chinese-menu approach of Optical Systems may be popular. In San Diego, once a viewer pays his basic service charge, he has a variety of options at a variety of prices: A "season pass" for everything offered, or a sports package, or a movie package; or he can select various individual items in advance. If the viewing urge strikes late, he can simply dial a special phone number and then plug a special "wild card" into the converter on top of his set. Immediately, his selection appears. He'll be billed later.

What's to prevent him from using his ticket over again? Pay-TV operators all have some sort of basic security arrangement. The most intriguing is that of TheatreVisioN, a venture of Chromalloy-American Corp. TheatreVisioN's black box swallows up the ticket and chews it until it's unusable.

Does the American Family
Need Another Mouth to Feed?

ARTHUR R. TAYLOR

Reprinted with permission of Columbia Broadcasting System, Inc., from a booklet produced by CBS/Broadcast Group, undated. Copyright Columbia Broadcasting System, Inc. Arthur R. Taylor is president of CBS.

From the invention of movable type to the development of television, every potential advance in communications has had to offer its services in the marketplace of ideas. The ones that have succeeded have always represented a broadening of service, either by providing new forms of information and entertainment, or by introducing techniques for wider distribution, or simply by reducing the cost to the point where more people could afford the service. The most successful of all communications media in this nation's history, television, meets all these criteria.

Today we are confronted with another self-proclaimed revolution in communications; it is one that meets none of the criteria. It is not providing new forms of information and entertainment, it is not expanding the total audience for those communications and, far from decreasing the cost, it is seeking to raise the cost while decreasing the audience.

This proposition is called pay cable television. It meets none of the criteria because it is sheltered from the normal American standards of fair competition. As a result, there is a real possibility that millions of American families will be denied the movies, sports events and other television attractions that now form an integral part of their lives. Millions of others will be allowed to view these attractions only at the expense of a large and continual drain on their family finances.

What we are speaking of, in short, is less a revolution than a sneak attack on the family pocketbook. The basic notion of pay cable television, as it is now developing, is nothing more than that the average television viewer should pay for the programs that he now receives free. The effect of this change in the free broadcasting industry would be an incalculable disservice to the American viewing public.

Let us agree at the outset that we have no quarrel with the growth of cable television in its original form. We welcome it for the two real contributions it was intended to make to our society. The first is obvious. Because of remoteness, mountains, skyscrapers, and the like, broadcast television cannot promise every viewer a perfect picture at every moment. Cable television often can promise and deliver better reception of local, over-the-air signals to its subscribers.

Cable television systems have already been built in most places where they are necessary to provide a good television signal. Now that industry is turning toward larger cities where television reception is, by and large, rather good. To attract subscribers in these cities, cable operators must offer another service.

This brings us to cable television's second potential contribution. There are only so many channels on the broadcast television dial. Broadcasters are charged with serving mass audiences; there is simply not enough time in the day to offer all the programs for which small, specialized audiences exist. Cable television offers an abundance of channels—24 to 40 in many places, with reports that the number may someday rise to 100. Thus, cable television can bring to the public a wide variety of services that broadcast television does not offer at this time, ranging from presently untelevised cultural events to new services like shopping-by-television. Perhaps most important, cable's multiplicity of channels promises access to a vital medium of special communication to such groups as doctors, educators, local governments and community organizations.

Cable television's founders consistently said that they would develop new programs and services. However, most cable systems have never originated programs of their own. A number of others which did so at one time in anticipation of rules that would require origination halted their origination activities after it became clear the rules would not immediately be implemented. Instead, the industry's current leaders have announced their intention to concentrate their efforts on the presentation, for a price,

Taylor

331

of exactly the same type of movies and sporting events people presently see on free television.

If pay cable television service were entirely separate and independent of over-the-air television, it would be a legitimate competitor. Broadcasters would meet it in the market place, just as they meet newspapers and movie theaters and other media. The public would choose between the services offered by each.

Cable television, however, is not this sort of competitor. The programs that it uses to gain entry into the American household for its wires and its tuning box are not its own, but those of free television. Once it has gained that entry, cable television proposes to add more charges.

To put this proposition in its simplest form, consider the football fan who subscribes to a cable service in the hopes of improving his television reception of football games (or any other program) broadcast by CBS. For this improved picture he contracts to pay a fixed monthly fee. This football fan then brings the cable television wires and tuning box into his living room. As the cable service adds subscribers by promising to deliver better reception of free television programs it is creating an asset—a distribution system.

The fees cable television has received for distributing free broadcast television programs (for which privilege incidentally it has paid nothing to the free broadcaster to begin with) have allowed the cable system to gain access to an audience which is exclusively its own. The cable system can then proceed to approach the distributors of programs now seen on free television, calculating that by charging its subscribers an additional fee for the exclusive right to see certain programs, it can generate sufficient revenues to outbid CBS for the rights to football games or movies or other forms of entertainment. Cable television systems can do that right now under existing regulations. All the cable system has to do is include the games in its locally approved general monthly charge to its subscribers.

Now our friend the football fan must pay more to see the football games he used to see free, or he must do without the games. His friends who had not subscribed to cable television would not be able to see the games at all. If our fan had not wanted to see free television broadcasts of football games more clearly he would never have subscribed to the cable system, but it is his very subscription to this system which could permit the cable system to take these games off free television and to increase his monthly

subscription charges.

It is important to understand the several meanings of the phrase "pay television." In the most basic sense, all cable television is pay television. Every subscriber must pay for the privilege of receiving what is furnished on the cable. But cable subscribers may also pay, either separately or as part of their regular monthly charge, for other programs. Some of those programs lack the mass audiences needed to justify their appearance on free television. It is a legitimate goal for pay television to bring these specialized attractions into homes that otherwise would be denied them.

The form of pay television to which we are specifically opposed is that by which free television's attractions are to be diverted to pay cable television. We use the term "siphoning" to describe this process. It is a descriptive term and an apt one. When gasoline is siphoned from one car to another, the car that receives the fuel may work beautifully, but the other is at a severe disadvantage.

The economic logic of siphoning was never better illustrated than when Joe Frazier fought Muhammad Ali for the heavyweight boxing title in 1971. About 1.5 million people paid more than $16 million to see the fight on closed-circuit television in auditoriums in the United States and Canada. Overseas, hundreds of millions saw the fight on free television, but returned only a fraction as much revenue to the promoters. That sort of lesson is easy for a promoter to remember. What benefits a promoter, however, doesn't always benefit the public. Throughout the country there are innumerable areas where families are so isolated that it is uneconomic for cable operators to build systems. These predominantly rural families depend on television as virtually their sole source of entertainment. They would be denied many of television's most popular attractions—no matter how much money they were willing to pay—if those attractions should be siphoned off to pay cable television at a time when no cable system existed in their areas.

The situation would hardly be better for families in areas where cable television systems did exist. For the first time, the amount and kind of television they could watch would be determined by their financial situation. *TV Guide* has already found families paying more than $20 a month for a very limited pay television schedule. With the addition of a full line of sporting events and movies to the schedule, many families could have to pay $30 or more every month for the program features they now receive free.

Even for the affluent, this is a needless cost. But how many less affluent families can afford at all that large an inroad into their limited spending power? The burden would be a heavy one for young couples just starting to build a family, and for older ones living on fixed pensions and Social Security benefits. The burden would be heavier still in communities in which unemployment and poverty are widespread; and a great many of our citizens live under exactly these conditions.

The effect of siphoning would be to make these minorities into second-class citizens in terms of access to their basic source of entertainment and information.

One in every four American families has an income under $5000 a year; but the best information available to us indicates that only one in eight families that subscribe to cable television has an income below that level. More than one family in every three has an income under $7000; but among families that buy original sports and movies on cable television, only one in nine has an income under $7000. These comparisons suggest that the economic discrimination inherent in pay television has already begun.

This discrimination is a matter of public concern, because cable television, like broadcast television, is a public communications medium. Acting through the Congress, our nation has determined that these media should be used in the public interest. It is hard to imagine how the public interest would be served if millions of viewers were denied access to television entertainment and information programming, while millions of others were compelled to pay for programs they now receive free. We are determined that this must not happen.

Based on performance to date, if pay television sports and movies were offered to each of the nation's 7.8 million cable television subscribers, about a fourth would sign up. If each of those homes paid the modest fee of one dollar for a movie, and if the cable television operator split that dollar 50-50 with the movie producer, the movie producer could receive about a million dollars for the pay television rights to his movie. Free television presently pays about $750,000 to show a typical movie two or three times on a national network. In other words, without adding a single new subscriber, cable television already possesses the bargaining potential to buy almost any movie it wants. We could perform the same calculation for the rights to sporting events; the conclusion would be the same.

The Federal Communications Commission has rules intended to protect the public from this siphoning of popular free television attractions. In recent years they have provided in part that most movies can be shown on pay television only if less than two years, or more than 10 years (under certain limitations), have elapsed since their first theatrical release, and that sporting events may be shown only if they have not appeared on free television within the previous two years. Series-type programs may not be siphoned at all. But the Commission was asked in 1973 to weaken these rules, even though they already contained loopholes so great as to offer grossly inadequate protection to both broadcasters and their public.

To cite a prominent example, a cable television system can circumvent the rules entirely by integrating its pay television charges into the basic locally approved monthly price for its subscribers, rather than charging for pay television attractions on a per-program or per-channel basis. In New York the cable television systems serving Manhattan offer New York Rangers and Knickerbockers home games as part of this basic monthly charge; recently the cable operators asked the city for a 33⅓ percent increase in that basic monthly charge. If siphoning is permitted, that is the pattern we are likely to see.

Even though keeping major attractions free and available to the entire public would seem obviously to be in the public interest, some FCC commissioners appear to look favorably on pay cable television as a means to further the Commission's stated intention to "get cable going." No one disputes the goal because the social value of the diversity cable television might offer the public is incontestable. But there are two flaws in the notion that siphoning is needed to get cable going. The first is the growth cable has already achieved. It has today enrolled one out of every nine television homes in the United States, compared with one out of every 700 twenty years ago; it is estimated that in another 10 years cable will claim at least one out of every five homes, and perhaps as many as three out of every five.

Second, if a cable operator can earn huge profits by diverting the attractions of free television to his own uses, what incentive has he to develop diverse new programming? Cable operators often argue that siphoning is necessary, because the resultant profits would support this new programming especially in the public service area. That argument startled Congressman Torbert Macdonald, Chairman of the House Subcommittee on Communications and Power, who told the industry late in 1973, "When the cable industry promised the country a great diversity of programs and services, they never mentioned that it could be attained only by doubling the admission fee."

We have always believed that public service is a specific obligation of any broadcaster, not a favor to be granted in return for profitable concessions by governmental entities. However, if that is to become the battleground,

Taylor

let us note that free television profits have supported a vast range of public service programs of very material social value. Television's news coverage of elections, moon landings and wars has touched the lives of hundreds of millions of people, while its spectrum of public affairs, cultural, educational and religious programs has in a quieter way also contributed much to the worth of our society.

Pay television advocates often argue that free television isn't really free because the cost of the advertising is added to the cost of the products viewers purchase. To the contrary, most advertisers believe and can demonstrate that their advertising makes possible mass distribution that brings down the cost of products. When advertisers are denied commercial time on television, they do not reduce their prices; they spend their money on other media or marketing techniques. But when they do advertise on television, their expenditures allow the public to receive their preferred forms of entertainment and information without cost.

Representative Macdonald has emphasized "the cardinal principle that what is now being offered to TV audiences at no extra charge won't be forced off the air into a coin box in the home, and thus restricted to those who can and will pay for it." In this society, our first hope would be that this principle could have been implemented through the free competition for program attractions between two separate, independent media—broadcast television and cable television. As we have seen, the institutional structure which presently governs the relationship of these two media makes any genuine competition impossible.

If the present structure is maintained, only government regulation will protect the public from having to pay for those attractions. We do not believe the anti-siphoning rules issued in 1972 provide sufficient protection for the public. But they do contain sound principles that belong in any overall effort to protect the public interest in its favorite attractions. These rules should be retained and the loopholes in them should be plugged. There are three specific additional steps that warrant very serious consideration as protections of the public interest.

First, cable television's liabilities under the copyright laws must be clearly defined. This definition may be provided by cases now before the courts, or specific legislation may be required. In either case the principle must be established that cable television, like every other entertainment medium, may transmit a program to an audience only when it has obtained permission of that program's copyright owner.

Second, pay cable television should not be permitted to siphon any program that has appeared on free television in the past five years. That is the standard the FCC has imposed upon over-the-air pay television for sports programs, and we believe it is equally appropriate to pay cable television. By pay cable, we mean any form of cable television that offers programs otherwise unavailable to its audience, whether the audience is required to pay for the programs by the event, by the channel or by the calendar period.

Third, before the owners of programs that have not appeared on free television in the past five years may sell those programs exclusively to pay cable systems that also carry free television's broadcasts, the programs must be offered to over-the-air free television. Such offers must be at a cost that is equitable and consistent with what free television pays for comparable attractions. There are difficult questions inherent in such a rule, but there is no reason a standard cannot be formulated that fairly balances public and private interests. Once implemented, such a rule would ensure that, no matter how public tastes might shift, the most popular attractions would be accessible without cost to every television viewer, no matter where he might live or what income he might have.

But as we discuss means to safeguard the public interest, let us remember that the public, too, must be heard from. Broadcasters and cable operators, theater owners and movie producers are quite able to make their positions known. But it is the public that will be most affected if its favorite attractions are diverted from free television to pay cable television, and it is the public's willingness or unwillingness for that to happen which must be communicated to legislators and regulators, in Washington and closer to home.

PUBLIC
BROADCASTING

Public radio and television have been considered the "alternate media"
—they represent the alternative to commercial broadcasting. Audiences
can turn to public broadcasting for programming not available from the
advertising-supported system. These public broadcasting stations,
formerly known as "educational stations," offer news, documentaries,
discussions, drama, and instructional programs on varied subjects.

Capital and operational funds for stations generally have come from the
licensing organization, a college or university, or a municipal, state, or
community administrative entity. A large amount of money was provided
by the Ford Foundation in the early years of educational television to
develop facilities and to support programming. The Department of Health,
Education, and Welfare in the Federal government makes matching funds
available annually for television facilities grants. But such support was not
given at a level high enough to build and support a high quality, truly
alternative system that would reach all of the American people.
A broader financial base was needed, and educational television leaders
sought and received federal legislation providing an organizational
structure and a financial commitment to the media. A new era began with

the Public Broadcasting Act of 1967, signed by President Lyndon B. Johnson. While it satisfied the educational community in many ways because it embodied the greater federal commitment that had been sought, the legislation was weak in that it failed to provide long-term financing. It required annual congressional appropriations. Tying the financial base of public broadcasting to annual approval by Congress and the president has created problems concerning governmental and political review of programming policy and practices.

Les Brown's article summarizes this financial problem and ties it into the Nixon administration's efforts, when Clay Whitehead was director of the Office of Telecommunications Policy, to "dismantle" PBS and to put control of public television back into the hands of local broadcasters. He also raises, in passing, the issue of corporate support of programming over public television stations. John O'Connor picks up that theme and suggests that the dependency of public television upon programs financed and *produced* by corporations is a serious weakness in public broadcasting. He, too, attributes the problem to the lack of adequate long-range financial support, independent of governmental control, for a national public broadcasting system.

Tania Simkin's article on public radio offers not only an historical perspective of this medium and its current state but also suggests new prospects for public broadcasting.

BIBLIOGRAPHICAL ESSAY

Two useful books on public television are Robert J. Blakely, *The People's Instrument: A Philosophy of Programming for Public Television,* 1971, and Fred Powledge, *Public Television: A Question of Survival,* 1972, both published by Public Affairs Press, Washington, D.C. Blakely's study concentrates on the creation of a programming philosophy for public television; Powledge deals with the need for financing in his 46-page study. A typescript study by Wilbur Schramm and Lyle Nelson, *The Financing of Public Television,* Aspen Program on Communications and Society, Aspen, Colorado, 1972, gives an excellent review of the various arguments advanced for supporting public television. While our readings indicate that the government finally has come to realize that long-range, reasonable support for public broadcasting is necessary, students will need to review these books to see how public broadcasting has arrived at its current economic position. They also will need to continue reading *Public Telecommunications Review* to keep abreast of changes in the field. Another excellent, ongoing source of information on public broadcasting, as well as commercial broadcasting, is the annual *Survey of Broadcast Journalism,* published by Alfred I. Dupont and Columbia University, New York, and edited by Marvin Barrett, issued under various titles since 1968 and 1969. For a recent summary of the effort to create the present public broadcast system, see John Macy, Jr., *To Irrigate a Wasteland: The Struggle to Shape a Public Television System in the United States,* University of California Press, Berkeley, Calif., 1974. The appendices to this book also are valuable for organizational and statistical information on the system.

Most people in public broadcasting were worried about the Nixon Administration's resistance to long-range financing of the medium; some were concerned about the administration's attempt to break up PBS in the process and to restore economic and programming control to local station managers. Sources mentioned above deal with some of these concerns. The article by Les Brown, however, deals specifically with the *effects* of the new funding arrangements on PBS programming. It deserves careful reading. In his article, Brown raises a problem that has received little public discussion, that is, the influence corporate support of programming has over public broadcasting. John J. O'Connor's article on the potential effects of such support is included to elaborate on Brown's statement. Just as public radio (see Tania Simkin's article) has received little attention in the professional and scholarly journals, so too has the issue of corporate support for programming received little attention. We hope that reprinting these articles will stimulate further investigation and publication in both areas.

STUDY QUESTIONS

1. Elaborate on what you believe is H. Rex Lee's point in his statement that "You would be naïve to believe, though, that permanent financing will free you from the potential of government interference. Only by fully exercising your rights and responsibilities as individuals and groups will you be able to do this." Do you view this as a threat by a man who was an FCC Commissioner at the time?

2. Since public broadcasting stations are grounded in education, public affairs, and quality drama programs, isn't the FCC asking for unnecessary work and expense by requiring such stations to undertake formal studies to ascertain community needs?

3. In what ways can public broadcasting serve to (1) upgrade audience tastes and (2) improve programming on *commercial* television?

4. Should federal funds be used for the support of public television? Why or why not?

5. What are the distinct problems of public radio compared with public television?

6. Do you feel that public television compromises its noncommercial status by accepting program grants? What is your reaction to public television accepting programs produced by corporations interested in improving their public image?

Public Telecommunications: The Task of Managing Miracles

H. REX LEE

Reprinted from *Public Telecommunications Review*, vol. 1, 3 (December, 1973), with permission of the publisher. Copyright 1973 by Public Telecommunications Review. At the time he delivered this address at the 1973 national convention of public broadcasters, H. Rex Lee was the FCC commissioner whose name was most often associated with public telecommunications; he was, in fact, the Commission's officially designated educational commissioner. He resigned from the Commission late in 1973 after five years of service.

[In late 1966], following a long campaign led by the NAEB [National Association of Educational Broadcasters] and others, President Johnson signed into law the Public Broadcasting Act. At the ceremonies in the East Room of the White House, the late President said, "Today our problem is not making miracles, but *managing* them." He then urged that we [the FCC] stake a claim on the combined resources of communications, and enlist the computer and the satellite, as well as radio and television, in the cause of education. Those were the words of a man who fervently believed in education and understood how the media could be used to advance human knowledge and help solve some of our pressing problems.

Perhaps it is timely to ask how effectively and efficiently have the miracles of telecommunications been managed? And where do we go from here?

Those can be unsettling questions. If some of you are squirming in your seats, let me assure you that I'm not standing here in the guise of a friendly government official who in reality fears the true independence of a strong public broadcasting system. Rather, I ask these questions as a long-time admirer and supporter of your efforts.

It's my sincere hope that public broadcasting may soon come of age without pressure from any outside source. That will only happen after, first, you resolve your internal dissensions and shift your attention to the people you were intended to serve—some 210 million Americans. And secondly, when you recognize that you are no longer educational broadcasters but public telecommunicators, and rely not just on rhetoric but the many tools of communications to deliver information and programming.

The time is ripe—and long overdue—for this to happen.

Never have so many well-intentioned, dedicated, and experienced people been given so great an opportunity to use these modern means of communications and had so little effect on education.

Never have so many public entities and organizations cajoled, argued, and maneuvered for their own points of view with so little impact on their audiences.

Never have so many people spent so much time talking about what public broadcasting might become—and had so much trouble translating their words into action. (I sometimes wish we could have a new matching grant formula: for every 100 hours of debate about who or what you are, the public could be guaranteed one hour of quality programming.)

Six years after the Public Broadcasting Act became law, you're still trying to define your basic goals. If a commercial broadcaster were to manage his business with the same indecision that plagues public broadcasting, he would possess not a license to print money but a one-way ticket to bankruptcy.

The blame for this sad state of affairs cannot and must not be placed entirely on your financially weak shoulders. You did not bring many of these problems upon yourselves. Unfortunately, public broadcasting became tangled in the web of a fierce anti-media assault. (Though, in fairness, it might be said some of your most vocal critics had respect for you. Otherwise, they would not have become so angry with your programming and organizational structure.)

While stressing that local stations should be the bedrock of public broadcasting (which they should), the Administration sought only a one-year authorization—a sure-fire guarantee for weak local stations.

While encouraging the development of programming to serve local needs, you were urged to stay away from public affairs—a subtle form of censorship.

While urging the further use of television in the classrooms, your efforts were undercut by insufficient funding at all levels.

If we have learned anything from the past two years, it is that public broadcasting must be adequately financed on a permanent long-term basis and that it must be completely free from governmental interference. The trauma of recent events proves this conclusively.

The CPB Long-Range Financing Task Force Report is a step in the right direction. But it will be only that—a mere step—until legislation is signed into law. Permanent financing must be of sufficient magnitude to remove your yearly funding hassle.

You would be naive to believe, though, that permanent financing will free you from the potential of governmental interference. Only by fully exercising your rights and responsibilities as individuals and groups will you be able to do that. At present this is a difficult but crucial necessity. The basic ideals of a free press—both print and broadcast—are being challenged by some people in all branches of government and other quarters as well.

Public broadcasting has felt the full thrust of these attacks, and their effect was—sad to note—very evident. In this regard, it is well to remember Benjamin Franklin's warning to the colonial newspapers; "They that can give up essential liberty to obtain a little temporary safety deserve neither liberty nor safety."

Our country was uniquely founded upon a constitutional premise guaranteeing a free press. It is the cornerstone of the democratic process. Now at this time of grave national crisis there is an even greater need for full, robust debate. However, the basic tenets of a free press are not entirely understood by the public. Rather than caring about their right to know (no matter what the message), some would rather stifle the bearer of bad tidings.

Public TV and radio have the duty, as broadcasters and leaders in their communities, to bring home to the American people the issues of a free

Lee

343

press in terms they can fully understand. Commercial broadcasters and the printed press have taken on this task. You must also. Our nation must be awakened to the fact that their basic liberties are threatened every time the press is threatened.

A recent fairness complaint about a public TV show raised the question about our jurisdiction over CPB. We denied the fairness complaint, but sought comments from you about this question. We just issued a ruling which declared that the statutory language of Section 398 of the Communications Act prohibited us from overseeing any of the Corporation's activities. We declined to exercise jurisdiction with respect to the so-called "super-fairness" doctrine of Section 396. We did, however, rule that the individual stations are fully responsible for all programs broadcast— regardless of the source of funds for these programs.

By the way, you should be congratulated for broadcasting perhaps the greatest civic lesson—the Watergate hearings. However, let it be said that this program which fell into your laps and increased your ratings and contributions does not excuse you from broadcasting more national and public affairs programs. If anything, your success with the hearings should be an incentive to carry more programs directed towards the needs of your community.

Our recently issued *Notice of Inquiry and Proposed Rulemaking* concerning ascertainment of community needs is directed toward that end. Unlike your commercial counterparts, you have not had any formal ascertainment requirements. Nevertheless, the law is clear that you have an affirmative obligation to determine the needs and interests of your communities and to program to serve those needs. Many stations presently assess community needs as a matter of policy, and have found it to be an effective way of stimulating a dialogue with their communities.

The crucial question, though, is whether formal ascertainment requirements should be imposed on educational broadcast applicants for initial licenses and renewals and, if so, what specific obligations should be assessed. We want to hear how you can best ascertain those needs and whether there should be special procedures for determining instructional needs as opposed to general community needs. We also want to know if radio and television stations should be treated differently.

In no event do we wish to impose requirements that will be costly, time-consuming, or ineffective.

There's another area of concern. Several noncommercial broadcasters recently heard from the Commission regarding their poor minority employment records. More stations can expect to hear from us unless they improve their hiring efforts at all levels.

Your accomplishments in this regard have been less than commendable. As Dr. Everett Parker's recent public TV study indicated, six states still have no minorities in official or managerial positions. Public radio's record probably isn't much better.

I fail to see how public broadcasters and their national organizations can self-righteously seek public support when their minority employment records indicate a less-than-vigorous effort to advance our national goals.

In terms of programming, public broadcasters should also take note. Ask yourselves, whether or not most public TV and radio fare has measured up to the goals of diversity and quality foreseen by the Public Broadcasting Act.

This is an important issue to the American people. Because when you present such an outstanding program or series as *Hollywood Television Theater, V.D. Blues*, the local newsrooms, *Sesame Street, The Electric Company*, and radio's *All Things Considered*, you have an immense impact on both commercial broadcasting and the public.

This has been a somewhat unexpected dividend. You have become a valuable experimental proving ground for innovative programming ideas and concepts—many of which have later been tried on commercial TV.

I cannot stress too much that you—the public broadcaster—should be the bellwether for the entire industry—both commercial and noncommercial. It is up to you to demonstrate that well-designed children's programs can attract an audience, that innovation is good for business, and that non-violent and wholesome programming can gain sponsorship and ratings. When you demonstrate these—by action and by serious discussions within the community—you put great pressure on the commercial system to meet this standard of excellence.

You can succeed by example where the FCC and Congress would fail by exhortation. And this is the way it should be.

Public broadcasting has painfully learned that quality programming not only takes time and money, but also an environment which is totally free from political and artistic constraints. Creative talent cannot and will not thrive in an atmosphere fraught with tension and antagonisms as parties seek to settle standing disputes. These disagreements can and must be resolved so you can get on with the task of serving and enlightening the American people.

The time has also come to rekindle the dreams of the founding architects of public broadcasting: to find ways to build a network for knowledge—to establish a system based not just on broadcast facilities, but one that employs every economical means of storing and distributing information that an individual or institution can use.

Whether you like it or not, you are no longer educational broadcasters. You are in the new profession of public telecommunications. Only by recognizing your true role will you be ready to take advantage of broadcast and cable TV, satellites, videocassettes, ITFS, broadband distribution methods, and the forgotten medium, radio. . . .

These new technologies present you with many opportunities. But if you don't take advantage of them, new communications structures and functions will begin to vie for available frequencies and audiences. You'll then find today's opportunities have become tomorrow's competition.

This may already have happened with satellites. Although the experiments with the ATS-F are moving along and others are planned, the educational establishment and public broadcasting have failed by-and-large to plan beyond the experimental stage for a fully operational system. The cost for this inaction will be very heavy.

The time has passed to urge you to action through metaphors and blue-sky projections. I'll leave that to the equipment manufacturers and suppliers and the many soothsayers of educational myths.

The time for urging has given way to the time for warning. Unless you broaden your horizons and perspectives, the communications revolution— call it what you may—will leave you pondering possible technological miracles.

We must begin to test these new services through pilot projects instead of studying them to death.

We must begin to understand what these new services mean and what their impact on society will be.

We must begin to design new curricula and systems of learning for formal and non-formal education.

And most importantly, we must begin to develop a new professionalism: one based not upon technological and professional antagonisms, but based upon trust, understanding, and a commitment toward the full utilization of communications.

For the past 49 years the NEAB has been in the forefront in advocating these goals. Its contributions have been substantial and important both in the United States and around the world. The NAEB must continue to play a major role in managing the miracle of communications for humanistic and artistic learning experiences.

For only when we work together, can we honestly say that we are embarking on a journey to enrich man's spirit.

The Breakup of PBS

LES BROWN

The New York Times, September 29, 1974, sec. 2. Copyright © 1974 by The New York Times Company. Reprinted by permission. Les Brown, formerly of *Variety*, now writes on media topics for *The New York Times*. He is the author of *Television: The Business Behind the Box*.

Public television will be offering some interesting programs this season [Fall, 1974], but also it will *not* be offering some. A number of operas— among them *La Traviata*, the Brecht-Weill *Seven Deadly Sins* and Stravinsky's *L'Historie du soldat*, which WNET in New York hoped to produce—have been scratched. So has the package of news documentaries that had been proposed by Washington's National Public Affairs Center for Television (NPACT). They have been passed up for programs on cooking and Yoga.

The direction the program line-up has taken in public television this fall is part of the legacy of the Nixon Administration which, in its heady years, had determined that it would remove control over national programming from the production centers in New York and Washington and disperse this authority among local stations. And now, the principle of "grassroots localism" championed by the Nixon Administration threatens to be written into law by an otherwise admirable bill, currently making its way through the Senate. The so-called Long Range Funding for Public Broadcasting bill would guarantee federal financing of public television for the next five years. The catch in the bill is that it also guarantees a decentralized system,

Brown

347

which is having its first test this fall and under which some of the more innovative and controversial projects of public television will be carried in only a few score communities around the counrty, or carried not at all.

To appreciate how public television got into this situation, it helps to look back to 1967 when Congress passed the Public Broadcasting Act, superimposing a new industry upon an old one that had been known as educational television. Its purpose was to give noncommercial broadcasting a scope beyond merely instructional service. But because difficult questions surrounded the government funding mechanism for the new system, not the least of which was the question of how to keep government from intruding into programming, public television was allowed to be born without a long-range provision for its support. Thus cursed with an anemic life, public television has from year to year made do on limited annual appropriations from the Federal government, grants from private foundations and corporations and contributions from the public.

The Washington-based Public Broadcasting Service came into being in 1970 for the purpose of supervising the interconnection between the more than 200 public stations and to serve as the national programming authority. In effect, PBS became the network. It went into its dying phase, as a network, the following year. In 1971, when the public television industry was expecting news from the White House that it would recommend to Congress a long-range funding bill, station managers were given to understand that such a bill would not be forthcoming unless public television gave up all notion of becoming a fourth network. It eluded no one that the Nixon Administration was seeking to break up the New York–Washington axis that controlled national programming in public television and to shift the power to the localities, where conservative views are better represented.

The message was transmitted by Clay T. Whitehead, then director of the White House Office of Telecommunications Policy and the Administration's principal denouncer of the alleged liberal bias of the commercial networks. It was Whitehead who had coined such memorable phrases as "ideological plugola" and "elitist gossip" to characterize network news. At a meeting of the National Association of Educational Broadcasters, Whitehead charged that public television, too, had a liberal bias and he cautioned the industry to strike a better ideological balance if it desired favors from the White House.

Whitehead suggested that his office might be more disposed to drafting a funding bill for a public television system built upon "the bedrock of localism" than for one that aspired to become the fourth network. Since the public broadcasters were more interested in getting federal money than in resisting federal pressure, they pledged themselves at once to "localism."

Over the months that followed, as production responsibilities were decentralized, common sense fell victim to doctrine. "Wall Street Week," for example, came to emanate not from New York City where Wall Street is an address but from Baltimore. William F. Buckley Jr.'s "Firing Line" began to be produced in South Carolina, although Mr. Buckley resides in New York; the host, as well as most of his guests, therefore have to commute. A program based on Ms. Magazine was set to be produced in Dallas, until that was recognized as impractical—everyone connected with it was in New York.

"Grassroots localism," as it has developed since 1971, has turned the Public Broadcasting Service from a national network into a kind of traffic manager. PBS does much of the paperwork for the newly reorganized system, but it no longer produces programs nor commissions others to produce. Public television stations remain interconnected, but they are without a nerve center, a decision-making authority comparable to Britain's BBC or Japan's NHK.

In place of a network, there is now a congress of 246 stations that vote on much of the national programming for public television through a new mechanism known as the Station Program Cooperative. In an industry obsessed with committees, the cooperative is the ultimate committee. Among other things, it affords regional blocs of stations a degree of veto power over certain program ideas that enter the system from the East.

For example, this season's public TV schedule—the first to be created in the new manner—began with a large catalogue of proposed programs from the various stations, and that was thinned down by a series of ballots, to a manageable number of prospects. When a station voted for a program, it meant the station was willing to pay a portion of the cost of producing it.

Under the new system, when enough stations pledge financial support to a project—that is, when the pledges add up to what it costs to produce the show or series—the project is accepted for the PBS schedule. Given the limited funds available to the Cooperative (for 1974–75 only $13.3-million, or less than the cost of a single evening's worth of commercial television for a year), chopping up the financing in this fashion is not to encourage elaborate or costly projects. A Yoga show that will cover a half-hour in the program schedule for a year becomes preferable to six documentaries, which cost more and, with repeats, would only fill 12 hours.

Nine rounds of votes, tallied by computer, were required for the stations to settle on some two-dozen series—comprising one-third of public television's programing—that will represent the Station Program Cooperative's contribution this fall. Since only those stations that contribute to the cost of a show may carry it, a number of programs that will be fed out by PBS—which has been reduced to handling the distribution—will not be seen on many stations in the country.

WNET, for example, will not be carrying seven of the PBS shows, those entitled *Woman, Burglar Proofing, In Recital, Mele Hawaii, Consumer Survival Kit, Solar Energy* and *Aviation Weather*. In place of those, the New York station will carry a number of locally produced public affairs series. In addition, with a consortium of public TV stations on the eastern seaboard, WNET has purchased several program series from Britain and Canada, among them "Family at War" produced by Granada TV, a British Company; the BBC's comedy series, *Monty Python's Flying Circus*; and, from Canada, *Witness To Yesterday*, a series of simulated interviews with historical figures. Public television on the East Coast will not be typical of public television across the country.

The programs selected by the Cooperative will make up the basic schedule of public television—the children's shows, such as *Sesame Street,* the service and educational shows, some cultural offerings, some minority-oriented programs and a few standard public affairs series, such as *Washington Week in Review*. Because the Senate Watergate Hearings last year proved a highly successful instrument for fund-raising by local public stations, the Cooperative voted to allocate a substantial sum to NPACT for other live special-events telecasts as might arise. *Black Journal* made the schedule but will only be carried by 41 stations.

Among the shows axed were *The Advocates, WNET Opera Theater,* the NPACT documentaries and a new documentary, *Primates,* by three-time Emmy winner Frederick Wiseman. But since the Wiseman documentary has already been shot, and its production paid for by WNET under an earlier contract, there is every likelihood that it will be televised on a number of stations, courtesy of WNET.

Public television's most glamorous shows—such as *Masterpiece Theatre,* the science series, *Nova,* and the health series, *Feeling Good*—will be carried by virtually every station in the system because they are underwritten, either by the Corporation for Public Broadcasting, a private foundation, a commercial corporation, or such federal agencies as the National Endowment for the Humanities or the National Endowment for the Arts. Whenever a series is so donated, virtually the entire public broadcasting system accepts the gift. (Indeed, where business corporations are involved, the grant often is contingent on a favorable time-period and distribution over the full system. The corporations get donor's credit, both audio and visual, before and after the program.)

Therefore, although the new arrangement in public television rules out any central programming power, all stations will nonetheless be carrying programs provided by government and corporate benefactors. On noncommercial television this fall, commercial enterprises such as Mobil Oil, Exxon and Atlantic Richfield—with almost a dozen program grants between them—will be calling many of the shots.

At any rate, having ostensibly "localized" the system, public television got its funding bill. Last July, Clay Whitehead, keeping his end of the bargain, came up with proposed legislation under which the government would contribute $1 for every $2.50 raised from nongovernmental sources by the industry. The bill calls for a maximum federal share of $70-million in the first year (fiscal 1975), graduating to $100-million in the fifth year. Public broadcasters currently are lobbying to raise the scale of grants, which they deem insufficient. A few weeks ago, a Senate committee, in approving the bill, did raise the ceilings; they would start at $88-million for fiscal 1975 and go to $160-million by fiscal 1980.

Scarcely noticed in the bill, however, is a provision that effectively would prevent the development of a public TV network and make as permanent as the funding act itself the still untested networkless form of public television. Between 40 percent and 50 percent of all the federal money is to be distributed directly to local stations, giving them the buying power that would perpetuate the Station Program Cooperative—but not such buying power that they could engage in the kind of expensive programming that PBS, and NET before it, had been known to generate. Many have observed that an innovative, and controversial, series such as *An American Family*, which played two years ago, could never have come into being under the Cooperative.

In the years when the Public Broadcasting Service operated as a real network, it succeeded in drawing away from commercial television a significant number of viewers for many of its programs. "Grassroots localism" being no match for the polished and highly promoted productions of ABC, CBS and NBC, the destruction of the public TV network is bound to reduce public television in the United States to a feeble alternative to the commercial system.

Can Public Television Be Bought?

JOHN J. O'CONNOR

The New York Times, October 13, 1974. Copyright © by The New York Times Company. Reprinted by permission. John J. O'Connor is television critic for *The New York Times*.

The warning signals for public television were there for some time, but with *The Way It Was* they no longer could be politely ignored.

First of all, the series of 13 half-hours offers still another variation on a sports theme, something commercial TV will provide at the drop of an available time slot. Second, and most prominently conceded in each program's final credits, the series was "created by" Herb Schmertz, vice-president of public relations for Mobil Oil. Needless to say, the series is also being "underwritten" by Mobil at a cost of about $30,000 per installment.

This raises some sticky questions. On one side, how much clout should corporations be allowed to exercise in a system that, if not quite totally public, is at least supposed to be noncommercial? On the other, how much control can public TV relinquish over its content before it becomes little more than a common carrier, willing to carry any outsider's slickly produced package?

The answers for public TV are tangled in a skein of problems, all of them financial. From the beginning, the system has been underfinanced. Government funds were deliberately kept to a minimum by the Nixon

Administration, which presided over a plan to bring "democracy" to the smaller stations by taking away from the bigger stations. The latter were more likely to have the facilities and personnel to create more "sophisticated," perhaps even tough programming. In addition, the Ford Foundation, a long-time and major contributor to the system, announced that it would begin to "phase out" its support.

With the amount of government funding tied to "matching monies" from other sources, the larger stations are scrambling for feasible alternatives. One is to boost the number of paying "subscribers" to a station. Some substantial progress has been made in this area, but the final total could prove limited.

The other, of course, is corporate funding. The corporate role in public TV is hardly new, going back at least to the early days of *Masterpiece Theater* and frequently being quite impressive. In the beginning, however, Mobil's participation was limited to a simple "billboard" credit at the start and close of each episode. The company occasionally took out a modest advertisement in a newspaper or magazine to remind readers of its "sacrifice."

It quickly became apparent, though, that no sacrifice was involved. The British imports featured on *Masterpiece Theater* were attracting widespread attention from both critics and public. As the Emmy awards began to accumulate, Mobil and other corporations began to realize that the public TV audience was likely to be more educated, more affluent and more discriminating. Public TV, in the words of the trade, became a "good buy."

It's an especially good buy when the product is an import, which can usually be picked up for a fraction of its original cost. But even domestic series such as *Theater in America* or *The Killers* can be "underwritten" for as little as $100,000 a program, which might run to 90 minutes or two hours.

Granted, in absolute terms $100,000 is still not paltry. But consider the competing economics. On commercial TV, *Born Free* is costing $275,000 per hour episode; *Harry O* is over $300,000.

Public TV officials are quite aware that many of their new corporate friends are those that have trouble with public images in matters like energy crises or antitrust suits. These officials can argue that they take only the badly needed money, that they don't worry if the programming helps or hurts the corporation's image.

The skeptic, after listening to innumerable examples of corporate pressures inside public TV, can only conclude: sometimes, yes; sometimes,

O'Connor

353

no. In fact, the pressure can sometimes spill out of the public TV orbit. After writing a favorable review of *Upstairs, Downstairs*, I received a letter from a Mobil official complaining that I hadn't given credit to the corporation. In that case, however, the pressure quickly wound up in the waste basket.

There is a public TV requirement, trotted out with tedious regularity by anxious executives, that all projects "produced" by a station must be "supervised" by that station. So *The Way It Was* series is billed as a production of KCET in Los Angeles, although it was created by an official of Mobil and made by an independent West Coast production company. That kind of supervision is as effective as the nonexistent "McGuffin" in an Alfred Hitchcock film.

Like several other corporations, Mobil is now probably spending more to advertise its participation in public TV programming than it is spending on programming itself. The simple billboards have gradually been supplemented with massive publicity campaigns. Now there are full-page proclamations of something called "The Mobil Season." Recognition of the local station in this process is limited to the small type at the bottom of the page.

It's understandable. Self-interest generates powerful rationalizations. The balance, however, seems in danger of tipping, perhaps to the point that corporate self-interest could overwhelm the supposedly public interest of the system. Public TV was created, after all, to provide a serious alternative.

The system may never work, stumbling again and again into the old adage: He who pays the piper, plays the tune. And it doesn't matter if the piper is the government, the Ford Foundation or large corporations. A tax on TV sets, similar to the British system, might have guaranteed more independent funding and an opportunity for public TV officials to concentrate on programming as the top priority. But, opponents say, that would never work in this country. Meantime, the debilitating power plays will continue. It remains to be seen who will win.

Public Radio: Coming Out of Hiding

TANIA SIMKINS

Reprinted from *Educational Broadcasting* (May/June, 1974), with permission of the publisher. Copyright 1974 by Acolyte Publications Corp. Tania Simkins is feature editor for Brentwood Publishing Corporation, publisher of bi-monthly trade journals.

As recently as the early '60s, an NAEB-commissioned report on the status of public radio labeled it the "Hidden Medium," although it has been around (albeit leading an improvised and impoverished existence) since 1919. In that year, the first educational radio station in the United States, 9 XM in Madison, Wis., began airing its program of farm news. Actually, it could just as well have been called the "Forgotten Medium."

Eclipsed by commercial television and radio and by public television and left largely to its own devices, educational radio struggled along for the next 50 years, managing somehow to provide a good deal of meaningful and innovative listening with second-hand equipment in converted studios, little professional staff assistance but plenty of ingenuity. It lacked some of the important elements enjoyed by its electronic competitors—principally a network and its own trade association and, of course, funding. NAEB, although for many years solely a radio association, was 25 years old before it undertook a national tape exchange program (in 1950) and later set up a radio division, National Educational Radio (NER) to distribute the tapes and act as mentor to the more than 275 stations it served.

Now, at last, public radio is emerging from "hiding." The advent of CPB was the turning point, and the subsequent establishment and funding by CPB in February 1970 of National Public Radio (NPR), the much-needed network, provided another boost. Finally, the replacement of NER, in effect, by the newly formed (in 1973) Association of Public Radio Stations (APRS), Washington, D.C., gave public radio its own unified "voice" in national affairs. Although NER was instrumental in bringing about many positive actions (*i.e.*, securing the reservation of FM frequencies for noncommercial, educational use; establishing an educational broadcasting branch within the FCC; advocating the inclusion of radio in the Educational Broadcasting Facilities Program of HEW through the Public Broadcasting Act of 1967; and encouraging the formation of CPB as a funding agency for radio as well as television), NER was no longer enough. As Ruane

Simkins

355

B. Hill, PhD, former NER Board member and currently on the APRS Board, puts it, "NER served a purpose, but it could not go beyond that. As one of four not quite autonomous divisions of NAEB, it was hamstrung—it simply could not be responsive to all the needs of an expanding public radio system, and it was not free to provide a vital Washington representation service, which APRS has already begun to do in really strong fashion."

IN SIX MONTHS, SIXTEEN ISSUES

Not a lobbying organization per se, APRS attempts to ". . . simply put coalitions of people together who have a common interest in our concepts, so that they will support them," according to Matthew B. Coffey, President of APRS and a man ideally suited to the job, as former Director of Planning and Research for CPB and Executive Assistant to former CPB President John Macy during his tenure, as well as ex-Staff Assistant to Lyndon B. Johnson at the White House for four-and-a-half years.

Matt Coffey was bringing his wisdom in the ways of radio and politics to bear on behalf of the 108 APRS members within a short time of the group's formation. In six months, APRS had something like ". . . sixteen issues in front of the FCC, including everything from setting standards for the dispensing of educational licenses to trying to get some resolution of the Channel 6 interference problem with television . . ." says Coffey. (Educational stations, particularly those near the lower end of the FM band, are subject to interference from Channel 6 broadcasting in the VHF television spectrum, a problem which can only be solved, according to Coffey, by the television channel allowing the radio station to use its antenna.)

A prime project for 1974, says Coffey, is to

. . . get Congress to concentrate on passage of the all-channel legislation. If we can do that, we'll really make a whole new breakthrough. Two bills have been introduced, one in the Senate and one in the House. The purpose of both is to make it mandatory for all radios in excess of $15 retail value to have both AM and FM capability. It is almost word-for-word like the television all-channel bill which passed 12 years ago. The effect of this would be to raise the penetration rate of FM radio, where most public radio stations (85%) broadcast, particularly in automobile radios, from its present 12% up to more like 88% where it should be. The FCC has stopped thinking of AM

and FM as two separate services. There should now be some requirement that manufacturers produce radios with FM reception.

At present, because of pricing policies of the major auto manufacturers, FM costs twice as much as AM and AM/FM stereo costs
three times as much as AM, when in fact the actual cost difference
between AM and FM is about $7 per radio. This pricing factor
severely limits the ability of the public to have FM in their automobiles. Yet here we are, a public news information medium, and our
principal audiences wind up being in automobiles. . . . The all-channel
bill is just as important as any funding bill, although obviously funding
is important. Funding bills, however, have a more favorable outlook
in terms of getting over all the humps.

One major objective of APRS is to reach 90% of the population of the
United States in the next five years. "We still have 35 major markets in the
U.S. without a public radio station. We're going to get one in every one of
them in the next five years," asserts Coffey.

Although this compares quite favorably with coverage in only 36 of the
top 100 major markets in the U.S. in January 1970, the many markets as
yet without public radio service are of concern to every organization
involved with public radio. Entire states (including Alabama, Delaware,
Idaho, Montana, Nevada, New Hampshire, Vermont and Wyoming) are
without a "full-service" public radio station.

Explains Lee C. Frischknecht, President of NPR,

There are over 700 noncommercial radio stations in the country, but
the overwhelming majority of them are very low power, student-
operated stations at colleges and universities. They are not part of this
system and they don't want to be—they are not interested in broad
community service. They exist to serve the student body and as
grounds for training programs. NPR has 143 members operating 163
stations in 38 states and the District of Columbia. Seventy percent of
them are operated by colleges and universities, except that they do
meet our criteria which are those established by CPB for financial
assistance and which have been adopted in an informal way by the
educational broadcasting facilities program in the HEW and by
the FCC.

However, it is not only sparsely populated areas, such as Idaho or
Montana, which do not have stations meeting our minimum criteria,
but also some of the so-called larger metropolitan areas, such as
Newark, N.J.; San Antonio; Las Vegas; Charlotte, N.C.—the list

Simkins

357

goes on and on. There are 38 cities in the top 100 population areas that are yet unserved by public radio service. This is probably one of the major weaknesses of public radio—it is not available to a large part of the population yet.

Meeting the criteria established by CPB in order to qualify for grants up to $17,000 is one of the hurdles many stations still face. Says Thomas C. Warnock, Director of Radio Activities for CPB,

In 1969, the majority of stations operating were on the air only when school was in session—they'd sign off for the Christmas vacation and for three months in the summer, and many would operate only five days a week. Those licensed to secondary school systems operated from 9:00 to 3:00 because they were primarly used as a means of distributing programs to their classrooms. Only a handful were professionally run and adequately financed.

Before setting up qualifying criteria for grants, we sent a questionnaire to stations asking them to indicate what their staffing situation and hours of operation were. A group of advisors, consisting of station representatives, have concluded that to perform an effective service to the public, a station ought to be operating at least 18 hours a day every day, and should have at least five full-time professional staff. Only 25 stations met those criteria at that time, and many of the others were at much lower levels. Obviously we had to compromise. We set up a scale which requires reaching the minimum by 1976. ... At the time, we had about 76 stations broadcasting eight hours a day, six days a week, 48 weeks a year, with at least two full-time personnel or equivalent, and we set the lowest level there. Our original grants were a flat $7500. In the second year, when we had some additional funds, we went into a graduated scale as a further incentive, so that the sooner a station met the criteria for a given year, the more money it received. Our scale in the second year ranged from $8000 on the low end, to $15,000 at the high end. That range held until this year, when we are now ranging from $10,500 to $17,000. We are also reserving some funds for Coverage Expansion grants, competitive awards in unserved areas where there is no existing station meeting our criteria. These usually result in the creation of a new station from scratch.

The grants have had the effect, adds Warnock, of making public radio a professional career possibility at long last. He comments,

There was no job market in public radio until about four years ago when we started to implement our policies at CPB and grants became available. Many brilliant and talented young people who served as volunteers at public stations owned by universities had to turn to commercial broadcasting at the end of their four years in college. There was just no place they could go and continue to do public radio, because there was nobody to pay them. What we have done, and will continue to do is create and expand a job market for professionals in public radio, which, in turn, will greatly increase the scope and quality of the service.

Noting that 147 stations now meet the standards set by CPB, Matt Coffey comments, "We expect to have 210 meeting them next year. We will be at a point where we can start thinking about the next step when we have 210 stations able to serve 60% to 70% of the population with a first-class public broadcasting service. The next step is multiple channels in every market."

PROGRAMMING PLUS

The strength of public radio lies in its programming potential. Unhampered by commercial sponsor pressures, it has the freedom and flexibility to explore in depth a broad variety of issues, sensitive, controversial, stimulating. It may, in fact, offend some as it informs others, notes the promotional brochure of Minnesota Educational Radio (MER), St. Paul, a system which, with four maximum-power FM stations in operation and two under construction, is the largest state-wide system of public radio stations in the country capable of local and interconnected broadcasting.

Furthermore, unlike other networks, NPR looks to its member stations for more than one-third of the network programming: decentralization is a cornerstone of NPR policy. Comments NPR's Frischknecht,

We are a mutual network in the truest sense, because our stations produce material—about 50% of it—for the network service. We are fairly successful at obtaining input and material for our programs from a wide variety of geographical, political and and economic spectra in this society—the program material stems from the grassroots. The two-way nature of the system is one of its strengths—there is not nearly the degree of material being produced by local stations in any of the other broadcast media.

Simkins

359

As a two-way network, NPR uses ATT long lines to provide the means for transmitting member-station-produced programs to the entire NPR membership. Each station is required to initiate most of its own programming, and is restricted from using more than 40 hours of NPR programming each week. NPR's 90-minute news magazine, *All Things Considered* . . . won the coveted George Foster Peabody Award for 1973 for "an innovative use of investigative reporting." Columnist Richard K. Shull wrote in the *Indianapolis News* in June 1973,

> . . . the most impressive of all on the NPR network is its daily news show, *All Things Considered.* . . . A news event isn't covered with the reading of the lead paragraph from a wire service story. The event is tossed in the air like a balloon, examined from various sides and maybe even punctured or shot down. . . . That's in contrast to the news operations of commercial networks which lean primarily on information from a few major cities where the networks own and operate stations. . . . How (does) NPR differ from commercial "all-news" stations. . . . (They) don't carry any more news than the other stations. They may repeat the hot headlines more often, but it's still the same superficial treatment. . . .

NPR has also provided live coverage of more than 600 hours of testimony at Congressional hearings: notes Frischknecht,

> We were doing Congressional hearings long before Watergate came along, and we do it in the kind of depth and complete gavel-to-gavel treatment that only occurs in other media where there is something as compelling as Watergate. Even there, when other people dropped out, we kept going. The profit motive simply precludes commercial media from spending the amount of time in covering an activity that we can and do.

In 1973, the network undertook a legislative study entitled *The Biography of a Bill,* following each stage of the national no-fault motor vehicle insurance act as it worked its way through the Senate and the House into becoming a law concerning every motor vehicle operator in the nation.

Despite programming and other strides in public radio, money continues to be a problem, and bigger budgets could certainly solve many of the medium's remaining problems. Although the CPB support grants can be ". . . life-savers—$15,000 a year at the right time can make all the difference between the success or failure of a station," in the words of

William H. Kling, President of MER, the model state-wide community radio system, they are still slim in terms of the need. The total CPB appropriation, about $45 million in 1974 (which must also cover the agency's administrative costs), represents about 20 cents per person for every U.S. inhabitant. This compares unfavorably with England's $3.30 per person, Japan's $3.10 and Canada's $7.70 in the public broadcasting kitty. Furthermore, radio receives only 18% of the total appropriation, compared to 33% in Canada and England.

Thus, public radio stations are either destined to be a line item in an institutional budget, competing for dollars with all the other things a university is doing, or they must seek support from listeners and/or develop other sources of income. MER started out in a private college, St. John's University, in Collegeville, Minn., as station KSJR, which still operates in the system at 90.1 Mc/s. Kling notes, "The station very quickly discovered that the costs of providing the kinds of service that they wanted in the area were far more than they were able to commit to it. So we reorganized as a separate corporation with participation from a number of different individual institutions. We pooled resources, thus giving us greater strength for going out in the community and seeking funds. It takes interested community leaders who have the vision to see what public radio can be and the power to interest others in it."

MER qualifies for CPB grants, has successfully sought community support (some $100,000 a year), has found backing from local trusts and foundations, and also uses, for example, the cassette tapes it produces of public affairs programs to boost the budget: Kling, considered a remarkable public broadcaster by his colleagues, reports that the hour-long tapes are sold for $4 an hour, ". . . which is quite reasonable for an hour tape, and probably double what it costs us to produce them. So there is the dual benefit, of added income *and* the potential for the getting the word out about our programming via the libraries, schools and individuals who buy them."

PROMO PARADOX

"Getting the word out" is an extremely important by-product: many public broadcasting spokesmen point to a programming-versus-promotion paradox. What good is quality programming on public radio, they argue, if no one is listening! Bill Kling puts it this way:

People don't know what public radio is, or *where* it is. We find at MER that the more promotion we do, the more people become wildly enthusiastic about us. They are terribly loyal and will go to great lengths to help support the station—once they start listening. Our corporate support goes up, too, as listeners start going out of their way to let firms which are behind us know that they are behind them. Many will open a savings account, for example, at a bank which provides funds for a given program, or will write a letter to X company which has helped fund a certain broadcast.

Promotion comes high, concedes Kling.

You have to make judgments about spending money on programming versus promotion. Spending money strictly on the former makes for great programs, but nobody knows they are occurring. We have been putting more and more money into newspaper advertising, bus posters and billboards. We make a fairly substantial allocation for several promotional campaigns each year. At that, we have the support of an advertising agency, which does all our design work free, and some outdoor billboard companies which put our designs up free as long as we pay for having them printed.

Dr. Hill, who devotes two-thirds of his time to managing University of Wisconsin at Milwaukee public radio station WUWM-FM . . . agrees that

. . . visibility, to borrow a television term, has been the single greatest problem of public radio, excluding funding. Our major problem at WUWM is one shared with every other station—simply "How do you let people know you are *there*?" How, when you do not have the budget to do it, do you publicize a superior product that tries to do much more for an audience than commercial stations can? And we have been told our budget is finite—last year's level will very likely be the ceiling hereafter. Costs go up, though, We have never considered a fund-raising drive on the air as many stations do, but we are thinking about it now for the first time. . . .

MER, on the other hand, has sought listener support by ". . . simply going on the air and asking listeners to become members of the station, just as many public television stations do," says Bill Kling. "It has been successful. In 1972 we had 1800 members. Currently we have 5600, quite a dramatic growth in two years. This represents a little over $100,000 a year—the average contribution is usually $20 per person. Our audience statistics look good, too. Between October/November 1972 and 1973, we had a 287% increase in audience, according to the ARB survey, which indicates something is beginning to work."

MER subscribers receive a handosme 48-page monthly program guide, *Preview,* containing literary articles, book reviews and general cultural information, if they contribute $18 or more a year to MER. . . . (Advertising in *Preview* yields an additional $20,000 to the budget.)

Bill Kling believes that many public stations could tap their community and area trusts and foundations for financial support, as MER started doing in early 1972. Some 21 Minnesota foundations contributed $43,280 to MER's $544,080 operating budget for fiscal 1974, and Kling feels that most states have this well-endowed philanthropic potential.

Kling lists MER's development in 1968 of Subsidiary Communications Authority (SCA) capability as one key to the corporation's success. Best known in its commercial Muzak form, SCA is a technical capability unique to FM transmission. It allows simultaneous transmission of two signals: explains Tom Warnock,

> Any station that broadcasts in stereo is using a portion of the SCA capability, which is aside from their main frequency in the spectrum but part of their licensed band width, which makes it possible to broadcast a separate and distinct signal from the main channel mon-aural signal. The SCA transmissions aren't quite in the high fidelity range of the main channel broadcast, and more importantly, they can be heard only on special receivers.

MER broadcasts 19 hours daily on SCA; there are 3000 receivers in the listening area, says Kling, representing more listeners than that. The programs are reading services for the blind—magazines, newspapers, current novels and other material, produced by the Minnesota State Services for the Blind. "That has been a great boost in terms of interest in our system," Kling maintains.

Tom Warnock of CPB is enthusiastic about SCA possibilities:

> Several state-wide networks are broadcasting two-way discussions between doctors who are continuing their professional education, to bring them up to date on new techniques. And the reading service for the blind—which includes much material that is never translated into Braille, on a continuous 18-hour-a-day basis, or in some cases 24 hours a day—provides a national service increment in public radio. We'd like to find some funds to improve some of the technical problems—the signal could be cleaned up a little bit if money were spent

Simkins

on reasearch, and there is an opportunity to bring the cost of the special receivers down dramatically. Right now a good one runs about $50—they ought to be down to $10 or $12.

FM PHENOMENON: 10 W AND $97

Other problems remain. Like SCA, the 10 W station is a phenomenon of FM, and there is concern in the field about the crowding of the available spectrum with a multitude of small, 10 W stations which operate within a seven-mile radius of their transmitter and prevent a high-powered station from coming in to serve an entire area. Although recommendations for regulation of the educational FM band date back to the CPB public radio study of 1969, the FCC has been benevolently lenient about allowing 10-watters to proliferate: a recent case in point was the granting of a license to an Oklahoma station which submitted a total construction cost figure of $97 and a yearly operating budget of $130—clearly not a station which will be able to offer the kind of upgraded public service which CPB, NPR and other noncommercial radio bodies are trying to encourage.

CPB filed a comprehensive recommendation with the FCC last year, says Warnock, for revising the rules relating to noncommercial FM stations.

> We were looking for a solution that would not put us in the position of attempting to eliminate the 10 W stations, but rather permit them to exist side-by-side with the high-power stations by adjusting the existing allocations of the 10 watt transmitters. While we are pleased that more new stations are meeting our qualifying criteria, we're a little disturbed, too, because in the same space of four years, the 400 stations have gone up to 650, and most of them are in the 10 W variety.

> Bill Kling notes, "The FCC has allocated 20 channels for educational radio stations, yet they have never really defined clearly what an educational radio station *is*. They never seem to have challenged any applicants for a station as long as they said they wanted to do noncommercial programming. As a result, we have a hodge-podge of little stations, most of which are laboratories for university communications departments or entertainment media for the dormitories. It is pretty much of a mess." He adds that although 10 W stations are eligible to join APRS, they ". . . may very well find that the Association is filing against them in some FCC proceedings. APRS represents the interests of qualified public radio stations."

Another technical problem, continues Kling, is that ". . . the distribution of programming by NPR is on five KC audio lines, which are of very limited audio quality. You need stereo capability for good music transmission. This will come with satellites, and I think within a year or so we'll find that NPR is transmitting some experimental broadcasts on network stereo."

NPR's Frischknecht confirms,

> Communications satellites will permit us to improve vastly the quality of program distribution which is limited to ATT circuits far below the quality that the average FM station broadcasts. The sound is about one-third as good, so when the network programs come into the station, they don't sound good. From a technological point of view, satellites are going to be what will really make this public radio system work properly.
>
> They are going to have another advantage in addition to quality. We will be able to have live access to the network stations from any of our stations, so that we can really make this decentralization work. Right now, most of the stations cannot feed to us live, so they either have to send in a poor quality report by telephone or send it on tape, which is not immediate. We see satellites as the complete answer to our two-way, decentralized system.

Frischknecht adds that the satellites will make possible a resurgence of live music on radio—"Classical music tends to predominate in this system, but we will include a wide variety, with jazz high on the list. Country, Western, Bluegrass and soul and other ethnic music will be done live again and in high quality. Right now, we do very little of that simply because the network lines do not permit us to do it with any essential good quality."

Frischknecht also expects to get much closer to the needs of the people. He says, "Ascertaining the needs of the public has been almost non-existent in public broadcasting or any kind of broadcasting for that matter. Our processes of research in determining what people need to hear are going to get a lot better, and we are already hard at work on ways to find out what these specialized needs are, and then design services that will fulfill them."

After coming almost full circle from a medium which could well have been called "university radio," not only owned and operated by colleges but dedicated to serving the needs of the licensee, to a medium which is truly *public,* designed to serve the audience and not the station owner, noncommercial radio may be taking another look at its educational possibilities. Veteran broadcasting expert James Robertson, former director of NER and now an independent consultant ("Having spent 36 years in commercial and noncommercial television and radio, I decided I'd like to try it on my own"), observes, "There has been a lot of interest in reexamining the role of radio in instruction. NER did a rather comprehensive report on this and came to the predictable conclusion that radio has great potential and is being under-utilized (as an educational tool). The research hasn't really gathered momentum across the country yet, but there are a number of places where radio is being used very effectively in training. There is a growing interest in this, and it may well be a trend that will develop in the next four or five years."

INTERNATIONAL
BROADCASTING

The flow of communications between and among countries has been a source of frustration and resentment for many people since news agency services began early in the nineteenth century. For years, nations of the world have depended upon Western news agencies for much of their information; indeed, in some continents, particularly Africa and parts of Asia, communications between countries on the same continent have had to go through international news agencies such as Agence France Presse, Associated Press, Reuters, Tass, or United Press International.

In the early twentieth century, Western countries that began to make movies soon found that other nations often were reluctant to show them because the political, cultural, and social content of the films sometimes was distasteful to the people or the governments of the nations in which they were to be shown. News agencies had been criticized because of the "nationalistic" content of the news they carried, and now film was criticized because of its nationalistic *culturalism*. For example, films produced in Hollywood frequently exemplified ideals of manhood or womanhood that were not shared by other cultures such as that of India. In addition, the obvious professional quality of Western-made films tended, in some cases, to hinder the development of indigenous movie industries.

The widespread development of radio in the decades following World War I brought about another problem. Whereas news from the wire services could be controlled at the point of reception, which was either a newspaper office or a radio station, and films could be controlled by import restrictions, which permitted theaters to show only certain films, radio transcended those boundaries. Radio could reach directly into the homes with shortwave radio receivers no matter what country they were in. All that the state could do to reduce such border "violations" was to either restrict the number of shortwave receivers in the population or "jam" the incoming signals by some electronic means. Thus, in the chaotic state of international politics, from 1920 through the "Cold War," international radio became a political propaganda tool as well as a means of exporting culture.

Television's rapid worldwide development in the years following World War II has brought us to a repeated situation: problems reminiscent of the distribution (continued distribution, it should be added) of movies have been recreated in the wide distribution of television programs. As a visual medium, television powerfully moves from culture to culture; dub in dialog in the local language or use subtitles and one country's programs can be understood and enjoyed by the people of any other country. The specter of widespread dissemination of anticultural values ("anti" to the country in which they are appearing) has arisen once again. As with film, the popular use of imported television programs has created a situation where local programs may not be produced because they cost too much for the quality that results. The availability of imported programs, then, also restricts the development of native talent in a powerful medium.

Television facilities in most countries of the world are owned and operated by the state or by some agency of the state, and it has been possible for national governments to set policies that restrict the use of foreign television programs. New technology, however, creates a situation where international communications may overcome that means of control. That is, direct satellite communications from a transmitter in the United States, for instance, to a community receiver with a relatively inexpensive antenna is now technically feasible and will become increasingly so in the next decade. What then? How will nations control the reception of these signals—signals that most likely will be used for national propagandistic purposes and that will compete with local programs? Will they limit the kinds of antennae people can use or will they "jam" the signals? Or, perhaps an answer will be found in international law, where nations already have demonstrated their strong concern for television control.

These two paramount issues in international communications today, the flow of television programs among countries and their affects on culture and local industry and the fear of direct satellite television are discussed in the articles that follow. Tapio Varis, a researcher in Finland, carefully outlines the direction of the flow of television communications in the world today, the methods used for distribution, and the reasons for the current import and exchange practices. Herbert Schiller, who seemingly coined the expression "media imperialism," gives a brief overview of the issues involved in direct telecasts from communications satellites.

Other issues also trouble the field of international communications. The relationship between Comsat (Communications Satellite Corporation), an American agency, and Intelsat (International Telecommunications Satellite), a consortium of about ninety nations using the Intelsat satellite communications system, has been more clearly defined in recent years so that American control no longer is quite as dominant as once it was. The ongoing issue, however, is what relationship the Communist systems will have with Intelsat. Right now the USSR's Orbita system serves several members of the Eastern Communist bloc through Intersputnik. Whether the nations can bring these communications systems together so that most of the nations of the world will be involved in international satellite communications is a question that only the events of the future will answer.

A related problem is the exchange of programs between Eurovision (the West European telecommunications network) and Intervision (the East European and Soviet Union telecommunications network). Progress of a sort had been made by 1972, the latest year for which figures were available. Almost 5000 news items were offered by Eurovision to Intervision; 60 percent of those items were used by Intervision. In return, however, of the 3083 news items offered by Intervision to Eurovision, only 220 were used—just 7 percent. A more balanced situation exists in the exchange of programs; "nearly four hundred TV hours originate in Eurovision countries and go to the Intervision exchange, and more than two hundred TV hours flow in the opposite direction," according to a UNESCO report. Most of the programs deal with sports. The flow of television program material and information will continue to be an issue of great moment in international communications.

BIBLIOGRAPHICAL ESSAY

The concept of a "free flow" of communications between and among countries has come under increasing fire during the past decade. Herbert Schiller, in *Mass Communications and American Empire,* Augustus M. Kelley, Clifton, N.J., 1969, was one of the early American critics of American involvement overseas through mass media: television programs, public relations and marketing surveys, and advertising. Since the publication of his book, many other critics have become involved in the field and the research needed to test some of Schiller's assertions has gone on. The reading by Tapio Varis should be supplemented by other articles appearing in the *Journal of Communication* (Winter, 1974), from which the Varis article was taken. For further details on the same issue, read Kaarle Nordenstreng and Tapio Varis, *Television Traffic—A One Way Street? A Survey and Analysis of the International Flow of Television Programme Material,* Paper No. 70, in the Reports and Papers on Mass Communication Series, UNESCO, New York, 1974. Supplement this report with Olof Hultén, "The Intelsat System: Some Notes on Television Utilization of Satellite Technology," *Gazette* (1973), 29–37. For a different view of the same problem, see Alan Wells, *Picture-Tube Imperialism: The Impact of U.S. Television on Latin America,* Orbis Books, Maryknoll, N.Y., 1972.

The advent of the communications satellite has created an international means of communication unsurpassed in previous history. It also has created monumental problems in international relations. Our selection by Herbert Schiller focuses on the problem created by the advent of the *direct broadcast satellite* (UNESCO refers to them as *broadcast satellites*), meaning a communications satellite that is able to circumvent existing state controls over incoming communications. See *A Guide to Satellite Communication,* Paper No. 66, in the Reports and Papers on Mass Communication series, UNESCO, New York, 1972. While already dated by events, this brief survey gives the important background without getting involved deeply in technology. The threat of direct broadcast satellites to a country's political and cultural well being is expressed in greater detail by Schiller in his "Freedom From the 'Free Flow,'" *Journal of Communication* (Winter, 1974), 110–117. Carroll V. Newsom, "Communication Satellites: A New Hazard for World Culture," *Educational Broadcasting Review* (April, 1973), 77–85, expresses his concern for the effects of American and European television programs on the culture of the undeveloped countries and, through his discussion of this effect, warns of the possible effect of direct broadcast satellite communication on nascent political systems and traditional cultures.

A brief, but excellent discussion of our direct broadcast satellite by FCC Commissioner Robert E. Lee, the one member of the Commission who has concerned himself for years with the satellite communication issue, can be found in "Direct Broadcast Satellites: A Reality This Year?" *Television/Radio Age* (March 18, 1974) 58–59+. In a companion piece in the same publication (April 29, 1974), 78–80+, Commissioner Lee deals with the problems of international and national regulation of direct broadcast satellites in an article entitled "Direct Broadcast Satellites: Their Future." For a vociferous rejoinder to those who would allow national control of direct broadcast satellites, see Dr. Frank Stanton, "Freedom and Satellites," *Television Quarterly* (Winter, 1973), 67–70.

STUDY QUESTIONS

1. Why is it possible that imported United States television programs could have a significant impact on foreign viewers when such programs account for only 20 percent or less of the total programming?

2. What television programs now on the air in the United States would you consider to be accurate reflections of our society and therefore warrant export? Are there any programs that should not be exported because they distort American society?

3. What are the arguments for and against the "free flow of information" between nations?

4. Should there be international controls to protect individual nations from direct satellite television? Why?

Global Traffic in Television

TAPIO VARIS

Reprinted from *Journal of Communications*, vol. 24, 1 (Winter, 1974), with permission of the publisher. Copyright 1974 by Journal of Communication. Tapio Varis is a researcher at the Institute of Journalism and Mass Communication of the University of Tampere, Tampere, Finland. This article summarizes some of the findings of an ongoing research project, which is reported more extensively in UNESCO's Reports and Papers on Mass Communication, N. 71, *Television Traffic: a One-way Street?*

Very few attempts have been made to compare the television program structures of different nations, or to measure or study the flow of information among nations via the television screen. A prevalent view emphasizes the free flow of information—an ideal system in which sovereign national networks distribute the best programs from all over the world, balanced by their own productions. This system, however, has never been shown to exist; in fact, evidence tends to show a quite different effect.

International broadcasting research has mainly dealt with radio broadcasting. The content, reception, and jamming of external radio service have been studied, although much of this research could be called "Cold War scholarship." World television has until recent years been largely unexplored.

The term "international broadcasting" as used here includes both direct broadcasts from one country to another and the use of foreign material in domestic radio and television services. International broadcasting is one form of transaction among nations—not only a social and cultural transaction, but also an economic one: television programs are produced, sold, and purchased as one commercial commodity among others.

An inventory of international program structure was begun in 1971 by the University of Tampere and the Finnish Broadcasting Company with UNESCO support. The original objective was to obtain a global view of the composition of television programs, based on information from countries representing various political and cultural systems and at various stages of economic development. The television stations of nearly 50 countries were surveyed about their program schedules, the sources of their programs and the conduits through which international program transactions are conducted.

A broad summary of the survey results is presented in Table 1. The results can best be discussed in terms of the production, distribution, and consumption of TV programs on a worldwide scale.

In international TV program production the United States led markets in the mid-60's by exporting more than twice as many programs as all other countries combined. The U.S. is still the leading originator of programs, but changing production conditions and the outflow of production capital from the United States make it difficult to estimate the aggregate total of American programs sold or produced abroad and distributed to various countries.

Other major originators of TV programs for international distribution are the United Kingdom, France, and the Federal Republic of Germany. Certain countries are major producers of programs for limited international distribution: for example, programs produced in Mexico are widely distributed throughout Latin America and in Spanish-speaking areas of the United States. Lebanon and the United Arab Republic are major producers for the Middle East. Programs produced in socialist countries are used mainly in other socialist countries, although the U.S.S.R. and the German Democratic Republic originate a large number of television programs which are used outside the socialist world—for example, in some Arab countries.

The production of television programs for international distribution (unlike that of radio programs, which are often used for propaganda purposes) is primarily aimed at making money. Commercial competition in the world market has led to concentration. In the United States, for example, where more than 150 companies are active in the producing and exporting of TV programs, the nine companies which form the Motion Picture Export Association of America account for about 80 percent of the total U.S. sales abroad.

Most programs in international circulation were originally made to satisfy the tastes of audiences in the countries where they were produced and first marketed. These programs were most often made for viewers in the U.S., Canada, Australia, Japan, and Western Europe. Later, they were adapted for worldwide commercial distribution—or for "cultural distribution."

Our analysis of direct sales of television programs indicates that the exporting corporations often aim at enhancing the national image of the

Varis

373

Table 1

Percentage of imported and domestically produced television programming (including repeats) by hours, 1970-71

Legend:
☐ Domestic % (A) = annual figures
▨ Imported % (W) = data based on sample weeks

*In Dubai, domestic programs refer to those in Arabic; imported programs are not in Arabic.

	NORTH AMERICA / LATIN AMERICA AND CARIBBEAN / WESTERN EUROPE	Domestic %	Imported %
NORTH AMERICA			
Canada/CBC (W)		34	66
Canada/RC (W)		46	54
United States/16 commercial (W)		1	99
United States/18 non-comm. (W)		2	98
LATIN AMERICA AND CARIBBEAN			
Argentina/Canal 9B.A. (A)		10	90
Argentina/Canal 11B.A. (A)		30	70
Chile (W)		55	45
Colombia (W)		34	66
Dominican Republic/Can. 3/9 (A)		50	50
Guatemala (W)		84	16
Mexico/Telesistema (A)		39	61
Uruguay (W)		62	38
WESTERN EUROPE			
Fed. Rep. of Germany/ARD (A)		23	77
Fed. Rep. of Germany/ZDF (A)		30	70
Finland (A)		40	60
France (A)		9	91
Iceland		67	33
Ireland (A)		54	46
Italy (A)		13	87
Netherlands (A)		23	77
Norway (A)		39	61
Portugal (A)		35	65
Sweden (A)		33	67
Switzerland/Deutschw. (W)		24	76
United Kingdom/BBC (A)		12	88
United Kingdom/ITV (W)		13	87

(scale: 10% 20% 30% 40% 50% 60% 70% 80% 90%)

Country	Top value	Bottom value
German Democratic Rep. (A)	68	32
Hungary (A)	60	40
Poland (A)	83	17
Romania (A)	73	27
Soviet Union/Cen. 1st (W)	95	5
Soviet Union/Leningrad (A)	95	5
Soviet Union/Estonia (A)	88	12
Yugoslavia/Beograd (A)	82	18
Australia (A)	43	57
People's Rep. China/Shanghai (W)	99	1
Rep. of China/Enterprise (A)	78	22
Hongkong/RTV&HK-TVB English (W)	60	40
Hongkong/RTV&HK-TVB Chinese (W)	69	31
Japan/NHK General (A)	96	4
Japan/NHK Educational (A)	99	1
Japan/Commercial stations	90	10
Rep. of Korea/Tong-yang (A)	69	31
Malaysia (A)	29	71
New Zealand (W)	27	73
Pakistan (A)	65	35
Philippines/ABC CBV (A)	71	29
Singapore (W)	22	78
Thailand/Army TV (W)	82	18
Dubai (A)	28	72*
Iraq (A)	48	52
Israel (A)	45	55
Kuwait (A)	44	56
Lebanon/Telibor (A)	60	40
Saudi-Arabia/Riyadh TV (W)	69	31
Saudi-Arabia/Aramco TV (W)		100
United Arab Republic (A)	59	41
People's Rep. Yemen (W)	43	57
Ghana (W)	73	27
Uganda (W)	81	19
Zambia (W)	36	64

producing country, in order to receive financial support from that state. Thus, only part of the foreign distribution of the French ORTF, for example, is classified as commercial; the rest is called "cultural distribution." "Cultural distribution" means that only the rights for the programs are paid for—either by the French foreign ministry or by the recipient nation; the distribution itself is on a nonprofit basis. This noncommercial distribution is aimed mainly at developing nations. Exporters in other Western countries report similar practices.

Governmental subsidies to program exports explain the low cost of imported programs in some countries. The prices of American films on TV vary considerably from area to area, and it is difficult to give a meaningful range of prices charged for U.S. feature films around the world. Some of the "blockbuster" films have been sold for as much as $50,000. But the effective distribution systems in the Western countries—particularly of the U.S. film industry—makes it easy for poor countries to purchase cheap programs. The lack of a similar distribution system in socialist countries makes it more difficult for the poor countries to buy programs from them.

Agencies which act as middlemen between program buyers and sellers are often located in third countries. In Finland, for example, more than one-third of the feature films imported in 1971 for television showing were purchased somewhere other than the producing country. London has been a center of traffic in American films, and similar local centers for distribution are found elsewhere. Direct travel by program purchasers to the producing countries is an important method of acquiring programs but is too expensive for the small countries. Viewing sessions and film festivals serve as meeting places for producers and purchasers.

Conditions for effective program exchange through broadcasting unions do not yet exist in most parts of the world. Even in Europe, where the systems of program exchange are most developed, the total amount of exchanged entertainment and news programs is not very large. In 1971, Eurovision (originating in Western Europe) produced about 1,200 hours and Intervision (originating in Eastern Europe) about 1,400 hours of programming. The total outgoing exchange (multilateral, bilateral, and unilateral) of the BBC to Europe in 1970 was only 15 percent of its direct sales to Europe.

The origination of news items by Eurovision is heavily concentrated in London; almost half of all news items originate in the United Kingdom. This is partly because London is the newsfilm distribution center for

American and British agencies. Worldwide distribution of newsfilm is so organized that U.S. and Central European subscribers may often receive a newsfilm of an event on the same day it occurs, while subscribers outside Europe receive the film four days after the event.

The distribution of Western news material to the socialist countries, and of those countries' news material to the West, is done through Austrian television.

Because the production of television programs is expensive, television stations in most countries of the world are heavily dependent on imported material. Although the average share of imported material in many areas is one-third of total output or less, some countries import more than two-thirds of their programming.

Many of the developing countries use much imported material, but—with the exception of a number of Latin American countries and a few Middle East countries—television is still of minor importance in most parts of the developing world; when it is available, it is for the most part merely a privilege of the urban rich.

The United States and the People's Republic of China are examples of countries which currently use little foreign material—at least compared with the total amount of their own programming. Japan and the Soviet Union also produce most of their own programs. Most other nations, however, are heavy purchasers of foreign material. Even in an area as rich as Western Europe, imported programs account for about one-third of total transmission time.

Most nonsocialist countries purchase programs mainly from the United States and the United Kingdom. In Western Europe, for example, American-produced programs account for about half of all imported programs, and from 15 to 20 percent of total transmission time. The socialist countries also use American and British material, but only TV Belgrade uses as large a share of American programs as the Western European countries.

The real social and political impact of imported programs may be greater than might be inferred from the volume of imported material, because of audience viewing patterns and the placing of foreign programming. Available studies about prime-time programming in various countries tend to show that the proportion of foreign material during these hours is considerably greater than at other times.

For each country surveyed, we looked at the categories into which imported programs fell. Program imports are heavily concentrated on serials and series, long feature films, and entertainment programs. In importing sports programs and in the selection of most entertainment programs, ideological considerations do not play much of a role, but many countries exercise greater selectivity in purchasing information-type programs.

Comparisons of types and amounts of imported programming were especially interesting in countries with both commercial and public or noncommercial TV stations (notably the U.S., U.K., Australia, Japan). Because most commercial stations would not release data on the sources of their imported programs, they could not be systematically studied. In the United States, the TV audience has been introduced to foreign programs mainly through the noncommercial public television system, although even those stations use a minimal amount of imported material. During the test week of the study, the U.S. public broadcasting stations were showing a British documentary, the British production of *The Forsyte Saga*, and a Soviet feature film. U.S. commercial stations showed series, feature films, and drama from the U.K., Australia, the Federal Republic of Germany, Switzerland, and Scandinavia.

In the United Kingdom, 90 percent of the foreign programming used by the BBC during the test week was of U.S. origin, and all of the imported material used by commercial ITV was American. Available data suggest that Japanese and Australian commercial stations purchase more of their foreign programs from the United States than do their noncommercial counterparts.

In the importation and exchange of newsfilm, distribution is concentrated in three worldwide agencies: Visnews (British), UPITN (joint British and American ownership), and CBS-Newsfilm (American). The fourth important newsfilm distributor is the West German DPA-ETES, but it has not gained a similar dominant role in world distribution. There are practically no other worldwide newsfilm distributors, and nearly all broadcasters in the world have to use film from these agencies.

The flow of information through television news is one-sided both between Western Europe and the developing countries and between Western Europe and the socialist countries. In the regular newsfilm exchange via satellite between Eurovision and four Latin American countries (Brazil, Colombia, Peru, and Venezuela), the flow between March 1971 and June 1972 consisted of 2,461 news items from Europe to

Latin America, and only 45 news items from Latin America to Europe. Of the 252 news items dealing with the Arab world carried by Eurovision in 1971, only 16 originated in the Arab nations themselves; 209 came from the Big Three newsfilm agencies, and the rest came from other European or American correspondents. The situation is much the same with news from other developing areas of the world.

The flow of information through news items between Western and Eastern Europe (through Eurovision and Intervision) is also one-sided— at least when measured in quantity. Athough both Western and socialist countries have increased their offers of material to each other since the beginning of regular news exchanges in 1965, only the socialist countries have increased their reception of Western material; the Western European countries have kept their reception of material from the socialist countries steadily low. The total flow of television news programs (including both news and feature films) from Western to Eastern Europe amounted to roughly 3,000 hours in 1970, while the reverse flow from Eastern to Western Europe amounted to about 1,000 hours. (See Table 2.)

Table 2

	From East to West (1000 TV hours)	From West to East (3000 TV hours)
Entertainment films	65%	50%
Sports	25	35
News and documentaries	10	15

Our survey tried to supplement plain statistics with some qualitative aspects. Our data are not sufficient for total understanding of international television. We did not, for example, examine audience exposure to imported programs. Regular audience ratings from various countries suggest that foreign programs are watched by large audiences, but these data have not been compared among countries.

The information we have gathered, however, does increase our knowledge of the present state of affairs in the flow of information among nations through television. The small and even the middle-sized nations of the world have been placed in remarkably similar positions under the pressure of foreign material.

Varis

379

One solution to the present imbalance in the market situation for TV programs might be new efforts on the parts of small and middle-sized producers to coproduce programs. The small producers cannot distribute packages of programs, and they are usually forced into black and white production and into high prices which make international distribution difficult. Coproductions can decrease costs and improve quality.

The technical and practical problems are important in the present-day television industry, but the basic problem has been and remains to be the social and political role of television communication: what is the real communication policy of this medium in various societies, and how much real choice is available and used in acquiring programs?

The Electronic Invaders

HERBERT I. SCHILLER

Reprinted from *The Progressive,* vol. 37, 8 (August, 1973), with permission of the publisher. Copyright 1973 by The Progressive Publishing Co. Herbert I. Schiller is professor of communciations at the University of California in San Diego. He wrote *Mass Communications and American Empire,* and his most recent book, *The Mind Managers,* was published late in 1973 by Beacon Press.

For twenty-five years, the "free flow of information" between nations has been a widely sought objective of the United States, generally supported in the international community. Enunciated and promoted by the United Nations Educational, Scientific, and Cultural Organization (UNESCO), with more than a little U.S. prodding, there was general, if not unanimous, agreement that an unimpeded communications traffic was a good thing and that people everywhere benefited when it occurred. If the concept was not always respected in practice, at least it was never frontally attacked as a principle.

A dramatic reversal of this outlook is now underway. It is becoming apparent to many nations that the free flow of information, much like free trade in an earlier time, strengthens the strong and submerges the weak. In the case of information, the powerful communicator states overwhelm the less developed countries with their information and cultural messages.

Though information that moves internationally flows through many channels—movies, books, periodicals, television programs, radio broadcasts, tourists, merchandise exports, cultural exchanges—the medium which has brought the issue into focus is the new technology of communications satellites, broadcasting from space. Communications satellites which will soon bring television programs *directly* into individual living rooms across the globe (an informed guess puts direct satellite broadcasting less than ten years away) is forcing a long hard look at just what imagery already is flowing across national boundaries through more conventional means.

Currently, television is either imported on film or tape and used locally; moves across contiguous national frontiers (most Canadians, for example, can and do watch U.S. programs from stations across the border); or is picked up from communications satellites by ground receiving stations, under *national* control, and distributed to local audiences through national networks. Broadcasting directly into home receivers from sky-borne satellites which respect no national frontiers will be accomplished with more powerful satellites and modified receivers, both of which are already technologically feasible but not yet operable.

Two decades of exposure to U.S. television exports (*I Spy, Mission Impossible, Laugh In*) make the possibility of direct, unmediated television transmission from the United States to *any* home in *any* nation a cause for traumatic anxiety in international communications-cultural circles.

After all, television is a global phenomenon. In 1970 more than 250 million television sets were in use around the world in 130 countries. The United States had 84 million, Western Europe had 75 million, the Soviet Union 30 million, and Japan 23 million. China had only 200,000 sets, Indonesia had 90,000 and India a mere 20,000. Yet other developing nations had considerable numbers of receivers. Brazil, for example, had 6.5 million sets; Argentina, 3.5 million; Venezuela, 720,000; the Philippines, 400,000; South Korea, 418,000; Nigeria 75,000, and Egypt 475,000.

The President of the United Nations General Assembly, Poland's Stanislaw Trepczynski, expressed anxiety over unrestricted transmissions at the opening of the 27th General Assembly last September: "In an age of unprecedented development of information media, of tremendous flow of ideas and of artistic achievements, concern for preserving the characteristics peculiar to the different cultures becomes a serious problem for mankind"

UNESCO itself, the acknowledged guardian if not parent of the free flow of information concept, has had some second thoughts recently about its hitherto favored principle. In October, 1972, it adopted a declaration of "Guiding Principles on the Use of Satellite Broadcasting for the Free Flow of Information." Article IX of the draft read: ". . . it is necessary that States, taking into account the principle of freedom of information, *reach or promote prior agreements* concerning direct satellite broadcasting to the population of countries other than the country of origin of transmission." (Emphasis added.)

The U.N. General Assembly passed a similar resolution in November by a vote of 102 to 1—the United States was the single dissenting voice.

A sample of national views, expressed in the United Nations' Political Committee before the vote, is illuminating for what it reveals about the widespread feelings and fears over cultural matters of which we hear or see little in our own mass media. For example, the French delegate asserted that "each state has the right to protect its culture." The delegate from Colombia expressed fear of "an ideological occupation of the world by the superpowers and their advertising mentality." Zaire's delegate said his country had been subject to subversion by private radios and was therefore aware of the possible danger of direct television broadcasting by satellites. His country, he added, wanted to be able to have control over information from outside. The Minister for Home Affairs of India said direct television broadcasting could be used to generate mistrust and conflict or for undesirable or harmful propaganda, and such use "would certainly constitute interference in the internal affairs of States." The delegate from Chile said that if new space techniques were not subjected to international rules, Latin America would be subjected to the political, economic, and cultural contagion of the large imperialist monopolies of North America. He added that the people of Latin America were rebelling against imperialism which was trying to impose on them a culture contrary to their well-being.

Aware of the extent and depth of these national sentiments, in both UNESCO and the U.N. General Assembly, that cut across ideological lines, the official U.S. position has tried to deflect the argument into a discussion of technological feasibility. Former Ambassador George Bush in the

United Nations and chief U.S. delegate William Jones in UNESCO minimized the dangers of cultural invasion and insisted that direct broadcasting was many years away and therefore no cause for immediate concern or organizational effort to regulate it.

Ironically but predictably, the U.S. diplomatic effort, formulated to sidestep an issue which unites most of the world against America as the foremost source of global communications pollution, incurred the wrath of the media moguls in the United States. Unwilling to accept a tactical retreat, insistent on their right to dominate world information flows, and indifferent to the needs and opinions of weaker states no matter how numerous, the no-nonsense American media managers reacted sharply.

Frank Stanton, then CBS president, member of the Presidentially appointed U.S. Advisory Commission on Information, and longtime chairman of the Radio Free Europe organization, wrote a lengthy article, "Will They Stop Our Satellites?" published in *The New York Times* October 22, 1972. In it he claimed that "the rights of Americans to speak to whomever they please, when they please, are [being] bartered away." His chief objection to the UNESCO draft of Guiding Principles on the Use of Satellite Broadcasting is that censorship is being imposed by provisions which permit each nation to reach prior agreement with transmitting nations concerning the character of the broadcasts.

Stanton finds the right of nations to control the character of the messages transmitted into their territories both dangerous and a gross violation of the U.S. Constitution's provision for freedom of speech: "The rights which form the framework of our Constitution, the principles asserted in the Universal Declaration of Human Rights, the basic principle of the free movement of ideas, are thus ignored."

Stanton apparently believes that the U.S. Constitution, fine document that it is, should be the binding law for the international community, whether it wishes it or not. Yet as long ago as 1946 the Hutchins Commission on Freedom of the Press rejected the easy assumption that the espousal of free speech in the U.S. Constitution was the basis for insisting on an unrestricted international free flow of communication.

"The surest antidote for ignorance and deceit," the Commission noted, "is widest possible exchange of objectively realistic information—*true* information, not merely *more* information; *true* information, not merely, as those who would have us simply write the First Amendment into international law seem to suggest, the *unhindered flow* of information!

There is evidence that a mere quantitative increase in the flow of words and images across national borders may replace ignorance with prejudice and distortion rather than with understanding." (Emphasis in text.)

Moreover, is the freedom of speech that the U.S. Constitution guarantees to the individual applicable to multi-national communications corporations, of which Stanton is so powerful an advocate? Are CBS, ABC, and RCA "individuals" in the sense that most people understand the term? And, if a nation does not have the right to regulate and control the information flowing into and past its borders, who does? CBS? ITT? Stanton?

Stanton's view assumes an identity between the profit-making interests of a handful of giant communications conglomerates and the informational needs of the American people. The error is compounded when the same corporate interests are placed above the needs of all nations for cultural sovereignty. The great majority of Americans have absolutely no capability, financial or technological, of speaking "to whomever they please, when they please," outside their own country (or inside, for that matter). The voices and images which are now, and will be, transmitted overseas are those produced by our familiar communications combines, scarcely grassroots organizations.

Stanton, in the best prose of the Cold War decades, argues that "leaders of too many countries have a deadly fear of information which could lead their people to topple the regimes in power." Possibly. More likely, many leaders have a "deadly fear" of the cultural effects of the programming the major U.S. commercial networks would be pumping into their countrymen's television sets. Some leaders are aware that many Americans are troubled with the character of the material that floods their homes. They know that there is an increasing number of parents who are outraged with the daily television shows that assault their children's minds (and from which, incidentally, CBS in 1970 derived $16.5 million in profits).

Perhaps those who are concerned with national cultural development in other countries do not want to wait the twenty-five years it took before Americans began to question the effects of exposure of their children and themselves to cartoons, commercials, and the likes of *Dragnet, Mod Squad, I Spy,* and other well known commercial offerings.

Arthur Goodfriend, a former State Department consultant, recently wrote in *The Annals,* "In an era of electronic communication . . . what is imperialism? Is it simply a policy of territorial extension? Or does it embrace the invasion of human minds?"

Should the international community be criticized for also asking this question? International regulation of direct satellite broadcasting is not an example of censorship that strikes at "the fundamental principle of free speech." It is a necessary measure to enable all societies to have a role in determining their cultural destinies.

Stanton and his friends—*The New York Times* supported his position editorially and complained about "censorship of the global air waves"— have it wrong. Liberty is not threatened. CBS profits could be. Freedom of thought is not challenged. RCA's markets may be.

The UNESCO declaration of "Guiding Principles" and the U.N. General Assembly's resolution regulating space broadcasting will not eliminate the cultural domination by a few that already exists in the world. They do signify, however, that the brief era of American global/cultural hegemony, established under the seemingly innocuous principle of "the free flow of information," is coming to an end.

There will be difficulties in the transitional period ahead. Some arbitrary national actions are inevitable. But the worldwide homogenization of culture is too high a price to pay for the maintenance of an arrangement which produces benefits for only a tiny cluster of U.S. communications conglomerates.

TECHNOLOGY AND ITS APPLICATION IN BROADCASTING

Since broadcasting is a product of technology, it is not surprising that people in the field are alert to technological developments that will affect their ability to perform well. When feasible, they are quick to adopt and adapt technical advancements that become available from a source outside of the field of broadcasting. However, when new technologies such as cable television and direct satellite communications are seen as threats to the existing economic structures, those in broadcasting often are just as quick to set up restrictions which will protect existing media organizations. While some of the issues growing out of the changing technology may not be readily apparent to the observer outside of the field, they may indeed have far more powerful effects on the consumer than those that are obvious, such as changes in programming.

Our entire section on Cable Television is a reflection of some of the issues growing out of this new technology. The advantage of the medium is related to its ability to offer multiple channels to the consumer, so that for the first time there would be spectrum space enough for all messages. But the social use of a technical development such as cable television depends upon conditions other than the technology itself. Lynn White, in his fascinating book *Medieval Technology and Social Change*, concluded that "a new device merely opens a door; it does not compel one to enter. The acceptance or rejection of an invention, or the extent to which its implications are realized if it is accepted, depends quite as much upon the conditions of society, and upon the imagination of its leaders, as upon the nature of the technological item itself." * A recent Rand study edited by H. Goldhamer, *The Social Effects of Communication Technology*, came to virtually the same conclusions, couching them in words which were more appropriate to the electronic media in the United States. Goldhamer suggested that the social effects of the new technologies, including cable television, computer-implemented communication systems, and "wired cities," will be great; he argued, however, that the possible social effects are not to be determined solely by the technical dvelopments in communications. They are, instead, to be determined in part by "cost considerations, public policy, and entrepreneurial and consumer pressures and choices."† We already have seen this statement to be true in the spread and adoption of cable television in the major cities.

Our readings in this section deal with two other technological developments and their professional and social use. They are the new minicameras, which are used to tape news events or to cover remote news events live, and the automation of radio stations so that programming can be produced at less cost or can be improved by supplementing existing industry practices. Robert H. Mulholland, with NBC in New York City, discusses application of the electronic "cameras" to network news operations, and Joan Sweeney gives a national report of the application of automation technologies to radio broadcasting.

Although Mulholland does not mention the problem in his study of the new technology, moving the electronic cameras directly into a news event has exacerbated problems that were not quite so obvious before. Early in 1974, television news covered live a fire-fight between Los Angeles police and SLA members, in which six members of the underground organization died. One station received an Emmy award nomination for its coverage. During the summer of 1974, newsmen, especially television remote units, created a problem for the police by reporting a confidential police stakeout of a building which supposedly housed SLA members and by sending so many units into the area to cover the story that the police were hampered getting in themselves. The faux pas created a climate where the television and radio newsmen and the police department finally had to sit down together to work out a system for avoiding the problem in the future. The new cameras did not create this problem—they added to it.

*Lynn White, *Medieval Technology and Social Change*, Oxford University Press, New York, 1966, p. 28.

†H. Goldhamer, Ed., *The Social Effects of Communication Technology*, The Rand Corp., Santa Monica, Calif., 1970, Introduction.

Broadcasting Technology

387

Related issues, already discussed in the section on International Broadcasting, include the controversy growing out of the use of the satellite for news transmission, programming of culture and sports, and direct broadcasting to homes in different countries. We have yet to determine the possible effects of the direct satellite system on our own television system, cable and broadcast. Will networks be enhanced by satellite-to-home broadcasting? Will independent and network affiliate stations both be destroyed because there no longer will be a need for their signal? Will cable television be more successful because it can pick up any signal from a satellite and retransmit it to homes already hooked into its system? Certainly, the role of the FCC and Congress in determining what takes place with such a satellite will be paramount. These are just a few of the issues that need to be explored and resolved in the years immediately ahead, for the direct broadcast satellite already is experimentally operational, far sooner than the experts had anticipated. How federal policy and economic factors will affect its use are the imponderables.

BIBLIOGRAPHICAL ESSAY

The impact of technology on the mass media and on society has received less attention than it deserves. Our selections by Robert Mulholland and Joan Sweeney offer broad, detailed surveys of some of the accomplishments and some of the issues involved when new technology is applied to the broadcast media. For views that go beyond these surveys to a discussion of some of the outcomes created by the new technology, particularly the use of cable television in conjunction with computers, see Ben Bagdikian, *The Information Machines: Their Impact on Men and the Media*, Harper & Row, New York, 1971, and Herbert Goldhamer, *The Social Effects of Communication Technology*, Rand Corp., Santa Monica, Calif., 1970. Goldhamer's study is dated now by technical developments, but his research and analysis was so thorough that it stands the test of time—it still is a highly useful survey of the possible effects of the new technology. A special issue of *Viewpoint (1972)*, a labor publication, offers useful insight into fears and expectations created by the new technology, from the aspect of the effects on workers. An overview of where we stand and of future applications can be found in Brenda Maddox, *Beyond Babel: New Directions in Communications*, Simon and Schuster, New York, 1972.

For a look at the experimental use of television technology, see the special issue of *Print* (January/February, 1972), which has several articles and case studies on the application of the computer and videotape to television graphic design and programming. The best single source of information on the current trend, however, is Kas Kalba, *The Video Implosion: Models for Reinventing Television*, Aspen Institute Program on Communications and Society, Palo Alto, Calif. Unfortunately, the 46-page typescript does not contain illustrations, which are included in the *Print* edition mentioned above. The Kalba paper does contain an extensive bibliography. To keep abreast of changes in the field, see especially *Radical Software*, a magazine published by Raindance Foundation.

Finally, students who wish to explore the potentials of new developments for the future should consult J. S. Cook, "Communication by Optical Fiber," *Scientific American* (November, 1973), 28–35, an illustrated, fairly technical article dealing with the present state of this fantastically large signal-carrying technology. According to Cook, the optical fiber coupled with lasers can become, sometime in the future, "One hundred individual, signal-carrying fibers bundled together [which would] occupy a space that has the diameter of the lead in an ordinary wooden pencil. *Each fiber* might carry 1,000 telephone conversations or several television programs at a time." (Italics added.) How and with what will we fill those channels?

STUDY QUESTIONS

1. Are there any disadvantages to be found in the new technological developments in television news coverage? What are they? What advantages do you see other than those enumerated by Robert Mulholland?

2. Watch your local television stations to determine if the new electronic cameras are now in use. Can you see significant differences in technical and journalistic qualities of those stories covered by the new equipment?

3. Which radio stations in your area use automated programming equipment? How does this programming compare to the nonautomated stations?

4. Joan Sweeney's article on automated radio poses this question: "Do you want local programming that sounds terrible or national-type programming that sounds professional?" How do you react to the local versus professional sound on radio?

Toward Totally Electronic TV News

ROBERT MULHOLLAND

Reprinted from *The Quill,* vol. 61, 11 (November, 1973), published by the Society
of Professional Journalists, Sigma Delta Chi, with permission of the publisher.
Copyright 1974 by The Quill. Robert E. Mulholland is vice president of NBC News
in New York City.

If you watch a television news program tonight, the odds are you'll see a
report you couldn't have seen one year ago.

Then, you would have seen that report tomorrow. Or maybe the day
after tomorrow.

In simplest terms, that's what the new technology means to the television
news viewer—more news now, not later.

Satellites, computers, microminiaturization, solid state components—all
these fancy space-age terms now mean something to electronic journalism
and journalists.

And more important, they mean something to the 90 million Americans
who watch television news each day.

Satellite transmission of foreign news is now commonplace. What that
means to a viewer is same-day coverage of an event in Europe or Japan.

Just 10 years ago, satellites were not available full-time. They could be
available as little as 13 minutes a day.

Now, fixed position satellites over the Atlantic, Pacific and Indian oceans,
plus nearly 90 earth stations for sending up pictures and sound, make it
possible to transmit news to the United States from every continent, 24
hours a day.

However, most of what is transmitted by satellite for television news is
film. And before you understand what the new technology means and where
it can take electronic journalism, you must understand the difference
between film and videotape.

When the Allende government was overthrown in Chile, the junta
sealed borders and closed airports. Reporters couldn't get into Chile. Film
couldn't be flown out.

A Santiago television station had covered all the fighting. Via satellite,
from a ground station in Santiago, Chile, American television viewers saw
their first report of what was happening.

But it was a film report. Film cameramen had covered the fighting. Then, after processing and editing, the film was satellited to the United States for broadcast on the network news programs.

Yes, new technology—the satellite—got the report here faster. Otherwise, the film would have been flown to New York, showing up possibly days after the actual event.

CAMERAS WITHOUT FILM

But now, there is a faster way. The networks are experimenting with it. And what the satellite has done for foreign coverage, even though it is film coverage, the new technology in hand-held electronic cameras will do for domestic coverage.

NBC News calls its camera the PCP-90. . . . CBS has dubbed its camera the Minicam.

The names are not important. What is important is that these new cameras are in the process of changing the way news is covered in this country.

First, these cameras do not use film. They record their pictures on magnetic tape. Just like home tape recorders. This means no processing time is needed. And that means news can be covered later in the day and still broadcast on the evening news programs.

Second, these cameras can be used to cover news "live." By either hooking into a telephone company line, or using a portable transmitter, a major story can be put on the air as it is happening as a bulletin or special report.

A SIX-OUNCE TV CAMERA

The new technology has made these cameras possible. Ten years ago, the lightest electronic color camera available at NBC weighed over 200 pounds. Now, electronic color cameras are on the market weighing as little as 30 pounds. And two companies, RCA and Fairchild, have announced development of a six-ounce television camera. Right now, though, it is black-and-white.

The lightweight electronic cameras were originally developed by the networks for use at the political conventions. Then, they became part of most sports coverage.

Mulholland

391

But, in both cases, they were used "live," cable connected. And they were used to cover a given event in a given location.

Then, the new technology came along with small, powerful batteries. And small portable videotape recorders. And the camera itself got smaller and lighter. As a result, the camera could be used to cover breaking news. And that's what is being done now.

In Washington, both NBC News and CBS use electronic cameras every day.

If you are a sophisticated viewer, you can tell what is film and what is electronic on the evening news programs. And when you see a correspondent or a major government official "electronic" on the news, the odds are that was a late story—too late to do on film.

In New York, Chicago and Los Angeles, some network-owned stations are now using the new cameras for their local news coverage. And as the price of the equipment drops, as it will, more stations throughout the country will be adding portable electronic cameras for news.

But all of this will soon pose a problem for the networks and the stations that start to go electronic. That problem is—how far do they go?

Do they go all-electronic? Do they go half and half? Or do they continue film as the basis for television news coverage, using electronic cameras only in special situations.

Each system requires a separate support system, and they are totally incompatible. The entire support system already exists for film. Networks and stations own their own processors. They have their newsfilm editing equipment. They are currently investing in new lightweight film cameras with solid-state sound systems.

TOTALLY ELECTRONIC NEWS

To go totally electronic for news will require, for example, expanded videotape editing facilities. News producers complain videotape can't be edited as quickly as film.

Computer-controlled videotape editing systems exist. But they are expensive compared to newsfilm editing equipment. Yet, competition has a way of either forcing the price down, or making it seem not quite so important.

If the opposition network or station can do something you can't, because of a piece of new equipment, there's usually a fast way to get it—especially if you've been beaten on a story once or twice.

Incidentally, although the new excitement in television news is electronic cameras, the new technology is also at work on film and film cameras.

Film speeds are now faster than ever before. Color film processing is faster. Film cameras are lighter and more versatile. And all of this means more news, covered faster and better, for the viewer.

Our reporters, in Washington for example, can stay on their beat an extra hour in the afternoon if they know an electronic camera is hot in the hallway. Rather than bringing our White House correspondent back to our studio, he can step outside after a late briefing and do a report that can be taped on the spot, or fed directly back to the studio and into a news program live.

FLIP SWITCH, PUSH BUTTON

The new technology makes all of this possible. And it isn't over yet.

A friend of mine at NBC News whose job it is to keep abreast of the new developments that might help us cover news faster, predicts this for the future: The television reporter will wear a small hearing aid device, actually a microminiaturized satellite receiver, that will keep him in constant contact with his office.

He'll have a small electronic camera, about the size of today's home movie camera.

And he'll carry a small videotape recorder the size of today's small audio tape cassette recorders.

To get his story on the air, he'll open his briefcase, flip a switch, push a button on his recorder—and that's it.

His briefcase will contain a satellite transmission terminal. And that will allow him to get on the air from any location.

So, the new technology is here, at work every day helping us get news to the people of this country. What we didn't think would be possible 10 years ago, we do every night without thinking twice. And what we dream about now, we'll be doing in the future. Maybe next year.

Mulholland

393

Radio Stations Dial "A" for Automation

JOAN SWEENEY

Reprinted from *Calendar Magazine, Los Angeles Times,* June 16, 1974, by permission
of the publisher. Copyright 1974 by Los Angeles Times Company. Joan Sweeney
is a staff writer with the *Los Angeles Times* on general assignment.

On a winter day a traveler tuning into a radio station in the Midwest might
hear disc jockey Don McMasters warning about black ice on the local
roads. At that identical moment, a listener to a station in the South might
hear the same Don McMasters announcing the time.

The ubiquitous McMasters, who is heard on nearly 100 radio stations
from Singapore to Casper, Wyo., is a manifestation of a quiet revolution
in radio stations—a trend to automation and computerization.

Disc jockeys spinning records on turntables in front of live mikes have
been replaced by banks of tape decks, cartridges and audio clocks for time
checks, all controlled and played automatically by a computer in more
sophisticated cases or by simpler automation system. Even news can be
inserted automatically from a network news service.

The capability exists for stations to operate without a human being on
the premises, according to Larry T. Pfister of International Good Music, a
manufacturer of computer systems for radio stations, but the Federal
Communications Commission does not permit it in the United States.

"It requires that a licensed operator be on duty at all times," he said. "It
can be a high schooler with an FCC license, but you need someone to
babysit the transmitter."

In Canada, however, several radio stations do operate for hours at a time
with no one at them, he said.

"If the system has sufficient tape reel capacity you can walk away from
it," he said. "The computer is fully capable of watching the system and
taking its own corrective action if a tape breaks. If a transmitter goes off
the air it can turn on a standby transmitter."

Some owners of automated stations do not even do their own
programming. Instead they hire a service that provides it for them on tape.
They can buy a personality like McMasters or a format like country and
western or hit parade prepackaged on tape.

Automation is merely assembling automatically prerecorded material, notes Andrew P. McClure, sales manager of Schafer Electronics Corp., in Santa Barbara, which manufactures computer and automation systems.

Generally disc jockey patter, intros and outros are on one tape reel; other reels contain music, generally segregated by tempo or type; commercials are in tape cartridge carousels.

Many systems have an audio clock in them, which has every minute of the day prerecorded, to announce time checks, according to McClure.

"It's an idea similar to what you get when you telephone for the time, but we like to think we don't sound as dead as the phone company."

The computer is programmed to play the tapes in whatever sequence the program director desires. It turns the tape machines on and off through subliminal tones and then rescues them automatically.

To someone watching the banks of tape decks and cartridges starting, stopping and rescuing—seemingly by themselves—next to an empty broadcast studio, it carries a hint of 1984.

Some critics complain automation turns programming into an assembly line process, like putting together a car at a GM plant. Proponents say it can mean better programming, especially on smaller stations.

"Radio suffered from a lack of air talent," McClure said. "It falls into the same type [of] thinking the FCC is concerned about in television. It would like to have a lot of programming originating from local TV stations. They can't afford this and don't have the talent to do it. Radio is the same kind of thing. Do you want local programming that sounds terrible or national type programming that sounds professional?"

He estimated about 1,000 of the nation's 7,000 radio stations are automated.

"One out of seven stations is fully automated and that can be anything from beautiful music to all news stations," he said. "Rock to Bach can and is being automated."

Automation originally began mainly in smaller stations, he said, but since services selling packaged programming started, stations in major markets have been switching to it to be competitive.

"All of our systems have network-join features," McClure said. "At a predetermined time each hour, the system automatically fades out of what it's doing and picks up news off the network line, puts it on the air automatically and, when the news is over, goes back to playing local preprogrammed material."

Station owners embrace automation generally for one of two reasons: to save money or to improve programming quality and thus hone their competitive edge.

In the beginning, Pfister said, "automation was considered the salvation for dying FM stations that did not have the money to hire people. That isn't the case anymore."

"There are two things you can do with automation: save money or improve quality," said John H. Garabedian, president and general manager of station WGTR in the Boston suburb of Natick, Mass.

"You can save money if you want to do it from the cheapo standpoint—fire all the announcers and have one guy do everything," he added. "We have a competitor station 10 miles from here which has the same basic computer we do. They did it to save money. We don't do it to save money."

The computer gives Garabedian greater quality, flexibility, control and efficiency. One industry source said he believed the station made the most creative and fullest use of the computer's possibilities of any station in the country.

Said Garabedian: "With the computer we have absolutely perfect control over executing whatever program design we want. The only mistakes we ever have are human mistakes. Any manufacturing process can be broken down into its component steps."

"Break down what an hour is made of—45 minutes of music, five minutes of news, eight–nine minutes of commercials and about one–two minutes of talk," he said. "So why does the announcer who only talks have to sit there hour after hour when all he does is talk about two minutes?"

With computerization, Garabedian said, a disc jockey can do a four-hour show in 15 minutes. He records his talk, sans music, on a tape. The automation system then mixes it with music on other reels.

"If he makes mistakes, he can go back and do it over," he added. "It gives us much better control over the format. You can design the most perfect format in the world and have an announcer foul it up because he interjects his own tastes."

His staff of 19 includes four newsmen and three disc jockeys, who work five days a week, but whose shows are heard seven days thanks to automation.

But with the computer, he said, "We can afford to pay the highest wages and, therefore, get and keep the best people, which makes us far superior to the competition with budget problems because they don't get the mileage out of people that we do."

Station KWOW in Pomona has one of the most advanced computer setups in the Los Angeles area and John Wickstrom, who does the station's programming, said:

"We can hire professional talent 24 hours a day and have a very consistent sound, 24 hours a day, seven days a week—that's the purpose [of computerized programming]."

KWOW does its own programming and has its own disc jockeys, but now instead of spending all their time spinning records, they are more involved in production—"enhancing the sound of the station, writing copy for clients," Wickstrom said.

Wickstrom estimated the station has nearly $100,000 invested in its computer and supporting equipment such as tape decks, carousels, etc.

While stations like KWOW and WGTR do their own programming, some other automated stations buy prepackaged material—personality shows or a special format. In addition to manufacturing automation equipment, IGM, headquartered in Bellingham, Wash., syndicates personalities like Don McMasters..

McMasters, who lives in Wenatchee, Wash., does not believe his show sounds "canned." He localizes it by making cuts that deal with local situations. . . . He also has recorded a time check tape.

This material is fed into the station's automation systems for insertion at the proper time, he explained.

"I use localized material that fools even professionals," he said.

He recalled the time a broadcaster, driving through the Midwest, heard him on a very small station in the backwoods, believed he was too good to be there and decided to hire him.

"He drove over 150 miles to find me going around on a reel of tape," said McMasters.

IGM's Pfister said, "We are for smaller markets that need to sound like bigger markets and can't afford it."

There are two schools of thought in programming, according to Pfister.

"One is the Bill Drake concept of having a consistent format all day long. The other concept is blocs of programming appealing to different audiences at different times of the day (which IGM provides). Both can be successful."

Drake, a high-priced radio consultant, is the Drake of Drake-Chenault Enterprises, Inc., one of the most successful of the programming packagers for automated stations. From offices on Topanga Canyon Blvd. [in Los Angeles] it provides programming for stations from Ventura to Gardiner, Me., and Harlingen, Tex. It does not divulge how many clients it has. An industry source estimates the number at about 100 stations.

It offers the station a choice of four formats: Hitparade, Great American Country, Classic Gold (hit oldies) and Solid Gold (both old and current hits). Emphasis is on music, not personality.

"We cannot and do not develop personalities for automated stations," said Pat Shaughnessy, executive vice president and general manager of Drake-Chenault. "We feel there are very few really strong personalities, and they are paid very handsomely for being personalities. . . . We employ more music, less chatter. It seems to be a very winning formula."

Each station receives a basic music library (which is changed periodically) of 50 reels with 28 songs per reel. In addition, it gets a reel of current hits each week.

Each station subscribing to a format receives the same nucleus of raw material, but the difference is in the embellishments—promos, ads, jingles— according to Shaughnessy. The music flow is different too, tailored for a particular station by the computer.

"Maybe in one classic gold town, you hear down-tempo music; you go to another town, it's all up-tempo. It depends on the competitive situation. But both stations have the same basic libraries."

Automation also makes it easier for stations to switch formats if the one they are using bombs.

"With automation all it needs to do is change tapes," said McClure. "It stops its country service and picks up progressive rock."

Garabedian believes that in 10 years 70–80% of the stations will be completely automated.

"Television is taking the really great people away from radio, and it is more and more difficult to find quality people at any price," said Pfister. "A lot of broadcasters see automation as making better jobs for guys who deserve to stay in broadcasting and weeding out guys who shouldn't be there anyway."

Many disc jockeys, however, are not enamored of automation, though disc jockeys in major markets sometimes moonlight for automated stations outside their area.

"It's a great way to pick up extra money for a guy holding down a regular job that doesn't pay him particularly well," disc jockey Mark Elliott said. "I know several other people currently involved in this kind of work who are doing very well."

Elliott, formerly on KHJ, contracted to do a series of programs for KWOW after he left KHJ. He drove to Pomona once a week from his Culver City home to do a full week of five-hour shows.

"I'd go in once a week to record seven or eight shows without the music," he said. "It takes approximately 40–45 minutes to do each show."

He figures it took him six–seven hours to do eight shows, "which is a long time to talk because for all practical purposes you're talking continuously with perhaps a five-ten second pause between each wrap."

"You do the first three–four shows in a given session and you're very sharp, very witty," he said. "By the time you get into the fifth, sixth or seventh show, you're getting tired, punchy, backing off a little. It's not something you have any control over."

He agrees with proponents who say automation makes for a more professional sound, but [he] is not necessarily sure that's entirely good.

"It's true you come off sounding very professional and very polished, but one of the criticisms I got most frequently on a live show was that it had too much of that quality to it."

But according to WGTR's Garabedian, his disc jockeys like the computerized system. The station recently did a live remote broadcast using conventional facilities from a large shopping center in eastern Boston.

"It was hilarious," he recalled. "The announcers felt like they were going back to the crank telephone."

APPENDIX 1

Performance of Network Affiliates in the Top 50 Markets

FCC Commissioner Nicholas Johnson,* in dissent to earlier renewal of station licenses in Arkansas, Mississippi and Louisiana, issued [a] 264-page report, "The Performance of Network Affiliates in the Top 50 Markets" (*Broadcasting*, July 9). No other commissioner joined in Mr. Johnson's dissent and report. Presented here is [a] table showing all affiliates by alphabetical order of ownership, with individual rankings in the several

*Former Commissioner Johnson was regarded by commercial broadcast interests as one of the gadflies on the Commission. He has published several books on broadcasting, one of the most successful being *How to Talk Back to Your Television Set*.

categories Mr. Johnson used. Composite rank (first column after call and location) was computed as follows:

Licensees were ranked first according to local-programming indicia computed by the sum of the prime-time local programming and total local programming in [a] composite week divided by two.

Second ranking is in order of the licensees according to the sum of the quantities of their news, public affairs and "other" programming, as depicted on FCC Form 303.

Third ranking is according to [the] number of public-service announcements carried in [a] composite week.

Fourth ranking is according to [the] number of hours in [a] composite week containing more than 12 minutes of commercials. The last ranking is ordered from lowest to highest.

Financial ranking is in order of magnitude of the ratio of programming expenses to broadcast revenues.

Composite ranking is a conglomeration of four different ranking criteria: (1) local programming, (2) news, public affairs and "other," (3) commercialization and (4) financial evaluations. In order that each element have an equal weight or have equal effect on composite ranking, licensees were assigned a number between zero and 100 for each of the four evaluation criteria, and the composite ranking is then based on an average of those four numbers.

For local programming, the number-one licenses sets the scale, *i.e.*, the indicia of 20.92 (hours and minutes were converted to hours in decimals for computer programming) represents 100/100. An indicia of zero is represented by zero; however, the lowest indicia, 1.71, is 8.71/100, representing the station in the top-50 markets with the least local programming.

A similar analysis is made with the news, public affairs and "other"; 48.53 hours represents 100 and 12.40 hours represents 27.05/100, zero being the lowest.

In commercialization ranking, the licensee with most hours containing more than 12 commercial minutes is assigned a value of zero on the scale between zero and 100. A licensee with zero segments having 12 or more minutes of commercials is assigned a value of 100; however, the licensee at the top in this report is rated 96.61/100, with two segments having 12 or more minutes of commercials.

In the financial factor ranking, the licensee having the highest program-expense/revenue ratio is assigned 100. A ratio of zero is assigned zero on the scale.

Once all of these factors were computed, the composite rank was calculated as an average of the four factors.

Owner	Station and market	Composite rank	Local	News	Commercialization	Financial	Minorities	Women	PSA
A. S. Abell Co.	WMAR-TV Baltimore	34	11	25	78	104	110	105	41
American Broadcasting Co.	KABC-TV Los Angeles	102	123	115	96	17	34	6	43
	KGO-TV San Francisco	76	94	70	99	30	42	34	106
	WABC-TV New York	13	63	77	56	1	98	65	62
	WLS-TV Chicago	115	53	61	143	68	63	25	87
	WXYZ-TV Detroit	117	89	116	135	26	97	18	141
Arizona Television Co.	KTVK-TV Phoenix	97	88	122	49	75	91	16	111
Avco Corp.	WLWC-TV Columbus	131	99	67	121	118	15	27	91
	WLWD-TV Dayton	83	30	42	137	83	36	81	79
	WLWI-TV Indianapolis	65	64	26	130	37	47	8	50
	WLWT-TV Cincinnati	25	1	118	129	44	36	87	36
	WOAI-TV San Antonio	58	58	88	31	93	123	92	38
Bonneville International	KIRO-TV Seattle/Tacoma	114	66	83	109	125	39	122	140
	KSL-TV Salt Lake City	33	57	90	88	6	145	147	118
Buffalo Evening News	WBEN-TV Buffalo	38	55	21	80	80	130	136	35
Capital Cities Broadcasting	KTRK-TV Houston	64	18	95	69	100	102	106	101
	WKBW-TV Buffalo	73	78	106	21	109	25	123	31
	WPVI-TV Philadelphia	50	14	62	113	45	56	51	10
	WTNH-TV Hartford/New Haven	95	81	81	57	124	65	141	28
Carter Publications	WBAP-TV Dallas/Ft. Worth	93	132	50	36	115	96	100	30
Chronicle Publishing	KRON-TV San Francisco						114	63	
Columbia Broadcasting System	KMOX-TV St. Louis	27	59	11	105	36	31	32	49
	KNXT-TV Los Angeles	40	21	8	128	88	112	72	85
	WBBM-TV Chicago	74	33	18	141	65	81	33	52
	WCAU-TV Philadelphia	46	42	9	127	73	59	1	38
	WCBS-TV New York	26	75	4	111	27	75	13	22
Columbia Pictures Industries (Screen Gems Broadcasting)	KCPX-TV Salt Lake City	109	142	136	16	40	85	116	29
	WVUE-TV New Orleans	79	107	112	44	34	117	15	72
Combined Communications	KBTV-TV Denver	142	91	128	142	42	113	95	123
	KOCO-TV Oklahoma City	91	62	124	81	53	17	117	33
	KTAR-TV Phoenix	23	8	64	66	48	45	62	88
Cosmos Broadcasting	WDSU-TV New Orleans	36	20	55	82	55	115	77	136
	WTOL-TV Toledo	98	87	71	65	122	38	20	103
Cox Broadcasting	WHIO-TV Dayton	126	45	123	133	87	23	114	143
	WIIC-TV Pittsburgh	15	17	53	101	8	24	22	56
	WSB-TV Atlanta	31	5	56	54	116	101	74	78
	WSOC-TV Charlotte	57	122	75	18	47	90	110	109
Dallas Evening News	WFAA-TV Dallas/Ft. Worth	85	47	114	75	85	95	37	67
Dispatch Printing	WBNS-TV Columbus	22	22	19	85	61	39	45	14
Dun & Bradstreet	KHOU-TV Houston	70	25	30	110	127	105	82	60
	KXTV-TV Sacramento/Stockton	105	101	36	122	66	125	50	74
	WISH-TV Indianapolis	104	73	65	80	135	57	26	67
Evening News Assn.	WWJ-TV Detroit	69	9	31	131	112	94	109	83
Evening Star Broadcasting	WMAL-TV Wash., D.C.	7	4	6	30	57	87	2	17
Fetzer Communications	WKZO-TV Grand Rapids/Kalamazoo	138	108	100	91	142	147	134	129
Fisher Companies	KOMO-TV Seattle/Tacoma	24	32	66	61	28	61	10	25
	KATU-TV Portland	18	50	96	25	13	21	68	54
General Electric	KOA-TV Denver	113	56	79	108	132	138	71	61
	WSIX-TV Nashville	61	82	125	32	22	70	9	138
	WRGB-TV Albany-Schenectady/Troy	118	100	121	39	129	135	97	26
John T. Griffin	KWTV-TV Oklahoma City	54	77	82	77	25	12	61	8
Harte-Hanks Newspapers	KENS-TV San Antonio	130	106	93	83	134	104	84	64
Hearst Corp.	WBAL-TV Baltimore	48	19	33	95	101	61	56	21
	WISN-TV Milwaukee	132	97	98	123	82	118	90	58
	WTAE-TV Pittsburgh	8	52	60	10	15	32	93	18
Houston Post	KPRC-TV Houston	41	29	22	79	94	132	107	12
Hubbard Broadcasting	KSTP-TV Minneapolis/St. Paul	59	43	91	62	71	91	73	126
Jefferson Pilot	WBTV-TV Charlotte	82	46	52	93	120	134	52	63
Journal Co.	WTMJ-TV Milwaukee	74	13	92	107	89	44	76	135
Kelly Broadcasting	KCRA-TV Sacramento/Stockton	20	27	14	73	69	86	124	77
King Broadcasting	KGW-TV Portland	16	67	35	53	2	7	88	32
	KING-TV Seattle/Tacoma	3	76	48	6	3	6	35	133
KOOL Radio-Television (Gene Autry)	KOOL-TV Phoenix	140	96	76	140	119	67	115	11
Landmark Communications	WFMY-TV Greensboro/High Point/Winston-Salem	9	96	38	2	76	83	75	91
	WTAR-TV Norfolk/Newport News/Hampton						105	39	
Lee Enterprises	WSAZ-TV Charleston/Huntington	124	119	58	71	139	5	139	91
Life & Casualty Insurance Co. (half-owner)	WLAC-TV Nashville	86	39	101	114	49	98	85	136

Owner	Station and market	Composite rank	Local	News	Commercialization	Financial	Minorities	Women	PSA
Lin Broadcasting	WAVY-TV Norfolk/Newport News/Hampton	81	121	54	37	84	88	58	20
Loyola University	WWL-TV New Orleans	11	7	24	72	31	139	99	95
McGraw-Hill	KGTV-TV San Diego	112	111	102	89	62	79	104	121
	KMGH-TV Denver	99	44	73	118	98	75	98	51
	WRTV-TV Indianapolis	37	65	39	40	64	49	44	88
Mecklenburg Television Broadcasters	*WCCB-TV Charlotte	144	133	129	84	137	133	21	112
Media General Inc.	WFLA-TV Tampa/St. Petersburg	127	120	51	134	78	41	113	54
Meredith Corp.	KCMO-TV Kansas City	87	54	69	102	97	61	140	109
	WHEN-TV Syracuse	108	127	89	90	54	9	64	115
Metromedia	KMBC-TV Kansas City	135	102	133	94	90	53	5	47
Metropolitan Broadcasting	KOVR-TV Sacramento/Stockton	44	134	120	20	5	108	131	97
Midcontinent Television	*WCCO-TV Minneapolis/St. Paul	84	12	74	139	72	28	29	116
Midwest Television	KFMB-TV San Diego	96	51	20	132	128	71	30	37
Multimedia	WFBC-TV Greenville/Spartanburg/Asheville	72	104	63	14	130	60	36	85
	WXII-TV Greensboro/Winston-Salem/High Point	63	118	105	29	21	137	26	112
Newhouse Broadcasting	KOIN-TV Portland	21	84	29	59	12	27	89	5
	KTVI-TV St. Louis	68	86	140	26	19	78	146	137
	WAPI-TV Birmingham	52	126	46	17	63	143	129	17
	WSYR-TV Syracuse	47	117	127	13	10	14	143	17
New York Times	WREC-TV Memphis	128	131	108	58	114	109	111	130
NTL Corp.	*WSM-TV Nashville	28	24	97	67	16	129	54	142
Orion Broadcasting	WAVE-TV Louisville	106	95	85	92	86	64	127	83
Outlet Co.	KSAT-TV San Antonio	78	90	131	28	38	118	48	128
	WJAR-TV Providence	94	114	47	70	91	35	144	7
	*WNYS-TV Syracuse	107	144	143	8	18	2	102	73
Overmeyer	WDHO-TV Toledo	100	139	144	7	29	142	31	117
Pacific and Southern Broadcasting	WQXI-TV Atlanta	143	129	126	112	99	75	23	44
Peninsula Broadcasting	WVEC-TV Norfolk/Newport News/Hampton	137	137	135	42	95	141	40	91
Plains Television	*WHNB-TV Hartford/New Haven	103	116	23	64	136	69	78	144
Poole Broadcasting	*WPRI-TV Providence	51	115	94	3	113	3	91	105
	*WTEN-TV Albany/Schenectady/Troy	90	110	103	76	39	20	120	52
Pulitzer Publishing	KSD-TV St. Louis	66	36	68	74	108	121	83	45
Rahall Communications	*WLCY-TV Tampa/St. Petersburg	70	61	44	86	96	140	137	4
RCA	KNBC-TV Los Angeles	14	3	3	138	35	54	38	99
	WKYC-TV Cleveland	116	113	86	126	43	26	67	88
	WMAQ-TV Chicago	43	41	2	136	74	51	41	101
	WNBC-TV New York City	39	60	17	97	58	67	17	65
	WRC-TV Washington	12	49	15	103	7	43	66	96

Owner	Station and market	Composite rank	Local	News	Commercialization	Financial	Minorities	Women	PSA
Reeves Telecom.	WHTN-TV Charleston/Huntington	110	140	107	19	102	8	12	59
RKO General	WHBQ-TV Memphis	141	138	139	52	111	110	119	134
	WNAC-TV Boston	17	37	41	27	59	19	112	22
Rollins	WCHS-TV Charleston/Huntington	121	85	132	24	140	10	60	69
Scripps-Howard Broadcasting	WCPO-TV Cincinnati	42	40	49	98	33	127	108	127
	WEWS-TV Cleveland	125	92	134	100	56	107	138	124
	WMC-TV Memphis	89	38	80	115	92	136	96	100
Southern Broadcasting	**WAST-TV Albany/Schenectady/Troy	30	135	119	9	4	12	11	48
	WLKY-TV Louisville	92	136	142	11	23	84	4	130
Southern Broadcasting	WBGM-TV Birmingham	139	125	117	50	143	118	103	119
	WGHP-TV Greensboro/Winston-Salem/High Point					39	7		
Spartan Broadcasting	WSPA-TV Greenville/Spartanburg/Asheville	129	103	57	117	121	74	101	104
Springfield Television Broadcasting	WKEF-TV Dayton								
Standard Corp.	*KUTV-TV Salt Lake City	53	83	104	63	11	144	94	106
Storer Broadcasting	WAGA-TV Atlanta	60	70	5	124	79	71	126	100
	WITI-TV Milwaukee	45	72	111	22	41	93	69	120
	WJBK-TV Detroit	133	93	99	116	106	40	132	132
	WJW-TV Cleveland	77	69	43	104	77	52	128	71
	WSPD-TV Toledo	119	124	113	41	107	54	142	108
Sunbeam	WCKT-TV Miami	56	71	27	46	117	123	47	45
Synercom Communications	WZZM-TV Kalamazoo/Grand Rapids	35	112	45	43	14	22	133	24
Taft Broadcasting	WBRC-TV Birmingham	49	23	12	51	144	121	55	81
	WDAF-TV Kansas City	134	34	72	144	131	103	135	81
	WGR-TV Buffalo	123	141	109	45	81	29	79	25
	WKRC-TV Cincinnati	120	74	138	34	133	30	86	41
	WTVN-TV Columbus	136	128	130	68	105	18	46	76
Time Inc.	WOTV-TV Kalamazoo/Grand Rapids	62	48	37	106	67	16	145	74
Times Mirror	KDFW-TV Dallas-Ft. Worth	101	26	34	125	141	80	49	45
Travelers Corp.	WTIC-TV Hartford-New Haven	16	68	28	5	110	48	42	13
20th Century-Fox	KMSP-TV Minneapolis-St. Paul	122	109	141	15	126	147	43	122
Washington Post	WPLG-TV Miami	6	10	1	87	52	126	19	56
	WTOP-TV Wash., D.C.	55	79	10	120	50	66	3	40
Westinghouse	KDKA-TV Pittsburgh	4	4	6	30	57	11	125	9
	KPIX-TV San Francisco	1	31	13	1	103	58	53	14
	KYW-TV Philadelphia	5	2	7	23	123	73	70	3
	WBZ-TV Boston	31	15	16	55	138	4	24	17
	WJZ-TV Baltimore	2	6	59	4	24	128	57	2
WGAL-TV Inc.	WTEV-TV Providence	88	130	110	48	32	1	80	33
WHAS Inc.	WHNS-TV Louisville	19	35	84	33	20	131	130	65
WKY Television System	WKY-TV Oklahoma City	29	16	78	38	70	46	118	1
	WTVT-TV Tampa-St. Petersburg	80	80	32	119	51	100	121	6
Wometco Enterprises	WLOS-TV Greenville/Spartanburg/Asheville	111	143	137	12	60	50	59	125
	WTVJ-TV Miami	66	105	87	35	46	115	14	112

APPENDIX 2

The CPB-PBS Agreement

Reprinted from *Public Telecommunications Review*, vol. 1, 1 (August, 1973), with permission of the publisher.

On May 31, 1973, the boards of the Corporation for Public Broadcasting and the Public Broadcasting Service reached a formal agreement to govern their joint operation of the national programming system. The "partnership agreement," which ended nearly six months of internal dispute, insured public television licensees a crucial measure of control over their national service. Here is the full text of the boards' joint resolution.

Resolved, by the boards of the Corporation for Public Broadcasting and the Public Broadcasting Service, that:

In order to effect a vigorous partnership in behalf of the independence and diversity of public television and to improve the excellence of its programs;

405

To enhance the development, passage by Congress, and approval by the Executive branch of a long-range financing program that would remove public broadcasting from the political hazards of annual authorizations and appropriations;

To further strengthen the autonomy and independence of local television stations; and

To affirm that public affairs programs are an essential responsibility of public broadcasting,

The Boards of the Corporation for Public Broadcasting (CPB) and the Public Broadcasting Service (PBS) do hereby jointly adopt the following agreement:

1. CPB will, in consultation with PBS, other interested parties, and the public, decide all CPB-funded programs through a CPB program department. The consultation prior to CPB's decision is vital so that the CPB programming department will understand what the licensees' needs are and thus avoid any possibility that CPB will fund programs that the licensees do not want. By such a consultation, well in advance of CPB program decisions, time and vitally needed dollars can be saved and the public can be best served. In the event that the PBS program department dissents from any particular program decision of the CPB program department, the PBS program department may appeal to the chief executives of CPB and PBS. Should these executives fail to agree, final [appeal] may be made to the respective chairmen of the two organizations whose joint decision will be final.

2. All non-CPB funded programs, accepted under PBS Broadcast Journalism Standards and normal PBS procedures, will have access to the interconnection.

3. Should there be any conflict of opinion as to balance and objectivity of any programs, regardless of the source of funding, either group can appeal to a monitoring committee consisting of three CPB trustees and three PBS trustees. It will take four votes of this committee to bar a program's access to the interconnection.

4. PBS, on behalf of the stations, will prepare a draft schedule of programs for interconnection. The draft schedule will be for one year divided into four quarters. It will be resubmitted each quarter for the ensuing four quarters. To preserve the mutual interests of both CPB and

PBS, CPB will be advised and consulted in the development of the draft schedule, and when each such four quarter schedule is completed, it shall be submitted for approval of CPB. In the event that the CPB program department does not agree to the draft schedule, it may appeal to the chief executives of CPB and PBS. Should these executives fail to agree, the issue shall be presented for final decision to the board chairmen of CPB and PBS. Should they fail to agree, they shall choose a third person to whom the issue will be presented and whose decision shall be final. Emergency scheduling decisions will be made in accordance with procedures approved by the chairmen of the CPB and PBS boards. In any event, the draft and final schedules shall reflect the arrangement of programs for interconnection service to stations, and shall not be regarded as a schedule of programs for broadcast by the stations.

5. There is hereby created a Partnership Review Committee consisting of an equal number of trustees of CPB and PBS. Such committee shall assess the working of the partnership on a regular basis with formal meetings to be held not less than four times per year. For a five-year period beginning with the adoption of this joint resolution, this committee will be charged with the responsibility of making recommendations to the boards for any modifications which they deem desirable.

6. CPB and PBS shall formalize an annual contract for the physical operation of the interconnection not later than August 31, 1973. Physical operation of the interconnection will be by PBS and will be funded by CPB. Any dispute as to the terms of the contract will be resolved by the chairmen of CPB and PBS no later than September 30, 1973. CPB will continue to finance PBS activities as it has in the past until September 30, 1973. Following that date, PBS will finance its own activities, receiving from CPB only the funds necessary for the physical interconnection services which it will render under the contract.

7. CPB and PBS hereby agree that CPB will provide the mutually desired bedrock of localism by unrestricted grants to the public television stations, under a formula accepted by CPB and PBS, aggregating annually not less than 30% at a $45 million level, increasing proportionately to: 40% at the $60 million level, 45% at a $70 million level and 50% at an $80 level. CPB and PBS will express this commitment to the Congress in connection with the pending legislation.

APPENDIX 3

Factsheet on the
PBS Station Program Cooperative

This factsheet was prepared by the Public Broadcasting Service in June-July 1974. Reprinted by permission.

What is the "station program cooperative?"

The station program cooperative is a unique system of public television program selection and financing through which the nation's public television stations may participate in the funding of those nationally-distributed programs they wish to broadcast.

How did it become PBS policy?

The cooperative concept, which has been under consideration by the PBS staff for at least two years, was approved by the Executive Committees **408** of the PBS Boards of Governors and Managers for a one-year trial basis at an April 5-6, 1974 meeting. The cooperative was subsequently accepted by the PBS member licensees who agreed to the plan on a one-year basis by a vote of 140 to 5 with 3 abstentions. Thus, 95 percent of those voting (93 percent of all licensees) voted to ratify the Executive Committee's action, exceeding the requirement (75 percent of those voting) set by the Committees. The full Board of Governors ratified the Executive Committee's action at a meeting May 13, 1974.

How does it work?

Implementation of the station program cooperative involves four steps:

1) Determination of national program needs of the stations which includes station surveys, audience research data, program carriage data, and consultation with advisory panels within and without the public broadcasting community.

2) Solicitation of program proposals from potential producers based on the results of the determination of national program needs.

3) Preparation and distribution of a catalog of program proposals for the use of participating licensees in the selection process.

4) The selection by the licensees of those programs they wish to carry. This process consists of : (a) bidding rounds in which licensees express interest in specific programs but do not commit to them; (b) elimination rounds in which programs begin to be purchased or dropped from the selection process; and (c) purchase rounds in which final purchase selections are made by the licensees.

When did it take place?

The first three of these four steps were completed by May 1974. The final step, the computer-assisted selection process, began May 21, 1974, and lasted through June. Some of the programs in the 1974 summer schedule and several in the 1974–75 fall and winter schedules are funded through the cooperative.

How large a proportion of the PBS schedule will the cooperative provide?

The station program cooperative *will not* supply the total schedule of programs transmitted by PBS, but will contribute from 30 to 40 percent of the total national programming schedule. The rest of the schedule will come from programs underwritten by corporations, foundations, the HEW Office of Education, and the Corporation for Public Broadcasting.

Why was the cooperative formed?

The concept of a cooperative, which was first proposed by PBS President Hartford N. Gunn, Jr., in an October 1972 article in *Educational Broadcasting Review,* has resulted from some fundamental structural and economic incentives.

First, it gives more local control in programming decisions to the nation's public television stations, something PBS has consistently sought for its member stations.

Second, the total dollars for new evening programming are dwindling rapidly. It has dropped from a total of $22 million in fiscal 1971, to $16 million in fiscal 1974, and is anticipated for fiscal 1975 to be between $13 and $14 million. These figures do not take inflation into account so the actual amount is declining even faster than the raw figures indicate.

While the total dollars for evening programming have been declining, funds to the nation's public television stations in the form of Community Service Grants administered by the Corporation for Public Broadcasting have increased. These funds have grown from $5 million 1973 to $15 million in fiscal 1974. In fiscal 1975, depending on what happens to the Federal appropriation, that amount will be between $15 and $24 million.

The Community Service Grants are direct and unrestricted to the stations and can be used for whatever purpose the stations choose. The station program cooperative provides to the stations with the option to use a portion of these funds, or any other funds they wish, to join together with other stations to underwrite programs they wish to carry.

Will there be any assistance for the cooperative beyond the stations' revenue?

To assist the cooperative in its first year, the Ford Foundation is providing a grant of $5.5 million, and the Corporation for Public Broadcasting a grant of an additional $4.5 million, for a total of $10 million to be used to provide discounts from the price that the stations otherwise would have to pay for cooperative programs. Each participating station will receive a 75 percent discount on its program purchase, up to a certain limit. In order to take full advantage of these discount funds, the stations will need to commit $3.3 million of Community Service Grants or other local monies.

STATION PROGRAM COOPERATIVE STATISTICS

1) A total of $13,332,467 has been committed to programs offered through the station program cooperative. Of that total, the following amounts were committed to the three program categories:

$6,315,756	educative programs (including children's programs)—47%
$4,293,058	public affairs programs—32%
$2,723,644	cultural programs—21%

2) Twenty-five program offerings were selected from among a total offering of 93 programs or series. Of these:

8 are cultural programs—32%
10 are public affairs programs—40%
7 are educative programs—28%

3) The following are the dollar figures and percentages of the total cooperative purchase each producing agency whose programs were selected will receive:

$4,708,000	35%	CTW (Children's Television Workshop)
1,999,402	15	NPACT (National Public Affairs Center for Television)
1,245,821	9	WGBH, Boston
1,118,150	8	FCI (Family Communications, Inc.)
856,000	6	KCET, Los Angeles
731,880	5	SECA (Southern Educational Communications Association)
616,003	5	WNET, New York
611,882	5	MCPB (Maryland Center for Public Broadcasting)
486,138	4	KQED, San Francisco
385,778	3	WTTY, Chicago
293,073	2	WHYY, Philadelphia
138,030	1	WNED, Buffalo
83,460	.6	WCET, Cincinnati
32,100	.2	KNME, Albuquerque
26,750	.2	WXXI, Rochester

Appendix

411

4) Of the programs purchased through the cooperative, the following are the percentages of funds going to the producing agencies according to program categories:

Public Affairs	Cultural	Educative
47% NPACT	44% WGBH	74% CTW
17 SECA	31 KCET	18 FCI
14 WNET	14 WTTW	5 MCPB
7 MCPB	10 KQED	1 WCET
7 WHYY	1 WXXI	1 WGBH
5 KQED		1 KNME
3 WNED		

5) The following are comparisons between the percentage of dollars committed this year through the cooperative and the total FY 1974 program expenditures in the three program categories:

	FY 1974	Cooperative
Public Affairs	23%	32%
Cultural	29	21
Educative	48	47

6) Programs selected through the cooperative are:

CTW	*Sesame Street* and *The Electric Company*
NPACT	*Washington Week in Review, Washington Straight Talk* and *Special Events*
WGBH	*Evening at Symphony, Zoom,* and *The Romagnoli's Table*
FCI	*Mister Rogers' Neighborhood*
WNET	*American Chronicles, Black Journal*
KCET	*Hollywood Television Theatre*
SECA	*Firing Line*
MCPB	*Wall Street Week* and *Consumer Survival Kit*
KQED	*The Japanese Film, World Press,* and *International Animation Festival*
WTTW	*Book Beat* and *Soundstage*
WHYY	*Black Perspective on the News*
WNED	*Woman*
WCET	*Lilias, Yoga and You*
KNME	*Solar Energy*
WXXI	*. . . At the Top*

7) The following is a listing, according to program category, of the selected programs showing the number of licensees (of a possible 152) which purchased each program:

Educative (including Children's)

Sesame Street	145
The Electric Company	143
Consumer Survival Kit	139
Mister Rogers' Neighborhood	135
The Romagnoli's Table	127
Solar Energy	114
Lilias, Yoga and You	92

Public Affairs

Washington Week in Review	144
Firing Line	143
Wall Street Week	139
Woman	132
Special Events	129
World Press	128
Black Perspective on the News	127
American Chronicles	87
Washington Straight Talk	82
Black Journal	39

Cultural

The Japanese Film	149
. . . At the Top	146
Book Beat	143
Soundstage	142
Evening at Symphony	140
Hollywood Television Theatre	103
Zoom	88
International Animation Festival	36

INDEX

415

Index

421

Index

423

Index

429